Doing History

Investigating With Children in Elementary and Middle Schools

Third Edition

Doing History

Investigating With Children in Elementary and Middle Schools

Third Edition

Linda S. Levstik
University of Kentucky

Keith C. Barton
University of Cincinnati

Routledge
Taylor & Francis Group
New York   London

Senior Acquisitions Editor:	Naomi Silverman
Assistant Editor:	Erica Kica
Cover Design:	Kathryn Houghtaling Lacey
Textbook Production Manager:	Paul Smolenski
Composition:	LEA Desktop Production
Text and Cover Printer:	Victor Graphics

First published by
Lawrence Erlbaum Associates, Inc., Publishers
10 Industrial Avenue
Mahwah, NJ 07430
www.erlbaum.com

Reprinted 2008 by
Routledge
Taylor & Francis Group
270 Madison Avenue
New York, NY 10016

Routledge
Taylor & Francis Group
2 Park Square
Milton Park, Abingdon
Oxon OX14 4RN

Library of Congress Cataloging-in-Publication Data

Levstik, Linda S.
   Doing history : investigating with children in elementary and middle schools / Linda S. Levstik, Keith C. Barton.—3rd ed.
      p.   cm.
   Includes bibliographical references and index.
   ISBN 0-8058-5072-4 (pbk.)
   1. History—Study and teaching (Elementary)—United States. 2. History—Study and teaching (Middle school)—United States.   I. Barton, Keith C.   II. Title.
   LB1582.U6L49 2005
   372.89'044—dc22

                                        2004056283
                                        CIP

Printed in the United States of America
10 9 8 7 6 5

To our respective spouses,
Frank Levstik and Shaunna Scott

CONTENTS

PREFACE

As we did in the first two editions of *Doing History*, we invite you to take a mental journey with us—to picture primary students debating whether Christopher Columbus should be considered a hero or eighth-grade students producing a video to examine whether a historic document—the Bill of Rights—speaks to current issues. We ask you to further imagine classrooms where students regularly, and actively, *do* history—frame questions, gather data from primary and secondary sources, organize and interpret that data, and share their work with different audiences. Finally we ask you to imagine a history curriculum that reflects the rich diversity of people in the United States and around the world.

We have been fortunate to spend a number of years working with teachers and students in just such classrooms, both in the United States and in other countries, particularly Northern Ireland, New Zealand, and Ghana. We have seen powerful historical study in classes where many of the children were recent immigrants, as well as in classes where children's families have lived in the same area for generations. Some classes are full inclusion programs where the special education and "regular" teachers collaborate; most include students with special needs, at least for social studies. The classrooms range from urban and suburban to rural settings. But despite their many differences, these communities of inquiry have several things in common. In each one, even the youngest children describe historical study as interesting and important. Moreover, historical study in each of these classrooms deals with important content and engages students in authentic inquiry. *All* students are invited to be historical participants. Throughout the book, we draw on these classrooms to provide models of instructionally sound, thoughtful, and thought-provoking history teaching with students from a wide variety of backgrounds. Most chapters also begin with a vignette from one of these classrooms.

Many of the teachers cited in this book worked with us on research related to the development of historical thinking. Some continue to do so. We met others through our work with teacher education programs or through professional meetings. All of them generously shared their time, ideas, and classrooms. Although we would prefer honoring each of them by using their real names, confidentiality agreements sometimes preclude that possibility. Many appear under their own names—Amy Leigh, Dehea Smith, Jeanette Groth, LeeAnn Fitzpatrick, Rebecca Valbuena, Rhoda Coleman, Ruby Yessin, and Tina Reynolds—whereas others are identified by pseudonyms. Similarly, all children's names are pseudonyms except where we had permission to credit a child for a specific piece of work. Again, we wish we could identify all of the students who so generously indulged our curiosity and answered questions that often must have seemed foolish, who lent us their work, and who shared their time and ideas. Our experience has been that children enjoy discussing their ideas about history and that they want to find out more about how things have changed over time. In addition, our conversations with children and adolescents in other parts of the world remind us of how tightly our conceptions of the past are linked to national contexts—to our sense of national agency, of the possibility for change, and of hope or hopelessness as we face the future.

As you read the vignettes, think of them as snapshots of history in action—including some of the obstacles even good teachers face. As with a snapshot, each vignette is a glimpse of a particular experience teaching and learning history. The rest of each chapter puts the vignette in perspective, explaining why it is sound instruction and sound history, and providing examples of activities ranging from the first years of primary school through the end of the middle grades. Although we have not tried to present a complete set of activities or recommend a specific curriculum, we have tried to suggest a framework for rethinking history instruction in elementary and middle schools. Our goal is to stimulate your thinking so that you can decide how to apply these ideas to your own classrooms and your own students. One way to begin thinking about how to adapt these ideas is to refer to the list of related children's literature at the end of each chapter. These lists are by no means exhaustive. Rather, selections are specifically intended to represent diversity of perspectives and different levels of difficulty. Other works mentioned in the margin notes are included in the reference section at the end of the book.

Continuous and constructive assessment takes on a special role in teaching history. By *continuous* and *constructive* assessment, we mean that evaluation occurs throughout instruction, not just at the end of a unit or grading period (or book) and that the effects of assessment on teaching and learning are positive. Moreover, assessment in history attends to specifically *historical* aspects of students' work. Against what criteria, for instance, do we assess students' progress in perspective-taking or building supportable interpretations? How do we use assessment to help students think more carefully about evidence or about cause-and-effect relationships? Rather than locating assessment in a separate chapter, then, you will find this topic woven throughout the book. We introduce the principles of constructive assessment in chapter 2, so that you have a basis for evaluating the assessment techniques that follow. In subsequent chapters, you will find examples of rubrics for assessing students' progress in both perspective-taking and developing historical interpretations. Other chapters provide a variety of techniques for evaluating students' history presentations—from position papers and history museums to oral performances. Each of these techniques is embedded in actual classroom practice, so that you can see how real teachers work to make assessment not only continuous and more constructive, but an authentic part of teaching and learning in history.

NEW IN THIS EDITION

As with any approach to teaching, ideas change and grow over time. So it is with this book. Some of the changes are relatively minor—we have updated the bibliographies, incorporating new scholarship on historical thinking and learning, and have suggested new children's literature to support good teaching. Other changes are more substantial. Research on children's and adolescents' historical thinking across cultures, as well as continuing debates about the place of history in the curriculum, led us to address more specifically some of the ways that doing history prepares students for participation in a pluralist democracy. From our perspective, the aims of history teaching and learning have less to do with meeting standards established by an academic discipline than with helping citizens more intelligently deliberate an   ng common good. We introduce this citizenship perspective and its t   etical framework in the first two chapters of the book. In subsequent chap.ers you will find examples of techniques for scaffolding discussion about controversial issues and for grounding that discussion in historical study. You will also find international comparisons—points, for instance, where history teaching and learning benefit from ideas or emphases more common to historical thinking in other cultures.

The teachers in this book—and others like them, in the United States and abroad—continue to renew our conviction that history *is* relevant to the lives of even the youngest school children and that disciplined, reflective historical inquiry *is not* the sole province of university historians, but rather the obligation of all of us who seek a more inclusive and responsive common good. We hope this third edition continues to do justice to the lives and work of these teachers and to the students in their classes. We also have been gratified, since the publication of the first edition, to find ideas from the book used successfully by other teachers, in other schools, and in other parts of the country and the world. We also hope that their example supports you and your students as you build communities of historical inquiry in pursuit of the common good.

ACKNOWLEDGMENTS

This book grew out of a series of collaborations—with teachers and students, with each other, and with the many colleagues with whom we have discussed and debated the issues surrounding the teaching and learning of history. The teachers and students with whom we work have been incredibly generous, giving us feedback on many sections of the book and always providing a reality check on our theorizing. In addition, we want to thank the administrators who let us observe in their schools, supported our research, and welcomed our university students into their schools. Several people also read and responded to portions of the original manuscript. Corinna Hasback, Terrie Epstein, Raymond H. Muessig, and Noralee Frankel provided encouragement, insightful reviews, and useful suggestions. Lynne Smith offered technical assistance as well as a good "language arts" perspective. Frank Levstik assisted in locating a variety of sources. He and Jennifer Levstik read, listened to, and commented on numerous drafts of chapters. Marge Artzer also provided valuable assistance, and Larry Newton provided at least one good line. Jennie Smith, Elaine Conradi, and Paula Bayer provided indispensable help in finding good children's literature, and Leslie King allowed us to investigate the impact of some of our ideas in new settings. In addition, Melissa Simonds provided valuable help in updating the children's literature bibliographies for this third edition.

Each new edition benefits from contacts with teachers and university educators. In addition to continuing to grow through our conversations with innumerable colleagues in North America, we have learned much from educators in other countries, particularly Neil Anderson, David Turner, and Deborah Elliot in New Zealand; Yao Quashiga, Naah Yemeh, Teresa Tuwor, and Jeanette Groth in Ghana; Alan McCully and many other professionals in Northern Ireland; and Maria Luisa Freitas, Isabel Barca, Marília Gago Quintal, and their generous friends, families, and associates in Portugal.

Sadly, we acknowledge the loss of Frank Levstik, whose support helped make this book, and so much else, possible.

Author Biographies

Linda S. Levstik is a professor in the Department of Curriculum and Instruction at the University of Kentucky. She is co-author with Christine C. Pappas and Barbara Z. Keifer of *An Integrated Language Perspective in the Elementary School* (Allyn & Bacon, 1998) and co-editor with Cynthia A. Tyson of *Handbook of Research on Social Studies* (Lawrence Erlbaum Associates, 2006). She conducts research on children's and adolescents' historical thinking in national and cross-national settings. She also researches, writes about, and conducts workshops regarding the development of gender-equitable classroom practices, promoting classroom inquiry, and engaging elementary and middle school students in archaeological study. She currently works with several Teaching American History grants in Eastern Kentucky as well as with a nationwide program funded by the National Council for the Social Studies and Learn for America and designed to enhance civic participation in K–12 settings. Prior to earning a Ph.D. from The Ohio State University, she taught in public elementary and middle schools and at the Columbus Torah Academy in Ohio.

Keith C. Barton is Professor in the Division of Teacher Education at the University of Cincinnati. Prior to earning a doctorate from the University of Kentucky, he taught elementary and middle school in Los Angeles and near San Francisco, where he also served as president of his teachers' union and as a teacher-consultant for the Bay Area Writing Project. Currently, he conducts research on elementary and middle school students' historical understanding, both in the United States and internationally, as well as on classroom contexts of teaching and learning in history and social studies. His recent research has focused on connections between history and identity in Northern Ireland and on U.S. teachers' ideas about the purpose of social studies and the nature of students' learning. His work has appeared in national and international research and practitioner journals, and he authored the review of history education in the *Handbook of Research on Social Studies* (Lawrence Erlbaum Associates, 2006). He teaches graduate courses on elementary and middle level social studies, educational research, and theories of teaching and learning.

Linda S. Levstik and Keith C. Barton have published joint research on history education in *American Educational Research Journal, Journal of Curriculum Studies,* and *Teachers College Record.* They have written about the role of history in preparing students for participation in pluralist democracies in *Teaching History for the Common Good* (Lawrence Erlbaum Associates, 2004).

1

PAST, PRESENT, AND FUTURE

The Sociocultural Context for Studying History

We learn [in history] ... how people's views change over time. A lot of people's views change, but not everybody. We still have things like the KKK around ... so obviously their views haven't changed since like the Civil War and stuff, but I think most people's have. Not necessarily everybody. ... There's definitely still prejudice around, not necessarily just about Blacks and Hispanics, either.

—Caitlyn, Grade 6

You may remember a very different history from the one Caitlyn describes. Too often history instruction is simply a march through time that never quite connects to the present. History becomes, as one second grader explains, "a main date." The dates may mark interesting stories, but the stories are finished—beginnings and middles established, climaxes identified, and endings predictable. Figures from a pantheon of heroes and villains step forward briefly, take their bows in stories that often fail to distinguish between myth and history, and disappear back into the pictures displayed above chalkboards. George Washington was the first president, had wooden teeth, and chopped down a cherry tree. Abraham Lincoln was honest, read by firelight, and walked a mile to return a nickel. It is little wonder that children sometimes ask what the point in all this storytelling might be.

Consider the kind of history Caitlyn's comments suggest. She clearly struggles to make sense of the prejudice she sees around her—both to explain how it is that prejudice exists and to separate herself from it. She uses her study of history to identify prejudice as an enduring human dilemma and to understand that "a lot of people's views change, but not everybody. ... There's definitely still prejudice around." In other words, we are still in the middle of the story. The ending isn't predictable, and the story unfolds in our own time and in our own lives. The point of history is that this is, after all, an enormous family drama. Each of us develops the plot twists with which future generations will have to cope. From this perspective, history forces us to consider what it means to be a participant in this human drama.

HISTORY INVOLVES MULTIPLE ACTIVITIES AND PURPOSES

History is used for multiple purposes. *Barton & Levstik (2004)*

Identification involves looking for connections between present and past. *Barton & Levstik (2004)*

Moral responses to history involve judgments about the people and events of the past. *Barton & Levstik (2004)*

Historical analysis involves identifying patterns or examining causes and consequences of events. *Barton & Levstik (2004)*

Exhibition involves the display of historical information, whether in school or out. *Barton & Levstik (2004)*

As Caitlyn's comment indicates, the past is complex. There are many ways of making sense of history, and no single purpose takes precedence as the sole reason for studying the subject. History involves a number of different activities, each of which can be used for a variety of ends, and these combinations of activity and purpose constitute four distinct "stances" toward the past. One of the most familiar is the *identification stance*, in which we look for connections between ourselves and people in the past. "You have Aunt Eliza's laugh," a father in New York tells his daughter, "and a stubborn streak just like your grandmother!" In a classroom in East Los Angeles, a girl explains that her mother has told her about leaving school as a child in El Salvador to help support her family; a classmate has learned that his uncle was once "the greatest truck driver in all Mexico," able to make it through flooded roads when no one else could; and yet another has heard her family recall the homes and businesses they owned before leaving Vietnam. And throughout the United States, students learn how "we" became a nation or how "our" ethnic group has struggled to achieve its dreams. In recognizing family characteristics, sharing family stories, and locating ourselves within a larger community, children (and adults) are expected to affirm connections between their own lives and those of people in the past.

Other times we take an explicitly judgmental attitude toward the people and events of history. This is the *moral response stance*. Sometimes we remember the sacrifices and hardships of those involved in tragic events, such as the Irish Famine, the world wars, or Vietnam. Other times we hold up events for condemnation (slavery, the Holocaust, the McCarthy hearings) or celebration (the Women's Suffrage Movement, Civil Rights, the end of apartheid). And still other times we single out people we regard as heroes or role models—George Washington, Harriet Tubman, Rosa Parks, or the police and firefighters of September 11. Judging the past as good or bad—or simply deserving of reverence—is another fundamental way in which people relate to history, both in school and out.

Two other approaches are less personal and less emotional. The first is the *analytic stance*. Students engage in historical analysis when they look for historical patterns or examine the causes and consequences of events in the past—how life has changed over time, the causes of the American Revolution, the effect of World War II on daily life, and so on. Sometimes, this kind of analysis is aimed at understanding the historical origins of contemporary society, as when students study the origin and development of their country's legal and political structure. Other times, the past may serve as a source of lessons or analogies; notice, for example, how often historical examples are used in discussions of the possible consequences of foreign policy decisions. Students also take part in analysis when they learn how historical accounts are constructed; working with primary sources, comparing conflicting sources, and reaching conclusions based on evidence are all part of the analytic stance.

Finally, one of the most common approaches to history in schools involves the *exhibition stance*. Here, students are expected to display what they know about the past by answering questions at the end of a textbook chapter, responding to teachers' questions in class, or taking achievement tests. This is the kind of history people seem to have in mind when they decry how little children know about history these days or how standards have fallen. The exhibition stance is also the easiest to dismiss, in part because it is driven more by demands for accountability than by a concern with developing deep understanding of history and, in part, because it reminds most of us of our own worst encounters with the subject. Yet exhibition is an important part of how history is used in society, and knowledge of the past is often displayed in museums and historical re-enactments as well as through hobbies such as genealogy or antique collecting. All these stances—identification, moral response, analysis, and exhibition—influence the teaching and learning of history, and we must keep each of them in mind as we think about how to develop students' understanding of the subject.

HISTORY HELPS US PICTURE POSSIBLE FUTURES

Any approach to history is as much about the present and future as it is about the past. When we identify with groups in history, we stake out identities in the present; when we look at where the world has been, we hope we will understand where it is going; when we judge the decisions of the past, we promise to make better ones next time. In order for history to fulfill such roles, though, students need a broad and inclusive exposure to the subject. By marking out particular paths to the present, history also points to some possible roads to the future and forecloses others. To the degree that history instruction limits students' views of the multiple paths leading from the past, it also inhibits their perceptions of the future. Students who do not see themselves as members of groups who had agency in the past or power in the present, who are invisible in history, lack viable models for the future. Consider, for instance, the impact of traditional history instruction that emphasizes the agency of some men—conquering the wilderness, establishing governments, leading social movements—while presenting most women as acted on—following husbands to new lands, invisible in government, silent on public issues. Particularly when such instruction matches school practice, where girls are often taught to be passive and boys active, there is little modeling of alternatives for the future. Not only is this problematic for girls, but it limits all students' access to the full range of choices open to human beings across time and among places. Ignoring the complexities and controversies inherent in the gendered interplay of public and private life leaves stereotyped ideas about gender unexamined. Unmediated by careful curricular attention, stereotypes and their accompanying misunderstandings lead females to limit their aspirations as well as their classroom participation and may encourage males to view information about and from females as insignificant. Of course, similar examples could be used for other groups who have been less visible in traditional history. When history is silent about these sorts of issues, it is often perceived as separate from ordinary life, divorced from the puzzles of culture and change that absorb us on a daily basis.

Shifting the focus of the history curriculum to a pluralist perspective presents a more inclusive and authentic vision of the futures available to all students. Studying a range of perspectives helps students understand discrimination, marginalization, and opposition, as well as power and privilege. It opens up a broader range of possible ways of acting in the world—and acting in the future. To help students envision such a history:

- Focus on enduring human dilemmas. Emphasize that the dilemmas of the present have their roots in the past. Untangling those roots can be both freeing and empowering.
- Focus on human agency. Emphasize the ways in which people have acquiesced to, ignored, or acted against oppression and injustice, as well as the ways in which people have worked to build the futures they desired.
- Focus on subjecting interpretations to scrutiny and skepticism. Emphasize the "authored" nature of historical interpretation. Whose voice is heard? Whose is left out? How else might the story be told?
- Connect to the microlevel. Emphasize bringing historical perspective to bear on current issues both in the classroom and the larger society.
- Connect to the macrolevel. Study discrimination, marginalization, and opposition as global phenomena that require global as well as local and national responses.

History points to some possible paths to the future and forecloses others. Holt (1990a)

Brophy (1990), Downey (1982), Epstein (1991, 1994a), Lerner (1997), Levstik (1999), Schuster & VanDyne (1998)

Gardner & Boix-Mansilla (1994), Kessler-Harris (1990)

Gagnon and the Bradley Commission on History in the Schools (1989), Penyak & Duray (1999), Zinn (1990), Allen (1998), Gordon (1990), Greene (1993a, 1993b)

O'Reilly (1998), Penyak & Duray (1999), Merryfield (1995, 1997)

HISTORY IS ABOUT SIGNIFICANT THEMES AND QUESTIONS

Exploring significant themes and questions is a basic activity of history. Evans (1988), National Council for the Social Studies (1994), Downey & Levstik (1991)

If history helps us think about who we are and to picture possible futures, we cannot afford a history curriculum mired in trivia and limited to a chronological recounting of events. Instead, we need a vibrant history curriculum that engages children in investigating significant themes and questions, with people, their values, and the choices they make as the central focus. In the past, we have assumed that students needed "basic skills" before they could engage with big issues. The trouble with this is that time lines, names, and memorized "facts" are not history, and they certainly are not compelling. The enduring themes and questions that humans have struggled with over time are, however, more compelling history (see Table 1.1). In the past, we have reserved these for historians and then wondered why children too often found history insignificant. By shifting the instructional focus from hearing about one historical story to asking questions worth pursuing, children have an opportunity to engage in the real "basics" of history.

Table 1.1 provides one set of suggested themes and questions. You would, of course, have to adjust the questions to fit particular grade levels. For instance, a primary class might begin with a question such as, "Why do people move from one place to another?" rather than with "How has human movement been encouraged and inhibited?" Their study might begin with the students' own experiences and then expand to consideration of community patterns over time. In contrast, a middle school class might consider the question, "How have our decisions about the environment changed other communities?" Again, students might begin by analyzing local conditions, then trace them back in time, and finally study the impact of local conditions on the larger community, nationally and internationally. As you look over the themes and questions in Table 1.1, consider how you might adapt them to engage students in thinking about who they are, where they came from, and where they might go in the future.

Most of us probably don't remember this kind of history. At worst, we may remember a string of isolated dates and questions at the end of a deadly dull textbook chapter. At best, we may remember a teacher who told impassioned stories about times long ago. But even at its best, we heard a single story, we already knew how it would come out—and some of us weren't in it. In fact, history always stopped long before it got to us. Therefore we had no role in history. Always excluded in time, often excluded because we were the "wrong" gender, class, race, ethnicity, or language, we weren't invited into the story—unless we were willing to identify with the main characters. And we were rarely encouraged to think about why the story was being told that way, or how it might have looked from a different perspective. In other words, we were unlikely to see history as either authored or interpretive.

Many students have been excluded from the story of history.

HISTORY IS INTERPRETIVE

All history is interpretive.

No historical account can be entirely objective, because historical knowledge always involves interpretation. At the most basic level, anyone interested in knowing what happened in the past faces a problem peculiar to history: The events are already over with and cannot be directly observed or repeated. As a result, finding out what happened always involves indirect methods (such as using primary sources and artifacts), and indirect methods require interpretation: The historian has to decide which sources to use, how reliable they are, and what to do when they contradict each other. We all know the same event can be explained differently by different people, and anyone who has listened to family stories grow and change over time knows that interpretation shifts with the teller. When Uncle Christopher tells the story of Scottish emigration, for exam-

4

TABLE 1.1

Significant Themes and Questions in History

The Development of Human Societies and Cultures

Why have people developed organized societies and cultures?
How have environmental factors influenced sociocultural developments?
How have cultures differed in social, economic, and political organization?
What elements do societies/cultures have in common?
How have cultures influenced the way people perceive themselves and others?
How have continuity and change been reflected in and across societies over time?

Movement and Interaction of People, Cultures, and Ideas

What forces have created, encouraged, or inhibited human movement?
What factors have enhanced and inhibited the spread of ideas, goods, and cultures?
How has human interaction led to conflict and/or cooperation?
How has the spread of ideas, goods, and cultures influenced societies?
How has the transmission of disease influenced societies?

Human Interaction with the Environment

Over time, how have societies viewed their physical environment?
How have humans changed the environment to suit their needs?
How have humans adapted over time to meet environmental realities?
How have decisions about the environment had cumulative and complex effects on societies?
How have competing interests within a society viewed resource allocation?

Patterns of Economic and Technological Organization and Change

Why have different societies and cultures developed different economic systems?
How and why did some societies develop agricultural economies?
What factors are critical to the emergence of technologically advanced societies?
How have societies with different economic systems included or excluded people/groups from decisionmaking and the allocation of benefits?
How have societies with different economic systems adapted to changing conditions and demands?
How have scientific developments led to technological and/or economic changes?

The Relationships Among Values, Beliefs, Ideas, and Institutions

How have religion and philosophy influenced individuals and groups?
How have these influences been expressed in the arts and other institutions?
How have values, beliefs, and ideas shaped culture and social institutions?
What leads some cultures to influence others?
How have some cultures imposed their values, beliefs, ideas, and institutions on others?
How have cultures attempted to maintain their values, beliefs, ideas, and institutions?
How have values, beliefs, ideas, and institutions come into conflict with each other, and how have these conflicts been expressed?
How have cultures defined the relationship between the individual and society?

Note: Adapted from National Council for the Social Studies Focus Group on the NEH History Standards (1993).

ple, it is a tale of brave ancestors wrapped in their clan tartans. In Aunt Kathryn's rendering, the tartans are more tattered and the family roots more humble. As one group of historians notes, "History is never either a neutral force or a complete world view; history is always *someone's* history." All of us, then, start with our own diverse social histories—the stories of who we are as interpreted through the experiences of daily living, family stories, pictures, and artifacts.

Appleby, Hunt, & Jacob (1994, p. 11)

People in the past were also influenced by their backgrounds and biases. There are dozens of firsthand accounts of the Battle at Lexington Green, for example, and no two of them are alike. Faced with conflicting sources, the histo-

Bennett (1967)

The historical record is incomplete.

rian must decide which descriptions seem most plausible, and such decisions necessarily involve judgment and interpretation. The historical record is more often incomplete than contradictory, though, and so we must piece together fragments of information to construct a complete description. This inevitably involves speculation, because some facts can never be recovered. Consider, for example, the assassination of President Kennedy. No single source contains enough information to know exactly what happened at the scene, and so the historian has to pull together evidence from films, recordings, firsthand accounts, and medical reports. The fact that this event has generated decades of controversy indicates just how impossible it is to establish what happened: There will always be gaps in the record, and people will disagree over the most reasonable way of filling in those gaps. For many historical events, it is impossible to separate description from interpretation.

History instruction has traditionally deemphasized diversity. *Downey (1985), Epstein (1991, 1994c, 1994e), Lerner (1997), Loewen (1995)*

For much of the past century, however, school history has been limited to a narrow range of interpretations. Much history instruction has begun with the assumption of a unified society and has told a story that tends to deemphasize racial, ethnic, gender, and class distinctions. As a result, many of us have become invisible in history. If our students are to be visible—able to see themselves as participants in the ongoing drama of history—then we have to rethink the ways in which we conceive of history. Specifically, we should:

Barber (1992), Zinn (1990, 1994)

- Begin with the assumption of a pluralist society. All of us belong to many groups that are intricately related to each other. Some of us have exercised more power than others; others have more often been excluded from power.

White (1982)

- Recognize that no single story can possibly be our story. Instead, our multiple stories, braided together, constantly speak to and against each other. Each of us is a strand but not the whole.

Lerner (1997), Tuchman (1981)

- Remember that history is alive. All our stories are only partially known, always unfinished, and constantly changing as we speak and act.

HISTORY IS EXPLAINED THROUGH NARRATIVES

Historical narratives explain how events are causally related. *Barton & Levstik (2004), Danto (1965), Gallie (1964), White (1965)*

Historical accounts also involve a more important kind of interpretation—not just in establishing what happened but also in showing how events relate to each other. A simple list of events from the past is usually referred to as a *chronicle*. *History*, however, is something more: Historical explanations frequently explain events in a narrative form. A historical account, then, often is a story about the past—with a beginning, middle, and end, and a setting, characters, problem (or problems), and resolution. Think, for example, about accounts of the American Revolution. The story begins at the end of the French and Indian War, as Britain imposes taxes to pay for the defense of the colonies. As the colonists become increasingly upset about the unfairness of taxation without representation, they begin a series of protests, which England meets with increasingly repressive responses. The colonists eventually declare their independence, a war results, and the colonists are victorious. This historical episode has a structure similar to any narrative, fictitious or otherwise—a setting, characters, a problem, and a resolution. Several historians have argued that this kind of narrative structure is the basis of all historical explanation.

Historical narratives are authored. *Danto (1965), Gallie (1964), Ricoeur (1984), H. White (1978, 1982, 1984), M. White (1965)*

But whenever history is told as a narrative, someone has to decide when the story begins and ends, what is included or left out, and which events appear as problems or solutions. As a result, historical narratives always involve interpretation: Someone decides *how* to tell the story. To take a simple example, it would be impossible to tell everything that happened during the American Revolution (even if complete records survived). That would mean explaining how Thomas Jefferson sharpened his pen each time he sat down to write, how Crispus Attucks buckled his shoes each morning, how Abigail Adams lit candles in her home—

and millions of other details about every person in the colonies and in England, every minute of every day for decades. No historian tries to write such a "complete" account, and no one would have time to read one. Instead, every historical account is selective—someone decides which events are important enough to include in the story. Deciding which events to include and which to leave out forms one of the most basic aspects of historical interpretation.

At an even more significant level, however, historical interpretation involves deciding not just what events to include, but how they relate to each other. Explaining that "taxation without representation" caused the American Revolution, for example, is an example of interpretation: The historian selects one reason as a more important cause than others. The facts themselves cannot explain why the war took place; explaining the war is a matter of interpretation. To take an even more familiar example: What was the nature of American involvement in the Vietnam War? Some would tell the story of a military hampered by weak politicians and ungrateful protesters, whereas others would tell of the triumph of the Vietnamese people over a brutal dictatorship and a vicious superpower. What appears as failure from one perspective appears as victory to another. The events of the war remain the same, but their meaning changes depending on the story being told. Even when the factual events of history can be firmly established, their meaning—their arrangement in a narrative—is always a matter of interpretation.

The historian engages in interpretation, then, whenever she shapes the events of the past into a story. Because no account of the past is ever complete, and because any event can be told as part of more than one possible story, interpretations vary from one historian to another. One may see progress where another sees decline, one may find the importance of events that others ignore, and so on. Far from being avoided, debates over interpretation are at the very heart of the historical profession. Historians know that more than one story can be told about the same events and that interpretations will change over time; there simply is no single, unchanging story of history. Such ambiguity is regarded as an inevitable, productive, and desirable part of the search for historical knowledge. That is not to say, however, that any interpretation is as good as any other. Any story about the past must, for example, account for the available evidence. A narrative of the World War II era that denies that the Holocaust occurred will not garner much respect, because the facts of the Holocaust can be conclusively established.

HISTORY IS MORE THAN POLITICS

Unfortunately, the range of interpretations traditionally found in textbooks and school curricula has been extremely small. The historical narratives that students encounter at school, for example, focus almost exclusively on the political and diplomatic history of the United States—the history of laws, presidents, wars, and foreign relations. Information that does not fit into these categories is rarely afforded much (if any) importance. As a result, those who traditionally have had little access to politics—such as women, people of color, and the poor—have largely been excluded from the narrative interpretation of American history.

Women, for example, appear infrequently in the curriculum because for much of the nation's history they have had only indirect access to politics—and as long as politics remains the focus of history, women will appear only when they influence that predominantly male realm (as, for example, during the abolition or women's rights movements). There is no objective reason, however, for history to concern itself so exclusively with the public political arena. For several decades now, academic historians have been turning their attention to other areas of life—such as family relations, domestic labor, and religion—and not sur-

No historical account is complete.

Historical interpretations vary from one historian to another. *Cohen (1994), Novick (1988), Ricoeur (1984), Shama (1992), Zinn (1990)*

Not all historical narratives are equally valid. *Kansteiner (1993), White (1992)*

School history has usually focused on politics and diplomacy.

Elshtain (1981), Lerner (1997)

Women have often been omitted from the history curriculum. *Crocco (1997), Gordon (1990), Lerner (1997)*

prisingly have found women to be significant historical actors. Even more recently, historians have explored the connections between the spheres previously regarded as public and private, and again they have found that gender has played a more significant role than was long recognized. As long as these topics remain absent from the study of history, however, so will most women.

People of color often have been omitted from the history curriculum. *Kessler-Harris (1990)*

Deciding to limit one's attention to politics, then, amounts to excluding large portions of the population from U.S. history; it is one way of deciding what is left in and out of the story. Not only women, of course, but many other segments of the population have suffered from this exclusion. African Americans, for example, have been considered an important part of history only when their presence had an impact on European American politics; the political, economic, and cultural developments within African American society have not been considered a part of the country's story (and still less have Latinos, Asian Americans, or other people of color been accorded a prominent place within that story). Again, however, academic historians have been devoting attention to such issues for well over a quarter of a century—but as long as this more inclusive interpretation of U.S. history remains outside the school curriculum, so will most groups other than European Americans.

Both *Native American* and *American Indian* are acceptable to most, but not all, people of native ancestry; usage varies somewhat according to geographic region. The names of specific nations are preferable to either. *Harvey, Harjo, & Jackson (1990)*

Native Americans often interpret the history of the United States very differently than do European Americans. *Axtell (1992)*

The traditional stories of history have been particularly severe in their treatment of Native Americans. For many years, the history of the United States was roughly equivalent to the triumph of European American settlement. In that story, the presence of Native Americans appeared as an obvious problem to be solved through their removal or relocation. Native Americans, of course, saw the story very differently: From their perspective, the problem was the forced surrender of their land (and often their way of life), and armed resistance, peaceful settlement, and collaboration all represented attempts at solutions. A historical map showing the expansion of European American settlement, then, has precisely the opposite meaning for Native Americans: It shows the contraction of their own territory. Again, the facts of the encounter between Native Americans and European Americans can be established in most cases, but their significance changes greatly depending on the story being told.

Interpretation is an inseparable part of historical understanding. *Cohen (1994), Novick (1988)*

Put simply, there is not a single story of history but many stories. Native-European relations, the American Revolution, slavery, changes in domestic labor, immigration, the Vietnam War—all these will look different from varying perspectives. Each point of view will regard some events as more important, others as less so; each will include some details while omitting others; what appears as progress in one story will seem like decline in another; and solutions in one will be regarded as problems in others. Each story will invariably contain the kind of interpretation that is an inseparable part of historical understanding.

HISTORY IS CONTROVERSIAL

The combination of interpretation and importance makes for a volatile mix. If historical truth were handed down to us on a stone tablet, the meaning and significance of the past would be certain and unchanging, and there would be no room for controversy. Not only would we know what happened in the past, but we would know just what story to tell about it; anyone who suggested alternative explanations could be dismissed as an unenlightened crank. And if history were unimportant, if it were not so central to our individual and collective identity, its interpretive nature would hardly matter. Historians and others could be relegated to the remote confines of archives and libraries, where they would be free to argue over their conflicting narratives, out of sight and out of mind. But history has a more vital fate: Because many stories can be told about the past and because those stories powerfully influence our understanding of who we are and where we come from, history is destined to be among the most controversial areas of human knowledge.

History is one of the most controversial areas of knowledge.

8

Such controversies are nothing new: They have been a constant feature of the public understanding of history in this country throughout the last century, as some groups have struggled to become part of the story of U.S. history and others have fought just as hard to keep them out. Regional tensions produced many of the most impassioned historical debates in the first decades of the 20th century, as Westerners argued that the Eastern United States dominated textbooks and public celebrations, and Southerners maintained that New England received too much attention at the expense of their own section. The legacy of the Civil War lent a particular fervor to debates between North and South, as each strove to establish its own interpretation as the accepted and "correct" one. In 1920, the New Orleans chapter of the United Daughters of the Confederacy warned mothers not to let their children celebrate Lincoln's birthday at school, and other Southerners promoted Robert E. Lee as the country's preeminent "man of honor." Northern veterans, meanwhile, threatened to boycott a joint reunion at Gettysburg in 1938 if Confederate veterans were allowed to display their flag, and they condemned the use of the phrase "War Between the States" instead of "Civil War." Clearly, the symbols of the past had an important and enduring legacy that still produced serious disagreements.

Sectional rivalries may not be completely dead, but it's hard to imagine the memory of Abraham Lincoln inspiring such a high level of feeling these days; the demise of everyone directly involved in the Civil War makes it a much less emotional issue than it was 85 years ago. Other historical controversies seem even more fleeting. In the 1890s, Anglo Americans protested the proposal to make Columbus Day a legal holiday because only "the Mafia" would be interested in celebrating the life of an Italian; in 1915, prejudice against German Americans forced the removal of a statue of Baron Von Steuben at Valley Forge; and the 1920s saw a movement to condemn American history textbooks as full of pro-British propaganda. These debates, of course, just seem silly today: Historical controversies always result from contemporary concerns, and few people now care about the issues that inspired such strong feelings against Italians, Germans, or the British. It's hard to imagine anyone getting upset about a monument to Baron Von Steuben anymore.

But as we all know, there are other contemporary issues that still inspire fierce passions. Racial tensions, both spoken and unspoken, permeate every sphere of our society and invariably affect our understanding of how the story of American history should be told. Since the beginning of Black History Week in 1926 (and before), teachers, parents, students, and scholars have argued that African Americans deserve a more prominent place in that story. This perspective has grown even more inclusive in recent years, as it becomes apparent that all racial and ethnic groups—as well as women, working people, and others—should be part of the story of American history and that they should be included as full and active participants rather than marginal "contributors."

Because issues of race, gender, and class still divide our society, though, every attempt to tell a more inclusive story of American history is met with fierce resistance, as defenders of the status quo argue that these attempts minimize the achievements of the men who made our country great. Ironically, though, it's rare for anyone to admit that this argument is one of interpretation; doing so would lead to controversy, and historian Michael Kammen argues that Americans have never wanted their history to be controversial; he maintains that Americans have always looked to history to provide a kind of comforting and guilt-free nostalgia and that they have consistently "depoliticized" the past.

THE GOAL OF HISTORY EDUCATION

Teachers may consider history education a daunting task, with its multiple activities and purposes, its interpretative basis, its controversial nature, and so on.

Historical controversies have been a regular feature of U.S. life. Kammen (1991), Nash, Crabtree, & Dunn (1997), Novick (1988)

Kammen (1991)

Kammen (1991)

Contemporary concerns lead to controversies over historical interpretations.

Racial controversies influence our understanding of history.

Attempts to tell a more inclusive story of American history are met with fierce resistance. Casanova (1995), Cornbleth & Waugh (1995), Evans (1988), Ravitch & Schlesinger (1990), Thornton (1990)

Kammen (1991)

And indeed, it is a complex undertaking, and the best history teachers struggle throughout their careers to get a better handle on this stubborn subject. In the face of such challenges, it may seem easiest to dismiss the issues raised in this chapter and simply conform to tradition. Many teachers do precisely that: They plod through the content of the curriculum, and they spend their time trying to keep the students quiet and submissive. But that's no way to teach. If teachers do no more than cover content and manage behavior, their students will learn little and care less, and teachers themselves will become frustrated and cynical. To avoid such depressing developments, teachers must have clear goals to drive their instruction, goals that focus their work and inspire their students. Teachers who do things differently—who resist the temptation of conformity—have a sense of purpose that extends beyond covering content or controlling students' behavior.

We believe one overarching goal can and should drive history education in the United States: Preparing students for participation in a pluralist democracy. Throughout this chapter, we have outlined aspects of historians' work, as well as the multiple purposes that influence history in school and out. All these perspectives help us better understand historical activity and the influences on students' understanding, yet none can tell us how we should teach history. Schools are not miniature research universities, nor do they simply mirror what goes on in the outside world. Educational decisions must be made on the basis of educational values, and there is a long tradition in the United States of educating students for democracy. This has always been the primary objective of the social studies, and of course history is part of that broader subject. Yet although most teachers would accept that students should be prepared for democratic citizenship, they may not always have a clear image of what that means. In order for the goal of democratic participation to provide the direction that teachers need, we must be clear about what it involves.

First, democracy requires participation, and this means more than voting in elections once in a while. Traditional civics education has focused primarily on the relationship between individuals and the state, and thus students have learned about political representation, legal rights and responsibilities, and the management of conflict. Yet participatory democracy is characterized as much by collaboration as by competition, and this collaboration takes place in a variety of settings—in unions, churches, neighborhood groups, professional associations, faculties, parent–teacher organizations, political parties, and so forth. In each of these settings, people reason together to take action in pursuit of a better future. This points to a second characteristic of participatory democracy: concern for the common good. We cannot simply pursue our own private interests or attempt to impose our will on others; we must be concerned with what is best for all the communities of which we are a part. Without such concern, people are little more than members of a loose association of selfish individuals, and they can hardly consider themselves part of a community at all. Moreover, in a pluralist society such as the United States, we must take account of multiple perspectives on what constitutes the common good and how to get there. This emphasis on pluralism is the third characteristic of democratic participation and perhaps the hardest to achieve. There is no preexisting consensus that tells us what to strive for or how we should live together; these are issues that must be worked out by carefully listening to each other, even when we disagree. Especially when we disagree.

History education cannot single-handedly produce a democratic society, nor can it guarantee that students will reason together, care for the common good, or listen to each other. However, the subject should be able to contribute toward each of these. It can do so, first, by giving students the chance to take part in reasoned judgment. Citizens in a democracy must look at evidence together and decide on the best course of action, and this strategy is precisely what is involved in analyzing historical information: We have to make choices about what information is reliable and how it can be used to reach conclusions about the past. Second, history can engage students in consideration of the common good, an activity that depends on identification with larger communities—ethnic, national, global, or all these at once—and on a sense of right and wrong. By considering historical events that affected their communities, and by considering the justice of these events, students should be better prepared, and perhaps better motivated, to engage with such issues today. Finally, history can play a critical role in helping students understand perspectives that are different than their own. Whenever we consider the actions of people in the past, we have to come to grips with ideas, attitudes, and beliefs that are no longer prevalent. We cannot simply dismiss such differences, or else we would be unable to understand anything that happened in history. To make sense of the subject, we must strive to see the logic of ways of life different than our own—and this should have some payoff in understanding diverse perspectives in the present. At the very least, it's worth a try.

The study of history can give students experience reaching conclusions based on evidence.

The study of history can engage students in deliberations over the common good.

The study of history can help students understand perspectives different than their own.

CONCLUSIONS

From our perspective, the desire to avoid controversy leads to one of the most serious weaknesses in the discussion of history—the refusal to admit that all history is interpretive. Those who defend the status quo portray their version as the "real" story (since it's already in the textbooks) and condemn all other interpretations as somehow weakening the "truth" of American history. Given that these arguments are usually made by precisely those people who benefit most from ignoring issues of race, class, and gender, that position is hardly surprising. But if schools are to prepare students for active citizenship in a democracy, they can neither ignore controversy nor teach students to passively accept someone else's historical interpretations. Being a citizen of a democracy means much more than that. Education for democratic citizenship requires that students learn to take part in meaningful and productive discussion with people of diverse viewpoints. Consequently, throughout this book, we portray history as a subject in which students learn how people create accounts of the past and how those accounts could be told differently. Far from being limited to some select group of students, we think this kind of instruction is practical for all children in the elementary and middle grades, and in the next chapter, we explain the principles of teaching and learning that guide our approach.

Lerner (1997)

Hahn (1998), Parker (1996)

2

IT'S NOT JUST A MISHAP

The Theory Behind Disciplined Inquiry

Understanding theory to me was like "Ah ha!" Teachers hear so much about theory, and when they go to a workshop or an in-service, they usually say, "Skip the theory, just get to the practical stuff." And so much of what I used to do I just did by instinct—I knew what worked, what would bring results, but I never knew why. Theory helped me understand why it worked, why A plus B equals C. I understood how cooperative learning and integrated instruction and sheltered English all went together; it was like the pieces of a puzzle—they all made sense together. I realized the things I was doing weren't just disconnected pieces, but were part of a design. I found out all these practical ideas I was using had a theoretical foundation behind them.

Knowing theory makes my teaching better. I can pick and choose better—I have a better sense of what will work and what won't. A lot of what I used to do was hit-or-miss; I would try something, and I would never use it again. Now when I consider a new teaching idea, I can filter it through what I know about theory: I can decide whether it adds to my program or whether it's just busy work. When I go to a conference, I can say, "Oh, that helps build schema," or "That's integrated language"—versus some program that's just a hundred questions or something, where I say, "That wouldn't work, it's not authentic." And theory helps me make sure I'm not doing something just because it looks cute, like, "Oh, gee, I'll have them make a scrapbook." Now I might have students make a scrapbook from the point of a view of a character in a novel, because I know it helps them pick out main ideas, develops their ability to understand characters, provides an authentic assessment—it actually teaches something, it isn't just a cute idea. I don't think, "Oh, isn't that cute! Oh, a bear!" I understand why teaching thematically isn't just having a heart or a bear on every handout.

—Rhoda Coleman, Fifth-grade teacher
Buford Avenue School, Lennox, California

Rhoda is right: Sometimes teachers hear a lot of theory, and usually it doesn't seem as important as the practical ideas—the good stuff. And some theory really isn't very useful: We've all heard or read theories that obviously came about in a laboratory or office, developed by people who didn't seem to have any idea what real children do in real classrooms. But theory, like teaching, can be good, bad, or somewhere in between. From our perspective, good theory helps teachers make sense of their own experience: It provides them with a clearer understanding of what they see in their classrooms every day—the "Ah ha!" Rhoda mentions. Good theory also helps teachers plan more effective and meaningful lessons for their students: Just as Rhoda explains, theory allows teachers to sep-

Useful theory helps teachers make sense of their own experience.

arate ideas that teach something important from those that are simply cute, novel, or well packaged. Rather than devoting years to trial-and-error attempts to find the best lesson ideas, a teacher who understands the theory behind how students learn can more consistently develop effective plans.

In this chapter, we lay out the basic theoretical principles that guide our understanding of how to teach history. On the one hand, these principles represent our reading of sociocultural perspectives on learning and contemporary cognitive psychology. On the other, they also reflect key aspects of the best history teaching we've seen. Rather than being removed from the realities of the classroom, the theory described in this chapter draws on what we know from our experience with teachers and students. We find these ideas useful in understanding what makes for good teaching, and we think they will help teachers plan their own instruction. Without these principles, the activities we describe in the rest of the book are good but isolated lessons, and teachers may or may not be able to use them in their own classes. But by understanding the theory that guides this approach, teachers can apply and adapt these suggestions to meet the needs of their students.

The research base for much of this chapter is summarized in Bruer (1993), Gardner (1991b), Good & Brophy (1999), especially chapter 10, Wertsch (1998), and Wood (1998)

TEACHING AND LEARNING MUST HAVE PURPOSE

Levstik & Groth (2005)

There is a saying in our language that we correct our mistakes from the past. From history we are able to correct the present.

—Junior Secondary student, Ghana

We want to know [history] because everybody has a different culture—how they did each thing …. And then we can learn from them.

—Lena and Leah, Fifth-grade students, U.S.

From their earliest years, children willingly engage in a wide array of learning experiences, many of them quite challenging. As they grow up, they practice for hours to qualify for a team, try out for a play, or play in a band. A child may struggle to read a school text but manage a complicated computer maneuver with ease. What makes the difference? Certainly children learn some things solely for a grade and with little or no expectation that they will ever use what they have learned outside of school, but as we can all attest, a good deal of the knowledge acquired in this manner quickly fades. Reading the computer manual or practicing for a play, team, or band, on the other hand, serve a variety of real purposes for many students. This sense of purpose motivates study, of course, but it also aids memory. Unfortunately, few children experience school history as similarly useful. Instead, as one fifth grader of our acquaintance explained, school history is "usually something you're supposed to *know*, not *do*." History, at least as children experience it in school, is too rarely connected to any important purpose and too often simply something to know for a test.

For further discussion of the purposes of history, particularly in schools, see Barton & Levstik (2003, 2004), Calclasure (1999), Husbands et al. (2003), Lowenthal (1998)

Barton (2001), Barton & McCully (2005), Levstik & Groth (2003), Levstik (2000, 2001)

Asked to reflect on why history might be worth learning, students in the United States tend to rely on humanistic purposes—developing a deeper understanding of self and, less often, of others. We find little evidence, however, that they connect the study of history to the kind of participatory democratic citizenship we discussed in the previous chapter. In this regard, U.S. students are not so different from children in other parts of the world. Children we have interviewed in other democratic societies may put more emphasis on learning others' history than do students in the United States, but like their U.S. counterparts, they rarely link history and citizenship. Ghanaian students represent an interesting and provocative exception. Ghana's national curriculum explicitly links history with democratic and humanistic goals in order to promote peaceful coexistence, cooperation, tolerance, and interdependence among different nations and cultures. As did other students we have interviewed, Ghanaian children understood history as deepening their understanding of themselves and others, but they also thought that history prepared them to help develop and strengthen Ghana's democracy. By learning the history of each other's ethnic groups, one girl explained, "perhaps we will not have the troubles [interethnic warfare] of other countries in Africa."

Levstik & Groth (2003)

As we explained in chapter 1, we share these students' hope that historical education, well directed, will support better-informed democratic participation. The Ghanaian experience suggests that when this goal is adopted by teachers and shared with students, students are more likely to see historical study as purposeful and significant—and worth learning. Being explicit about purpose has other benefits, too. First of all, clear purposes direct content selection, encourage a sense of agency among students, and create an environment that supports continued intellectual growth. In Ghana, for instance, students learn about the connections between past and present political, economic, and social realities of different ethnic and religious groups because a primary purpose of history in this pluralist democracy is developing a sense of common identity—and citizenship—while respecting existing loyalties and identifications. Similar purposes in the United States might direct us to more fully explore race, class, gender, and ethnicity, moving beyond stories of collective oppression to more fully address individual and group agency—spending time on how people have resisted oppression, worked to build coalitions to solve problems, lived rich and full lives. An investigation of *Brown v. Board of Education,* for instance, could call student attention to how the courts interpret law—perhaps inviting a lawyer to class to explain how the Supreme Court works—but also to the power of collective action—sit-ins, boycotts, teach-ins, letter writing. Many communities have members who participated in these activities and who would be more than willing to share their experiences with students. Students might also investigate current manifestations of collective action: building a community garden, political campaigns, and the like. This kind of purposeful history teaching provides some of the background necessary for more thoughtful and informed citizen participation. It also provides children with evidence that even difficult struggles can have positive outcomes.

Buah (1998), Ninsin (1996)

Purpose directs content selection, encourages a sense of agency, and supports intellectual growth.

Fertig (2003), Jackson (2003), Nasir & Saxe (2003), Payne (2003)

Menkart, Murray, & View (2004)

Education without purpose not only robs children of the desire to learn, it undermines their ability to learn. Learning occurs when students make sense of their choices and actions. If their actions are pointless—directed at nothing so much as pleasing a teacher, or earning a passing grade—than their capacity for intellectual growth is stunted. Good teaching focuses on helping students connect what they are learning to some overarching purpose that suggests questions for investigation, provides a reason for in-depth understanding, and suggests uses for the results of those investigations, supporting intellectual growth as well as civic competence.

Garrison (2003)

LEARNING MEANS IN-DEPTH UNDERSTANDING

You have to go into a topic in depth, not just see who can get to the American Revolution by May; otherwise, they won't remember it. I may be slow because I'm just on Jamestown, but my students still remember what they learned about Native Americans. It's important that they're actually *doing* history, not just memorizing information.

—Rebecca Valbuena, Fifth-grade teacher
Baldwin Park, California

I don't remember very much about the Revolution, but it doesn't matter. We'll get it again in junior high.

—Fifth-grade student (one month after studying the topic)
Fort Thomas, Kentucky

Experts have more organized and well-developed schemas than novices. Chi (1976), Chi, Feltovich, & Glaser (1981), Sternberg & Horvath (1995)

In any subject, some people achieve more than others. An engineer can build a better bridge than a college undergraduate, for example, and an experienced doctor diagnoses illness better than a first-year medical student. Among younger students, some read better than others, some solve math problems more easily, and some are better dancers, musicians, basketball players, and so on. Psychological research that investigates differences between *experts* and *novices* in various fields indicates that those who are more capable do not simply know more, nor do they necessarily have any greater general intelligence or reasoning ability; rather, they have a better understanding of the key concepts in their field and a more developed understanding of when and how to apply those concepts. In the language of cognitive psychology, experts have more organized *schemas*, or mental representations of knowledge, than novices.

Memorizing facts rarely results in conceptual understanding.

From this perspective, simply knowing more facts does not necessarily mean greater understanding; students may learn facts without having any idea what they mean or why they're important. In elementary school, for example, many children memorize multiplication and division tables to perfection but have no idea how to solve real-life problems; even though they know plenty of "math facts," they don't know enough about what the operations mean to use them in real situations. They know facts about division without really understanding what division is all about. Similarly, many students memorize the names of state capitals in fifth grade, but few have any idea what a state capital is or what goes on there. They have retained some trivial facts about place-name geography but have no understanding of geographical principles.

Effective teaching helps students learn important organizing ideas. Bamford & Kristo (1998), Good & Brophy (1999), Prawat (1989a, 1989b)

National Council for the Social Studies (1994), National Council of Teachers of Mathematics (1989), National Research Council (1996)

Good teaching, then, focuses on helping students learn important organizing ideas, rather than simply covering massive amounts of factual information. Teaching writing, for example, means teaching students to communicate—how to write for an audience, how to organize information, how to revise, and so on—not how to diagram sentences; diagraming sentences simply doesn't have anything to do with becoming a good writer. Similarly, teaching geography means focusing on human–environmental interactions, the movement of people, goods, and ideas through space, and so on—not the names of state capitals; knowing the names of state capitals has nothing to do with the key concepts of geography. The standards issued by national organizations in science, math, and social studies all focus on developing this kind of in-depth understanding.

In-depth understanding requires sustained study. Newman, Secada, & Wehlage (1995), Wells & Chang-Wells (1992)

Such learning does not involve the same all-or-nothing mastery as remembering isolated facts: Either you know the capital of Wyoming or you don't, but understanding complicated concepts like culture, environment, and society develop gradually over time; students learn more each time they encounter them. In-depth understanding also requires the time for sustained attention: Students have to study topics in enough depth to understand them and reflect on the meaning and significance of what they've studied. Although it's certainly possible to cover a great deal of information by going through a textbook one week at a time, students are unlikely to learn anything important from doing so. Unfortunately, the study of history has been one of the worst offenders in this regard; too many students experience history as part of a "race to get to the American Revolution by May," in Rebecca's words. When students rush through dates and events without understanding their reasons or significance, the best they can hope for is to "get it again in junior high," as the fifth grader said earlier.

History involves the sustained study of important topics.

To develop an in-depth understanding of history, students have to engage in sustained study of the kinds of topics identified in the first chapter. Instead of moving through the major events of world history chronologically, for example, a teacher might devote a two-month unit to the history of human interaction with the environment. A unit like that would not mean identifying every time people and the environment have interacted—obviously impossible!—but developing students' understanding of the variety of ways people throughout time have adapted to the environment, changed it to meet their needs, competed for resources, and so on. And rather than learning a list of names, dates, and events (to be forgotten quickly), students would be *doing* history, as Rebecca suggests—questioning, collecting data, interpreting, explaining. Admittedly, a teacher may cover less material that way, but students will learn more of the things that make for expert understanding.

INSTRUCTION MUST BUILD ON STUDENTS' PRIOR KNOWLEDGE

You have to start with what the kids already know. Just reading the text and answering the questions at the end of the chapter doesn't work for my LEP [limited English proficient] students, and I really don't think it works for any students. You can't just let them go in and read a chapter cold. If you can't build on something they already know, they can't learn it. They can't understand it if they have no background; they don't get a thing out of it, and you're wasting your time. Students need to put themselves in the place of someone at the time, or read a diary entry—something more personal. A lot of times history is "untouchable," and if I can say, "This is what an eleven-year-old girl really wrote," they're like, "Wow!" That really makes it come alive. They like to read about everyday people who lived a long time ago, even more than famous people, because they can compare it more to their own lives.

—Rebecca Valbuena

No one these days seriously believes that children enter schools as "blank slates" or that the purpose of instruction is simply to fill them up with information. Before they ever arrive in a classroom, children have developed an understanding of the world around them: They have their own ideas about language, counting, the natural world, and even social relations. These intuitive theories are based on their direct experiences with people and objects and often are quite accurate: Preschoolers know that fire is hot, that three cookies is more than one, that sometimes people don't tell the truth, and so on. Other times, their ideas are inaccurate—or at least incomplete—as when they believe that the world is flat, that there are no more Native Americans, or that banks store their customers' money in individual boxes.

> Children do not enter school as blank slates.

To help students develop their understanding, teachers must directly address the knowledge they bring with them to school and build on it whenever possible. To learn, people have to link new experiences to previous understanding: They have to restructure their mental schemas. Sometimes people simply add new information; an automobile mechanic who knows how engines work adds to her schema when she works on a model she's never encountered before. Other times, restructuring involves more complete shifts in understanding, as when young children start to understand that plants are alive just like animals. In either case, learning is not passive: People have to compare what they encounter to what they already know. As Rebecca notes, if you can't build on what students know, they can't learn.

> Instruction builds on the knowledge and experience children bring to school.
>
> *Carey (1985), Piaget (1952)*

Unfortunately, textbooks and other materials rarely devote much attention to students' prior understanding. Of course, every child, every class, and every community is different, and no textbook could address their variety of experiences or range of understandings. But research on learning and instruction consistently shows that when school experiences aren't linked to prior understanding, students learn very little: When they can't connect what they're supposed to learn at school to their own schemas, their understanding is notoriously superficial. Every teacher has thought her class learned something new, only to discover they had forgotten it a week later or couldn't apply it in a new situation. This kind of superficial learning occurs precisely because students have only memorized information or procedures, rather than actually modifying their understanding.

To understand information—not simply repeat it—students must connect it to their previous understanding. Textbooks cannot do that. Instead, teachers—the people who know students best—have to find out what they know and how to build on that knowledge. In science, having students make predictions before conducting experiments is an obvious way of finding out what they know, and having them compare their observations to those predictions helps connect new knowledge and old. In history, teachers can also ask students what they know about a topic before they begin studying it or ask them to make predictions about what they will learn—KWL charts, in which students discuss what they know, what they want to know, and (later) what they have learned, are one way to activate this prior knowledge. A teacher can also build on students' background knowledge by making a web of their ideas about a new topic on a large sheet of chart paper; not only does this allow her to identify what students already know, but it also can help students make connections as the class returns to the web throughout the lesson to discuss information that was correct, to correct mistakes, and to add new information. It is important to keep in mind that the usefulness of discussions, predictions, webs, and KWL charts in linking new knowledge to old depends on teachers' attention to integrating them into instruction throughout a lesson or unit, rather than simply introducing them at the beginning of a topic and then dropping them.

Another important way to connect history to what students already know is by focusing on the everyday lives of people in the past. People are one of the subjects children understand best; even from a very young age, they can reason about the beliefs and intentions of others. Margaret Donaldson goes so far as to maintain that for something to make sense to young children, it must make human sense: Children, she argues, understand situations in terms of how they involve people. Historians also focus on the human sense of situations: Much of their work involves studying the beliefs and intentions of people in the past. When the race is on to make it through the textbook, though, the human element is first to get pushed aside, and students wind up studying the things they know the least about, such as politics, diplomacy, and government. The absence of people in the study of history may account for the lack of enthusiasm that has been attributed to the subject. By focusing on people, teachers can both build on what students know best and give them a better sense of what historians actually do.

PEOPLE LEARN THROUGH DISCIPLINED INQUIRY

There's the synergistic effect of minds working together, hearing what others are doing—it gets *my* neurons sparking, it multiplies what everybody can do. Then there's also the democratic process: Everybody having a say, everybody participating, not just the teacher standing up and lecturing. It also gives them a chance to discover, instead of just *telling* them; they get to hear different points of view, and discuss outcomes on their own, rather than just you connecting the dots for them.

—Rhoda Coleman

Although teachers can activate students' prior knowledge and call attention to the way those ideas relate to new experiences, they cannot directly teach understanding—they cannot do the mental work for their students. Both research on human learning and our own experience as teachers directly contradict the

See especially Caine & Caine (1994), Gardner (1991b)

Teachers must help students connect the curriculum to their prior knowledge.

Ogle (1986)

Children strive to make human sense of the world. Donaldson (1978), Wellman & Gelman (1992)

See, for example, Brooks & Brooks (1993), Caine & Caine (1994), Duckworth (1987), Taylor (1993), Wells & Chang-Wells (1992)

"transmission" model of learning, which assumes knowledge goes directly from one source (whether a teacher or textbook) to another (the student). We cannot simply fill children up with information, no matter how elaborate our system of rewards and punishments; we can't "connect the dots" for them. People learn when they seek answers to the questions that matter to them; their understanding changes only when they become dissatisfied with what they know. The process of asking meaningful questions, finding information, drawing conclusions, and reflecting on possible solutions is known as *inquiry*.

Fortunately, children are naturally inquisitive learners who strive to make sense of their world. Anyone with young children knows the challenge of keeping up with their urge to explore and their ever-present question, "Why?" Older children, meanwhile, often devote their energy to demonstrating just how much they do know. But although humans are naturally inquisitive, most people do not sit around and memorize trivia just for the fun of it. Outside school, learning almost always takes place within the context of *purposeful* activity: People learn because they need to know how to do something important, and they can see examples of what it looks like to accomplish those tasks. Young children, for instance, learn to talk because they need to communicate, and they continually see people doing exactly that. Similarly, adolescents who hope to become dancers, musicians, or athletes learn the skills necessary to accomplish those goals, and there is no shortage of expert performances from which they can learn. Not surprisingly, people learn best when they know why they are learning and can see what it looks like to do it successfully.

This kind of purposeful learning always takes place in a sociocultural context that determines what knowledge is worth having, how to acquire it, and how to use it. Scientists, for example, do not pursue their investigations in isolation: The questions they ask, the standards they apply, and the way they report their results are the product of on-going debate and discussion among a community of scholars (and the concerns and values of the wider society also influence that community). In every field, knowledge has meaning only in the context of the questions, procedures, and debates in which it develops. Nor does any single community have a monopoly on producing knowledge; understanding of the environment, for example, may come about very differently depending on whether one is a farmer, research scientist, or environmentalist. Meaningful learning involves not just mastering the content of a subject (no matter how deeply), but understanding the nature and purpose of that subject—the diverse ways of thinking and acting mathematically, historically, or scientifically in our society. We use the term *disciplined inquiry* to refer to purposeful investigations that take place within a community that establishes the goals, standards, and procedures of study.

Teachers can capitalize on children's natural enthusiasm for learning by making their classrooms places where students explore important and meaningful questions. For most of the last century, educators have argued for the importance of teaching students how to use and apply knowledge in authentic situations (rather than simply expecting them to learn isolated or irrelevant information). The tasks students encounter at school should be similar to those people face outside school. By engaging in the same kinds of challenges as scientists, citizens, artists, business people, and so on, students will better understand the purpose of their studies and will be more likely to understand, retain, and apply what they learn. Seeing their peers, teachers, and other community members engaged in these processes is a central feature of this approach.

Unfortunately, schools rarely engage students in authentic inquiry; their experiences are usually determined by the content of textbooks or curriculum guides rather than the pursuit of meaningful knowledge. Children have few chances to investigate questions that have meaning for them or that engage then in realistic challenges. As a result, schools rarely provide students with any clear

People learn when they seek answers to questions that matter to them. *Dewey (1933, 1956)*

Inquiry is the process of asking meaningful questions finding information, drawing conclusions, and reflecting on solutions.

Children are naturally inquisitive learners.

People learn best when they understand the purpose of their learning.

Learning takes place within a sociocultural context. *Lave & Wenger (1991), Resnick (1987), Rogoff (1990), Vygotsky (1978), Wertsch (1998)*

Disciplined inquiry takes place within a community that establishes the goals, standards, and procedures of study. *For more on disciplined inquiry, see Newmann et al. (1995)*

Students should use and apply knowledge in authentic situations. *Wiggins (1993)*

sense of purpose. As we said earlier, many students have no idea why they are expected to study history, or any other subject, because they rarely see what it means to use these subjects. Although students may sometimes be admonished that they will "need this later," they rarely see examples of expert performances in science, history, mathematics, and so on. Instead, they too often see artificial exercises removed from meaningful application.

Once again, the study of history has been one of the worst offenders. In the middle grades, studying history all too often means reading a chapter in a textbook and answering the questions at the end (or, worse, memorizing the names of presidents). In the early grades, history rarely amounts to more than learning a few isolated facts about famous people connected to major holidays. In neither case do students have the opportunity to ask and answer questions important to them; in neither case do they learn how historians go about their work; in neither case do they see examples of the authentic use of historical knowledge. In fact, when asked why they think history is a subject at school or how it might help them, students sometimes can think of little except that it might be useful if they were ever on *Jeopardy!*

Barton (1994a), VanSledright (1995, 1997)

To get more from history than preparation for a game show, students must take part in disciplined inquiry, not just repeat isolated trivia. The study of history must begin with the concerns and interests of students and must help them find answers to questions that grow out of those concerns and interests. This means that students have to learn what it is to ask and answer historical questions—how to find information, how to evaluate sources, how to reconcile conflicting accounts, how to create an interpretive account. And students certainly must learn what the authentic application of historical knowledge looks like: They must see how history can explain the present, and they must see this in the most authentic of ways—through the comparison of conflicting ideas about the nature and significance of the past.

Authentic historical study involves the comparison of conflicting ideas through disciplined inquiry. *See also* Seixas (1993a)

TEACHING MEANS SCAFFOLDING

You have to provide them with structure. You don't just say, "Write a paragraph"; you introduce them to some vocabulary, brainstorm about the topic, make comparison charts and graphic organizers, and then help them use those to write a paragraph. If you want them to produce something, you have to provide structure; you have to take them where they are and move them one step further.

—Rebecca Valbuena

People learn through interaction with more knowledgeable members of a community. Lave & Wenger (1991), Rogoff (1990), Vygotsky (1978), Wertsch (1998)

Outside school, learning almost always involves ongoing collaboration among the members of a community, as more knowledgeable members help newcomers become full-fledged participants in activities they both consider worthwhile. Consider, for example, how young children learn to talk. The process extends over many years and involves countless thousands of utterances, as the child tries to speak and the adult accepts and encourages the attempt while also modeling a more fluent way to express what the child wants to say. Although the precise kinds of interaction may vary from one culture (or subculture) to the next, a child who has no opportunity at all to interact will not learn to talk; she constructs her understanding of language through interaction with fluent speakers.

To take a somewhat different example, professional schools require prospective practitioners—doctors, teachers, and so on—to engage in extensive field experiences where experts help them learn to deal with real-life situations. No one would trust a doctor who had learned medicine only from a book; to treat patients, doctors must undergo a lengthy period of practical training. During this time, experienced practitioners model the practical use of medical knowledge, and novices are gradually given more responsibility for treating patients on their own. Most learning outside the classroom follows a similar pattern. Whether related to traditional economic tasks (farming, cooking, quilting, hunting), the work of modern careers, or pursuits such as sports or the fine arts, learning usually involves a kind of *apprenticeship*, in which those who are more knowledgeable gradually help novices develop expertise. They provide them with the structure Rebecca mentions.

Unfortunately, children rarely have the chance to take part in this kind of sustained interaction at school. Most often, they are expected to listen while teachers transmit information to them. Participation is usually limited to the common *initiation-response-evaluation* pattern: The teacher asks a question, a student responds, and the teacher tells her whether the answer was right. The purpose of such interactions is to assess students' retention of information, not to help them pursue questions or issues that interest them. Other times, students may be given independent assignments or expected to "do research," but they aren't taught how to go about the process of learning. As every teacher knows, few students have the skills necessary to conduct inquiry on their own. Although inquiry is essential to education, simply assigning such tasks won't guarantee meaningful results. Most students need direct help to make the most of their experiences, and teachers' most important responsibility is to provide them with the structure they need to learn—a process known as *scaffolding*. Just as scaffolding on a construction project supports people as they work, scaffolding in the classroom supports students as they learn. Children learn best when they take part in joint activities with teachers (and more knowledgeable peers) who help them go about their studies.

Scaffolding takes many forms. First, teachers have to encourage students' interest in accomplishing tasks; although children are naturally inquisitive, they are more likely to follow through with their investigations when teachers help them develop and maintain interest. Second, teachers must actively support and encourage students as they work through assignments. This support often involves breaking a task down into manageable components; although we certainly don't advocate a behaviorist "task analysis" that teaches small and isolated skills, students can write a better paragraph when they become familiar with vocabulary, engage in brainstorming, and plan their compositions (as Rebecca explained earlier) rather than simply being told, "Write a paragraph." Similarly, students learn more from inquiry when teachers give them experience developing questions, identifying resources, and planning presentations than when they are just sent to the library and told to "do research." Graphic organizers often play a key role in providing the structure for these tasks because, as Rebecca says, if you want students to produce something, you have to provide them with structure.

Another crucial element of this scaffolding is the teacher's modeling of procedures. As suggested earlier, teachers must demonstrate what it looks like to do history; just as students need to see their teachers reading and writing, they need to see them grappling with historical questions, collecting information, making generalizations, and so on. Teachers must show students what it looks like to accomplish a task successfully; if they don't see examples, they won't know what they are supposed to do. In addition, teachers have to work closely with students as they try out these procedures; this involves constantly using "probing questions" to help students discover how to apply historical skills in their own work. Finally, teachers have to give students critical feedback on their performances: They must help them understand how their work compares to ideal versions. Without such feedback, many students will not know whether they are accomplishing a task successfully. The ultimate goal of all these forms of scaffolding is to transfer control from teacher to student by enabling students to plan their learning and monitor their own progress—abilities sometimes referred to as *metacognition*.

In apprenticeships, those who are more knowledgeable help novices develop expertise.

Cazden (1988)

Teachers have to help students develop the skills necessary to engage in inquiry.

Good & Brophy (1999), Rogoff (1990)

Teachers scaffold students' understanding by providing the structure they need to be successful.

Teachers' modeling of procedures is a crucial element of scaffolding.

Teacher use probing questions to help students discover how to apply historical skills in their own work.

Providing critical feedback improves achievement.

Metacognition refers to students' planning and monitoring of their own learning process.

CONSTRUCTIVE ASSESSMENT

Assessment and evaluation are used interchangeably throughout this chapter.

Assessment, evaluation, testing, and worst of all, *grading*—for many educators, these are three of the most unpleasant words in their professional vocabulary. They conjure up a host of negative associations—from stanines and percentiles to long evenings spent poring over countless versions of the same assignment, redlining and correcting ridiculous mistakes, pleading for insight into why students just don't get it. Considering how much importance schools attach to grades and other forms of evaluation, students are usually shocked to discover that their teachers don't enjoy the process and would just as soon jettison the whole enterprise. For most of us, it's not evaluating but instructing—the scaffolding we discuss throughout this book—that provides our image of what teaching is all about. Evaluation seems, at best, a necessary evil to be tacked onto the end of units so we can come up with a grade for report cards. At worst, it can ruin a perfectly good relationship between a teacher and her students.

Evaluation can be meaningful and even enjoyable.

But it doesn't have to be that way. Instead of an unpleasant add-on, evaluation can be a meaningful and sometimes—believe it or not—enjoyable task, a set of practices at the very heart of teaching and learning. To fulfill such lofty expectations, however, evaluation must play a different role than we usually imagine. If the primary purpose of classroom evaluation is to produce a set of grades, then neither students nor teachers are likely to see much benefit in the practice. When grade books, rather than students' needs, determine the form of assessment, assignments become little more than an attempt to trip students up—to force them into revealing what they don't know so the grades will resemble a normal distribution. This obsession with sorting students out virtually guarantees that evaluation will be a negative experience, one designed to uncover the deficiencies in students' knowledge and understanding.

Hart (1994), Johnston (1992), Shepherd (1991)

In the kinds of classrooms described in this book, the primary characteristic of evaluation is that it is *constructive*. By constructive evaluation, we mean first and foremost that it serves a constructive purpose—it has beneficial effects on teaching and learning. For students, this means that evaluation tasks allow them to show what they know rather than what they don't know. The teacher is not an adversary who tries to ferret out what they have failed to accomplish but an advocate who helps students demonstrate their achievements. Most teachers at one time or another worry that students' performance doesn't accurately reflect what they have learned; they believe (or hope) that students know more than they have been able to show on tests or other assignments. Constructive assessment confronts this problem head-on by giving students as many ways of showing what they know as possible—through formal and informal measures, through tasks chosen both by teacher and student, through speaking, writing, and other forms of presentation. When students and teachers work together like this—looking for the best means of demonstrating what's been learned—students' self-esteem benefits because they have every chance to live up to their potential. The teacher's instruction is better, meanwhile, because she gains more complete insight into what students know and what they still need to learn.

In constructive assessment, teachers are advocates for students. Hart (1994), Johnston (1992), Wiggins (1989)

To gain this kind of insight, a teacher needs more than one way of tapping into students' achievement. By combining several means of assessment, she can be more confident of finding out what they know and can do. Three of the most useful ways of finding out about students are through their discussion, their writing, and their performances or presentations. No one of these tasks provides a complete picture of learning: Some students may remain silent during discussions but write fine essays, some may give insightful presentations but never finish their writing, and so on. Relying on just one measure means that students who do well in that medium—writing, speaking, drawing, or whatever—will do well, but those whose strengths lay elsewhere will seem deficient. Using multiple

Multiple forms of assessment, and opportunities for student choice, provide a more complete picture of students' progress. Harp (1993), Hart (1994), Johnston (1992)

means of assessment gives each student a chance to show what he or she knows. This approach also frequently involves giving students choices. In some cases, students may choose the form their assessment takes—a student might be allowed to decide, for example, whether an inquiry project will result in an essay, a poster, a videotape, or a presentation to the class. Other times it may be the topic of study that students choose; within a broader unit chosen by the teacher (such as the American Revolution or the Westward Movement), each student might decide which specific questions he or she would like to investigate and be evaluated on. When given choices, students are more likely to capitalize on their opportunities for learning than if they are simply answering questions posed by the teacher, using methods assigned by her.

Assessment activities should also be authentic—they should be similar to the tasks people do in their communities, in businesses, or in scholarly disciplines. This often involves preparation for an audience beyond that of the teacher. When the teacher is the only audience for a task, students have little motivation to show what they know. When children retell a story they have heard to someone who doesn't know the story, for example, their explanations are much more complete than when they know the listener has heard it as well. Similarly, when students communicate for a real audience, they perform at a much higher level than when they complete an assignment only to turn it in to the teacher; students are motivated to show what they know because of the necessity of getting their audience to understand them. This use of authentic activities highlights another characteristic of constructive evaluation—its continuity with instruction. Traditionally, teachers think of assessment as what comes after instruction: You teach students about something (or they read about it on their own) and then you test them to see if they learned it. In most classrooms, it's easy to tell the difference between teaching and assessment. In fact, schools often go to great lengths to make the two situations as different as possible: When students are being tested, they don't talk, they don't move around, they don't work together, they don't get help from the teacher. But in the kinds of classrooms described in this book, there is no such split between instruction and assessment. An observer walking into one of these classes would not be able to tell whether it was a "teaching" day or a "testing" day, because they're one and the same thing. Teachers take notes while students are talking, observe their presentations, review their projects, and read their written reports; all these are part of the ongoing assessment of learning. There are few separate times set aside for assessment because assessment is always taking place.

Perhaps the most important principle to keep in mind in assessing students' historical understanding is that constructive evaluation must be consistent with a constructivist perspective on teaching and learning. People learn new information by linking it to what they already know; their understanding, then, is never a simple reproduction of the information they encounter but always an interpretation in light of prior understanding. A student's understanding at any given time represents the interaction between external sources of information and her prior knowledge. As a result, no two people's understanding will be identical, nor will a child's understanding be the same as an adult's. Anyone's understanding of history will vary depending on what she brings to her studies; learning about history is not an all-or-nothing process in which you either "know" a topic or you don't, but a lifelong process of schema building that involves not only a greater quantity of information but also increasingly sophisticated insight into the connections and relationships among concepts. Constructive evaluation seeks to provide teachers and students a picture of how this schema-building process is going, rather than assessing whether students have "caught" discrete pieces of factual information.

Assessment tasks should involve authentic historical activities.

Hart (1994),
Wiggins (1992)

Hart (1994),
Johnston (1992)

Constructive assessment does not focus on the simple reproduction of information.

Historical understanding develops in the interaction between new sources of information and prior experience.

CONCLUSIONS

In this chapter, we have identified the aspects of human learning that we think provide the best guidance for teaching history. Based both on contemporary research in cognitive psychology and our own experience, we have argued that the best teaching makes the purposes of history explicit; focuses on in-depth understanding of important ideas related to those purposes; builds on what students already know; engages students in collaborative, disciplined inquiry, in which they investigate important questions in authentic ways; involves extensive scaffolding; and is assessed through a process of constructive evaluation. Although we have tried to describe these principles separately, they have little meaning in isolation. Teachers will not succeed if they focus on important ideas but do not build on students' prior knowledge, if they require inquiry but don't teach students how to do it, or if they teach problem solving but never address significant content. By devoting consistent attention to these principles in an integrated way, however, teachers can develop meaningful and effective instruction for students from a variety of backgrounds in a variety of circumstances. As Rebecca explains in our final quotation, understanding this theoretical background ensures that good teaching isn't just a mishap.

> I can't tell you how much [knowing about theory] has changed me; it all makes sense. Being a good teacher means you know what to do and you have a purpose for what you're doing. Everything you do has to have a theoretical base, from classroom management on. I think a lot of teachers do things naturally, but if you know the theory beforehand, it's so much more satisfying: It's not just a mishap, you're doing it on purpose. Knowing the theory takes you to a level beyond.
>
> —Rebecca Valbuena

3

THERE AREN'T A LOT OF "FOR SURE" FACTS

Building Communities of Historical Inquiry

It is 11:10 on a cool October morning and 26 seven- and eight-year-olds are gathered around their teacher, listening to a story about Johnny Appleseed. At one point, the teacher stops to talk about what is known about the historical Johnny Appleseed:

Teacher: What kind of a story is this? Remember we said that some stories were tall tales?

Jennie: And folktales!

Teacher: Right, some are folktales. And Johnny Appleseed is a le … ? le … ?

Choral: Legend!

Teacher: Legend. That means some parts of the story are?

Ryan: True.

CeCe: But some are just made up.

At this point, the children engage in a general conversation about why parts of stories might be made up. One boy suggests that the real story probably wasn't exciting; others think that people probably didn't know "the real facts" and so simply made them up.

Teacher: What parts of this story do we *think* are true?

Gabriel: Well, there *was* a man who planted apple trees. It said so in that other book.

Avram: Yeah, but his real name wasn't Appleseed, remember!

Several of the children recall that John Chapman was the "real" Johnny Appleseed. The teacher draws them back to the original question: Which parts of the story do we think are true? Again, she puts the emphasis on *think*, and the students begin to discuss "facts" versus "exaggerations." The conversation bogs down as some children repeat suggestions others have already made. Lucy and Gabriel appear to be having an argument over whether "Appleseed" can be a "real" name, because it was a nickname used by Chapman's contemporaries.

Lucy: See, it says here [in the encyclopedia entry] that he was "popularly known as Johnny Appleseed." I think that's what people called him then.

> *Gabriel:* Uh-uh. That's what's popular *now*.
>
> *Teacher:* I'm getting mixed up. Is there some way we can keep track of our ideas here?
>
> *Lucy:* We could make a list!

Two children get the large pad of chart paper that hangs in the front of the room. Another grabs the plastic cup of magic markers.

> *Avram:* Let's take the story in pieces! We can put each fact we find under "facts" and have exaggerations on another paper.

For the next 20 minutes, the children analyze the story, event by event. They use two other books about Johnny Appleseed, along with a brief encyclopedia entry, but there are several places where they aren't sure whether something is a fact. At the teacher's suggestion, they use red markers to circle these items. Someone else suggests underlining "for sure" facts in green and "for sure" exaggerations in black.

> *CeCe:* There sure aren't a lot of "for sure" facts!
>
> *Teacher:* No, there aren't. We seem to have a lot of questions about this story. What would it look like if we wrote it so that it didn't have any exaggerations? Could we write it so that it only said what we are pretty sure happened?
>
> *CeCe:* That would be a short story!

Hyde & Bizar (1989), Newmann et al. (1995), Wells & Chang-Wells (1992), Wertsch (1998)

The students in the previous vignette are members of the kind of community of reflective, disciplined inquiry already described in chapter 2. Such a community encourages participation with others in goal-directed activity, engagement with intellectual problems that cannot be resolved through the routine application of previously learned knowledge, and understanding and resolving problems with the aid of a variety of intellectual tools. Establishing a community of inquiry in a classroom that provides a meaningful, integrative, challenging, and active context for learning history, as Rebecca Valbuena notes in chapter 2, is not just a mishap. Whether primary children are investigating the facts and exaggerations of an American historical legend, fourth graders are writing the history of their school, or middle schoolers are debating the merits of nonviolent protest as a response to colonialism in India, communities of inquiry have certain things in common:

Characteristics of communities of inquiry.

- There is lively conversation and intellectual negotiation among participants who each have varying degrees of expertise in the topic at hand.
- Conversation focuses on questions and tasks worthy of sustained discussion and in-depth study.
- Students use both prior knowledge and newly gathered data to "master perplexity"—to make sense out of what seemed not to make sense when their study began.
- Teachers model and students practice "classroom thoughtfulness"—taking the time necessary to think carefully and thoroughly before responding to questions or attempting to resolve problems.
- Students *do history*—they pose, investigate, and at least tentatively answer historical questions and develop historical explanations and interpretations—they don't just memorize the history others have done.

This chapter introduces the kind of reflective, disciplined inquiry that sustains the communities of inquiry you will meet throughout this book. Well-constructed, integrated instruction presents students with tasks that require engagement with the content and methods of the discipline of history while providing the scaffolding necessary for students to engage in in-depth study.

Scaffolding is necessary for in-depth inquiry.

Consider how the teacher in the opening vignette structures her primary students' engagement with historical inquiry. First, because the Johnny Appleseed legend is a common children's story and an example of the kind of historical mythologizing that frequently appears in the elementary curriculum, it provides an appropriate forum for *talking historically*—communally analyzing the legend's historical roots. Second, the teacher scaffolds the historical talk so that it becomes a conversation, not a recitation. She calls children's attention to the genre—a legend—with which they are dealing and reminds them that legends have particular characteristics that are important for readers to know. Note, too, that the teacher does not ask which parts of the story are "known to be true"— known by someone else. Rather, she asks her students to call on their prior knowledge of literary genres and the historical Johnny Appleseed and consider what parts they "think are true."

"Talking historically" is conversation not recitation.

The choice of language is important here. By asking students what they think, the teacher models a more tentative language that invites speculation rather than final answers. She also encourages students to take intellectual risks that keep conversations alive and engaging. Who is Johnny Appleseed, anyway? Is this fiction or history? How can we distinguish between facts and exaggerations? What makes us think that one part of a story is true, but not another? As they participate in the conversation, these children not only think about what counts as history but also consider why people might exaggerate beyond the historical data and how different genres use historical information—important questions about the ways in which history is used in the larger world. They also learn that some of the most interesting questions don't have single, or easy, answers. These questions are central to reflective, disciplined inquiry, but just as important is the historical talk surrounding them.

TALKING HISTORICALLY

As already mentioned in chapter 2, all of us learn how to "mean" in a variety of social contexts. In addition, we learn how to express what we mean through various symbolic forms—literature, art, music, dance, drama, writing, and conversation, among others. Symbolic forms are not, however, simply windows through which meaning shines clearly. Instead, symbolic form both expresses and shapes meaning. A photograph of a family standing beside a covered wagon (Fig. 3.1) shows us how small a space early pioneers had for all their possessions. We can analyze other details as well: the military uniform that one man wears, the prairie stretching behind the family. But the photograph also freezes what would otherwise have been a fleeting moment, giving it weight and meaning it might not otherwise have had. The frown on the woman's face comes to represent more than simple weariness with posing or a response to bright sun; instead, we read in her face the rigors of the overland journey.

Lemke (1991), Van Oers & Wardukker (1999), Wells (1999)

Arnheim (1981), Levstik & Barton (1996)

As do photographs, written texts store, shape, and transmit information, but they use words rather than visual images. The use of imagery and analogy, the choice and arrangement of words, and the expectations we have for a particular genre shape how we interpret written texts. Both the descriptions in Fig. 3.2 describe the same man, General James Longstreet, a Confederate officer who fought at Gettysburg, but the first is from Michael Shaara's Pulitzer Prize-winning novel *Killer Angels*; the second from Mark Boatner's *Civil War Dictionary*. As you read each description, consider how language shapes your image of this historical figure. What are the differences you can identify between Shaara's and Boatner's descriptions?

Purves (1990)

Boatner (1969), Shaara (1974)

Language shapes our views of history.

In the first excerpt, Longstreet is willing to lose it all; in the second, he is accused of holding back. Shaara's Longstreet is fearless; Boatner's lethargic. The first account has a more personal voice; the second more distanced and impersonal. Yet neither is objective. What if Boatner had described Longstreet's reluctance to send men to certain death, rather than his "lethargy?" Or if Shaara described a man frozen by his fear of "blind stupid human frailty?" In reading each of these passages, you can't ask the authors for further explanation, hear

Purves (1990)

FIG. 3.1.   On the prairie: Family with covered wagon, 1886.

their tone of voice, or read body language. You negotiate meaning with the text rather than with the author. In other words, the text does not "mean" by itself. Rather, you rely on your own life experience, including your experiences as a reader of other texts, to make sense out of the semantic clues provided by the text. If this seems confusing, think about a book you have read more than once. Perhaps it was a story you read when you were younger and returned to as an adult. You probably found that the book took on new dimensions with a second reading. The words did not change, but you did, and so you understood it quite differently at a second reading. In part, this is what the students in the vignette are learning to do. But they are also shaping their historical understanding through another symbolic form—talk. By talking historically, students *do* have an opportunity to ask for further explanation, hear tone of voice, or read body language. They can negotiate meaning, try out ideas, keep or discard them—jointly making sense of history. This process is at least as challenging and important to historical thinking as learning to read either written texts or visual images.

In discussion, children jointly make sense out of history. *Wells (1999), Wertsch (1998)*

Longstreet knew himself. There was no fear there. The only fear was not of death, was not of the war, was of blind stupid human frailty, of blind proud foolishness that could lose it all. He was thinking very clearly now. Mind seemed to uncloud like washed glass. Everything cool and crystal.

Michael Shaara, *Killer Angels*, p. 202

[Longstreet's] delay in attacking on the second day at Gettysburg, and his lethargy in organizing "Pickett's Charge" on the third exposed him to the most vindictive of criticism by Southerners after the war.

Mark Boatner III, *The Civil War Dictionary*, p. 490

FIG. 3.2.   Contrasting views of a historical figure.

Sometimes we take conversation for granted. Talk seems so common that we forget how intricate a really engaging conversation can be. First, the style of talk implies meaning beyond words. Certain styles signal playful engagement. Participants exchange what in other circumstances would be insults but in this context are not meant seriously. Other styles signal more serious intent—negotiations during a labor dispute, for instance. And this only scratches the surface of what you already know about conversation. You know, for instance, that forms of address signal status and tone of voice implies feelings not necessarily conveyed by words. In addition, different disciplines use different forms of oral discourse. Mathematicians may talk about "proofs," or the application of algorithms, and rely on mathematical concepts to support their ideas. History, too, has its own forms of oral discourse, including expositions, explanations, justifications, narratives, and dialogue. Each of these genres uses historical content and processes as the substance of discourse. Making sense in history, then, is at least partially constructed within (or in opposition to) this discourse as participants test out ideas, listen to other possibilities, ask questions, and challenge interpretations. For children to learn history, then, they need practice in using these oral genres as well as the written and visual ones we have already mentioned.

Conversations are intricate social interactions.
Oyler (1996)

Different disciplines have their own forms of discourse.

Bakhtin (1986), Leinhardt (1994), Swales (1990), Todorov (1990)

We are not suggesting that teaching history to elementary and middle school students is simply a matter of inducting them into the professional culture and discourse of historians. Although the conversation in the prior vignette has some elements that would be familiar to historians, elementary and middle school children are not—and need not be—full participants in the semiotic communities of professional historians. Instead, they employ meaning-making practices that work in their multiple communities, including the classroom. Some of these practices barely intersect with those of professional historians. In younger children's parlance, for instance, the term *history* can be a warning: "If you don't watch out, you're history!" Older students may also use the term *history* in this way, but they tend to be more adept with an academic history genre. In Fig. 3.3, you can see how a fifth grader is learning to employ this genre. As you read Kareem's comments on American history, notice how he talks about history in terms of cause and effect (if not necessarily multiple causation). Note, too, that he introduces a discourse of morality, using the personal pronoun *we* and passing judgment on the events he describes.

Levstik & Barton (1996), Levstik (2000)

History has intersecting discourse communities.

Levstik & Pappas (1987)

Kareem's interest in making historical judgments, and the primary students' enthusiastic participation in "deconstructing" the Johnny Appleseed legend, combine elements of literary, historical, and moral discourses as well as classroom protocols. This is rich and interesting talk. It is also the kind of talk that is

---

We had established 13 colonies and then the English started taxing us and we got fed up with that, that was after the French and English War. So then . . . we got our own independence and George Washington was our leader. [Later] people got in wagons and start moving westward to find new lands and settle and stuff because they didn't even know what was back there.... I think it's a shame that we tore down all those trees and ran off the Indians, 'cause it was their land in the first place.... We were trying to con 'em—tell 'em that if they signed this petition paper, they'd still have land, this small portion and they did that 'cause the colonists knew that the Indian's couldn't read. They could read their signs that they made but they couldn't read English.

Kareem, Grade 5

FIG. 3.3. Combining an academic history genre and the discourse of morality.

unlikely to occur if the only experience children have with history is filling in blanks on a worksheet or memorizing presidents in chronological order. Nor is it likely to occur where children are silenced because either what they have to say, or the way in which they say it, isn't valued. This is particularly important in classrooms where the children come from diverse linguistic or cultural backgrounds. Talking historically is more likely to occur where teachers and students value the multiple perspectives that diversity can provide, where conversation revolves around questions worthy of sustained discussion, and where conversation is supported by in-depth study.

Diversity is valued in communities of inquiry.

Hansen (1993), Levstik (1997), Peetoom (1991)

THE IMPORTANCE OF QUESTIONS

Anything that may be called knowledge, or a known object, marks a question answered, a difficulty disposed of, a conclusion cleared up, an inconsistency reduced to coherence, a perplexity mastered.

—John Dewey, *The Quest for Certainty* (1929, pp. 226–227)

If children are to enthusiastically engage in sustained conversation about history, four things are required:

Collingwood (1961), Degenhardt & McKay (1990b), Parker & Hess (2001), Penyak & Duray (1999)

- Questions that are worth discussing.
- Questions that do not have simple or single answers.
- Sufficient and appropriate data sources so that students can attempt to answer the questions.
- Imaginative entry into the past.

Questions are at the heart of inquiry.

Obviously questions are at the heart of this approach to history. But we are talking about very different questions than the ones many of us are familiar with from textbooks and workbooks. The point of these questions is not to see whether students have read a particular text; rather, it is to provide direction and motivation for the rigorous work of doing history. An example of this kind of direction and motivation can be seen in a sixth-grade classroom where the students are studying India. The class has just completed working with an artifact kit using a variety of resources to compare life in a modern Indian city with life in the students' hometown. A guest speaker previously told them that, to understand some of the differences between India and America, it is necessary to understand each country's history.

Jeanette Groth, the teacher, now asks the sixth graders to use their textbooks to identify eight events in Indian history that they consider pivotal. While the students read and take notes, Jeanette places on the board a large time line that runs from 2500 BCE to 1948 CE. She then asks students to suggest items for the time line. There is debate about whether farming in the Indus valley was pivotal and whether it could legitimately be considered to have a "main date." Soon, however, students move on to the establishment of the British East India Company, colonization by the British, and the eventual British withdrawal. They use time lines developed by the eighth-grade American history class to compare what was happening in each country during each time period. Jason points out that the colonization periods for both India and the American colonies overlap, "but our Revolution came sooner."

On the surface, this may not look terribly different than a good traditional history class. In fact, however, this activity is crucial for several reasons. First, it asks students to think about what is historically significant. Second, it makes clear that neither American nor Indian history exists in a vacuum. Finally, it establishes the historical background—prior knowledge—needed to raise the next, teacher-initiated, question: Were there any similarities in

CE (Common Era) and BCE (Before the Common Era) are used instead of AD (Anno Domini) and BC (Before Christ) by some historians, anthropologists, and archaeologists.

Some inquiries are teacher-initiated.

30

the ways in which the people of India and the people of the American colonies rid themselves of British rule? Iman exclaims, "Well, we kicked their butts!" Ainslie chimes in, "We tried to get the British mad, to get them started in a war, but the Indians tried compromise." The students draw on their fifth-grade experience in reenacting a trial of the participants in the Boston Massacre, they talk about the techniques the rebels used to end British rule, and they check dates on the time line to see what was happening in India during the same period. At this point, different groups are asked to develop comparative time lines showing British colonial rule and the independence movements in each country. By the next class, students are ready to compare colonialism and rebellion in India and North America. Their discussion is lively, requiring them to select relevant information, combine pieces of information, even though some of those pieces might at first have seemed unrelated, compare the problem under investigation with problems previously encountered, and use skills and concepts previously employed. In other words, their inquiry requires both prior knowledge in the discipline—their fifth-grade study of the American Revolution—and in-depth study—their investigation of British colonial rule in India.

Inquiry requires prior knowledge and in-depth study.

PRIOR KNOWLEDGE

We know that new knowledge builds on the learner's prior knowledge base. This seems self-evident, but it is certainly not simple, particularly in history. First of all, history might be more adequately described as a set of intersecting fields rather than as a unitary discipline. Thus, social historians, military historians, archivists, public historians, interpreters at historic sites, and genealogists, to name just a few, all deal with history, but their various fields are marked by sometimes disparate modes of inquiry, styles of communication, and perceived purposes. In addition, students bring much more background knowledge to the study of history than we sometimes credit them with. History is, after all, not confined to historians. Families construct histories as they interpret events through the lens of family involvement. The media also interpret historic events. They create documentaries and news programs that purport to explain—and sometimes make—history, but they also present fictionalized versions of the past. *Little House on the Prairie* or *Dr. Quinn, Medicine Woman*, for instance, present current sensibilities in period settings. There are also persistent historical myths and legends held dear by parts of the larger culture—Betsy Ross sewing the first flag, Columbus "discovering a new world," and so forth. For some students, these images are comforting; others may feel excluded by the popular culture's mythologies. In any case, these myths and legends are often part of the historical knowledge base that children bring to school. Once in school, students acquire historical information (and misinformation) from instruction. The sixth graders studying India, for instance, were able to think more clearly about resistance to British colonialism because they could draw on their prior study of the American Revolution. Notice, however, that their teacher did not rely on unassisted recall. Instead, there were prompts to trigger prior knowledge, most notably the American history time lines constructed by her eighth-grade class.

Because reflective, disciplined inquiry is rooted in what students already know and can do and gradually moves beyond the known, teachers must take into account the conceptions and misconceptions held by students and supported by popular culture, as well as the knowledge base provided by the fields of history. Historical inquiry develops most easily when the creation or discovery of a problem challenges prior knowledge, providing opportunities for students to outgrow what they already know. As they create and test hypotheses, explore variations on initial problems, and reflect on the consequences of an-

Levstik & Barton (1996)

Students bring background knowledge.

Barton (1995), Seixas (1993b)

History is interpreted publicly and personally, as well as by historians.

Historical myths are part of popular culture.

Barton & Levstik (1996), Levstik & Barton (1996), VanSledright (1997/1998)

Inquiry begins with challenges to prior knowledge.

swers as well as the processes of and purposes for their study, students engage in authentic historical work, building on prior knowledge to *produce* rather than *reproduce* knowledge. Although their interpretations may be naïve and are rarely new to the discipline of history, students are not simply reproducing knowledge that others have produced. Instead, they attempt to construct a coherent explanation for a set of historic events. The sixth graders' comparison of Indian and American independence movements, for instance, obviously owes much to prior studies in American history as well as to some of the facts, concepts, theories, and discourse that mark history as a discipline or field. In addition, students' attempts to construct this comparison should make them more interested in and thoughtful about other independence movements as well as other historical interpretations of the events they have just analyzed. Clearly this approach emphasizes in-depth understanding both of history and historical methods.

IMAGINATIVE ENTRY

In a fifth-grade classroom, Tessa discusses the outcome of a class trial based on the events surrounding the Boston Massacre:

> Tessa: The British won [in our class], but in the real trial the British didn't win. ... But I'm a colonist. I'm a patriot. She [the teacher] showed us all the evidence, and she showed us everything that happened and we studied it, but she didn't tell us anything that happened after that, and she said all right, are you for the British, because the British, on one hand were taxing the colonists and the colonists had no way of representing. They could not vote for people who were running in England and they had no say in their taxes they were going to do it upon them so that was on the colonists' side, but the British on the other hand, they were being thrown rocks at. My name was Archibald, and I didn't know that I had already broken my wrist on a British officer, so when I got on the stand and they said have you ever assaulted a British officer, then he said we have evidence you broke your wrists off a British officer, and I went OOH! I didn't know, but I shouldn't have said that, because in the book it said, "Bleep, you Yankee bloopers."

From Tessa's comments, we can see that she finds history neither boring nor irrelevant. Her interest in the different perspectives of British soldiers and American rebels is generated and supported by the opportunity to act historically—to take on the perspective of a participant in the historic drama. While in-depth understanding in history comes as students assess, organize, and interpret historical data in the ways already described, it is also grounded in the kind of imaginative entry into the past that is part of Tessa's experience. Students might, for instance, participate in simulations and role plays or recreate biographies or historical stories that require imaginative entry into a historical era or event. In doing so, they use historical information to help them either assume the role of historical actors or vividly describe historical events or people. We are not suggesting fanciful retellings of history. Rather, students must speculate on the motives, values, and choices of historical actors in order to build supportable, *discipline-based* accounts that explain events. In doing so, they must imagine the perspective of participants from another time and place without imagining beyond their data. Tessa, for instance, is well aware of the need for historical evidence. The fact that she missed an important piece of evidence altered the outcome of the trial. If this had been a test, she might have missed the item, taken her grade, and forgotten all about it. Because this was part of a simulation, her error was corrected in a context that made the correction important and memorable. Tessa's experience also pointed out how easily misinformation can alter interpretations—and how important it is to hold conclusions as tentative and to reevaluate ideas. Finally, Tessa's experience points up another feature of effective group inquiry. Although Tessa's study was done in community with other students, it was not a matter of each student investigating what every other student investigated, searching for a single right answer. Rather, each student's research provided one piece of a larger puzzle and served as at least a partial check against inaccurate or unsupportable interpretations.

Newmann et al. (1995), Pappas, Kiefer, & Levstik (1999)

Another feature of in-depth study is the application of new learning beyond the classroom. In other words, disciplined inquiry has value and meaning beyond success in school. Remember that we already said that history presents us both with stories of origins and possible destinations. These are not just school stories left behind when children exit the classroom. Instead, these are stories that have the power to transform students' understandings of themselves and their possible futures. The writer James Baldwin expressed his sense that historical stories could help children "know that just as American history is longer, larger, more various, more beautiful, and more terrible than anything anyone has ever said about it, so is the world larger, more daring, more beautiful and more terrible, but principally larger—and that it belongs to [the children]." In one sense, our lives become more meaningful when we see ourselves as actors within the context of a historical story—we look for the connections among past and current events, the lives of those around us, and our own lives. We begin to recognize that no society or group of people is wholly wise or virtuous, that all of us have the capacity for both good and ill. Wisdom develops as much from stories about human failure as from stories of success. In short, to see ourselves in historical perspective, we need stories about the range of human experience, and we have to learn to evaluate the meaning of those experiences from many perspectives.

History can be transformative.

Baldwin (1988)

Epstein (1993), Griffin (1992)

REFLECTION AND ASSESSMENT

The rich communities of historical discourse described in this chapter and throughout the book provide teachers an ideal opportunity for the kinds of constructive assessment described in chapter 2. First, these classrooms produce a wide array of data about students' developing historical understanding that give teachers insight into how students are progressing along the road to increasingly mature historical thinking. Second, this insight into students' thinking comes about in the context of purposeful historical inquiry and interpretation. Teachers learn what students can do historically by engaging them in authentic and purposeful historical activities; students' talk, question setting, research, and interpretations all offer insights into what they know, what they still need to learn, and what progress they are making toward the goals of historical study. Finally, classrooms like Ruby's and Jeanette's provide multiple pathways for assessing students' historical understanding. As we describe in the following chapters, constructive assessment in history can involve peer and teacher review, self-assessment, anecdotal records, formal scoring rubrics, checklists, and other formats for gaining insight into students' thinking. A teacher's "kid-watching" skills and a willingness to document her observations are the best tools she has for assessing this process.

Alleman & Brophy (1999), Segall (1999), Yell (1999)

One challenge for teachers is organizing this array of data so that it provides useful information, not just to the teacher, but to students and their parents and guardians. This need not be as burdensome as some teachers fear, but it does require planning. Most of the teachers with whom we work accomplish this complex task by using portfolios as a means of organizing assessment data. This involves not only collecting pieces of student work, but helping students learn to monitor their own progress by involving them in the task of assessment. Students, for instance, can manage much of their own organization if they understand the established protocols—such as knowing what records must be kept, where they are kept, and how they will be used. By simply taking time weekly (or

Portfolios help organize assessment data.

daily if needed) to make sure the system is working, teachers can obtain a wealth of data without running themselves ragged.

In general, teachers organize student portfolios into three levels. The first is a *learning portfolio*. Teachers and students jointly decide what should be included in these ongoing collections representing student work either across the curriculum (usually in elementary classrooms) or for one content area (more common at the middle school level). These portfolios are organized to correspond to the categories used in reporting student progress. Documenting historical thinking within a learning portfolio might include audio- and videotapes, samples of different genres of historical work, self-assessments, and the like. At the end of each week, students, in cooperation with their teacher, select a *Friday Portfolio* of work to share with parents and guardians. Although some teachers do not require the return of these materials, most ask that parents respond to the portfolios and that students return them on the next school day. If you use this technique, you might want to talk with students a bit about how to share their work with their family.

Ruby Yessin, for instance, describes trying to help her first graders decide what should go in their Friday Portfolios. It had been a busy week, and she wanted to make sure they would share something about the Russian dance company performance, learning Russian folk dances, or perhaps the maps they had worked on that showed some of the geography of Russia. "What" she asked her students, "will you say when your parents ask you what happened this week?" Almost as one, her students responded, "The Russian kissed Melissa."

In response, Ruby and her students developed some conversation starters to help students share their Friday Portfolios. They might want to start with "something I am proud of because … ," "something I did for the first time … ," or "something I didn't know before … ." In addition, because not all the adults in her students' lives could read, and it was good practice for her students in any case, Ruby asked students to read one piece of their writing to someone else. In this way, the Friday Portfolios became a source of communication between home and school, and the students had a way to share what they were learning.

A third level of organization is an *assessment portfolio*. This, like the Friday Portfolio, is a subset of the learning portfolio. It, too, is jointly constructed by the students and the teacher. Once this portfolio is completed, it becomes the grounds for whatever formal evaluation is required by the school or district. Students have an opportunity to select for inclusion in the assessment portfolio what they consider to be their best work in different categories and then to explain why they selected each piece. In addition, the teacher requires the inclusion of certain items—perhaps a sample of a particular genre of historical writing, a self-assessment of a project, or an annotated bibliography of sources used in developing an interpretation. Jeanette, for instance, might require students to include an argument for the importance of one of the events on the time line they developed, while Ruby might ask her students to include their pictures of "for sure" facts about Johnny Appleseed.

Assessment portfolios also provide a good opportunity for teachers to conduct conferences with students about their work. Abby Mott, one of the teachers you will meet again later in this book, goes over the assessment portfolio with each child, discussing strengths and areas that need to be worked on in the coming weeks. Her students write up a set of goals for the upcoming grading period; the goals are then put in the learning portfolio as a way to organize for the next grading period. Besides the obvious advantage of emphasizing evaluation as an opportunity to plan for the future, these conferences allay student fears about report cards. By the time the report cards are distributed, there are rarely surprises. The students have a pretty clear understanding of their progress to that point and what they can do in the upcoming term. Abby has found that these conferences not only reassure students and promote more accurate self-assessment, they

Learning portfolios are ongoing collections of student work. Hart (1999), Milson & Brantley (1999), Pappas et al. (1999)

Fredericks & Rasinski (1990)

Portfolios help structure reporting to parents and guardians.

Friday Portfolios and assessment portfolios are subsets of each student's learning portfolio.

Portfolios help structure student–teacher conferences.

When students help develop their own portfolios, they have a clearer understanding of their own performance.

provide another opportunity for children to engage in historical talk—to return to ideas introduced earlier in a study and to discuss them one-on-one with an interested and informed adult.

CONCLUSIONS

Although each encounter with history may not transform every child in quite the ways James Baldwin suggests, cumulatively, in-depth historical study is more likely to encourage children to recognize themselves as historical participants rather than passive recipients of the past and unwitting victims of the present. As have others before them, they can change both the present and future. Simply telling students the same myths and stories over and over again will not have this effect. As Oscar Wilde once noted, "the one duty we owe to history is to rewrite it." In-depth study invites students to critique the myths, rewrite the stories, and tell multiple stories. It asks them not just to memorize someone else's interpretations but to develop their own; not just to accumulate information, but to ask themselves and each other, "So what?" What difference does this information make in the world? What does it say about what it means to be human in other times and places and right now, in our world? If students cannot enter imaginatively into the past, if they lack in-depth information about the world around them and its myriad possibilities, they are also less likely to understand the people next door.

Baldwin (1988)

Wilde (1982)

Degenhardt & McKay (1988)

History organized around imaginative entry into the past, in-depth studies of enduring themes and questions, focused on tasks that have relevance beyond the classroom and tied to students' prior knowledge may seem an overwhelming task. Certainly communities of historical inquiry don't just happen; they require careful planning on teachers' parts, time to build a foundation of mutual trust and respect, and freedom from some of the constraints of "coverage." The following chapters provide specific research-based suggestions involving a variety of classrooms in magnet schools, urban, suburban, and rural schools, schools where many children are bilingual (or becoming so)—where doing history is intellectually invigorating for both teachers and students.

CHILDREN'S AND ADOLESCENT LITERATURE

Historical Mystery, Myth, and Legend

Alderman, C. L. *Annie Oakley and the World of Her Time.* Macmillan, 1979.

Altman, L. J. *The Legend of Freedom Hill.* Lee & Low, 2000.

Balit, C. *Atlantis: The Legend of a Lost City.* Henry Holt & Company, 2000.

Barboza, S. *Door of No Return: The Legend of Goree Island.* Cobblehill, 1994.

Baylor, B. *And It Is Still That Way.* Trails West, 1988.

Cashford, J. *The Myth of Isis and Osiris.* Barefoot, 1993.

de Paola, T. *The Legend of the Indian Paintbrush.* G. P. Putnam's Sons, 1988.

DeSpain, P. *Sweet Land of Story: Thirty-six American Tales to Tell.* August House, 2000.

Dorson, M., & Wilmot, J. *Tales from the Rainforest: Myths and Legends from the Amazonian Indians of Brazil.* Ecco, 1997.

Edmonds, I. G. *Ooka the Wise: Tales of Old Japan.* Linnet, 1994.

Fritz, J. *Brendan the Navigator.* Coward, 1979.

Hooks, W. H. *The Ballad of Belle Dorcas.* Knopf, 1990.

Irwin, C. *Strange Footprints on the Land: Vikings in America.* Harper, 1980.

Jaffe, N. *Patakin: World Tales of Drums and Drummers.* Holt, 1994.

Kellogg, S. *Johnny Appleseed.* Morrow, 1988. (Kellogg also has written and illustrated other picture book versions of tall tales, including Pecos Bill, Mike Fink, and Paul Bunyon.)

Kessel, J. K. *Squanto and the First Thanksgiving.* Carolrhoda, 1983.

Koger, E., Sr. *Jocko: A legend of the American Revolution.* Prentice-Hall, 1976.

Lauber, P. *Lost Star: The Story of Amelia Earhart.* Scholastic, 1988.

35

Lupton, H. *The Story Tree: Tales to Read Aloud.* Barefoot Books, 2001.

Manitonquat (Medicine Story). *The Children of the Morning Light: Wampanoag Tales.* Macmillan, 1994.

McCaughrean, G. *The Bronze Cauldron: Myths and Legends of the World.* McElderry, 1998.

Osborne, M. P. *American Tall Tales.* Knopf, 1991.

Sanfield, S. *The Adventures of High John the Conqueror.* Orchard, 1989.

Stanley, D. *Joan of Arc.* Morrow Junior, 1998.

Quackenbush, R. *Quit Pulling My Leg! A Story of Davy Crockett.* Simon & Schuster, 1987.

Van Laan, N. *Buffalo Dance: A Blackfoot Legend.* Little, 1993.

Zeman, L. *The Revenge of Ishtar.* Tundra, 1993.

4

To Find out Things We Didn't Know About Ourselves

Personal Histories

On the first day of school, Tina Reynolds asks her fourth graders to complete the sentence, "History is … " on slips of paper and to discuss their answers. At least half the class writes, "I don't know," while others give short answers like "long ago," "antiques and old stuff," or "presidents and other famous people." Tina asks if they have ever learned about history; a few recall that parents or other relatives have told them about the past, while others can't remember having learned anything about the topic.

She then asks if a *person* can have a history: "Could there be a 'History of Christy,' for example?" Some think yes, some no, but none can explain why. Tina says that she has a history of herself to show them and asks what they think it might look like. Again, students aren't sure. She shows the class a poster she has made with a time line of important events in her life, and students' interest begins to pick up; they eagerly volunteer to read out loud each of the milestones in Tina's life—when she was born, started school, got married, and so on. She then tells students they are going to make their own time lines to show the most important things that have happened to them, and that they will use these time lines to create a "History of Me" to share with the class.

After a discussion of what they might include, students begin working on a list of the five most important things that have happened in their lives. Although they are excited about the topic, writing is difficult for many; making a list like this takes a while. Seated at tables of four and five, though, they continually share their experiences as they write—telling each other about siblings being born, vacations their family has taken, or starting a new sport. Tina, meanwhile, talks to students as they work, asking them to explain why they chose the items they have or helping those who are having trouble. After completing their lists, students fill in the dates of each event on a blank time line of the last ten years. Because most have no idea when each thing happened, they had to take these home to complete with their parents' help. Tina also asks them to add any new events they discover in talking with their parents.

The next day, it is obvious that students have not only recorded a set of dates but have learned an entirely new set of stories from their parents. They are eager to share these in class—the time Martin rolled down the stairs on his tricycle, the time Lisa "almost drowned," and so on. Afterward, students begin creating their personal histories. All have to write narrative essays about their lives, but they can present these to the rest of the class in several different ways—by recording a video- or audiotape, making a poster with photographs (or drawings) and captions, or simply reading their essay. One student even acts as a "museum guide" to the important events of his life. The next several days are devoted to this assignment, as students write essays, design posters, and plan scripts for tapes. When the time comes to share these products with their classmates, even the shyest are proud to present, and students listen with careful attention to the stories of each others' lives.

Barton (2001b),
Barton & Levstik (1996),
Levstik & Barton (1996),
Levstik & Pappas (1987);
see also Brophy &
VanSledright (1997)

In our interviews with children from first grade through middle school, we have found that all of them know something about how things were different in the past. Less often do they have a clear idea what *history* means. Because students usually don't encounter the subject at school before fourth grade, they sometimes don't even clearly recognize the word; those who have heard it may link it with the past generally ("antiques and old stuff"), or may associate it with famous people or events. But rarely do they realize that they are part of history, or that they have a history of their own. A seventh-grader trying to explain the difference between science and history observed that he and the other students were *part of* science, because it was about them and the world around them—"We're *in* science," he pointed out, "but we're not *in* history." Because too many students do not see themselves as being "in history," developing a sense of what the subject is all about and how it relates to them must be one of the teacher's first and most important goals.

Students do not always see themselves as part of history.

ASKING HISTORICAL QUESTIONS

Understanding history begins with students' own pasts.

Beginning with students' own lives is an obvious way to develop an understanding of their place in history, and it also introduces them to key elements of disciplined inquiry. In the earlier passage, Tina engaged her students in the most basic of historical questions—How has my own past affected my life today? She did this by asking students to think about their past in terms of significance: She didn't want them to try to remember everything that had ever happened to them, but to select the five most important things—those that had the greatest influence on their lives today. This seemingly simple assignment thus introduced students to what it means to ask historical questions. Moreover, this was a highly authentic question. As we have already noted, history is concerned with explaining how we got to be where we are today, and knowing the story of one's own life is the most basic form of historical understanding. Note also that students became most interested once they moved away from a general and abstract discussion of history and began talking about specific people they knew.

History examines the effect of the past on the present.

Students are interested in history that focuses on people. *Barton & Levstik (2004)*

Making a list of important events, however, was not something that came easily; it didn't seem to be the kind of question students had ever been asked. Many had trouble deciding what to include on their lists, and a major part of Tina's responsibility was to help them think about how to answer the question; she stayed busy asking students how events in the past had affected their lives today and how their lives would be different if those events hadn't happened. Some students stared at blank pieces of paper until she came around to their desks and asked probing questions to help them think about the events that had been important to them; afterward, they were more prepared to commit their ideas to paper. The collaborative nature of Tina's classroom also helped students consider the question: Although they worked individually, students shared their ideas constantly and heard others explaining their experiences. Many weren't sure what was important until they heard their classmates sharing what was important to them.

Students benefit from collaboration among themselves and with their teacher.

COLLECTING HISTORICAL INFORMATION

This exercise also introduced students to the collection of historical data. They began with the most basic source of information—their own memories. By developing a list of events they remembered, they saw how they could serve as a

38

source of data themselves. They also began to notice the limitations of relying on memory: Although they remembered many of the things that had happened to them, few knew when they happened—either the dates or how old they were at the time. By having to combine their own memories with information from relatives, they learned that using multiple sources can lead to a fuller picture of the past than relying on any single source—one of the most basic principles of historical research.

Even the idea of consulting resources in order to learn something can be a new concept for children; they sometimes claim they couldn't possibly know anything they haven't directly experienced. In helping students develop a list of important events in their lives, for example, Tina asked one group to think about the things that excite parents when their children do them for the first time. One girl suggested getting a new tooth, another mentioned learning to talk, and both added these to their list of things to find out more about. Exasperated at these suggestions, one boy exclaimed, "How would *I* know any of those things happened!?"—he refused to write these down because (he believed) he had no way of knowing that he had ever gotten his first tooth or learned to talk. He couldn't remember it, he reasoned, so how could he know that it ever happened? Although it seems obvious to adults that a person can know something about the past without directly remembering it, this is an understanding that has to be developed in children through exercises like these.

Collecting information from relatives obviously gives students a comfortable and accessible way to move beyond their own experience. Even such familiar sources, though, begin to acquaint them with fundamental issues of historical interpretation. Students quickly learned that their sources might disagree and that they had to make judgments about reliability. Several found that relatives remembered events differently, and in explaining why they believed some sources rather than others, many noted that parents were more reliable because they probably saw the events firsthand, and more distant relatives would have heard about them later. Other students pointed out that mothers would know more about early events than fathers because they were around them more when they were babies. Still others found that "baby books" were a useful source of information when people disagreed, and one student found that both his parents had been wrong about when he lost his first tooth. His baby book, he explained, was the most reliable source because events were written down in it at the time, but people trying to remember events years later might forget exactly how they happened. In this simple assignment, then, students dealt with fundamental historical issues—how to reconcile conflicting accounts and how to judge sources' reliability.

Just as students needed Tina's help to develop a list of events, they needed some structure in collecting information about dates. This was their first exposure to time lines and to collecting chronological data, so Tina did not simply tell them to go home and find out when events had happened. With those instructions, students probably would have brought back papers with a random collection of words and numbers and little idea how they were connected. Instead, she gave each student a time line of the last ten years and explained how to record the information they collected—using her own life as an example. As a result, students appeared to have little trouble keeping track of their information, and the next day they could easily use their time lines to answer questions about when things had happened (see Fig. 4.1). Collecting data is a fundamental part of all research, yet it is enormously difficult for young children. Providing them with the structure necessary—in this case, in the form of a printed time line—is crucial to ensuring their success. The importance of this help became apparent when students made their presentations. Many of those who created posters of their lives developed larger and more elaborate time lines for them, and several remarked that making them—spacing the years evenly and so on—was the most

Historical inquiry can help students see the need for multiple sources of information.

Many students are unfamiliar with how people learn about the past. *Barton (1994), Brophy, VanSledright, & Bredin (1992), Shemilt (1987, 1980), Wineburg (1991)*

Relatives provide a comfortable and accessible way for students to move beyond their own experiences.

Sources sometimes disagree; some sources are more reliable than others.

Students need experience evaluating sources as evidence for historical interpretations. *Ashby & Lee (1998), Van Sledright (2002)*

Teachers can provide the structure students need to collect information successfully.

39

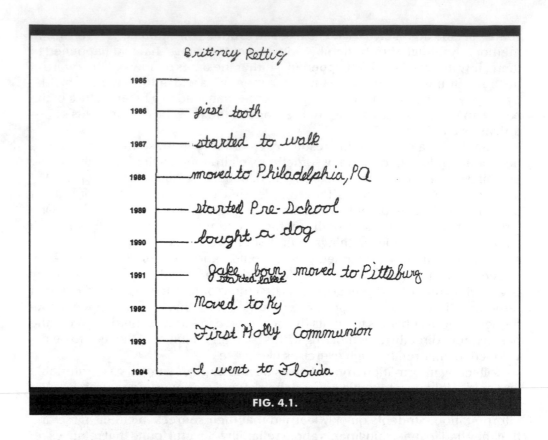

FIG. 4.1.

difficult part of the entire assignment. Without the help of a printed version to begin with, many students would never have been able to keep their information organized. Because they had that help, they not only completed the assignment successfully but tackled the more challenging task of making new time lines for their presentations.

DRAWING CONCLUSIONS AND REFLECTING ON LEARNING

Newmann, Secada, & Wehlage (1995), Scheurman & Newmann (1998)

As we noted in chapter 2, learning activities should be *authentic*; if students complete assignments only to please their teachers or get a grade, they're unlikely to understand the purpose of what they're doing or be able to apply it in new situations. In their "History of Me" assignments, students were not simply collecting information about themselves and filling it in on a time line; that would have been more or less a typical school experience (even if a more interesting one than answering questions at the end of a chapter in a history book). Tina, however, required her students to go further and use this information to create a narrative of their lives for an audience of classmates—and the creation of narratives is one authentic use of historical information in our society. Like the students in chapter 3, Tina's were not just learning skills or content but were using what they learned to create new knowledge.

Creating narratives is an authentic use of historical information.

History can be integrated with other subjects.

Producing this kind of knowledge, though, was no simple matter. After completing their initial time lines and discussing their results in class, students began creating written narratives and presentations about their lives. Because they were learning more about writing during other times of the day, they were familiar with the elements necessary for an effective narrative—putting events in order, including details, and so on. But when it came to taking the information from their time lines and putting it into a new form, many had great difficulty. Several didn't realize that their time lines contained the information they needed to begin, and they displayed an attitude teachers will quickly recognize: They acted as if they were supposed to pluck ideas out of thin air on a completely unexpected topic. The look and sound of "I don't know what to write" came from several students around the room. Of course, in some classrooms, students are expected to do assignments that come out of thin air, but Tina had just spent two days engaging her class in prewriting activities for this task. Most did indeed see the connection to their previous work and used their time lines to plan their essays. But others needed more explicit help: They needed someone to show them how to use what they had already learned. As Tina (and their classmates) helped them make this connection, the expectant sound of "Oh! Now I get it!" replaced the desultory "I don't know what to write." As always, scaffolding was critical. Teachers cannot simply throw an assignment at students and expect them to learn from it; at one time or another, most will need help figuring out how to use their knowledge and skills in their work.

Teachers need to help students apply their knowledge and skills.

An even more significant problem for some students was deciding which information from their time lines was important enough to include in their narratives. Although Tina led the class in a discussion of how to choose what to write and modeled the process using her own time line, many still weren't sure how to go about it. Again, teachers will recognize how difficult it is for students to take information from one form and put it in another; because many elementary children only learn about creative, fictional writing, they often have little understanding of how to use written language in other ways. Tina's students knew they shouldn't just rewrite everything from their time lines, but they didn't know what was important enough to include in their narratives. Just as she did when they first began the assignment, Tina had to help students (individually and in small groups) think about how to choose from among a list of events to include those that were most significant. In essence, she was scaffolding their understanding of historical significance.

Students have difficulty putting what they have learned into new forms.

Teachers focus students' attention on questions of historical significance.

Of course, students' understanding of significance will not be the same as an adult's. Many chose the events they had enjoyed the most (a favorite vacation, for example), rather than those an adult might think were actually the most important. Given that they hadn't run into this kind of question before, and because they were only nine years old, that's hardly surprising. But Tina consistently kept their attention focused on the issue of significance rather than simple storytelling. She never told any student, "Don't include that, that's not important," but she always asked, "Why did you include that—what impact has that had on your life?" As a result of this constant probing, students learned that history is a matter of what's important: By the end of the assignment, they could be counted on to explain their choices by beginning, "This has had an impact on me because. ... " Although not all their explanations were equally convincing, they knew that any justification for including an event had to refer to why it was important in the present—and they learned to use the word *impact* along the way.

Creating narratives involves making judgments about historical significance.

Understanding the purpose of schoolwork is also an important element of authenticity. Tina, however, consciously avoided telling students what they were supposed to think—she preferred instead to let them develop their own ideas about the assignment's purpose. Rather than telling them what she thought the purpose was, she periodically asked students to reflect on what they thought. Several times, for example, she began the history portion of the day by reading books like *Family Pictures–Cuadros de familia* and *This Land is My Land*, in which adults reflect on the events of their youth, and she asked students why they thought the characters found stories about their past so important. She also asked students why they thought they were doing this project. Their answers reflected a range of understanding—"To find out what year we did things and what we did," "To find out things we didn't know about ourselves," and "To find out what history is," for example.

Students need the opportunity to reflect on the meaning and significance of history.

Garza (1990), Littlechild (1993)

Other teachers might justifiably take a more directive approach and explain how a "History of Me" relates to personal identity, the impact of the past on the present, or the gathering and interpretation of data. Tina's approach, though, has the distinct advantage of allowing children to draw their own conclusions from their school experiences. One of the things about this project that most interested students—and surprised Tina—was their realization that each had his or her own unique history, different from everyone else's. Tina hadn't considered that they wouldn't already realize that, and she hadn't thought about emphasizing that as a goal of the assignment—yet for students it turned out to be perhaps its most important purpose. By placing responsibility for creating meaning with the students themselves, Tina thus allowed them to come away with the understanding they found appropriate. Her approach also lays the foundation for developing truly critical thinking: Instead of waiting to be told why something is important, Tina constantly teaches students to ask themselves, "So what?" This kind of reflection is a crucial—but frequently neglected—component of true historical inquiry.

Reflection gives students responsibility for creating meaning and engages them in critical thinking.

ASSESSING STUDENTS' LEARNING

One of a teacher's most important tasks is assessing student learning—not simply so she can establish accountability to parents or administrators, nor to shake loose a set of grades for the report card, nor even to reward students for a job well done. The purpose of assessment is to improve teaching and learning. Assessment fulfills that goal when teachers establish clear standards and criteria for achievement, when they help students understand the meaning of those standards, and when they provide feedback on how well students have mastered the goals of the class—including how far they still have to go. This kind of critical feedback is a key element of the instructional scaffolding mentioned in chapter 2, and the assessment strategies described in chapter 3 depend on such feedback. Letting students know what they have accomplished, and making them aware of the criteria for improvement, enables them to learn far more than if they are only given summative evaluations of their assignments.

The purpose of assessment is to improve teaching and learning.

Alleman & Brophy (1998)

In a world of multiple-choice tests and percentage grades, assessment appears to be a relatively easy process: Make out a test, see how many answers each student gets right, and assign them their grades. But no such simple procedures are available for the complex, real-world tasks found in classrooms where meaningful historical inquiry is taking place. A "History of Me" produces no single list of factual items that could be used on a test for the whole class. Not only will students have used a variety of sources and investigated a diverse set of experiences, they may have learned different things about history: Some may have come to understand how past events affect people's lives in the present, some may have learned about the reliability of sources, while others may have increased their understanding of dates and sequencing. All of these are valid and worthwhile achievements, yet no single test will be valid for all students in the classroom. Complicated and authentic tasks call for complicated and authentic forms of assessment, and these must take multiple forms. For the project described in this chapter, for example, Tina relied on both anecdotal records and formal scoring guidelines, and she gave students the chance to represent their learning in multiple formats.

Authentic tasks require multiple forms of assessment.

Anecdotal records provide the opportunity for on-going assessment during classroom activities.

Tina used anecdotal records throughout this project and, indeed, during all her teaching. She always has a pencil and a notepad at hand, and her observations of students as they work independently, discuss assignments in a group, or interact with her one on one provide rich insights into their understanding of the demands of the task. During the "History of Me" project, for example, when a student was able to explain how past events influenced her life in the present, Tina wrote that down on a slip of paper to add to the assessment folder she kept for the student. When another student appeared to understand the influence of past events but had trouble expressing it clearly, Tina provided scaffolding ("Try saying, 'If this hadn't happened, I would … '"), and noted in her records that he was able to provide an explanation when she helped with the wording. And for a few students, she observed that they were unable to give any examples at all of how the past had affected their lives. Similarly, Tina took note of students who had consulted multiple sources and those who had relied on only one, and she noted students who were easily able to match dates with events on their time lines and those who needed help from herself or their peers. All these observations arose naturally during the course of students' completion of classroom activities.

Anecdotal records like these did not result in a grade; they resulted in information on students' learning. They helped Tina see what help each student needed and provided a basis for deciding what kinds of ongoing instruction and assistance she should provide. Based on her anecdotal records, Tina knew that some students needed no more help with explaining the connection of past and present and that the next time she talked to those students (whether during this project or the next) she could move on to other aspects of historical significance—such as multiple causation or the interaction of past events. Similarly, she knew that students who had only consulted a single source would need to be reminded to use more in the future and that they might need additional assistance in doing so. Anecdotal records thus provided Tina a means of individually tracking students' progress on a variety of important historical skills, and she used this information in planning instruction, reviewing students' achievements with them, and completing the narrative section of their report cards. Although she did not include the anecdotal records themselves as part of students' portfolios, she used them as a basis for discussion while reviewing the contents of the portfolios with students.

Some aspects of the "History of Me" project also lent themselves to assessment through more formal scoring guidelines. All students, for example, had to write narrative essays about their lives, and these were an important part of their portfolios. Tina evaluated these compositions by using guidelines from the statewide assessment program (see Fig. 4.2). Such scoring guidelines—sometimes referred to as *rubrics*—have become increasingly common as a way to provide objective criteria for assessing complex student performances. Rubrics have no magical power of their own, but when used well, they can help students understand what is expected of them and can help them incorporate those expectations into their own work. The rubric in this assignment focused only on features of written composition—rubrics more directly tied to other aspects of historical inquiry are found in later chapters—but its use in the classroom reflected important characteristics of the role of any rubric.

Tina's chief task in making scoring guidelines useful was helping students understand the meaning of each component. Because the rubric in Fig. 4.2 was part of the state assessment program and was used to evaluate a variety of writing genres, its wording was somewhat more general than that found in many scoring guidelines. Tina had to devote sustained instructional time to ensure that students had a firm grasp of the criteria and could apply them to their own writing. She began by conducting mini-lessons on each of the components; the beginning of the language arts portion of the day usually began with brief instruction and practice on topics such as effective introductions, use of details, sentence structure, and various aspects of punctuation. Students followed up on these mini-lessons not by completing worksheets on isolated skills, but by actually writing—both during language arts and in the content areas. In order to ensure that students were applying the skills called for in the rubric, Tina conferred individually with them on a daily basis. During these conferences, she used the scoring guidelines to help students evaluate their own work (both in language arts and in the content areas). She talked to them about how many details they used; whether they used connecting words like *because*, *after*, and *then*; how

Assessment helps teachers plan for ongoing instruction and assistance.

Anecdotal records allow teachers to track individual students' progress.

Scoring guidelines or *rubrics* can provide criteria for assessing complex student performances. *Popham (1997)*

Teachers must help students understand the standards of achievement.

Goodrich (1996/1997)

Based on Kentucky Department of Education (1999)				
	Novice	Apprentice	Proficient	Distinguished
Audience	Limited awareness of audience and/or purpose	Some evidence of communicating with an audience for a specific purpose; some lapses in focus	Focused on a purpose; communicates with audience; evidence of voice and/or suitable tone	Establishes a purpose and maintains clear focus; strong awareness of audience; evidence of distinctive voice and/or appropriate tone
Idea Development	Minimal idea development; limited and/or unrelated details	Unelaborated idea development; unelaborated and/or repetitious details	Depth of idea development supported by elaborated, relevant details	Depth and complexity of ideas supported by rich, engaging, and/or pertinent details; evidence of analysis, reflection, insight
Organization	Random and/or weak organization	Lapses in organization and/or coherence	Logical, coherent organization	Careful and/or subtle organization
Sentence Structure	Incorrect and/or ineffective sentence structure	Simplistic and/or awkward sentence structure	Controlled and varied sentence structure	Variety in sentence structure and length enhances effect
Language	Incorrect and/or ineffective language	Simplistic and/or imprecise language	Acceptable, effective language	Precise and/or rich language

FIG. 4.2. Scoring guidelines for written composition.

they captured their readers' attention; and so on. A key goal in the use of rubrics is for students to internalize the standards of achievement, and Tina accomplished this through a combination of direct instruction, meaningful writing, and individual conferences.

A final characteristic of constructive assessment in this project was students' ability to choose from multiple formats for their presentations. All students were required to write narratives, and they had to complete this assignment before moving on to their presentations. Such compositions were a required part of the assessment system in the state, and like most people, Tina considered this kind of writing to be an important part of what students need to learn at school. But Tina did not assume that writing was the only way to display knowledge or that students who didn't write well yet couldn't learn history. Although they were required to write an essay, students had their choice of many different forms for their presentations—making posters, using photographs, recording videos or audio cassettes, and so on. It has become a commonplace observation that not all students learn the same way. Tina recognized that many students would benefit from using information in forms other than writing and that they were capable of making their own choices about what they wanted to do. Nor did Tina try to pigeonhole students into any single "style" or "strength." Most students, for example, chose to create a poster with a time line, photographs, and captions and to describe their work orally to the class; this required the use of both oral and written language as well as both visual and mathematical understanding. Although some students may be more visual, others more tactile, and so on, all students learn better when they have the chance to combine different modes of understanding.

Giving students a choice of forms for presentation also made the assignment more authentic. Although books and articles are an important source of historical information in our society, so too are museums, documentaries, and oral accounts. The forms available to students for their presentations introduced them

Students need the opportunity to display their understanding in a variety of forms.

Students should not be limited to a single learning "style."
Caine & Caine (1994)

Authentic tasks allow for student choices.

to the different ways of presenting historical knowledge and to some of the unique features of each. The popularity of photographs, for example, showed how interesting visual access to the past can be. Students also learned about its limitations. They found that they didn't have photographs of many of the events they wanted to include. As a result, they had to make choices about how to represent their lives. Some included whatever pictures they had and then revised their judgments about significance: The most important events in their lives turned out to be chosen from the photographs they had. Others took a different approach: They used the pictures that were available, but explained how they represented other events in their lives—a photograph of a vacation, for example, might actually represent the birth of a sister because she was still a baby in the picture. Again, that is exactly what historians do: They decide how the available resources can be used to tell a story. For years, historians based much of their work on letters, diaries, and diplomatic papers; as a result, they had to omit people who didn't leave behind these kinds of documents. In recent years, many historians have attempted to find other sources to represent the lives of people in the past—wills, court proceedings, tax records, and the like. Similarly, some of Tina's students based their ideas about importance on the sources that were readily available, whereas some used other criteria and the sources as indirect representations.

It is also important to note that these presentations were not simply an enrichment exercise or an activity for "early finishers." Too often, only students who do well at standard written assignments get to move on to those that involve creativity, problem solving, or other forms of learning. In Tina's class, though, all students were given the time and support to complete both kinds of task. The provision of material resources was as important as Tina's instructional help. The class included students from a wide range of socioeconomic backgrounds; many had their own video cameras and cassette recorders at home, but for others, just buying the materials to make posters may have been difficult. Rather than allowing students' schoolwork to mirror their families' economic status, the school supplied all the equipment they needed. We recognize that not all schools have the technology or supplies that students need to do their best work; fortunately Tina teaches in a state where schools have flexibility in deciding how to use their limited resources, rather than being hemmed in by regulations forcing them to buy expensive textbooks. In any event, providing students access to appropriate resources is an essential part of equitable and effective education.

THE "HISTORY OF ME" IN THE CONTEXT OF DIVERSITY

Interestingly, the students who can most easily describe how their own pasts have affected the present are often those whose parents have divorced and remarried; they are usually quite ready to explain how changing houses, being adopted, or getting new siblings have influenced their lives. Presenting a "History of Me" can be an enormously fulfilling experience for such students; we have been impressed with the way they can use this activity to affirm their backgrounds and proudly present their lives to their classmates. We have been just as impressed with their classmates' readiness to hear about and appreciate differences in family life.

As with academic skills, developing these values depends in large part on how well they are modeled by the teacher. A teacher who accepts the differences among students and their families as natural and who shows genuine interest in their uniqueness will find that many of her students do the same. But a teacher who regards deviations from some imagined norm as deficiencies—or who tries to ignore such differences—will rarely have students who demon-

Mizell, Benett, Bowman,
& Morin (1993),
Richards (1993)

strate even basic tolerance. When a teacher develops a supportive and caring environment in her classroom, "celebrating diversity" can become more than a slogan, and investigating personal histories can help children see how their backgrounds both converge and differ.

Nevertheless, the purpose of an assignment like this is not to pry into children's personal lives. Most students and their families will readily answer questions about important events in their lives, but others will refuse to address the topic. Students will not want to share some events that have had an impact on them—abuse by a family member, for example, or the loss of a loved one. In other cases, parents will resent participating in this assignment. For example, undocumented immigrants often fear that personal questions will lead to deportation or denial of services for their family, and many people of fundamentalist faiths believe schools should not ask questions about children's lives outside school. The solution to these dilemmas—we decline to call them "problems" because we recognize and accept the reasons for them—is not to avoid assignments about personal histories, nor is it to exempt some students and thus highlight what they may think of as an inadequacy. Rather, teachers must make such assignments flexible enough to accommodate the legitimate differences among students and their families in our extraordinarily diverse society.

To do this, teachers should never require students to share (with them or the class) anything they don't want to. In essence, a "History of Me" should include the most significant events children want to share, not those most significant in any kind of absolute sense. In addition, the teacher should always give students the option of investigating someone's life other than their own; the purpose of the assignment, after all, is to find out how the past affects the present, not to force students into putting themselves on display. Those who don't want to call attention to themselves should have the option of doing a history of a friend in another classroom, a teacher at the school, or someone else in the community. Rather than being forced to take part in an unpleasant assignment, they then have the enriching experience of learning about someone else's life—and classmates are invariably more attentive to these presentations than any other. However, it is important to keep in mind that all students must be given these options, not just those whom the teacher thinks may need them. Otherwise the mere presence of an alternative may seem just as unpleasant as the original assignment.

Some families decline to reveal personal information.

Assignments must be flexible to accommodate diversity.

Students should not be required to share personal information.

All students need choices in assignments.

EXTENSIONS

A project like the "History of Me" can be extended in several ways to develop further experience with asking and answering historical questions. An obvious follow-up is for students to use historical biographies to investigate the impact of an individual's past on his or her life. Such biographies are one of the most commonly available forms of historical literature. They range from books appropriate for young children—such as *Diego, Mary Bethune, Malcolm X,* and *The Last Princess: The Story of Princess Ka'inlani of Hawaii*—to those more suitable for the middle grades—such as *Eleanor Roosevelt: A Life of Discovery, Rosa Parks: My Story,* and *Quanah Parker: Great Chief of the Comanches.* (A more complete list follows the end of this chapter.) Using literature like this allows students to move beyond their own experiences and gives them the chance to examine the lives of people whose race, ethnicity, gender, socioeconomic class, or physical abilities may be very different than their own.

Teachers often assign students to read biographies and then "do a report"—but as a colleague of ours once noted, it's been a long time since most of us sat down and wrote a report on a book we've read. Book reports simply are not an authentic genre in our society; they're just a traditionally assigned (and tradi-

Winter (1991), Greenfield (1997), Adoff (1970), F. Stanley (1991), Freedman (1993), Parks (1992), Gonzales (1987)

Biographies allow students to move beyond their own experiences.

tionally despised) means to assess whether students have done their work. Outside school, people may discuss a book with others who have read it, or they may recommend it to those who haven't, and many teachers pattern their classrooms on these more authentic tasks—assigning students to take part in literature response groups, for example, or to make advertisements or other recommendations for the books they've read. Such assignments develop children's language skills in a more authentic way than writing a report, which has no clear purpose or audience.

How can students use biographies in a way that models the use of disciplined inquiry in a more specifically historical way? Certainly there's nothing wrong with using them in connection with discussion groups or other such assignments, in the same way any piece of literature would be used; people do read historical biographies for pleasure, they do discuss them, and they do recommend them to others. But in addition, using biographies along with projects like those in this chapter can focus students' attention on the specifically historical nature of the genre. Historians do not read biographies and then write reports on them; rather, they do one of two things—either they write such works themselves or they evaluate those that others have written. Both tasks are well within the abilities of children in the elementary and middle grades.

Students can write their own accounts, for example, by using published biographies, encyclopedias, CD-ROMs, and even oral memories or folklore to make a time line of important events in a famous person's life and then construct these into written narratives or other kinds of presentations. Just as they did with their own histories, the emphasis would be on establishing the impact of events on the person's life and explaining how things might have been different if those events had never happened. A six-year-old would produce a much different work than a fourteen-year-old, yet both would be engaged in a more purposeful assignment than "doing a report": They would be asking historical questions, collecting and interpreting information, and reflecting on what they found. Using multiple sources to create a historical account in this way is an important step in moving students beyond the simple recall of historical narratives toward a more critical and interpretive encounter with historical evidence. In addition, instead of making the teacher the sole audience for these student-created biographies, the class could compile and compare their findings. For example, they might discuss which of the figures they investigated has had the greatest impact on contemporary society—thus extending their understanding of the influence of events on individuals to the influence of individuals on society.

Students can critically evaluate published biographies or other accounts by examining the basis for authors' claims, just as the primary children in chapter 3 did with Johnny Appleseed. What statements are based on evidence? How good is the evidence? Which simply derive from folklore or legend? We mentioned earlier that in doing a "History of Me," students should only be asked to share what they want to share, not everything that has happened to them. At first glance, that may have seemed distinctly unauthentic: Surely history is about the truth, not covering things up. But as we explained in chapter 1, any history leaves some things out—that's the very essence of historical explanation. A student who has had to decide what to include and what not to include in her own biography may then recognize (with the teacher's help) that books about famous people do the same thing, and she can try to explain why some biographies of George Washington note that he owned hundreds of slaves while others ignore the topic. Students can compare different biographies of the same person and rank their authenticity and believability, just as historians do.

Older students can even examine how the writing of historical biographies has changed over time. Most of us probably remember common biography series from our childhoods, and school libraries are still full of dog-eared copies of them. Students in the middle grades could compare those to more contempo-

Book reports, like all assignments, need a clear purpose and audience. *Scheurman & Newmann (1998)*

In literature response groups, students meet together to analyze the works they are reading. *Daniels (2002), Smith & Barton (1997), Keegan & Shrake (1991)*

Students can use multiple sources of information to create biographies.

Mayer (1998), Perfetti, Britt, & Georgi (1995), Rouet, Marron, Perfetti & Favart (1998)

Students can critically evaluate published biographies.

Students can examine how conventions of historical writing have changed over time.

Wilton (1993)

rary accounts and try to explain what biographical conventions have changed, which have remained the same, and how these changes relate to larger changes in society. Biographies from the 1950s, for example, rarely included any consideration of the failings of their subjects; their purpose was less to teach about real historical individuals than to provide role models who were paragons of patriotism and proper behavior. Many contemporary biographies, on the other hand, treat their subjects in a more balanced way; although they may still serve the purpose of providing role models, they are certainly very different models than those of previous generations.

Of course, most popular biographies focus on famous people, but much contemporary historical writing uses the lives of ordinary people to highlight significant aspects of historical continuity and change, and students can do the same. Although information on famous people is more readily available, with a little bit of work, teachers and their students can locate the primary sources necessary to construct biographies of everyday people, particularly from their own communities.

CONCLUSIONS

From fifth grade through college, history is one of the most securely established subjects in the curriculum, and most students in this country will take the same survey of American history at least three times—in fifth, eighth, and eleventh grades, usually—and a fourth time if they go to college. Yet the amount of information they retain from these courses is shockingly small, as national tests and surveys have shown for more than 50 years. How can there be such a mismatch between what students study and what they learn? Tina suggests that part of the problem lies in the inappropriateness of the content of traditional school history. Even in schools in which teachers have great flexibility and control of their curriculum, there are enormous pressures to teach topics like "state history" in fourth grade and to do so in a way that mirrors the content of history textbooks or curriculum guidelines—having students learn when the state was admitted to the union, who the first governor was, and so on.

Ravitch & Finn (1987), Whittington (1991)

Academic researchers have suggested that teaching state history in fourth grade confuses children, but Tina's criticisms are stronger still: "It's ridiculous to go through a book reading about the founding of the state when students don't even have a sense of what history is, of what it means. Without knowing what history is all about, the rest of it will just go over their heads." We agree. At some point in their school career—hopefully in the primary grades, but later if necessary—students have to learn what history is all about, that they themselves have a history and that they are *in* history just as much as they are in the natural world. The activities in this chapter may seem simple, but they initiate students into an understanding of history and their role within it.

Brophy, VanSledright, & Bredin (1993)

For history to be meaningful, students must understand the meaning of *history* as well as their place in history.

Moreover, these activities help lay the groundwork for students' participation in a pluralist democracy. Although they involve no discussion of grand social and political issues, no debates over public policy and the common good, personal biographies do introduce students to important elements of such participation. As we have emphasized throughout the chapter, developing biographies requires selection, interpretation, and presentation of evidence, and these are indispensable for public deliberation. By learning how to find information and what to do with it, students should be better prepared to use evidence as they consider a variety of social issues, not only in school but throughout their lives. In addition, they should become more aware of how others have used evidence and of the choices that have led to particular selections, interpretations, and representations. One set of lessons in fourth grade won't accomplish that, of course, but if teachers consistently build on such beginnings, students' understanding of history—and democracy—should increase enormously.

CHILDREN'S AND ADOLESCENT LITERATURE

Personal History, Memory, and Identity

Alexander, S. H. *Mom Can't See Me.* Simon & Schuster, 1990.

Bahr, M. *The Memory Box.* Albert Whitman and Company, 1991.

Belton, S. *McKendree.* Greenwillow, 2000.

Bonners, S. *The Wooden Doll.* Lothrop, Lee, and Shephard, 1991.

Bunting, E. *Once upon a Time.* Richard C. Owen, 1995.

Cha, D. *Dia's Story Cloth: The Hmong People's Journey of Freedom.* Museum of Natural History, 1996.

Clifford, E. *The Remembering Box.* Houghton Mifflin, 1985.

Garza, C. L. *Family Pictures-Cuadros de familia.* Children's Book Press, 1990.

Giovanni, N., Ed. *Grand Mothers: Poems, Reminiscences, and Short Stories About the Keepers of Our Traditions.* Holt, 1994.

Greenfield, E. *African Dream.* Crowell, 1989.

Johnson, A. *Tell Me a Story, Mama.* Orchard, 1989.

Johnston, T. *Any Small Goodness: A Novel of the Barrio.* Scholastic, 2003.

Littlechild, G. *This Land Is My Land.* Children's Book Press, 1993.

Matas, C. *Sparks Fly Upward.* Clarion, 2002.

Myers, W. D. *Brown Angels: An Album of Pictures and Verse.* HarperCollins, 1993.

Nodar, C. S. *Abuelita's Paradise-El paraíso de Abuelita.* Whitman, 1992.

Pomerantz, C. *The Chalk Doll.* Lippincott, 1989.

Ringgold, F. *Tar Beach.* Crown, 1991.

Say, A. *The Bicycle Man.* Houghton Mifflin, 1982.

Schwartz, A. *Mrs. Moskowitz and the Sabbath Candlesticks.* Jewish Publication Society of America, 1983.

Shea, P. D. *The Whispering Cloth: A Refugee's Story.* Boyds Mill Press, 1995.

Stevenson, J. *When I was Nine.* Greenwillow Books, 1986.

Biographies

Adler, D. *A Picture Book of Helen Keller.* Holiday, 1990.

Adoff, A. *Malcolm X.* Harper and Row, 1970.

Brown, M. M. *Susette La Flesche: Advocate for Native American Rights.* Children's Press, 1992.

Bruchac, J. *Crazy Horse's Vision.* Lee & Low Books, 2000.

Cedeno, M. E. *Cesar Chavez: A Migrant Family.* Lerner, 1992.

Codye, C. *Vilma Martínez.* Raintree, 1990.

Coil, S. M. *Harriet Beecher Stowe.* Franklin Watts, 1993.

Cooney, B. *Eleanor.* Viking, 1996.

David A. *A Picture Book of Sojourner Truth.* Holiday, 1994.

Delano, M. F. *Inventing the Future: A Photobiography of Thomas Alva Edison.* National Geographic, 2002.

Faber, D., & Faber, H. *Mahatma Gandhi.* Julian Messner, 1986.

Fox, M. V. *Bette Bao Lord: Novelist and Chinese Voice for Change.* Children's Press, 1993.

Freedman, R. *Eleanor Roosevelt: A Life of Discovery.* Scholastic, 1993.

Garza, H. *Frido Kahlo.* Chelsea House, 1994.

Gleiter, J., & Thompson, K. *José Martí.* Raintree, 1990.

Gonzales, C. T. *Quanah Parker: Great Chief of the Comanches.* Eakin Press, 1987.

Green, C. *Elizabeth Blackwell: First Woman Doctor.* Children's Press, 1991.

Green, C. *Mark Twain: Author of Tom Sawyer.* Children's Press, 1992.

Greenfield, E. *Mary McLeod Bethune.* HarperCollins, 1977.

Greenfield, E. *Paul Robeson.* HarperCollins, 1975.

Greenfield, E. *Rosa Parks.* Harper, 1973.

Grimes, N. *Talkin' about Bessie: The Story of Avitor Elizabeth Coleman.* Orchard Books, 2002.

Haskins, J. *I Have a Dream: The Life and Words of Martin Luther King, Jr.* Millbrook, 1992.

Haskins, J. *Thurgood Marshall: A Life for Justice.* Henry Holt, 1992.

Kent, Z. *The Story of Geronimo.* Children's Press, 1989.

Klausner, J. *Sequoyah's Gift: A Portrait of the Cherokee Leader.* HarperCollins, 1993.

McDonough, Y. Z. *The Life of Nelson Mandela.* Walker & Co., 2002.

McKissack, P. C., & McKissack, F. *Sojourner Truth: Ain't I a Woman?* Scholastic, 1992.

Medearis, A. S. *Princess of the Press: The Story of Ida B. Wells-Barnett.* Lodestar, 1998.

Meltzer, M. *Dorothea Lange: Life Through the Camera.* Puffin, 1986.

Miller, W. *Frederick Douglass: The Last Day of Slavery.* Lee & Low, 1995.

Myers, W. D. *Malcolm X: By Any Means Necessary.* Scholastic, 1993.

Neimark, A. *Che! Latin America's Legendary Guerilla Leader.* HarperCollins, 1989.

Parks, R. *I Am Rosa Parks*. Dial, 1998.

Pinkney, A. D. *Dear Benjamin Banneker*. Harcourt Brace, 1994.

Roberts, M. *Cesar Chavez and La Causa*. Children's Press, 1986.

Sabin, L. *Roberto Clemente: Young Baseball Hero*. Troll, 1992.

Say, A. *El Chino*. Houghton Mifflin, 1990.

Selvin, D. F. *Eugene Debs: Rebel, Labor Leader, Prophet*. Lothrop, Lee and Shephard, 1966.

Selvin, D. F. *The Thundering Voice of John L. Lewis*. Lothrop, Lee and Shephard, 1969.

Simon, C. *Wilma P. Mankiller: Chief of the Cherokee*. Children's Press, 1991.

Stanley, D., & Vennema, P. *Bard of Avon: The Story of William Shakespeare*. Morrow, 1992.

Stanley, D., & Vennema, P. *Shaka: King of the Zulus*. Morrow, 1988.

Stanley, F. *The Last Princess: The Story of Princess Ka'inlani of Hawaii*. Four Winds Press, 1991.

Thompson, K. *Sor Juana Inés de la Cruz*. Raintree, 1990.

Turner, R. M. *Mary Cassat*. Little, Brown 1992.

Uchida, Y. *The Invisible Thread*. Simon & Schuster, 1991.

Walker, A. *Langston Huges: American Poet*. HarperCollins, 2002.

Wepman, D. *Benito Juárez*. Chelsea House, 1986.

Winter, J. *Diego*. Knopf, 1991.

5

TELL ME ABOUT YOURSELF

Linking Children to the Past Through Family Histories

After students have completed their personal history projects, Tina Reynolds begins a unit on family history by reading *The Patchwork Quilt,* a book in which a girl and her mother discover meaning in the way a grandmother's quilt "tells stories" about the family's past. Tina asks students whether their relatives have ever told them about the past, and nearly every hand is raised: One boy tells about his uncle who was in "the war"; a girl relates how her grandmother talks about the old things she owns; another student explains that his grandmother's World War II factory badge is in an exhibit at a nearby museum. The rest of the lesson focuses on the concept of "generation"—which relatives are in their own generation, which in their parents', and so on. The next day, Tina introduces students to a new assignment, creating a family history based on interviews with their grandparents. Although students can do a "Family History Chart" as an optional assignment, their primary task is to give a presentation that focuses on the differences between their grandparents' lives and their own. Tina assigns several questions for students to ask in their interviews and works with them to develop several more of their own. She also spends an entire lesson modeling how to conduct an interview, as well as how to take notes. Sharing the results of these interviews takes several days, as students feel compelled to share as many of the things they've learned as possible.

Rebecca Valbuena begins a unit on immigration by portraying her grandfather, a Latvian who immigrated to New York as a 10-year-old in 1910. She places photographs of him around the room, plays Latvian music on a tape recorder, and explains why he came to the United States and what he found here. After answering questions about his life, she asks students why their own families—almost all of whom are recent immigrants—came to the United States. They quickly produce a list with a variety of reasons—to find work, to be with relatives, for political freedom, to get away from war, and (the most common), "for a better life." This discussion leads into the first assignment of the unit: interview an immigrant. Working together as a class, they develop a list of questions that would be important to ask an immigrant—What country did you come from? Why did you immigrate? What difficulties did you have when you first arrived? Was the United States what you expected? And, at students' insistence, How much did it cost? Over the next few days, students develop written and oral reports based on their interviews, and then they compare their findings to the experience of other immigrants in history—such as the Irish on the East coast in the mid-1800s and the Chinese on the West coast in the late 1800s. At the end of each day's lesson, Rebecca reads aloud a different book about immigrants, such as *Who Belongs Here?* and *Where the River Runs,* and students discuss the feelings and experiences of immigrants.

One of the most crucial challenges in teaching history to children lies in linking the subject to their prior knowledge. As we discussed in chapter 2, people can make sense of new experiences only when they compare them to what they already know. Without such a connection, children are unlikely to understand the history they encounter at school. Yet it's not always obvious just how to make that connection; certainly many of the topics traditionally covered in history textbooks have no clear relation to students' own experiences, and texts rarely suggest how such topics might be relevant. The challenge for the teacher, then, lies in deciding what aspects of important historical content match up with elements of students' lives. Finding that link is the key to broadening students' understanding of history beyond their own experience, and family histories provide one of the most useful ways to do that. Tina's and Rebecca's classes show how the lives of students' families can introduce them to important and meaningful topics in history.

Teachers must decide how to connect students' experiences with important historical content.

CONNECTING STUDENTS TO IMPORTANT HISTORICAL THEMES

Pappas et al. (1999)

Sometimes classrooms are described as being either "teacher centered" or "student centered," but we find that most focus on the interests of neither students nor teachers but on whatever's in the textbook. To link important historical content to children's backgrounds, however, the primacy of texts will have to be replaced with teachers' own decisions about instructional content. Even when working within the framework of state academic standards, teachers must make countless decisions about the specific content they will teach, as well as about how to present it to students. From our perspective, it is up to teachers to determine what historical content is worth teaching and what aspects of students' experiences provide the best avenue for doing that.

Thornton (1991)

Rebecca's classroom provides a clear example of such an approach. Her school's textbooks don't start with a comparison of contemporary immigration to Irish and Chinese immigration in the 1800s; like most texts, they start with Native American life and early European explorers and proceed through time in strict chronological order. Given the amount of material to be covered and the limited time that can be spent on the topic, few fifth-grade teachers who base their instruction on textbooks get much further than the American Revolution. Limiting history to events hundreds of years in the past practically guarantees that students will have few opportunities to make connections to their own experiences. Rebecca, however, begins not with what is in the text but with her knowledge of history and her students.

Instruction must begin with students' interests and experiences.

Authentic history focuses on important themes.

Rebecca knew that the movement of people is one of the most important themes throughout both U.S. and world history (see Table 1.1, chap. 1), and that students would return to it throughout the year—when they studied the encounter of Native Americans with European settlers, for example, or when they studied the enslavement of Africans. Moreover, Rebecca focused not just on the bare facts of immigration, but on issues that would allow students to compare these different movements of people—questions like, "What motivated people to migrate?" and "Did they find what they expected?" By beginning the year with the study of an important theme, students were better able to see how the year's topics were related than if they proceeded chronologically through a textbook.

A thematic approach to history encourages students to make connections across time and place.

Rebecca also chose this topic because of the obvious ways it allowed children to make connections with their families. Nearly all her students had immigrated recently to the United States—some from Mexico, some from Central America, some from Southeast Asia—so they and their families were directly familiar with motivations for immigrating and the consequences of moving. (In other classrooms, students may not be immigrants from another country, but their families may still have moved from one place to another and for some of the same reasons—to find a job, to be with relatives, and so on.) But this is not to say that all teachers should begin with the topic of immigration and interview their relatives about why they have moved; our intent is not to replace the traditional beginning of elementary history (Early Explorers) with a new one (Immigration). Teaching history does not mean relying on a cookbook in which someone else has decided which topics are most appropriate for the children in all classrooms. Only teachers can do this, and they can do it only by knowing both history and their students.

Tina, for example, also followed her "History of Me" projects (see chap. 4) with family histories, but hers had nothing to do with immigration. Tina's students lived in a stable residential neighborhood, and some of their families had lived in the same town for generations. Interviewing their relatives would yield little or no information on why people move or what they find when they do. (Although her students did study immigration, it came later in the school year and was based primarily on children's literature.) Instead, Tina's students interviewed their grandparents to find out how life was different in the past. They found out what chores their grandparents did when they were young, what they did for fun, and so on. In Tina's class, this provided students with an introduction not to immigration in U.S. history but to the study of how material and social life has changed over the last century (see also chaps. 7 and 11). Despite the differences in topic, Tina and Rebecca developed their curriculum in identical ways: They chose important themes and helped students broaden their understanding through their use of family histories.

IMAGINATIVE ENTRY: PERSONALIZING HISTORY

As we discussed in chapter 2, children strive to make human sense of the world around them. Rebecca emphasized the importance of personalizing history for students, of helping them see how the subject involves real human beings. Her introduction to the immigration unit is a perfect example: Just as Tina's students were excited about reading her personal time line in chapter 4, Rebecca's students listened with rapt attention as she took on the appearance of her grandfather and described his experiences for students. In such a presentation, history is not about anonymous groups of immigrants, who moved for some vague reason at some distant point in history; it's about the teacher's grandfather who came to the United States when he was a kid like them.

The multisensory aspect of Rebecca's presentation was also critical. Students did not just hear about or read about an immigrant, they saw photographs of him, saw the way he dressed, and even heard the kind of music he listened to. (Even for teachers who do not have information from their own families, photographs of immigrants are easy to obtain because this is a richly documented era in American history.) Students can also take part in acting out the experience of immigrants. Tina's, for example, planned and acted out an encounter between immigrant families and government officials after reading *Immigrant Kids* and *If Your Name was Changed at Ellis Island.* Visual images, music, artifacts, and role-playing are second nature to any teacher whose students do not speak English as a first language, but in teaching history, these strategies should become part of every teacher's repertoire. The more avenues to the past available to students, the more likely they are to make connections to what they already know.

One of the most important ways to personalize history lies in helping students make connections with their own families. Simply assigning them to find out how life has changed over the past three generations, for example, is unlikely to inspire much interest. By having them interview their grandparents, however, Tina could be more confident that they would find the topic of change over time personally relevant. Indeed, students came back from these interviews with

Students are usually
interested in learning
about their families'
histories.

Students can study history
by beginning with the
recent past and working
backward.

Family histories help
students build on their
background knowledge.

Literature helps students
make personal
connections to history.
O'Brien (1998)

Elementary and middle
grade students enjoy
being read to.

Levinson (1985),
Hesse (1992),
Bresnick-Perry (1992)

Learning about abstract
concepts begins with
concrete examples.

Family histories introduce
students to important as-
pects of historical inquiry.

pages of notes and eager to share their stories with the rest of the class. It quickly became obvious that they had not limited themselves to the list of questions they developed in class but had conducted a much more personal and wide-ranging discussion of their families' pasts. Students also took an interest in their class-mates' presentations because they were hearing not just about history but about each others' grandparents.

Similarly, Rebecca's primary purpose was to develop her students' under-standing of the motivations for and consequences of immigration, but instead of starting with experiences remote in time and place and working forward, she began with what students already knew—why their families immigrated—and these reasons were much the same as those that have motivated people throughout history. By making a list of the motivations found within their class-room, students had a starting point that *they already understood* to compare with the motivations of other immigrants throughout history. Similarly, when they interviewed family members, they found out what kinds of problems they had when they first came to the United States—finding a job, finding a place to live, not being able to speak the language—and this gave them yet another basis for comparison with the experiences of other immigrants.

Literature also provides a highly effective way to help students make personal connections to history. Unfortunately, picture books and other works for reading aloud sometimes fall by the wayside after the primary years, perhaps because they somehow seem too easy or because reading aloud doesn't always involve students in the production of a tangible product. Yet nearly all children love to be read to; when the time for reading aloud arrived, the sounds of "Yes!" and "All right!" filled Rebecca's room. (Even eighth-grade teachers can be pleasantly surprised by students' positive reactions when they begin reading aloud.) As an adult, of course, Rebecca could read with much more expression than her stu-dents, and she tried to make the voices and dialects in the books as authentic as possible; as a result, her students heard what it sounds like to read fluently in English. For Tina's students, meanwhile, literature was absolutely essential for studying immigration. With little personal experience related to the topic, her students relied on books—short works like *Watch the Stars Come Out* and *Leaving for America* or longer ones such as *Letters from Rifka*—to provide them with an understanding of the personal dimensions of immigrants' experiences.

Finally, both Tina and Rebecca made history personal by including attention to what children know best—daily life. Having fourth graders ask their grandpar-ents directly about abstract topics such as economics or society would not be ef-fective, because children have only a rudimentary understanding of those concepts. But by asking about changes in chores, entertainment, school, and the like, students developed their understanding of social and economic changes by linking them to their own experiences. When they studied immigra-tion as well, Tina's students wanted to know about practical matters; discussion often focused on questions of what people ate while on immigrant ships, how they went to the bathroom, and so on. Rebecca's students were also interested in these seemingly routine details—witness their concern with the monetary cost of immigration—although they could readily identify with the hardships of immigration that Tina's students only wondered about.

COLLECTING AND INTERPRETING INFORMATION

Conducting historical research with family members has many of the same ad-vantages we discussed in chapter 4. Interviewing relatives is an accessible and comfortable way for students to move beyond their own experiences, and yet it allows them to see how accounts may differ, how sources can vary in reliability, and how conflicting accounts can be reconciled. Tina found that one of the most striking benefits of this project was that students saw that not everything they learned had to come from a book, and that people were a valuable resource for historical inquiry. Her students were amazed that they could get so much information from people.

As we emphasized before and will emphasize again, however, students need explicit help in learning how to collect and interpret information—no matter how familiar the source may be. Both Rebecca and Tina spent entire lessons teaching students how to conduct an interview. Tina, for example, talked to students about how some topics might be personally sensitive and how their grandparents either might not want to talk about them or might get emotional when they do. Her own grandmother, she explained, cries whenever she talks about World War II. Even more importantly, she provided a model for students of how to conduct interviews: She had students from the class practice by asking her questions, she responded as if she were the grandparent being interviewed, and other students took notes on what she said. Note-taking turned out to be very challenging for students: They wanted to write down every single word she said, and she had to explain how to focus on only the most important points and how to write down words and phrases that would help them reconstruct the interview later. That lesson was particularly eye-opening for students: They were shocked that they were allowed to write something other than complete sentence and paragraphs! Although as adults we recognize that different uses of language call for different conventions, children need explicit instruction in when to use these.

Teachers must help students learn to collect information.

Students need to learn to use language for a variety of purposes.

Rebecca also worked with students on conducting interviews, but language development was a much more pervasive aspect of instruction in her class than in Tina's. Few of Rebecca's students spoke English as a first language, and so every aspect of the unit required attention to the use of words. As she portrayed her grandfather, for example, Rebecca called students' attention to vocabulary cards containing key words for the unit—*immigrant, emigrate, motivation*, and the like. To ensure that students would be better able to write comparisons of immigrants' experiences, Rebecca modeled the use of sentences containing words like *because, although, when, before*, and *after* to express causal and temporal relationships. Explicit modeling of these vocabulary words and skills in authentic contexts helped students transform their conceptual understanding into more fluent prose.

A significant part of teaching students to collect and interpret information is providing them with ways to keep track of what they learn, and graphic organizers played an important role in both Tina's and Rebecca's classrooms. Sometimes graphic organizers help individual students organize information—for example, the time lines Tina provided for personal histories in chapter 4. Other times, graphic organizers are useful as a way to call students' attention to themes that emerge from the information they collect. As students reported what they learned from their grandparents, for example, Tina recorded the information on chart paper with headings like *technology, work, leisure*, and *school*. By seeing the information recorded in this way, students not only gained more insight into the meaning of concepts like *leisure* and *technology* but could also more readily identify the patterns that began to emerge from the interviews (see Fig. 5.1). Similarly, as Rebecca's students studied immigrants throughout history, they recorded what they learned on a chart that identified the motivations of each group and the consequences of their migration. Again, by seeing the information displayed in a visually organized way, students could more easily discern the similarities and differences in the experiences they learned about. Finally, leaving charts like these on the wall throughout the year allowed students to add new information whenever they encountered it, and thus to see the topics as issues of ongoing importance rather than isolated units of study.

Graphic organizers are a means of visually organizing information.

Wall charts help students keep track of information collected during ongoing units of study.

Leisure	Work
board games baseball dolls going to movies fishing tag	lots of chores cooking mowing the grass feeding animals pulling weeds

Clothes	Technology
blue jeans dresses Angora sweaters bobby socks overalls suspenders	didn't have VCRs black and white TVs no computers big cars with fins coal furnace no microwave icebox bicycles

FIG. 5.1. Wall charts based on grandparent interviews.

Students can use information to create authentic historical presentations.

In both classrooms, students also did more than collect information: They used what they had learned to create authentic historical presentations. Tina, for example, set aside time each day for students to share what they were finding out about their grandparents, and Rebecca's students developed formal presentations based on their interviews with immigrants. Both teachers also assigned written compositions: Students in Tina's class wrote simulated diaries from the perspective of their grandparents when they were children, and those in Rebecca's turned their interview notes into written essays. Historical inquiry in these classrooms provided an important opportunity for students to develop their ability to communicate through speech and writing, both of which are central to the use of historical information in our society. "Authentic genres" of historical presentation, after all, are not radical educational innovations—learning how to speak in public and write for an audience are among the most traditional goals of learning and are likely to be important for a very long time to come.

Authentic tasks include writing and speaking for an audience.

ASSESSMENT AND FEEDBACK

Formal scoring guidelines are most useful for evaluating skills that apply to a variety of tasks. *Popham (1997)*

Both Tina and Rebecca evaluated students in these lessons somewhat differently than in the way described in chapter 4. Anecdotal records were a continuing part of Tina's assessment, but in this case she did not use a formal rubric to judge their achievement at the end of the unit. Scoring guidelines like those in chapter 4 are most useful for evaluating skills that apply across a variety of tasks or performances. Attempting to create a full-scale rubric for every task students engage in would be unnecessarily time consuming and in many cases would result in guidelines so task-specific that they would contribute little toward helping students develop important skills or understandings. The usefulness of the scoring guidelines in Fig. 4.2 lies in the fact that students will encounter them again and again, in a variety of settings, and over time they become increasingly adept at applying those standards to their own writing. But when teachers want

56

to tie their assessment to the more specific demands of a particular project, a checklist can be a more useful evaluation instrument.

Checklists can take a number of different forms, but the one in Fig. 5.2 shows one way to evaluate students by assessing their performance on the specifically historical aspects of assignments. During their presentations, students in Rebecca's class were expected to do four things—explain three conclusions they had reached about the experiences of the immigrant who had been interviewed; back up each conclusion with evidence from the interviews; represent the person through clothing, artifacts, props, and so on; and speak loudly and clearly. Just as in a rubric, the different components of the assignment are listed along the left side of the evaluation form, but instead of specifying levels of performance for each, the form allows the teacher to assign a range of points based on how well the student has achieved the desired objectives. The differing number of points possible for each component makes it easy for the teacher to specify the relative importance of each. Although rubrics can also be weighted in this way, the use of varying point values helps students see more clearly which aspects of the task are most important and where they should focus their efforts. The diary entries written by students in Tina's class could be evaluated according to a similar checklist, one that included components related not only to students' explanations of conclusions and their use of evidence but also to their ability to take on the perspective of someone who lived in the past.

Checklists can guide evaluation of the specifically historical aspects of assignments.

Note that the checklist in Fig. 5.2 includes room for the teacher to write her comments on students' performance. A "Comments" section is an indispensable feature of evaluation checklists; it provides space for the teacher to identify exactly which characteristics of a student's performance were well done and which needed improvement. As we noted in chapter 4, this kind of critical feedback—letting students know what they have done well and what they still need to improve—is an important form of scaffolding. If students simply receive a number or letter grade with no comments—or with only vague notes like "Great job!" or "Try to do better"—they will not know what to continue doing and what to change. Teachers frequently come across a list of *100 ways to say "Good work"* ("All right!" "Wonderful!" "Tremendous!"), but none of the 100 ways is likely to improve performance, because such global praise provides no useful information to students except that the teacher approves of them. For feedback

Effective feedback specifies the relevant aspects of achievement. Good & Brophy (1999)

Name *Mercedes*		Points *35/40*	
	Points possible	Points awarded	Comments
Speaks in clear voice, makes eye contact	5	3	*You're getting better, but remember to look at your audience and to speak loudly and clearly. We're all on your side!*
Uses props or artifacts to represent the person interviewed	5	5	*Nice use of your aunt's scarf and jewelry—very authentic!*
Explains three conclusions about the experience of the person interviewed	15	15	*Your explanations of why your aunt immigrated and what she found made us feel like we understood her experiences. I can tell you spent a long time talking to her. Using phrases like "The first thing I learned…" was a good way of helping the audience follow your presentation.*
Supports conclusions with quotes or other information from interviews	15	12	*You used lots of details in your presentation, and that helped us understand how you reached your conclusions. I wasn't always sure whether you were mentioning things that your aunt told you or things you already knew about before the assignment—be sure to make it clear where you learned the information.*

FIG. 5.2. Checklist for evaluation of "Immigrant Interview" presentation.

to be effective, it must specify the relevant aspects of achievement. Rebecca's use of comments such as "Using phrases like 'The first thing I learned ... ' was a good way of helping the audience follow your presentation" is likely to result in more student learning than a thousand ambiguous exclamations of "Stupendous!" Including these checklists in portfolios gives teachers, students, and parents a concrete way to talk about students' achievements and progress.

Note also that the checklist in Fig. 5.2 introduces students to the evaluation of specifically historical skills, rather than only generic aspects of written language or oral presentations. During these projects, both Rebecca and Tina emphasized drawing different pieces of evidence together to reach more general conclusions, and they also noted the importance of clearly specifying where the evidence for these conclusions originated. These are critical components of historical thinking and understanding. Although standards for scholarship have changed over time, no historian today would simply list a set of isolated pieces of evidence without trying to draw them together into overarching themes or conclusions; the synthesis and interpretation of different pieces of evidence are what give a historical account its meaning. Similarly, no historian today would use evidence without identifying its source; clear citations are necessary for the audience to judge the validity of the conclusions. Yet few teachers evaluate such aspects of historical thinking among students; although they can be very perceptive in assessing students' understanding of important components of reading skills, mathematical reasoning, or written composition, most teachers limit their evaluations in history and social studies either to the retention of factual information or to measures of reading comprehension. But these are not enough; if teachers are to help students do history, they must pay attention to students' use of historical skills, not merely to their memory or their ability to answer questions on a reading passage. Rebecca's evaluation of how well students drew conclusions and used evidence to back them up represented an initial attempt to address these issues. Further evaluation of historical skills is taken up in following chapters.

LINKING STUDENTS TO LARGER NARRATIVES

Why use family histories to introduce students to these topics? Is it simply because they provide a way to personalize the past and give students an easy way to learn how to collect historical information? These are important considerations, but family histories serve a larger purpose as well. We have argued that a central role of history in our society lies in its ability to explain how the past produced the present. The personal histories discussed in chapter 4 may help students understand that they themselves have histories, but those histories become much more meaningful when they are linked to other stories—when students begin to see themselves as participants in larger narratives than those of their own lives.

The stories families tell about the past are one of the most important ways to introduce children to history. Many families tell these stories. Across race, ethnicity, class, and geographic region, children often learn about what has gone on before in their families and where they fit into that picture. Consider the eagerness of Tina's students to explain what they had learned about the past and the readiness of Rebecca's to share the reasons their families had immigrated. These were hardly new topics: Students had talked about these things with their families before. Passing on family history of one kind or another is a basic part of many cultural traditions. Using family histories as a part of instruction, then, represents the height of authenticity: It engages students in precisely the kind of historical understanding that exists outside of school.

Historical accounts involve the synthesis and interpretation of multiple pieces of evidence.

Teachers need to evaluate students' historical thinking in addition to more generic skills.

History helps students see themselves as part of narratives larger than their own lives.

Barton (2001b), Levstik & Barton (1996), Seixas (1993b)

As with most topics, students in the same classroom will develop different levels of understanding and awareness of this purpose. In Tina's class, for example, some students saw little more than that they had it easier than their grandparents, and so they should appreciate what they had. Others, however, recognized that the way they lived was directly dependent on what came before; for example, one student explained that he found history interesting because "I'm always curious, and history just answers zillions of questions, like 'How did we get here?'" Similarly, Rebecca found that her unit on immigration helped students understand their place within a nation of immigrants and see how they were fundamentally like other Americans. That wasn't always obvious to them: In a culture that rarely celebrates diversity, students may think of themselves as falling short of the American ideal. Moreover, they often are ready to assert their place in society by denying a similar place to others; Rebecca notes, for example, that students at her school often pick up on the general prejudice toward immigrants and refer to other students with pejorative racial terms—names they themselves may have been called only a few years earlier. In a basically intolerant culture, students cannot be expected to spontaneously understand the personal and political effects of such prejudice. She found, however, that after studying immigration and comparing the experiences of people throughout history, students were more likely to understand how they and their classmates were alike. History provided them an expanded perspective on their place—and the place of others—in American society.

> History helps explain, "How did we get here?"

> History can provide students an expanded perspective on their place in society.

FAMILY HISTORY IN THE CONTEXT OF DIVERSITY

Most of our recommendations on diversity in chapter 4 apply here as well. In general, it is important to keep in mind that the purpose of family histories is for students to learn historical content in a meaningful way, not to put themselves or their families on display. Tina, for example, allowed students to interview anyone about the same age as their grandparents if they preferred. Similarly, Rebecca simply required students to interview an immigrant; although most chose their parents, some interviewed other relatives or neighbors instead. Just as important, both teachers approached these assignments with an acceptance of, and respect for, diversity. During their discussion of what constituted a "generation," for example, Tina's students became interested in learning exactly how they were related to people in their families; many were just starting to see what made someone an uncle, cousin, and the like. This discussion naturally turned to questions of biological and step relations—what they were, how to refer to them, and so on. Tina emphasized that the existence of a variety of families was completely normal; she explained that there had always been plenty of people who don't live with two biological parents, but that in the past people sometimes regarded that as something shameful. The "Family History Chart" she used (see Fig. 5.3) is a good example of this approach: Rather than taking the form of a traditional lineage chart, in which each person has two and only two parents, it divides families into generations—thus allowing students to include only one parent if they want, or two or three or four. Because Tina modeled respect for the diversity of family relations that characterizes our society, her students felt free to discuss their own families without fear of shame or ridicule. Of course, some children still didn't want to share such topics openly, and she didn't require them to.

Rebecca modeled a similar respect for her students' family backgrounds. About half of her students' families were undocumented immigrants, yet Rebecca made no distinction between their experiences and those of families that had official sanction for their immigration. Certainly no students were made to feel ashamed of their backgrounds; as a result, they openly discussed and

> Students need to be given the choice of collecting information from people other than family members.

> Family history charts can allow for nontraditional family structures.

> Teachers who respect the diversity of family experiences do not treat differences as deficiencies.

Generations		
Yours (you, siblings, cousins)	Your parents' (parents, aunts, uncles)	Your grandparents' (grandparents, great aunts/uncles)
Name _____	Name _____	Name _____
Place of Birth _____	Place of Birth _____	Place of Birth _____
Date of Birth _____	Date of Birth _____	Date of Birth _____
Date Married _____	Date Married _____	Date Married _____
Name _____	Name _____	Name _____
Place of Birth _____	Place of Birth _____	Place of Birth _____
Date of Birth _____	Date of Birth _____	Date of Birth _____
Date Married _____	Date Married _____	Date Married _____
Name _____	Name _____	Name _____
Place of Birth _____	Place of Birth _____	Place of Birth _____
Date of Birth _____	Date of Birth _____	Date of Birth _____
Date Married _____	Date Married _____	Date Married _____
Name _____	Name _____	Name _____
Place of Birth _____	Place of Birth _____	Place of Birth _____
Date of Birth _____	Date of Birth _____	Date of Birth _____
Date Married _____	Date Married _____	Date Married _____

FIG. 5.3. Family history chart.

wrote about their experience hiding under a blanket in the back of a car, using a friend's passport, running across "the line," or paying a *coyote* $300, only to be caught anyway. As in Tina's class, though, no student was required to share such personal details.

Unfortunately, not everyone is so accepting of diversity. Rebecca taught the unit described here in the months immediately preceding the passage of a state-wide referendum that, had it been implemented, would have denied government services to undocumented immigrants. The climate of anti-immigrant feeling made some students hesitant to complete the assignment; the one student whose family were not recent immigrants was forbidden by his mother to interview an immigrant—she was afraid her son would "get into trouble." More important, Rebecca realized she might never be able to teach this unit in the same way again: The referendum would require a teacher to report any undocumented immigrants (so that they can be expelled from school) or have her credential revoked. Rather than face such an intolerable choice, Rebecca planned to avoid any situation that might provide information on how her students came to the United States. Although she would still be able to teach about immigration—by bringing in guest speakers who have immigrated from a variety of countries, and having students interview them in class—she no longer would have been able to use family histories in the same way.

Political circumstances sometimes force teachers to modify assignments.

EXTENSIONS

Because migration is such an important theme in history, there are many possibilities for expanding on the topic. In addition to studying voluntary migrations to the United States, for example, students could examine migrations that have been coerced; obvious examples in our own past include the trade in African slaves, the Japanese American relocation during World War II, and the Trail of Tears. Students could also study migrations that have been means of escape, such as the Underground Railroad in the United States or the movement of political and economic refugees here and throughout the world. (See the literature list at the end of this chapter.)

Students could also compare the experiences not only of Irish, Chinese, and contemporary immigrants (as they did in Rebecca's class) but also of immigrants from Germany, Japan, Italy, Russia, Poland, or any number of other countries. Such investigations can provide a meaningful connection to local history. For example, students near Cincinnati could examine the violence and discrimination faced by people of German ancestry during World War I; students in California could learn about the extradition of Mexican Americans during the Depression or prejudice against Japanese and Chinese workers in the 19th century; and those in the South could study the forced removal of African Americans in their communities in the early part of this century.

These are only a few isolated examples; the power of family histories lies in the way they can be adapted to local circumstances. Most students are required to study their state's history at some point (often in fourth grade), but unfortunately the topic usually amounts to little more than temporarily memorizing the names of early political leaders or other "heroes." (And from other perspectives—such as Native Americans'—these leaders are often anything but heroes.) Moreover, the study of state history generally reinforces the misconception that history is synonymous with progress—that the past has been marked by consensus and increasing prosperity. Rarely does state history acquaint students with the conflicts that have had a lasting impact on them. The topic would be much more vital, interesting, and meaningful if it focused on topics—such as immigration and its consequences—that actually help explain the present.

Similarly, a topic like *communities* in third grade will be more meaningful than learning about "Anytown, U.S.A." if it involves students in investigations of migration in their own communities. Not every community is fortunate enough to have as high a proportion of recent immigrants as Rebecca's, but people everywhere move. Students could collect information on the moves they, their parents, and their grandparents have made in their lifetimes and use the data to answer a variety of questions—Have most people lived in one place all their lives? Have more people moved from one county to another, one state to another, or one country to another? Why have people moved? Students can then post requests on the Internet (or contact pen pals through the mail) to collect similar information on the movement of people in other communities. Rather than an exercise on how to find the post office on a generic map, the study of community could help students develop an understanding of how communities are similar and different throughout the United States. (For a more detailed description of community study, see chap. 8.)

Using family members to learn about history, as Tina's students did, also has unlimited possibilities for extensions. Although her students focused on aspects of everyday life and rarely made connections to larger political or economic issues, teachers in the middle grades can help students learn about national and world events through the experience of their relatives, who often prove to be amazingly rich resources. One eighth grader in a class studying changing patterns of labor in the 20th century, for example, had assumed her family would

Focusing on important themes in history makes the study of state and local history more meaningful.

State and local history should include the conflicts that have influenced the present.

Community study should include attention to the historical development of specific locales.

Family histories can link students to national and world events.

have little insight into the topic. To her surprise, they knew a great deal: Her grandfather still had his union card from the International Tobacco Workers Union, and her great-grandfather's union card was in the family Bible; her grandmother had left the farm during World War II to work in a chemical factory; and a great aunt had saved pro- and anti-union pamphlets from the 1940s in her scrapbook. The personal insights of relatives and the further research they inspired led to a level of involvement that no textbook could have stimulated. Similarly, in one class, students did research for a "desegregation time line" that compared significant events nationally to those in their own school and community; information on the latter came primarily from their interviews with local residents.

Oral history and the experiences of families provide motivation for learning about modern history. Crocco (1998)

Collecting this kind of information can also help students understand more completely the evidentiary and interpretive nature of history. We noted in the last chapter that when children ask their parents questions, they quickly see that people disagree about the past. Students investigating truly significant issues (rather than when someone first learned to ride a bike) will encounter even more fundamental disagreements. Those in the middle grades, then, could compare the perspectives of family members on Vietnam, the Civil Rights Movement, or changing roles for women, and contrast these to accounts found in textbooks or the media. When students see historical interpretations on television or in movies, they may either uncritically accept or uncritically reject what they see—but when they have a chance to compare these interpretations to those of family members, they gain a better understanding of just how complicated history is. Students come away not only knowing more history but coming closer to understanding how history is interpreted and presented.

Family disagreements help students see history as controversial and interpretive.

Students in the middle grades can also use their families to learn about historical evidence other than oral histories. Several eighth graders, for example, extensively documented their families' involvement in World War II with draft notices, transfer orders, newspaper clippings, gasoline rationing forms, and factory identification badges. By combining these with the interviews they conducted, they put together a wide-ranging collection of historical evidence. Other students in the class used report cards, school yearbooks, and newspaper clippings to create histories of their parents' school careers. In both cases, students learned about the variety of sources on which historical accounts can be based.

Families may have a wealth of historical source materials.

Of course, as with any topic involving families, teachers must provide choices. Rather than expecting that every family will have experience with a war, unions, or any other single topic, teachers must recognize that each family's experience will differ. Some students may be able to investigate their relatives' involvement in the political events found in textbooks, but many others will benefit from looking at other topics more closely related to social history. The point of involving family members is not simply to provide some gimmick by which students learn more about textbook content but for them to understand how history is written and interpreted in order to learn how the past has produced the present.

Families have different historical experiences.

CONCLUSIONS

At first glance, history appears to be more remote from students' experiences than subjects like language, math, and science. Even young children are familiar with talking, counting, and nature, but the world of the past seems inherently more abstract and distant. Some educators have even argued that the subject is so far removed from children's experiences that they are not ready to study history until high school! Family histories, though, help students make concrete connections to topics that would be less accessible if they were introduced only through readings in a textbook. By learning about their families' experiences moving or the way their grandparents lived when they were children, students both build on the mental schemas they already have and begin to move outward to people further removed in time and place. Tina points to this as one of the most important benefits of the activities described in this chapter: "Students start to get interested in something other than themselves, other than their friends, their clothes, their bubble gum."

As we noted in chapter 1, one of the ways in which history contributes to democratic participation is by encouraging students to think about ways of life other than their own. By studying immigration, Rebecca's students had to consider the lives of people who came from different countries, whose circumstances were different than theirs, and who had different ideas, attitudes, and beliefs. They began by noting similarities between past and present, but they increasingly explored the differences as well. Similarly, Tina's students knew that their relatives were like themselves in may ways, but their family history projects also helped them understand how they differed—the fashions they wore, the games they played, the technology they used. Although we will discuss more complicated forms of perspective recognition in later chapters, the activities described here introduced students to a basic element of historical understanding and democratic participation—the recognition that we are both similar to and different from other people and that both are crucial to understanding each other.

<aside>Students need to understand both similarities and differences across time and space.</aside>

Focusing on families is also tremendously motivating for students and parents alike. Tina's students were excited about getting to interview their grandparents and to tell their stories in class; as one girl pointed out, "I learned things that my grandma did that I didn't know. You know what you have now, but you don't know what they had before." In Rebecca's room as well, students shared countless artifacts from their families' backgrounds, and parents sent in photograph after photograph for students to include in their presentations and papers. Successful schools recognize the importance of students' families and try to make them feel comfortable at school; family history projects take this recognition one step further by making family experiences a part of instruction. As Rhoda Coleman points out, "Parents love it, they love the interaction between the school and home. For once, this ten-year-old is asking them about their lives. Their child is asking them, 'Tell me about yourself.'"

CHILDREN'S AND ADOLESCENT LITERATURE

Family History

Arrington, F. *Bluestem*. Philomel, 2000.

Belton, S. *May'naise Sandwiches & Sunshine Tea*. Four Winds, 1994.

Cross, V. *Great-Grandma Tells of Threshing Day*. Whitman, 1992.

Flournoy, V. *The Patchwork Quilt*. Dial Books for Young Readers, 1985.

Greenfield, E., & Little, L. J. *Childtimes: A Three-Generation Memoir*. HarperCollins, 1993.

Hicyilmaz, G. *Smiling for Strangers*. Farrar, Straus & Giroux, 2000.

Howard, E. F. *Aunt Flossie's Hats (and Crab Cakes Later)*. Clarion, 1991.

Igus, T. *When I Was Little*. Just Us Books, 1992.

Johnson, A. *Tell Me a Story, Mama*. Franklin Watts, 1989.

Kurtz, J. *Faraway Home*. Gulliver, 2000.

Lasky, K. *Night Journey*. Viking, 1986.

Levoy, M. *The Hanukkah of Great-Uncle Otto*. Jewish Publication Society of America, 1984.

McDonald, M. *The Potato Man*. Orchard Books, 1991.

MacLachlan, P. *Three Names*. HarperCollins, 1991.

Peck, R. *A Year Down Yonder*. Dial, 2000.

Radowsky, C. *Jenny and the Grand Old Great-Aunts*. Bradbury Press, 1992.

Stevenson, J. *Don't You Know There's a War On?* Greenwillow Books, 1992.

Stolz, M. *Go Fish*. HarperCollins, 1991.

Weber, J. E. *Melting Pots: Family Stories and Recipes*. Silver Moon Press, 1994.

Anastos, P., & French, C. *Illegal: Seeking the American Dream*. Rizzoli International Publishers, 1991.

Anzaldna, G. *Friends from the Other Side/Amigos del otro lado*. Children's Book Press, 1993.

Ashabranner, B. *An Ancient Heritage: The Arab-American Minority*. HarperCollins, 1991.

Ashabranner, B. *Still a Nation of Immigrants*. Dutton, 1993.

Atkinson, M. *María Teresa*. Lollipop Power, 1979.

Avi. *Beyond the Western Sea: Book One—Escape from Home*. Avon, 1996.

Avi. *Beyond the Western Sea: Book Two—Lord Kirkle's Money*. Avon, 1996.

Bartone, E. *Peppe the Lamplighter*. Lothrop, Lee, & Shepard, 1993.

Beatty, P. *Lupita Mañana*. William Morrow & Company, 1981.

Bial, R. *Tenement: Immigrant Life on the Lower East Side*. Houghton Mifflin, 2002.

Bode, J. *New Kids on the Block: Oral Histories of Immigrant Teens*. Franklin Watts, 1989.

Breckler, R. K. *Hoang Breaks the Lucky Teapot*. Houghton Mifflin, 1992.

Bresnick-Perry, R. *Leaving for America*. Children's Book Press, 1992.

Brown, T. *Hello Amigos*. Holt, 1986.

Brown, T. *Lee Ann: The Story of a Vietnamese-American Girl*. G. P. Putnam's Sons, 1991.

Bunting, E. *A Day's Work*. Clarion, 1994.

Bunting, E. *Going Home*. HarperCollins, 1996.

Cazet, D. *Born in the Gravy*. Orchard, 1993.

Chetin, H. *Angel Island Prisoner, 1922*. New Seed Press, 1982.

Coerr, E. *Chang's Paper Pony*. Harper, 1988.

Cohen, B. *Make a Wish, Molly*. Doubleday, 1994.

Choi, S. N. *Halmoni and the Picnic*. Houghton Mifflin, 1993.

Crew, L. *Children of the River*. Delacorte, 1989.

Fisher, L. E. *Across the Sea from Galway*. Four Winds Press, 1975.

Fisher, L. E. *Ellis Island: Gateway to the New World*. Holiday House, 1986.

Freedman, R. *Immigrant Kids*. Scholastic, 1980.

Garrigue, S. *The Eternal Spring of Mr. Ito*. Bradbury Press, 1985.

Graff, N. P. *Where the River Runs*. Little, Brown, 1993.

Gundisch, K. *How I Became an American*. Cricket, 2001.

Harik, E. M. *The Lebanese in America*. Lerner, 1988.

Harvey, B. *Immigrant Girl: Becky of Eldridge Street*. Holiday House, 1987.

Hesse, K. *Letters from Rifka*. Henry Holt, 1992.

Hoobler, D., & Hoobler, T. *The African-American Family Album*. Oxford, 1996.

Hoobler, D., & Hoobler, T. *The German-American Family Album*. Oxford, 1996.

Hoobler, D., & Hoobler, T. *The Japanese-American Family Album*. Oxford, 1995.

Hoobler, D., & Hoobler, T. *The Irish-American Family Album*. Oxford, 1995.

Howlett, B. *I'm New Here*. Houghton Mifflin, 1993.

Hoyt-Goldsmith, D. *Hoang Anh: A Vietnamese-American Boy*. Holiday House, 1992.

Katz, W. L. *The Great Migrations, 1880s–1912*. SteckVaughn, 1993.

Kidd, D. *Onion Tears*. Orchard, 1991.

Knight, M. B. *Who Belongs Here? An American Story*. Tilbury House, 1993.

Kraus, J. H. *Tall Boy's Journey*. Carolrhoda Books, 1992.

Kuklin, S. *How My Family Lives in America*. Bradbury, 1992.

Lech, J. *My Grandmother's Journey*. Bradbury, 1991.

Leighton, M. R. *An Ellis Island Christmas*. Viking, 1992.

Levin, E. *If Your Name Was Changed at Ellis Island*. Scholastic, 1993.

Levine, E. *I Hate English!* Scholastic, 1989.

Levinson, R. *Soon, Annala*. Orchard Books, 1993.

Levinson, R. *Watch the Stars Come Out*. Dutton, 1985.

Levitin, S. *Silver Days*. Atheneum, 1989.

Lim, G. *Wings for Lai Ho*. East West Publishing Company, 1982.

Maestro, B. *Coming to America: The Story of Immigration*. Scholastic, 1996.

Meltzer, M. *The Chinese-Americans*. Crowell, 1980.

Meltzer, M. *The Hispanic-Americans*. Crowell, 1982.

Mohr, N. *Felita*. Dial, 1979.

Moscinski, S. *Tracing Our Jewish Roots*. John Muir Publications, 1993.

Moss, M. *In America*. Dutton, 1994.

Moss, M. *Hannah's Journal: The Story of an Immigrant Girl*. Silver Whistle, 2000.

Murphy, E., & Driscoll, T. *An Album of the Irish Americans*. Franklin Watts, 1974.

Na, An. *A Step from Heaven*. Front Street, 2001.

Naff, A. *The Arab Americans*. Chelsea House, 1989.

Namioka, L. *Yang the Youngest and His Terrible Ear*. Little, Brown, 1992.

O'Connor, K. *Dan Thuy's New Life in America*. Lerner, 1992.

Paek, M. *Aekyung's Dream*. Children's Book Press, 1988.

Polacco, P. *The Keeping Quilt*. Simon & Schuster, 1988.

Poynter, M. *The Uncertain Journey: Stories of Illegal Aliens in El Norte.* Atheneum, 1992.

Rosenberg, M. B. *Making a New Home in America.* Lothrop, Lee, & Shepard, 1986.

Sagan, M. *Tracing Our Jewish Roots.* John Muir Publications, 1993.

Sandler, M. W. *Immigrants.* HarperCollins, 1995.

Say, A. *Grandfather's Journey.* Houghton Mifflin, 1993.

Shefelman, J. *A Peddler's Dream.* Houghton Mifflin, 1992.

Siegel, B. *Sam Ellis's Island.* Four Winds Press, 1985.

Stanek, M. *I Speak English for My Mom.* Albert Whitman, 1989.

Surat, M. M. *Angel Child, Dragon Child.* Scholastic, 1989.

Temple, F. *Grab Hands and Run.* Orchard, 1993.

Waters, K., & Slovenz-Low, M. *Lion Dancer: Ernie Wan's Chinese New Year.* Scholastic, 1991.

Woodruff, E. *The Orphan of Ellis Island: A Time Travel Adventure.* Scholastic, 1997.

Yee, P. *Roses Sing on New Snow: A Delicious Tale.* Macmillan, 1991.

Yee, P. *Tales from Gold Mountain: Stories of the Chinese in the New World.* Macmillan, 1989.

Yep, L. *Dragonwings.* Harper, 1975.

Forced Migration, Refugees, and the Underground Railroad

Barboza, S. *Door of No Return.* Cobblehill, 1994.

Bealer, A. W. *Only the Names Remain: The Cherokees and the Trail of Tears.* Little, Brown, 1972.

Beatty, P. *Who Comes with Cannons?* Morrow, 1992.

Bergman, T. *Along the Tracks.* Houghton Mifflin, 1991.

Bial, R. *The Underground Railroad.* Houghton Mifflin, 1995.

Fradin, D. B. *Bound for the North Star: True Stories of Fugitive Slaves.* Houghton Mifflin, 2000.

Fritz, J. *China's Long March: 6000 Miles of Danger.* Putnam's, 1988.

Haskins, J. *Get on Board: The Story of the Underground Railroad.* Scholastic, 1993.

Hopkinson, D. *Sweet Clara and the Freedom Quilt.* Knopf, 1993.

Johnson, D. *Seminole Diary: Remembrances of a Slave.* Macmillan, 1994.

Kushner, A. *Falasha No More: An Ethiopian Jewish Child Comes Home.* Shopolsky, 1986.

Levine, E. *If You Traveled on the Underground Railroad.* Scholastic, 1992.

Lois, R. *Steal Away Home.* Macmillan, 1994.

Mikaelsen, B. *Red Midnight.* RAYO, 2003.

Muñoz, R. P. *Esperanza Rising.* Scholastic, 2000.

Rappaport, D. *Escape from Slavery: Five Journeys to Freedom.* HarperCollins, 1991.

Rappaport, D. *Freedom River.* Jump at the Sun, 2000.

Schur, M. R. *When I Left My Village.* Dial, 1996.

Wilkes, S. *One Day We had to Run! Refugee Children Tell Their Stories in Words and Paintings.* Millbrook Press, 1994.

6

I THINK COLUMBUS WENT TO HELL!

Initiating Inquiry Into World History

> Name: _____
> Please help your child with this interview.
> Person interviewed _____ **GUS** _____
> How does someone become famous?
>   *They do something special for a person.*
> Who do you think is a famous American? Why?
>   *President Clinton. Because he's the president*
>   *& he does a lot of things that are famous.*
> Can I become famous?
>   *Yes.*
> How do you know when you are famous?
>   *Because the people you talk to when*
>   *you're famous tell you so.*
> Once you are famous, do you stay famous?
>   *Sometimes, but if you don't want to you don't*
>   *have to stay famous anymore but usually you do.*

Twenty-two kindergartners and first graders excitedly share their homework assignment. They had interviewed family members, neighbors, and friends. Some of them wrote their responses independently; others had an adult help them. They were trying to find out how people became famous. Some of their interviewees thought fame came when you were rich or when you did "something real cool," "headturning," "something out of the ordinary." Their list of famous Americans included President Clinton, Michael Jackson, Miss America, Shaquille O'Neal, Jimmy Carter, Abraham Lincoln, and Daniel Boone. Staying famous was, their survey helped them conclude, not a certainty. "Sometimes," Minna Gayle declared, "you can really blow it."

In classrooms across America, children study famous people. Rarely, however, do they consider how these or any other people became famous or what "fame" really means. Teachers sometimes fear that young children will be unable to deal with the controversies that surround some historic figures or events. Others worry that young children are not ready to study people from more distant times and places. LeeAnn Fitzpatrick shared these concerns, and she was also worried that her students—a number of whom were nonreaders—might have difficulty with disciplined inquiry. With some hesitation, then, she decided to test this approach with her students, but to do it in ways that would provide many links between the familiar and unfamiliar.

Oral history is accessible even to the youngest students.

Crook (1988), Penyak & Duray (1999), K. A. Young (1994)

Even young children can deal with historical controversies.

Evans et al. (1999), Levstik (2000), Sosniak & Stodolsky (1993), Thornberg & Brophy (1992)

Emergent readers can conduct disciplined inquiry.

See chapter 1, Table 1.1, "themes and questions" for more on the source of this topic.

Be sure to select manageable topics. *See also* Pappas et al. (1999)

Controversy generates interest and challenges existing schemas.

Newmann et al. (1995), Trout (1982)

Local issues can link students to global issues.

Anderson (1990)

A global context helps make sense of national history. Merryfield (1995), Merryfiled & Wilson (2004)

Barton & McCully (2005), Chua (2003), Levstik & Groth (2004), Levstik (2000), Thelen (1995), Willinsky (1998)

Making global connections requires teacher facilitation.

Anderson (1990), Levstik (1995), National Council for the Social Studies (1994)

Initially, LeeAnn planned to introduce a number of people whose values, beliefs, ideas, or explorations had influenced or changed America. She decided to start with famous people because fame would be a familiar concept for most of her students. Starting with something this familiar, she thought, provided a framework for understanding more distant people and events. As she began planning, however, it became apparent that a study of multiple individuals was too complex for her first attempt at disciplined inquiry with young children. There weren't enough sources at the right levels of difficulty, and the available sources did not represent the diversity of people that she had hoped for. Finally, juggling that many individual studies seemed unmanageable. LeeAnn began searching for a single individual on whom to focus.

At about this time, the local news began covering a series of protests surrounding the upcoming Columbus Day celebrations. Here was a famous person who had definitely influenced or changed America and one with whom the children were probably somewhat familiar. It was certainly easy enough to generate interest—in fact, all LeeAnn had to do was bring in one newspaper article and a cartoon pointing out that some Native Americans saw Columbus as a villain while some Italian American groups viewed him as a hero. The controversy about Columbus was authentic—real, important, and public—well enough known to generate conversation and different viewpoints that were accessible to children, and there was an abundance of resources at appropriate levels. Columbus seemed an excellent beginning point both for thinking about whether fame and heroism were synonymous and for considering the differences between "good" fame and "bad" fame. Local controversy provided another familiar, current connection that could help students make sense of Columbus and the time in which he lived.

In the wake of Columbus' explorations, culture contact between people from the Americas, Europe, and Africa altered the continents on which they met and from which they came. LeeAnn thought that studying Columbus might provide an opportunity to introduce history from this more global perspective. Such a perspective is important for two reasons. First, it helps students make better sense out of world history; second, a traditional history curriculum too often presents American history as almost entirely unrelated to the rest of the world. In an international survey, historians complained that American history had become too "insular and inward-looking, not international or comparative enough." In the past, we argued that national histories often presented history as if each country existed in a historical and geographic vacuum. Though it is true that some nations do present their histories in these ways, this is more often the prerogative of the powerful. Smaller nations cannot often afford insularity. Their survival more clearly depends on the actions of other nations—whether the World Bank forgives crippling debts, membership in the European Community is withheld, economic boycotts imposed, trade embargoed, or refugees flood across borders. *World* history is, for most nations, a daily reality.

Many of the teachers in this book actively work to connect national and world history. Remember in chapter 3, Jeanette Groth made explicit the connections between independence movements in India and the American colonies. She began with India and then linked events there to more familiar American history. LeeAnn Fitzpatrick began with a current event—the controversy over a U.S. holiday—and moved from there to connect with roots in American, European, and African history. These connections do not happen by chance. Rather, they require that teachers:

- Make explicit the connections between local and global events.
- Scaffold students' understanding of more distant times and places through the use of a variety of symbolic forms—pictures, maps, charts, fiction, nonfiction, mathematics, and writing.
- Make explicit the connections between past events that are history and current events that are making history.

START LOCALLY, CONNECT GLOBALLY

Christopher Columbus

christopher columbus rode on a sail boat called the Santa Maria. He was standing on the ship when a wave splashed over the boat. The ship sinked and he swam to land. He gave the indians fake jewelry and they gave him real gold. He took the indians back with him to Spain across the ocean to the castel. The king and queen gave him money to make other trips. He brought food like corn, potatoes, beans and tobacco. He also brought back gold. He was famous.

—Donte Morgan, age 6

Traditionally, there has been little emphasis on world history with young children. To some extent, this is related to the problem of ethnocentrism mentioned earlier. More generally, however, the lack of attention to world history can be attributed to theories that assume that young children can learn best those things directly experienced and closest in time and place. As we mentioned earlier, recent research on human cognition suggests that these assumptions are not well grounded; understanding is not so much a matter of physical proximity as it is the degree to which children can make human sense out of whatever history they are studying. Certainly Donte, in his story, makes interesting human sense out of Columbus' interactions with Native Americans. As were several of his peers, Donte was convinced that Columbus violated basic rules of fairness—he traded fake jewelry for real gold and he took human beings away from their families just to show them to the king and queen. The class had acted out this part of their study, with LeeAnn declaring that she was going to need "sample school children" to take home with her because her neighbors didn't understand what she did all day. She asked the children how they would feel if she just decided to keep a couple of them. They couldn't go back home, they'd have to be put on display for other people to watch, and maybe they couldn't understand any of the language or customs of this new place. This was an issue that made clear human sense to the children. It made no difference that the setting was distant in time and place; people should never be souvenirs nor taken unwillingly from their homes. Columbus had committed a historic wrong. As five-year-old James declared, "I think Columbus went to hell!"

Even before the children found out that Columbus had, in their view, behaved unfairly, their study was grounded in a familiar concept: fame. First, of course, the survey asked children to find out how other people in their environment viewed fame. These questions generated interest and discussion at home as well as in the classroom. Students compared their own responses to survey questions with those they received when they conducted the interviews and discussed the differences. Why, for instance, did so many men mention athletes, women name politicians, and children mention singers and actors? And no one had mentioned Christopher Columbus, despite all the newspaper coverage! Did that mean he wasn't famous? Or, maybe he just wasn't very important? The discussion lasted a good 30 minutes, and when LeeAnn suggested that perhaps they could study more about Columbus and answer these questions, the students were enthusiastic. At this point, she introduced a set of questions that encouraged children to consider how a voyage that began in Spain over 500 years ago touched their lives today:

Why do we celebrate Columbus Day?
Is Christopher Columbus famous?
Would we be here today in America if there had never been a Christopher Columbus?
What do you think it was like living 500 years ago?
How did people travel in those days?

Blythe (1989), Brophy & VanSledright (1997), Downey & Levstik (1991)

World history can make "human sense" even to young children.

Barton (1997a)

Linking experience, discussion, and substantive questions leads to student inquiry.

What would a person need in those days to travel across such a large body of water?
How long ago was October 12, 1492?
How long did it take Columbus to make his voyage to America?

START GLOBALLY, CONNECT LOCALLY

So far we have looked at introducing global connections by beginning with a familiar concept—fame—and a local controversy—celebrating Columbus Day. Although this is an effective technique, it is not the only way to make explicit the connections between local and global events. Consider, for instance, Walt Keet's seventh-grade class' study of South Africa and the transition from apartheid to a coalition government led by Nelson Mandela. As had LeeAnn Fitzpatrick, Walt had a topic that was current as well as deeply rooted in historic issues of colonialism and human rights. In addition, the history of South Africa is connected to U.S. history both by foreign policy issues and our own struggles with race and segregation. Walt wanted to make connections between his seventh graders in the present day American South and the struggles of South Africans half way around the world. There were obvious links, from colonialism and de facto and de jure segregation, to civil war and civil rights, but Walt wanted his students to start with the human sense of apartheid. He began by arranging with his team teachers for a block of time in which to show the film *Cry, Freedom*. This movie, set in South Africa in the 1960s, tells the story of antiapartheid activist Steven Biko and the newspaper publisher who befriended him and who, from exile, wrote about Biko's life and murder at the hands of the South African government. Anticipating that some parents might object to the film because of the violence of some of the scenes, Walt also prepared a list of alternative readings for those students unable to view the film. *Journey to Jo'burg* and its sequel, *Chain of Fire*, were both short enough to be completed in a week, and both dealt with the issues of separation of families because of restrictive housing and homeland laws (see literature list at end of chapter). In addition, the novels were written from the perspective of Black South Africans, whereas the film was presented from the White editor's perspective.

The film and books generated interesting responses from Walt's students: "How could people still let these things happen?" "Why didn't the Blacks just leave?" "Why didn't somebody go over there and stop them?" These students were too young to remember similar forms of legal segregation in their own country. Although they were well aware that race was an often divisive issue—there were racial tensions in the wake of a shooting in their own community—most were sure that the Civil War had ended legal discrimination in the United States. With this in mind, Walt showed excerpts from several documentaries dealing with race and civil rights in 20th-century America. "Now," Walt said, "I have a question for you. One of the issues that faces Nelson Mandela and the new South Africa is what to do about the past—about a difficult and often horrible part of history. Mandela's African National Congress has suggested establishing a 'truth commission' somewhat like the Nuremberg Trials we have already studied. Nationalist Party argues that this will lead to revenge rather than reform. They suggest drawing a 'veil across the past'—do not hold a truth commission, do not tell the story of apartheid. People in South Africa also look to the rest of the world to see how we have handled this sort of issue. After all, this is a human, not just South African, problem. What advice would you give to the people of South Africa? Should they learn the history of apartheid, or not?"

This is not a made-for-school question. Nor is it a question with a single, clear answer. Instead, it is a real question actually being asked by South Africans, that touches on the political and social uses of history. By grappling with this as a central concern of their study, Walt hoped his students would come to better under-

McGinnis (n.d.)

Older students also need to make human sense of historical controversies.

Boner (1995), Cuthbertson (1995)

Naidoo (1986, 1989)

Films and books can initiate inquiry and represent multiple perspectives.

Real questions are worth investigating.

70

stand why history is controversial and why it is important. Although this question is clearly researchable and has real world applications, its controversial nature and the kind of resources necessary for the research make teacher mediation—scaffolding—absolutely essential.

Allen (1999), Newmann et al. (1995), Wells & Chang-Wells (1992)

SCAFFOLDING INQUIRY INTO DISTANT TIMES AND PLACES

Young children generally haven't the slightest idea what "research" means, and for older students, as most of us remember all too well, research often means poorly disguised plagiarism and suffocatingly boring reports. It takes specific kinds of scaffolding to support student inquiry; the kind depends, in part, on the age and experience of the learners but also on the questions asked and the kind of resources used. In general, you should consider the following elements of scaffolding as necessary to disciplined inquiry:

Pappas et al. (1999)

Particular aspects of scaffolding are necessary for in-depth inquiry.

- Building a set of common experiences.
- Building in challenges to prior knowledge that provide models of multiple perspectives on and interpretations of data.
- Providing specific, in-class, help in selecting, collecting and organizing data.
- Providing specific help with how to report to real audiences.

Building Common Experiences

LeeAnn Fitzpatrick and Walt Keet were careful to determine what relevant knowledge students already had and to establish a set of common experiences for their classes. Although children come to school knowing all sorts of historical information, you cannot rely on their having either sufficient prior knowledge or much enthusiasm for any particular topic. Before students can or will conduct inquiry, teachers must generate interest in history and help students establish a working knowledge base. It is this continually growing knowledge base from which questions are generated and against which answers can be tested. Both LeeAnn and Walt used discussion to "prime the pump." LeeAnn used a KWL procedure. She began by asking students what they already knew about why there was a Columbus Day. As the children talked, she recorded their comments on chart paper under the heading "Know." Later, questions to investigate were recorded on chart paper under the heading "Want to Know," and the concluding discussion of the study was recorded under the heading "Learned." As a result, there was a public, running record of student conversation to which everyone could refer.

Harste & Short (1988), Hepler (1991), Jorgensen (1993), Ogle (1986), Reardon (1988)

Walt, on the other hand, assumed that the movie would generate considerable discussion. Concerned that everyone would not participate in a whole class free-for-all, he broke the class into response groups of three to five participants each. Each group was to discuss three questions: What most surprised you about the movie (or book)? Why do you think this movie or book was distributed outside South Africa? What issues in this movie (or book) do you think the class should discuss further? Next, the class moved into a circle so that everyone could see the other participants. Because Walt had several male students who tended to dominate conversations, he used a more formal model for full-class discussion, passing a "talking stick" (a wooden baton) from speaker to speaker. Although students could opt not to speak when it was their turn, everyone was required to make at least one substantive comment during a discussion. He also limited comments to three minutes each and forbade interruption, often holding up his hand for silence to give students time to think before responding. In conducting class discussion in this way, Walt found that the male students did

Response groups help organize discussion.

Sadker & Sadker (1994), Schuster & VanDyne (1998), Streitmatter (1994), Weikel (1995)

not monopolize the conversation, and several female students who rarely commented in general discussion were more likely to talk when their turn came.

Both LeeAnn's and Walt's approaches to classroom discussion helped establish what students already knew and got them thinking about the topic at hand. Making explicit the local connections also helped each teacher capture student attention. Following these initial discussions, each teacher set up a series of experiences to provide students with enough background knowledge to shape and motivate inquiry. With the younger children, for instance, the concept of "fame" needed a working definition. By having the children conduct their surveys, LeeAnn modeled one way to gather and display data, but she also made clear that people could have different ideas about the same concept. She laid the groundwork for students to feel comfortable about developing their own interpretation of Columbus and for their peers to expect that people might have different points of view. From the beginning of the unit, the students were helped to see that different people had different ideas about what constituted fame. Walt, on the other hand, went about things a bit differently. Rather than define the concept of apartheid for the students, he decided to let them see what apartheid looked and felt like to South Africans. The movie and novels captured the emotional weight of a concept with which students would have to grapple, graphically portrayed the clash of ideologies and emotions, and established the background for the organizing question about the place of history in the new South Africa.

LeeAnn also used film, but she chose an old filmstrip without sound or narration. She explained that "the terminology in a lot of the material on Columbus is too hard for an early primary student to understand. If you paraphrase the plot, though, the pictures make a good introduction to the study." The filmstrip provided visual images of the time and place and some of the people involved in the Columbian/Native American encounter. Now students had information against which they could test new ideas as well as some understanding that different people might have different ideas. In addition, LeeAnn was able to introduce common terminology—names of countries and their leaders and terms such as *cargo, voyage, exploration, encounter,* and *exchange* that would appear throughout the study. As new words were discussed, they were written on large pieces of chart paper so that the children would be able to use them in their writing and editing. Children also selected several of these words for their individual weekly spelling assignment.

Introductory activities such as these are particularly important when children have relatively little prior knowledge about a topic, which is often the case with world history. These activities establish a common vocabulary and generate discussion. But baseline data are meant to be built on, not preserved untouched. It serves as an intellectual seed bed in which new ideas are planted, transplanted, fertilized, or weeded out—and in which what might at first have seemed a weed may turn out to be a flower or the reverse. At its best, reflective, disciplined inquiry both builds and challenges what students think they know about history. It is essential, then, that new information be presented as a beginning, not an endpoint, and that teachers carefully scaffold the ways in which what is "known" is held up to challenge.

Challenge the Known: Multiple Perspectives and Changing Interpretations

All of us think we know some history, especially about our own country. We recognize, of course, that we could always learn more, but we don't usually look for proof of those things we think we already know. It is troubling, then, when what we thought we knew is challenged. Sometimes we reject the challenge—the new information is wrong! Sometimes we want proof—what evidence is there

Discussion helps establish what prior knowledge is available to students.

Teachers model date gathering.

Atwell (1987)

Multiple data sources provide richer background information.

Downs (1993), Greene (1995)

Attention to vocabulary building is important in enriching students' historical schemas.

Temple, Nathan, Temple, & Burris (1993)

Developing baseline data is crucial to supporting student inquiry.

Newmann et al. (1995), VanSledright (1997/1998)

History is always "in progress."

for this challenge? And sometimes we seek out more information—what did I miss before? Challenges to what we thought we knew happen all the time in history. Sometimes they come as the result of new information. More often they come because we are suddenly asked to look at something from a different historical perspective. Think about the controversy over the names of sports teams, for instance—the Braves or Redskins—and the symbols that accompany them—stereotypical images of Native Americans, hatchets, and the like. Or consider how you might interpret the battle at Little Big Horn.

Appleby et al. (1994), Novick (1988), Todorov (1984)

Little Big Horn Battlefield National Monument is a historic site and museum in Montana. You may remember it as the site of "Custer's Last Stand." From 1876 until 1976, that was the way the site was interpreted—Custer and the Seventh Cavalry made a last, desperate stand against the Indians who threatened settlement in the American West. The visitor center at the site was located close to where Custer died, and visitors viewed the battlefield from the perspective of the cavalry. Few visitors went to the site of the Indian village or were introduced to Native American views of the battle. Beginning in the 1960s, however, the U.S. Park Service began to change its interpretation. What happened? Well, Native American protests and changing ideas about a more inclusive history made people "see" Little Big Horn differently. This new view challenged old ideas so that Little Big Horn became less massacre and more battle, less triumphant march of civilization westward, and more conflict of cultures. Much of the information had been there all along, but its meaning changed dramatically. As a result, scholars asked different questions, sought out different sources, and found new information. Between 1983 and 1994, for instance, archaeologists working at Little Big Horn began comparing physical evidence—artifacts—with eyewitness reports from various combatants. Overall, they found that Native American reports closely matched the physical evidence. In consequence, any current history of the site must take this new information into account.

Linenthal (1994), Welch (1994)

Reinterpretations often challenge old assumptions and stereotypes.

Holt (1990a)

As you can see, challenging the "known" is not just cognitively sound instruction; it is also an authentic disciplinary model for doing history. As we already noted, children's schemas develop through generating questions and testing hypotheses. The same is true of historians; without challenges to existing schemas, they would have nothing to do. If the story of Little Big Horn were finished in 1876, there would be no need to rethink how the site is interpreted or for current historians to attempt to reconcile conflicting accounts to create a richer, more authentic interpretation. But the story is not finished, nor can it ever be; even if there were not conflicting accounts of what happened, historians would continue to interpret why it happened. Sometimes this interpretive restructuring involves minor tinkering—enriching but not significantly altering current schemas. Other times, it generates major restructuring of schemas, as when we stop telling the story of Columbus "discovering" a new world and start talking about culture contact, exchange, and conflict. Children's and historians' mental models of the past are constantly restructured—not just by learning more historical information but by regularly reflecting on what that information means, on what other points of view are possible, and on what light new historical knowledge throws on current events.

Fox (1993), Scott, Fox, Connor, & Harmon (2000)

For an interesting description of archaeological work and interpretive efforts at Little Big Horn, see http://www.custerbattle.com

Both LeeAnn Fitzpatrick and Walt Keet wanted their students to reflect on how perspective or point of view influences historical interpretation and leads to controversy. Each approached this task in different ways. LeeAnn decided that one way to help her students understand the controversy surrounding Columbus Day was to introduce them to different versions of the Columbus story. She selected three picture books and she, a teacher aide, and student teacher divided the class so that each of the three groups listened to a different book about Columbus. In the class discussion that follows, the students recorded information on a comparison chart. As you can see by reading Table 6.1, there were several places where the books did not agree or where one book gave information that another did not.

Table 6.1

Book Comparisons

Book Title and Author	Why did Columbus go on the ocean voyage?	What did people think the world was like?	What happened to the people who already lived in America?	What did Columbus accomplish?
Where Do You Think You're Going, Christopher Columbus? By Jean Fritz	Short route to the Indies (Japan & China) Wanted gold Wanted to make people Christians	Agreed that the earth was "round like a ball" Disagreed about how big the earth was Thought that there were gold, jewels, and spices in the Indies	Traded beads and bells for gold and parrots Indians were friendly Took 6 back to Spain on first trip Took 500 to sell as slaves Killed Indians for gold	Proved the sea was big Did not find Japan or China Did not know he was lost Found some gold Famous in Spain Named islands
Christopher Columbus by Ann McGovern	Wanted to reach "the east" by going west Wanted gold for Spain	Most people thought the earth was flat A few people thought the earth was round	Traded glass beads Indians were "gentle and friendly" Took 10 back to Spain on first trip	He was a hero in Spain He did not know he was lost He did not want to find a new world
The Columbus Story by Alice Dalgliesh	Wanted gold for Spain	Far away was the "Sea of Darkness"	Indians thought Columbus came from heaven Traded bells, beads, and caps for gold Indians were "gentle and friendly" Took "some" Indians back to Spain	He said all the land belonged to Spain He crossed the sea first

Walt was working with older students, so he began by presenting them with the African National Congress (ANC) and Nationalist positions and then asking them to go backwards in time to uncover the roots of dissension. In order to better help his student recognize the powerful emotions and perspectives behind the historic events, he used a graphic organizer (Fig. 6.1). This symbolic representation of perspectives helped students think about what points of view needed to be researched in order to understand the dilemma the new coalition

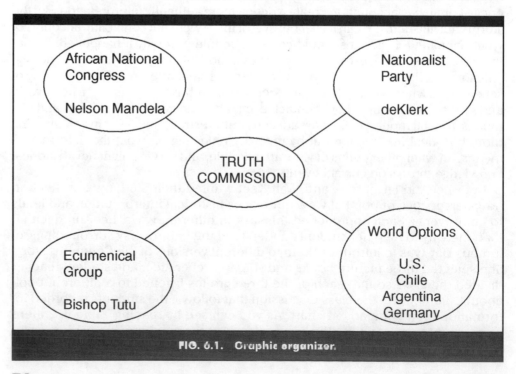

FIG. 6.1. Graphic organizer.

government faced. It also served as a way to organize inquiry groups. One group was assigned to each of the South African perspectives represented on the graph. A slightly larger group was assigned to provide a world perspective, with pairs of students given the task of investigating how the United States, Chile, and Argentina handled the issues of human rights violations and the national memory of these events. The class had already studied the aftermath of World War II and the Nurenberg Trials, so they had some historical precedent on which to base their current study. Chile and Argentina's history provided more recent examples of countries faced with major political changes following massive human rights violations, while a U.S. comparison encouraged students to think about what their own country faced in the aftermath of Civil War and in the midst of ongoing concerns over civil rights and terrorism.

Comparative world history helps develop historical perspective.

Selecting, Collecting, and Organizing Data

Both LeeAnn and Walt provided a variety of resources for their students to use, either in the classroom or in the school library. Each assumed different degrees of independence for student work. Both selected appropriate ways to help students be successful as researchers, given the age and experience of their students. LeeAnn's first problem was that none of her students had previously been involved in disciplined inquiry. A number of her students were not yet independent readers. She decided not to focus on the selection of resources at this point; rather, she organized activities that would help the children select information from sources she provided, then organize that information, and communicate it in ways that would be usable by their peers. In addition, her use of an integrated curriculum model led her to look for ways to incorporate other content areas such as mathematics into her instruction. She divided the class into five groups, based in part on what tasks seemed within reach for each group.

Foster & Yeager (1999), Freeman & Person (1992), Hyde & Bizar (1989), Pappas et al. (1999), Wells (1994)

Organize historical inquiry so that all students can be challenged as well as successful.

Group One: A Global Perspective. LeeAnn provided a large blank map of the world, globes, and flat maps. Students referred to the comparison charts they had already developed, used the globes and flat maps to answer the following questions, and transferred information to the blank map. Their map was then hung up in the classroom as a reference for further discussion. Questions included locating the following on a world map:

1. The countries the kings lived in who turned Columbus down when he asked for financial assistance. (England, France, Portugal)
2. The country that gave Columbus the money to finance the voyage. (Spain)
3. The countries that Columbus wanted to travel to. (India, China, the East Indies, and Japan)
4. The route Columbus followed to get to the Americas.

Group Two: Life in a Small Place. LeeAnn provided a large cross-section drawing of a ship, string, rulers, and the like. After measuring the size of Columbus' ship and cutting string to the appropriate length (90 ft), the children used books, illustrations, and the comparison chart they had worked on earlier to identify cargo (food, firewood, water, wine, clothes, ropes, sails). On the cross section of the ship (see Fig. 6.2), they then drew the cargo that they thought Columbus would need. Later, LeeAnn marked out an outline of the ship on the playground so the children could try to fit into the ship. Children were asked to think about what it was like living on the ships, with so many people, in such a small space, for such a long time.

Group Three: Seeds of Change. The task for this group was to find out what kinds of new plants—unfamiliar to Europeans—were found in the Americas.

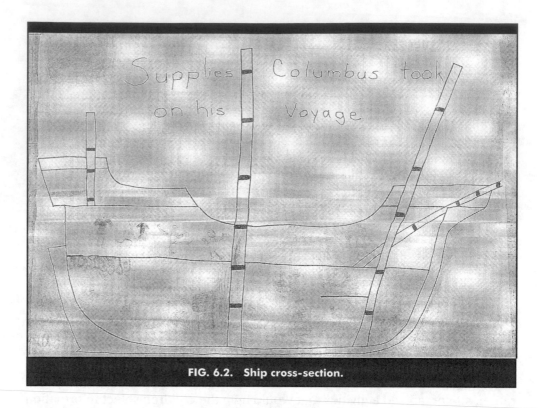

FIG. 6.2. Ship cross-section.

Again, LeeAnn provided appropriate books, along with a chart where the children categorized the plants as fruits, vegetables, and nonedible plants. Children drew pictures of the plants in each category and then labeled their illustrations. See Fig. 6.3.

Group Four: Counting the Days   Groups Four and Five had some of the youngest children, for whom the concept of time needed considerable support and visual reinforcement. Group Four's task was to make a time line showing how long Columbus' voyage lasted. They took calendars from August until October,

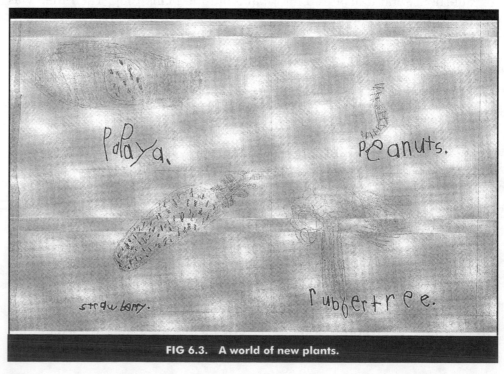

FIG 6.3. A world of new plants.

cut them apart, and put them on a time line, marked off the number of weeks, and then counted the days of the trip.

Group Five: How Long Is a Century?   This group also developed a visual representation of time, but their task was to make a time line showing how many hundreds of years separated 1492 from the present. They marked time in 100-year increments by first grouping unifix cubes in 10s, then placing markers after 10 groups of 10 to indicate a 100-year period. As the time line grew, it snaked down the hall and provided an impressive visualization of just how long a span of time separated the children from Columbus.

Walt's problem was somewhat different. His students had some experience with "looking it up"—selecting sources, note taking, citing sources appropriately, and the like—but less with researching a controversial topic. In particular, they had difficulty moving beyond simply reporting opinion—"What do you mean, where's the support? It's just his opinion!"—to trying to uncover the cultural and historical roots of opinions. Walt decided to try several techniques for helping students think about these historic sources of current perspectives.

Source Packets.   Because he wanted students to learn to use some sources that were new to them—demographic data, newspapers, magazines, cartoons, videotapes—Walt put together sets of primary and secondary source material and background information on South Africa, Chile, and Argentina. Each packet contained demographic charts (age, ethnicity, education, and the like), photocopies of newspaper and magazine articles, photographs, and novels. He was able to obtain videotapes of some events in South Africa, footage of Juan and Eva Peron in Argentina, and photographs of the aftermath of the collapse of Chilean democracy. For each item, he attached a short set of guide questions that helped students use and critique the source.

Double Entry Journals.   As each group began using the source packets to gather data on the point of view they were researching, Walt asked them to keep a double entry journal. At the top of each entry, students listed the source for the information. In the first column, they listed a position or argument along with supporting data. Opposite that position, in the second column, students made notes on what they thought the counter-arguments might be. So, for instance, the student citing deKlerk's position that a truth commission would lead to revenge and a possible coup noted in the first column that some people were already calling for public trials of the notorious state police, and that military leaders had threatened to overturn the coalition government if that happened. In the second column, he speculated that Mandela and the ANC might not be able to maintain their standing with people who had been victims of the state police if past atrocities were swept under the carpet. Using this technique, Walt hoped to help the students think about what support they would need to make their position more clear and/or compelling. "After all," he reminded his students, "people organized governments, arrested and executed other people, went into exile, and sacrificed their lives for these beliefs."

Charting Key People and Events.   Walt also asked students to record significant names in the graphic organizer categories as a way to keep track of people representing the different perspectives. Other students could then note where they might look for opposing viewpoints. A class time line also helped students organize information chronologically and made it easier to think about cause-and-effect relationships.

In order to help students connect individual pieces of information to the larger framework of South African history, Walt provided regular whole-group

Students need specific help in researching controversial topics.

Allen (1999), Carlisle (1995), Dickinson (1993), McGinnis (n.d.), Shemilt (1987)

Pappas et al. (1999)

Atwell (1987)

Journals help organize research.

Journals help students support positions.

Boner (1995), Cuthberston (1995)

experiences. He invited a guest speaker to talk about the new coalition government. He also required that each student select and read one novel set in South Africa (see reading list), conducted small-group discussions of the novels, and had students read background material on the colonization of South Africa, the Boer War, and the origins of apartheid. During one class, he provided political and resource maps of South Africa and led a discussion of regional differences in the country. Students were expected to draw on their research as they participated in the discussions.

It is crucial to conduct research in class rather than as homework.

It is important to note that although some assignments in each class were done outside of class—conducting surveys or reading books—most of the research was conducted in class. This is an equity issue as much as it is an opportunity to teach students specific research skills. Conducting research in class means that students with fewer resources to draw on at home are not at a disadvantage. In addition, it does not place the instructional burden for teaching students how to research on the home. Finally, conducting research in the classroom allows the teacher to help students think about appropriate forms for communicating what they are learning with different audiences.

Reporting Out: Who's the Audience?

As communities of inquiry such as those developing in Walt's and LeeAnn's classrooms grow, they need to develop strategies for sharing and assessing work. Students who have done substantial inquiry require more than a final grade to bring their study to closure; they need an opportunity to make public sense out of what they have learned. "Going public" means students organize what they have learned during their investigations in order to present their findings to others. You will recognize the importance of this part of inquiry when you think about how much you learn when you teach a subject, as opposed to when you simply study it for a test. As you will recall from Tina's experience in chapter 4, students often have difficulty sorting out what is important about their studies and then organizing that information for particular audiences. Such "presentational talk" takes practice and substantial support from the teacher. Because LeeAnn's students had little experience in presentational talk, she incorporated a number of small in-class presentations where students were able to use the different graphic organizers their groups had used. Thus, two groups referred to charts, the map provided a focus for a third group, and the time lines were used by the last two groups. After each group explained what they had learned, LeeAnn opened the discussion for questions and comments from peers. In a follow-up discussion, she also helped students further synthesize the results of their studies across groups. "Now that we have seen all the group projects" she said, "let's go back to our comparison chart and see if we still have conflicting information." In discussion, then, students noted where information from different sources agreed or disagreed. They found that some sources still claimed that Columbus' voyage proved the earth was round, other sources differed on whether Queen Isabella really sold her jewelry to finance Columbus' voyage, and not all the sources mentioned taking Native Americans back to Europe.

Atwell (1987), Flack (1992), Graves (1983), Jorgensen (1993)

Pappas et al. (1999)

With plenty of discussion and debate as foregrounding, LeeAnn then drew the students back to their first questions: Was Christopher Columbus famous, and if he was, why was he famous? "Now each of you will have a chance to be a historian and answer the questions we've asked," she told them, asking them, too, if they remembered how historians told people about the past. Students gave several suggestions—books, movies, speeches—and finally decided to write books about Columbus. "Remember that historians can have different

Historians have to use facts

ideas about the past, but they have to use the facts," LeeAnn explained. "Historians also think about who might read their books, and explain things so their readers will understand them. Who might read our books?" Students decided that because their parents and friends had helped them do the original survey, they might be interested in reading what the students had learned. The class decided to share their books with parents at a special "Christopher Columbus Presentation" at the end of October. With an audience in mind, a written genre—biography—selected, and the results of their study displayed throughout the classroom, the students were ready to write. During writers' workshop, a time set aside each day for student writing, editing, and publishing, those children who were independent writers began biographies of Christopher Columbus that would answer the question, "Was Columbus a hero?" Other students dictated their stories to an adult. Over about a two week period, children wrote, conferenced with an adult or peer, edited, illustrated, and then published their books. As editor-in-chief, LeeAnn made one suggestion about medium (mechanics) and one about message (content) components of each child's story prior to publication. At the Columbus Presentation, children shared their biographies, presented their projects, and discussed what they had learned, including:

Students can select appropriate historical genres.

"Books on the same subject can give you different information."

"Different maps can use different colors to tell you things. Oceans are usually blue, but could be brown, and Italy can be yellow or pink."

"We learned where France, Portugal, Spain, England, Italy, India, China, and Japan are. Also Africa, the Atlantic Ocean, the Pacific Ocean, Indian Ocean, and the Mediterranean Sea. And the United States and the Caribbean Islands."

"You need to take many of the same supplies on an ocean voyage today as you did 500 years ago."

"We learned that living today is more convenient compared to Columbus."

"Different countries grow different kinds of foods."

"It is easier to count to 500 if you count by 10s until you get to 100."

"Columbus did not treat the Indians fairly, so why was he considered a hero and named 'Admiral of the Ocean Sea?' He was famous."

Not every inquiry requires an outside audience in quite the way that LeeAnn arranged for her class. In Walt's case, his students tended to prefer peer audiences, and he wanted to focus on how individuals can take action on public issues. In addition, his state's assessment system required performance assessment, and Walt knew students needed individual, assessable products for their social studies portfolios. As a result, he organized "reporting out" at three different levels.

Assessment can match both state requirements and an inquiry perspective.

McGinnis (n.d.)

Round-table Negotiations. Walt held a class training session on consensus building as students completed their research into the different positions regarding a South African "truth commission." He then selected one student arbitrator and one student representing each of the different points of view on the issue for each round-table. Arbitrators were to keep negotiations on track and serve as time keepers. Once all students had been assigned to a round-table, they were given the remainder of the class period to lay out the major arguments for each position. During the next class session, negotiations began. Students were to see if they could reach some consensus in their groups regarding the establishment and functioning of a truth commission. As a homework assignment, students were asked to write a brief statement outlining their understanding of their group's results. What points of agreement were there? Of disagreement? In the next class, positions were again diagramed on the board and areas of agreement and disagreement discussed.

National Council for the
Social Studies (1994)

Letter Writing. Following the round-table negotiations, students were asked to consider what action they could take as a result of their inquiry. Now that they had opinions, what purpose did those opinions serve? At first there was dead silence in the room. Finally, one student suggested writing to "Congress or someone" to offer suggestions. Walt began a list of places where their opinions might be registered: letters to the local paper, to news magazines, to Congressional delegates, Nelson Mandela, and Desmond Tutu. Each round-table group selected one of these options, and wrote a letter offering their opinions and suggestions, along with supporting data.

Position Papers. Finally, Walt asked students to step back from their studies and reflect on how their own ideas had changed from the beginning of the study. He asked them to look over their research notes and dialogue journals and to think about what their study of South Africa told them about the kind of history people needed to learn. After a brief discussion, Walt passed out two articles: one criticizing school history for dwelling on problems such as the Ku Klux Klan, the other complaining that school history too often ignored problems in the past. "Now it's your turn to take a stand on this issue in your own country," he explained. "Use what you have learned about South Africa to help you respond to the critics in these two articles. What should American students know about the problems in our past?" In the criteria for this task, Walt emphasized that the quality of support for each position was the basis for assessment rather than the particular position a student might take.

Encourage students to use
what they have learned in
authentic ways.

Newmann et al. (1995)

Notice that both LeeAnn and Walt shuttle between the local and the global, trying to make connections between what happens in other parts of the world and what happens in children's historical backyard. LeeAnn asks children to consider whether we should celebrate Columbus Day; Walt asks them if what they think is good for South Africa is equally appropriate in the United States. There are many other ways of connecting children to more distant times and places that also relate the unfamiliar to the familiar. One way is inviting international guests or travelers to the classroom. First graders in Ruby Yessin's class, for instance, studied Scotland and England because their teacher arranged for an adult who was traveling to both countries to send postcards to the class and then visit the class after the trip. The guest brought artifacts representing both current and historical England and Scotland: coins, a brass rubbing kit, a police officer's hat, directions for building a Viking settlement. Children enjoyed trying out the artifacts, figuring out the money, and discussing the symbology used in brass rubbings. In addition, they became fascinated with illustrated resources, discussing the age of some of the buildings pictured in these materials:

Levstik (1993)

Darren: Some of those are real new, they just make them look like real castles.

Guest: Well, we do that in this country, don't we. The one you're looking at is pretty new. It's only 150 years old.

Catrina: 150 years! That's old!

Mitchell: The Vikings are older than that.

Teacher: How long ago were the Vikings? Does anyone remember?

No one can recall. They think it was "long, long ago, back when they had those ships."

This conversation led to more interest in Vikings, as students tried writing in Viking script and constructing models of a Viking village. They also spent the larger part of an hour asking about details in a set of slides of a Viking excavation in York. They calculated how long ago the village was lived in and talked about how the Vikings were European explorers like Columbus. They discussed the way in which Vikings used animal skins, antlers, and so forth. One child even turned in all his work with his name in Norse.

By starting with a person they knew (the guest) and artifacts from the places they had seen in postcards, the students' interest was captured. As they formed and reformed temporary interest groups, they sought out more information and were especially attentive to the information slides and books could provide. The guest helped establish a personal connection between students and the places they were studying so that England and Scotland became knowable places—it was possible for someone with whom they were familiar to go there; perhaps it was possible for them as well.

Walt Keet, you will recall, also made use of an international guest. He invited a South African university student to discuss the results of the round-table negotiations with his class. Once again, the guest's presence made South Africa more real and further personalized the issues under study in the classroom. The guest, after all, had seen first hand the transition from apartheid to a more inclusive democracy, and also knew enough about the United States to help students see some of the differences and similarities. This is one of the advantages of developing a more global perspective in history. Studying other countries is, of course, interesting in its own right, but it also allows us to look with new eyes at our own culture.

This approach is not without its problems. Encouraging cross-cultural inquiry challenges traditional interpretations and brings enduring myths into question. Other teachers may object to this approach. New interpretations may be thought to threaten national pride. Some parents, too, may find it disconcerting to learn from their five-year-olds that Columbus did not discover America or that Europeans did not treat Native Americans well, while others may not want explicit comparisons made between U.S. racial problems and those in other parts of the world. Teachers cannot ignore these potential problems, but you can plan ahead so that you respond intelligently to challenges. Present controversial issues in as balanced a way as possible, emphasizing what is supportable given the available evidence and what is representative of current scholarship. Journals such as *Social Education, Social Studies and the Young Learner, The Social Studies,* and *The History Teacher* provide help in making some of these judgments. In addition, documents such as the NCSS *Curriculum Standards for Social Studies: Expectations of Excellence* and the National History Standards provide support for the approaches described in this book, as well as help in deciding what constitutes a supportable interpretation. Kraus International Publications also produces a guide for K–12 social studies curriculum, *Social Studies: Curriculum Resource Handbook,* that provides further help in deciding on and defending the introduction of multiple perspectives in social studies (including history).

Finally, if you are presenting history as a process of interpretation, rather than as a single version of the "truth," you should be able to explain the grounds for that approach to concerned colleagues or parents. It often helps to explain that you are trying to help students develop supportable interpretations rather than requiring that they hold any single explanation to be the end product of historical thinking.

Most of the teachers with whom we work have found that when their students are excited and interested in historical study, most colleagues and parents are pleased and supportive. These teachers more often report that their most significant problem in challenging historical myths is the persistence of those myths in the larger culture. It is hard to challenge the myths surrounding Pocahontas, for instance, when they are enshrined in a popular animated film and reproduced in toys and commercial messages. The same is true for the persistence of the myth that Columbus proved the earth was round. (That the earth was round was, of course, a piece of information known to just about all educated people of the period.)

Interest groups are generally temporary configurations.

Wilson (1983)

K. Young (1994)

Plan ahead to respond to concerns about controversial issues.

Kraus (1992), National Council for the Social Studies (1994), National History Standards Project (1994a, 1994b)

Know the grounds for your own curriculum choices.

When students are fully engaged and enthusiastic about their studies, parents often are too.

Burton (1991)

THE PERSISTENCE OF HISTORICAL MYTHS

Christopher Columbus discovered America Oct. 12, 1492. The pirates attached him. His ship sank, but he had to leave others behind because there wasn't enough room on the other ships. The ship that sunk was called the Santa Maria. It was the best ship on the sea. Columbus survived and got on. He survived. All of Christopher's friends thought the world was flat. Christopher Columbus did not think so. His voyage proved he was right. It made him a hero.

—Steve, age 5 (dictated story)

In looking back on her first attempt at disciplined inquiry, LeeAnn noted that several aspects of her class' study had surprised her. First of all, she was pleased with the level of the children's enthusiasm and the ways in which the different age groups in her class worked together on the project. "By working in small groups, the children had to learn to work together. They had to locate their information by looking at pictures. The older children read what they could and shared their information with the nonreaders, so their project could be completed and understood. This developed a sense of pride and accomplishment by all children when the project was completed." But there were also problems. First, the project took more time than LeeAnn had anticipated. Her team teachers had moved on to other topics before her class had completed its study of Christopher Columbus. Second, it was very difficult for children who had been absent for more than a day or two to reenter the study. One child had been taken out of school for over a week to go on a trip with his parents. Although LeeAnn explained what the children would be working on and the boy's parents agreed to help him learn about Columbus, he was not part of the class experience, and his final book showed his lack of engagement—there were only two lines of story, and they did not deal with the question of fame. Other parents were quite excited about their children's work, and several commented that this was their child's best written effort of the year.

LeeAnn was also interested in the issues the children dwelt on in their books. Almost all the children noted that Columbus traded "fake jewels" for "real gold." More than half of them noted that Columbus took Indians back to Spain. On the other hand, LeeAnn was puzzled at the persistence of myths that she thought the class had clearly rejected in discussion. Despite having worked on developing comparison charts that pointed out discrepancies in accounts, several children, including Steve, wrote about Columbus "discovering" America and proving the earth was round.

The fact that some historical misconceptions persist really isn't surprising. As we mentioned earlier, school isn't the only place where children come in contact with history, especially with historical figures who have become cultural icons. Think about all the images of Columbus that appear just before Columbus Day. There are Columbus Day sales, advertisements on local television that emphasize "discovery," and some that spoof Columbus' proving the world was round. In addition, some of the stories the children read presented the myths as facts. Despite discussion to the contrary, some children focused on the more public parts of the story and missed the distinctions the teacher was trying to help them grapple with. Although it would be nice if students "got it" every time we taught, we know that isn't going to happen. Sometimes the myths persist because they are more appealing. As six-year-old Jake wrote, "Columbus waze the bravest. The uthers thoet there were sea monsters and big waves but Columbus woz the bravest .... Columbus was famous." There is something compelling in the story of braving sea monsters and proving others wrong. It is also a beginning point. These are, after all, five- and six-year-olds. They will meet Columbus again. It is important to remember that the development of historical thinking takes time and experience. Although one experience with disciplined inquiry is

In-depth inquiry take time.

*Blythe (1989),
Newmann et al. (1995),
Pappas et al. (1999)*

Myths can persist despite in-depth inquiry.

Pappas et al. (1999)

82

certainly better than none, it is likely to take multiple experiences to counter prevailing myths. This is especially so if those stories are bound up with some sense of identification—with Columbus' Italian nationality, for instance, or simply with the idea of brave ancestors settling a "new world." If students continue to encounter history as inquiry, they may alter their schema to account for different views of history. If, on the other hand, history is continually presented through myths and legends, early history schema may well remain intact.

Barton & Levstik (2004)

ASSESSING HISTORY OUTCOMES

Clearly it isn't enough to simply trust that arranging interesting and challenging experiences with history will result in growth in students' historical thinking. Teachers need to assess student progress so that they can plan for the most effective experiences for their students. As you can tell by now, neither LeeAnn nor Walt rely on a single measure of students' progress in thinking historically. By the time their students "report out," both teachers possess a wide variety of information on their students' inquiry and interpretive skills. Because so much of students' work in history is embedded in reading, writing, and speaking, however, it is easy to focus on assessing literacy to the exclusion of the specifically historical purposes of students' study. For LeeAnn and Walt, the historical aspects of their students' inquiry into world history include working with different data sources, recognizing different perspectives, making connections between local and global history, and building tentative historical interpretations. As you review the tasks they engage in with their students, you will notice that each activity allows the teachers to assess whether students achieved some part of these goals. As soon as LeeAnn's students complete their world map, for instance, she has information on how they conceptualize important parts of Columbus' story. Although students accurately identify the countries that turned Columbus away, where he finally received help, and where he hoped to end up, they also confuse "the Americas" with the United States, coloring in the present day United States, including Alaska, to indicate where Columbus actually landed. In response, LeeAnn spends time discussing what the Americas were like in 1492. Later, when students fill in the comparison chart, LeeAnn assesses what they are learning from different data sources. Similarly, Walt's three levels of "reporting out" provide increasingly detailed and individual information on how students understand the uses of evidence in constructing a historical argument. Walt uses a written set of criteria to help students understand his expectations for many of these tasks—and to remind himself of his goals for a particular activity. Early in the year, Walt writes the criteria himself. Once his students become familiar with the pattern, he invites them to help him develop criteria for their own work. Figure 6.4 shows the jointly created criteria for the position paper. Figure 6.5 shows a joint evaluation sheet used at the end of the unit.

Joint evaluation provides an opportunity for Walt to discuss specific aspects of the study with each student. When he first developed this evaluation, he hoped it would elicit important information from his students. He wanted to know, for instance, how well they understood the language of historical study used in the class—perspective, primary and secondary source, and the like. He also wanted to understand from the students' perspective what they were learning. Walt soon discovered that joint evaluation also provided important information to his students, especially about their teacher's goals and expectations. Over time, too, joint evaluations helped his students become more self-reflective about their own learning. Because this is a time-consuming process, however, Walt found that it was not practical to conduct joint evaluations after every unit of instruction. Instead, he decided to use them as a periodic gauge of student progress and especially as an opportunity to debrief controversial topics with his students.

Assessment helps teachers plan more effective experiences for students.

Yell (1999)

For more discussion of using generic rubrics, see chapter 4.

Teachers need to assess specifically historical aspects of inquiry.

Written criteria help students understand the standards for their work.
Nickell (1999)

Hart (1999), Jorgensen (1993)

Joint evaluations help debrief controversial topics.

Wertsch (1998),
Yell (1999)

Position Paper

Question At Issue: What Should American Students Learn About the Problems in Their Country's Past?

Turn in a 5-10 page position paper. This paper may contain a combination of words, pictures, graphs, and any other types of illustrations that make a persuasive case for a position on this question. The paper will be evaluated on the following criteria:

• The author clearly explains what he/she considers to be the purposes of learning history.

• The author clearly shows an understanding of the similarities and differences in the historical situations in South Africa, Chile, Argentina, and the United States and makes the differences clear to the reader through the use of words and illustrations (charts, pictures, etc.).

• The author clearly connects what is happening in the rest of the world to what is happening in the United States.

• The author takes a position and supports it with accurate information from at least 4 different sources used during our study and gives bibliographic information for each one.

• The author describes and counters the major arguments against her/his position.

FIG. 6.4. Position paper.

You have probably noticed, too, that LeeAnn's and Walt's assessment strategies evolved over time. They tried some techniques, adjusted them to suit their particular circumstances and students, and evaluated their effectiveness in use. Fundamental to this process is each teacher's desire to establish a particular kind of learning community. It is not just that they want students to learn history, although this is certainly a primary goal of their instruction; they also want assessment to contribute to inquiry, not interrupt it. Traditional test questions—questions that allow only one possible right answer or focus on reporting on what someone else thinks or has said—are less likely to foster this sort of community of inquiry. Authentic or constructive assessment—questions and prob-

---

Student/Teacher Evaluation

Name of student _____   Date _____

South Africa/Apartheid study

The student completes the left side of this evaluation and then the teacher will complete the right side. Afterwards we will discuss your work, identify areas of strength, and decide on the areas that need to be improved.

0=Outstanding	S=Satisfactory	N = Needs Improvement

Student Evaluation		Teacher Evaluation
____ I used a variety of relevant and challenging resources to learn about my subject.		_____
____ I gained confidence in my ability to evaluate historical sources.		_____
____ I used both primary and secondary sources to learn about my subject.		_____
____ I improved in my ability to construct a persuasive historical argument.		_____
____ I improved in my ability to identify different historical perspectives.		_____
____ I improved in my ability to discuss ideas with which I disagree.		_____

The most important thing I learned from my study was:

FIG. 6.5. Student/teacher evaluation.

lems with multiple acceptable responses—invite students to contribute something new—to change or modify an inquiry—while providing data on how students are progressing in that inquiry. Constructive assessment also signals to students that what and how they think and know is important. By differentiating tasks—offering choices in terms of tasks as well as how tasks are approached and reported on—and scaffolding tasks—providing appropriate structures to help students master the complexities of a task—teachers model powerful ways of knowing and doing history.

Barton & Levstik (1996), Levstik & Barton (1996)

CONCLUSIONS

As we mentioned earlier, world history is virtually invisible in U.S. elementary schools and receives scant attention thereafter. This pattern is reinforced in museums, the media, and in other sources outside the schools. Indeed, by adolescence, U.S. students have so internalized this pattern that they view world history as considerably less significant than national history. The experiences of teachers such as LeeAnn and Walt suggest, however, that inquiries into world history make an important contribution to students' developing historical understanding. Walt's class study of apartheid in South Africa, for instance, had a profound impact on students' views of race in the United States. Investigating racism and segregation in South Africa brought new perspectives to bear in thinking about similar issues in the United States.

Perhaps most significantly, studying world history makes the profound historical effect of people's differing beliefs, values, experiences, and knowledge clearer. Recognizing some of these differences challenges students' assumptions about the growth and development of human societies, laying a foundation for countering stereotypical thinking and enhancing cross-cultural communication. In addition, studying world history puts national history—and national identity—in a broader context, suggesting alternatives to current local and national practice. To the extent that such study makes explicit students' connection to other parts of the globe, it better prepares them to participate in the kind of decision making required of citizens in an increasingly interconnected world.

Davis et al. (2001), Gaddis (2002)

National Council for the Social Studies (1994), Peace Corps World Wise Schools (1998)

CHILDREN'S AND ADOLESCENT LITERATURE

Different Perspectives on Columbus

Adler, D. *A Picture Book of Christopher Columbus*. Holiday House, 1991.

Ceserani, G. P. *Christopher Columbus*. Random, 1979.

Conrad, P. *Pedro's Journal*. Caroline House, 1991.

Fritz, J. *Where Do You Think You're Going Christopher Columbus?* G. P. Putnam's, 1980.

Jacobs, F. *The Tainos: The People Who Welcomed Columbus*. Putnam's. 1992.

Landau, E. *Columbus Day: Celebrating a Famous Explorer*. Enslow, 2001.

Levinson, N. *Christopher Columbus: Voyager to the Unknown*. Dutton, Lodestar, 1990.

Maestro, B., & Maestro, G. *The Discovery of the Americas*. Lothrop, 1991.

Meltzer, M. *Christopher Columbus and the World Around Him*. Watts, 1990.

Pelta, K. *Discovering Christopher Columbus: How History is Invented*. Lerner, 1991.

Roop, P., & Roop, C. *Christopher Columbus (In Their Own Words)*. Scholastic, 2001.

Roop, P., & Roop., C. (Eds.). *I, Columbus— My Journal*. Walker, 1990.

Weil, L. *I, Christopher Columbus*. Atheneum, 1983.

Yolen, J. *Encounter*. Harcourt, 1992.

Books on South Africa

Angelou, M. *My Painted House, My Friendly Chicken, and Me.* Clarkson, 1994.

Biko, S. *I Write What I Like.* HarperCollins, 1979.

Ferreira, A. *Zulu Dog.* Frances Foster, 2002.

Gordon, S. *The Middle of Somewhere: A Story of South Africa.* Orchard, 1990.

Gordon, S. *Waiting for the Rain: A Novel of South Africa.* Orchard, 1987.

Harris, S. *South Africa: Timeline.* Dryad, 1988.

Krog, A. *Country of My Skull: Guilt, Sorrow, and the Limits of Forgiveness in the New South Africa.* Three Rivers Press, 2000.

Mathabane, M. *Kaffir Boy: The True Story a Black Youth's Coming of Age in Apartheid South Africa.* Macmillan, 1986.

McKee, T. *No More Strangers Now: Young Voices from a New South Africa.* DK Ink, 1998.

McKee, T. *No More Strangers Now: Young Voices from a New South Africa.* DK Publishing, 2000.

Meisel, J. D. *South Africa at the Crossroads.* Millbrook, 1994.

Naidoo, B. *Chain of Fire.* Lippincott, 1989.

Naidoo, B. *Journey to Jo'burg: A South African Story.* Harper, 1986.

Naidoo, B. *The Other Side of Truth.* Amistad, 2002.

Naidoo, B. *Out of Bounds: Seven Stories of Conflict and Hope.* HarperCollins, 2003.

Odendall, A., & Chilane, F. *Beyond the Barricades: Popular Resistance in South Africa.* Aperture, 1989.

Rochman, H. (Ed.). *Somehow Tenderness Survives: Stories of Southern Africa.* HarperCollins, 1988.

Sacks, M. *Beyond Safe Boundaries.* Dutton Lodestar, 1990.

Sparks, A. *Beyond the Miracle.* University of Chicago Press, 2003.

Stock, C. *Armiens' Fishing Trip.* Morrow, 1990.

Thompson, L. *The History of South Africa, 3rd Edition.* Yale University Press, 2001.

Williams, M. *Into the Valley.* Philomel, 1993.

7

RATS IN THE HOSPITAL

Creating a History Museum

After her fourth graders have completed family history projects, Amy Leigh introduces them to their next investigation—creating displays on how life has changed over the last hundred years. On the first day of the unit, she shows them an object she explains was a common tool about a hundred years ago. Most students quickly identify it as a hand-held drill, and several volunteer to demonstrate how it was used. After discussing how it differs from modern drills, the class gathers on the floor in front of Amy while she reads *I Go With My Family to Grandma's*, which she explains was also about a time almost a hundred years ago. Amy asks students to point out anything they find in the book that would be different today, and she keeps track of their observations on a sheet of chart paper on the wall. After discussing the book, students work in pairs with historical photographs to make further observations about change over the last century, and at the end of the day they report on these to their classmates and add new items to the chart.

Over the next several days, students examine physical artifacts Amy has brought in—old watches, purses, tools, clothes, and appliances. Guided by "Artifact Think Sheets," they record ways these differ from similar objects today. After everyone has worked through all the objects, the class meets together again to summarize what they have found and to develop a list of general categories of change—technology, clothes, transportation, etc. Each student then chooses two or three categories to find out more about. After several days of exploration with library resources—trade books, CD-ROMs, and encyclopedias—students choose partners and pick a single topic to investigate in more depth. Each group develops a set of specific questions they want to answer, and they collect information using not only print and electronic resources but also artifacts, interviews, and photographs. During the research phase of the project, Amy works with each group to help them locate and use information to prepare reports and displays, and afterward, students create exhibits for a History Museum in their classroom. They explain their exhibits for other classes who tour their museum and for parents and grandparents during a final performance.

One of the most common suggestions for teaching social studies (at any level) is to have students "do research." Yet as we have noted, simply sending students off on their own to engage in that vague activity rarely results in anything positive or productive. Younger children are unlikely to have any idea what they are supposed to do, while older ones will do what nearly all of us did when we were in school—go to the library and copy something out of an encyclopedia. In these days of electronic resources, many students simply type a query into an Internet search engine and hope it results in a site that answers all their needs. Neither of those strategies helps students learn about the past or about conducting inquiry. In contrast, the students in Amy's classroom learned both: They not only investi-

Lipscomb (2002), Milson (2003)

gated how things have changed over time, but they also learned to ask questions, collect information, draw conclusions, and present their findings.

Sometimes assignments are difficult, and students dislike doing them. Other times, students enjoy themselves, but the activities are too easy for them really to learn very much. But teachers know they're on to something when students enjoy doing an assignment that does not come easily. The "History Museum" project in Amy's classroom is a perfect example of such an assignment: Students immensely enjoyed it, yet none of it came easily. They spent nearly a month working on the activities, and nearly every minute of that time involved painstaking efforts by Amy to help students use resources to find information, reach conclusions based on their observations, and transform notes into reports and presentations. Having little or no previous experience with the process, students encountered numerous obstacles along the way. As a result, Amy could not tell them to do research; she had to teach them. In this chapter, we show how she met the challenge of teaching students to ask and answer historical questions.

Teachers must help students learn how to conduct inquiry.

IMAGINATIVE ENTRY

Family histories lead to further historical investigations.

Getting students interested in the topic of change over time was the easiest part of Amy's job. Like Tina's students in chapter 5, Amy's class had completed family history projects in which they asked their grandparents how life had been different when they were children. As a result, the topic of change over time was fresh in their minds, and they could call on these experiences for specific examples to compare with the information they encountered at school. Moreover, changes in material culture are among the historical topics students know the most about. In our interviews with children from kindergarten through sixth grade, for example, we have found that even the youngest know that clothes and transportation were different in the past, and older children have an even more complete inventory of generally accurate information about change over time. During the project described earlier, students frequently pointed out having learned about historical changes outside school—seeing an old shaving mug and brush in a local barbershop, for example, or seeing pictures of sod houses in a book. As we noted in chapter 2, instruction must begin with what students already know; thus Amy began with the details of everyday life—drills, shaving mugs, purses, and so on—rather than abstract topics like politics, economics, or society. (She did, however, eventually get to these topics; see chap. 11.)

Material culture provides entry into historical study. Barton & Levstik (1996), Hickey (1997), Levstik & Barton (1996)

The visual aspect of history is also critical in helping students understand what the past was like—particularly any time period before they were born. Amy thus began the unit (as well as several other lessons throughout the unit) with books such as *I Go with My Family to Grandma's, Ragtime Tumpie,* and *When Great-Grandmother was a Little Girl.* In most cases, she was concerned not with the language or thematic content of the books—*I Go with my Family to Grandma's* is written for young primary students and has only the most basic plot, for example—but with the information the pictures provided on historical changes. Amy also took care to call students' attention to aspects of the pictures that were vague or ambiguous, and she asked students to consider how they differed from photographs.

Visual images can help students learn about the past. Blythe (1988), Harnett (1993, 1995), Foster & Hoge (1999)

We cannot overstate the importance of using visual images (particularly photographs) with children. Visual sources tap into a much wider range of background knowledge than printed text or oral discussions. In Amy's class, the photographs were a popular part of the unit, as students examined them with great interest and enthusiasm and frequently called their friends over to look at unusual or surprising details. They had no difficulty using the pictures to develop a list of differences between a hundred years ago and today, and they eagerly shared their findings with the rest of the class. (Amy used a set of photographs from Scholastic Book Service's *The American Experience* series, but similar sets are available through other publishers of social studies materials, on CD-ROMs, over the Internet, or at sites such as those created by the Library of Congress or the National Archives and Records Administration.)

Just as important as photographs were the physical artifacts Amy brought in. The sight of the old drill in the first lesson was exciting for students, and all of them made sure they touched it and played with it before the day was over. While working on their Artifact Think Sheets (Fig. 7.1), students constantly played with the objects—rubbing a shaving-cream brush on their skin, flipping the handle of a cherry-pitter back and forth, fiddling with an old camera to see how it worked, using a cuff-maker to create creases in paper (again and again and again). Because school tasks often rely exclusively on written language, students' preoccupation with physical play can strike an observer as being "off task"; outside school, though, no parent would expect a child to sit still for hours on end. We agree with Dewey that children's behavior at school frequently appears in need of "management" precisely because they have so little chance to engage in their natural impulse toward activity. By encouraging them to handle and use the objects, Amy built on her students' inclinations rather than attempting to suppress them. As a result, they stayed interested in the objects for several days and developed clear ideas about how they could have been used. Of course, many teachers find themselves evaluated (implicitly or explicitly) on how quiet and physically inactive their students are, and they may need to be ready to explain why playing with a cuff-maker is more appropriate for an eight-year-old than writing quietly at all times. Fortunately, Amy's principal, Dan Kelly, encouraged—even expected—the kinds of hands-on lessons found in her classroom; he even walked in on the class one day during this project and joked knowingly, "Hey, there can't be any learning going on here—they're having too much fun!"

Amy's introduction to the History Museum project demonstrated several principles that are fundamental to developing students' interest. First, she related the topic to what they already knew, both by focusing on aspects of everyday life and by connecting the topic to their previous family history projects. Rather than being an isolated, "cookie-cutter" plan, it flowed naturally from students' background knowledge and from the issues they had already begun to investigate during the year. Second, Amy made sure that students had a variety of means of entry into the topic, rather than relying solely on oral and written language. Literature, photographs, and physical artifacts gave students a more concrete understanding of life in the past and helped stimulate their interest in the topic. Perhaps most important, this project had a significant element of authenticity. Outside school, people really do take an interest in how things have changed over time: People save artifacts and photographs, and they tell their children and

Students enjoy manipulating historical artifacts.

Dewey (1956)

Administrators can support and encourage inquiry.

Historical inquiry stems from students' interests and experiences.

Teachers can provide a variety of means of entry into historical topics.

Barton (2001b)

There are many artifacts from the past displayed throughout the room. Please write a paragraph for each of 5 artifacts. Your paragraphs should answer all of these questions:

a.   Make up a name for this artifact that tells its purpose. You may write more than just the name if you'd like to better explain its function.

b.   Explain what parts of the object gave you clues for its purpose.

c.   Tell when you think the object was used (1800–1849, 1850–1899, 1900–1949, or 1950–NOW), and tell how you decided when it was used.

d.   Name the object we now use instead of this artifact.

For each artifact you write about, please write the number of the artifact next to the paragraph you write. You only need 1 artifact think sheet completed per group.

FIG. 7.1.   Artifact Think Sheet.

grandchildren how things were different in the past. Understanding historical change is a basic part of each person's life, and that understanding often is passed down through families. Students' excitement about these projects indicates just how much Amy had tapped into the meaning and purpose history has in our society. For several weeks, students rummaged through their homes and attics (and their grandparents'), looking for their own artifacts to bring in and add to the visual time line in the class. Their interest motivated one girl to work with her parents to make a videotaped tour of the Victorian home she lived in and another to help her grandmother photograph and catalog the family's heirlooms. Even Amy's own grandparents were excited about explaining how to use the various artifacts she brought in for students. When a project stimulates this kind of intergenerational communication, it clearly has a purpose beyond simply pleasing the teacher or getting a grade.

TURNING INTEREST INTO RESEARCHABLE QUESTIONS

The first year Amy taught this unit, she proceeded directly from her introductory lesson to having students develop a list of questions they wanted to answer. At first glance, it seems that students who already know something about a topic and are interested and enthusiastic about learning more should have no problem sitting down and deciding what they want to learn. In fact, however, that task was tremendously difficult. Amy had students develop KWL charts on the topics they had chosen, and most encountered a roadblock when they got to the "Want to know" section. Many simply stopped working and apparently had no idea what to write. Others seemed to consider it a convenient time to sharpen their pencil collections or rearrange their desks, or they devoted their energy to making the physical layout of their charts as attractive as possible. Even with Amy's help and encouragement, most students weren't sure what it was that they wanted to know, and those who wrote anything at all confined themselves to simple questions about dates: When was the car invented? When did people stop wearing hoop shirts? When did milk stop coming in bottles? It seemed that most students didn't really understand the purpose of the questions. They were just eager to get to the library and start copying something down.

When it became clear that students weren't getting much out of this question-developing activity, Amy called them back together as a whole class to give them more direction. She wrote the words *Where, What, Why, Who,* and *How* on the board and told students they needed to come up with two questions beginning with each word; she then went on to model how to do that with the topic *schools*—a subject they had discussed in class but that no students had chosen to investigate in their projects. This was a kind of ad hoc solution to the problem, and it gave students enough structure to begin their research. It was clear, however, that students still failed to fully understand the role of questions in conducting research. For example, some tried to copy Amy's questions onto their own charts by simply changing a few key words. When that didn't work, they protested that it couldn't be done and were shocked when Amy explained that the questions would be different for each topic. Others didn't understand why they would come up with questions before doing the research, and one student asked incredulously, "Are we going to answer these questions ourselves?" With little prior experience in developing their own questions to investigate, the activity made little sense to students.

The next year, Amy was more prepared to help with this aspect of the investigation. As you can see in the description at the beginning of this chapter, she did not jump directly from sparking students' interest to expecting them to develop specific questions. Instead, she engaged them in examining artifacts for several days;

Authentic projects involve learning beyond school boundaries.

Students are not accustomed to generating questions.

Teacher scaffolding can help students develop more meaningful questions.

90

in the course of making their observations, students found a number of things they wondered about—How did they keep from getting the clothes dirty when they used this kind of iron? How did they keep it hot? Did everybody use this, or just rich people? The experience of observing and discussing the artifacts gave students the chance to come up with specific questions they wanted to know more about and to do so in a natural context. In addition, Amy gave students several days to explore library resources before asking them to specify either their topic or a list of questions. Although she had them narrow their interests to two or three (so their energy wouldn't be completely unfocused), she wanted them to have a chance just to play around with the available resources to find out what they wanted to ask. This turned out to be an enormously popular activity, as students excitedly scurried around the library, talking with Amy and each other about what they were learning. They were often very surprised at the differences they found; one group investigating changes in medicine, for example, was fascinated to find that hospitals were not as sanitary in the past as they are now. They told anyone who would listen, "Did you know that a hundred years ago, if you were in the hospital, you might wake up and see a *rat* in your room?! Today you'd probably wake up and just see a spider—*if* you're lucky."

Observation and discussion of historical artifacts lead to specific questions.

This time, there was no shortage of questions students wanted to investigate. When using science or math materials, students require exploration before working with them in a more systematic or teacher-directed way—otherwise they'll still want to play with the objects when they're supposed to be using them for a more specific purpose. Similarly, students need time to explore at the beginning of historical investigations. By giving them several days to examine artifacts and then several more days to explore library resources, Amy afforded students a much better chance to recognize what it was that they wanted to know. Once she asked them to come up with a list of questions they wanted to investigate, then, they didn't become stuck as they had previously. Even during this exploration time students were learning a great deal about history—not only information about the past, but also the process of making observations and drawing conclusions from historical sources.

Time for exploration leads to better questions.

That is not to say, however, that developing questions required no further help from Amy. As they moved from exploration to specific questions, Amy called the class together to find out what they wanted to learn in their research. As students suggested questions to investigate, Amy helped them rephrase the questions in such a way that they focused more clearly on "big ideas" (a concept she referred back to often) about changes over time. She asked for a sample question, for example, from students who were investigating the topic *houses*. They suggested, "What did they walk on, dirt, wooden floors, carpets?"—a question that by itself would have a fairly simple answer and would probably focus on only one time period. Amy responded, "So, 'How have floor coverings changed over the last hundred years?'"—a question that included what students wanted to know but considerably broadened it as well. After several similar examples, one member of a pair of students who had chosen *railroads* suggested, "What happened to James Watt?" Amy asked if he considered that a big question, and his partner said, "No, it would be, 'Why didn't trains run on electricity?' or 'Why did they stop making electric trains?'" Amy broadened it even further by suggesting, "How has the power used for trains changed?" and pointed out that the information they wanted to include about James Watt would be part of their answer to that question.

Teachers can help students develop and refine questions.

People often think of education in terms of exclusive opposites: Either students do what the teacher tells them, for example, or they do whatever they want. As we discussed in chapter 2, we find both those methods intellectually indefensible: Students are unlikely to learn anything important from either method. The assistance Amy provided students in developing their questions, on the other hand, was a clear example of scaffolding: She neither told them what to do nor uncritically accepted their first efforts. She knew that their projects had to grow out of their own interests and concerns, and she gave them several days to develop their ideas about what they wanted to do. But she also recognized that not all questions are equally significant: She knew that students would learn more from some questions than others, so she helped them rephrase their inquiries to address what they wanted to know within the context of bigger issues of change over time. In short, she helped them learn more than they would have solely on their own.

Students learn more with teachers' help and support than they would on their own.

FINDING THE ANSWERS TO QUESTIONS

For all its pitfalls, helping students develop questions was a simple matter compared with helping them find the answers to those questions. One of the first challenges Amy faced was helping students locate the information that would be useful to them. At the simplest level, this just meant reviewing the kinds of sources they could use. Students immediately recognized encyclopedias as a major source of information, but Amy also emphasized that they could use trade books, CD-ROMs, and resources outside of school—relatives, other people in the community, and even videos. A more important task was helping students understand *how* to locate information in such resources. For example, many of them returned from their first foray into the library complaining, "There is *nothing* on it!" or "The encyclopedia doesn't have *anything* about how transportation has changed over time." The reason for students' frustration was quickly apparent: Nearly all of them expected to find books or encyclopedia entries entitled "How transportation has changed over time" or "How floor coverings have changed over time." When they found there weren't any, they concluded that no information existed on their topics.

Information in inquiry projects comes from a variety of sources.

Students' difficulties may have stemmed, in part, from a lack of previous experience with finding information in reference sources. Although students in the primary grades are often assigned dittos or workbook pages on "Using Reference Sources"—and assessed on that ability on standardized tests—such exercises are often poorly designed. Students are shown a side view of a set of encyclopedias (or a sample table of contents from an almanac) and asked to identify the volume (or page numbers) where they would look to find information on *horses* or *volcanoes* or *frogs*. Unfortunately, such questions have almost no connection to the way people actually use encyclopedias or books; they certainly provide no assistance in helping students investigate how things have changed over time. As a result, much of Amy's effort was devoted to teaching them how to really use reference works.

Students often have little experience using reference sources to answer questions.

In part, this meant working with the whole class and with groups of students to develop lists of words and phrases they might use in finding information. Knowing that one group was investigating *entertainment,* for example, Amy brought in a book called *What Did You do When You were a Kid? Pastimes from the Past.* Yet students looked at the index and table of contents and—not finding the word *entertainment* in either—concluded the book had no relevant information. Somewhat surprised, Amy explained that the whole book was about entertainment—that pastimes are entertainment, and students would be able to find information on their topic by looking up other specific kinds of entertainment (movies, television, music, dance) rather than only looking for the word *entertainment*. Similarly, one group looked up *medicine* in the encyclopedia and found only information on present-day medicine. Amy suggested they look at the list of "related entries" at the end of that section; they saw that there was a separate entry under *medical care, history of,* and word spread like wildfire through the class that historical information could be found under similar headings. With each group, Amy had to provide assistance in developing possible al-

Sturner (1973)

ternatives to the main words they were looking for—helping the transportation group come up with *automobiles, railroads, ships, airplanes;* the fashion group come up with *clothing, jewelry, hairstyles;* and so on.

Once students found relevant books or encyclopedia entries, Amy also had to help them use them efficiently. Most students started reading a source at the beginning and continued through word for word until they got bored (which usually was quickly). Amy thus had to show students how to look at section headings and tables of contents to find which parts of a source would be most likely to address their questions and how to skim through those parts to find if they were indeed relevant. Although whole-class instruction on this skill seemed to make that idea clear to students in a general way, she still had to work extensively with individuals and pairs for them to apply it to their own work. Particularly during the early stages of their research, Amy spent most of her time directing students' attention to this process of evaluating the usefulness of sources—looking together with a student at a source, for example, and asking questions like, "*Early hospitals*—does that sound like it would have information on how medicine has changed over time?" and "If you want to know if this has anything on railroads, what words are you going to look for when you skim through it?" Without this kind of explicit help in reading reference works, it is unlikely that students would ever have gone very far with their research.

Interestingly, encyclopedias ultimately provided students with only minimal information. In the early stages of their research, many focused almost exclusively on encyclopedias, but most soon found that other works provided information in a more accessible form. In the end, most students relied on juvenile trade books more heavily than anything else, and the kind of books they found most useful were similar in form. Students rejected any work that contained several pages of uninterrupted text (such as *Prairie Visions: The Life and Times of Solomon Butcher* or *Children of the Wild West*). No matter how much information such a book might have contained, most students simply would not read through it to find what they needed to know. Instead, nearly all students relied on books that contained profuse illustrations on each page and short captions to accompany them. The most commonly used such books were those in the *Eyewitness* series—such as *Car, Sports,* and *Costume*—although there are other series with similar formats. (See the book list at the end of this chapter.) The advantage of such books clearly lay both in their visual appeal and the ease with which students could find the information they needed. As one girl remarked, "They get to the point better."

People—relatives and others in the community—also provided important sources of information. Some students decided from the beginning that they would interview people for their projects; one girl investigating changes in homes, for example, planned to talk to the interior designer who lived next door to her, and a boy whose project was on transportation knew the captain of a local steamboat. They had already interviewed relatives for their family history projects, and Amy reviewed with them how to plan out their questions for interviews. Because some of their questions were very specific, she also had to help them plan what they would do when people didn't know. For example, one group planned to call a local bank to ask questions about old money; Amy asked them what they would do when the answer was, "I don't know." Most students, on the other hand, had not initially considered humans to be an important source of information on their topics (despite their family history projects!), but once they began planning their centers, they developed a renewed sense of interest in them. Most of them wanted to display objects—old clothes, appliances, money, and so on—and when they started collecting these from people, they learned new information that became important to their papers and presentations.

Brainstorming words and phrases to locate can help students use reference sources.

Students need to learn to read selectively for information.

Conrad (1991), Freedman (1983)

Hammond (1988), Rowland-Warne (1992), Sutton (1990)

The most useful reference sources have rich visual information and short expository text.

People can serve as an important source of historical information.

REACHING CONCLUSIONS

In history, conclusions are based on evidence.
Barton (1997a), Barton & Levstik (2004)

A basic principal of conducting historical inquiry is that conclusions are based on evidence. Indeed, that simple proposition forms the intellectual foundation of the entire field of social studies—not to mention other disciplines—and even of democratic citizenship generally. For students to understand what it means to *know* something, they have to understand that knowledge is fundamentally different from either faith or simple blind opinion. History is not made up out of thin air, nor is it based on what we wish to believe or what has been revealed to us—it is based on evidence. Although in most cases different conclusions can be drawn from the same evidence, conclusions that are based on no evidence whatsoever have no place in history, social studies, or public debate. Basing conclusions on evidence, however, came no more easily for Amy's students than asking questions or collecting data.

Students often have simplistic ideas about how to find answers to historical questions. *Ashby & Lee (1998), Barton (1997a)*

One of the first challenges Amy faced was confronting students' belief that somewhere, in a single place, lay the answer to each of their questions, and their conviction that if they could only track down that source they could copy the answer and begin working on their displays. In this, Amy's students no doubt demonstrated the same understanding held by millions of schoolchildren who have developed their perspective from answering questions at the end of textbook chapters. We all know that most such questions can be answered by finding the sentences in the chapter that provide single and direct answers. In fact, most of us probably realized at some point that we could find the answers without ever having read the chapter in the first place. Outside the topsy-turvy world of textbook information, however, few questions have such simple and direct answers.

Important questions rarely have simple or direct answers.

Significant historical questions—like those in Table 1.1 and those students developed in this project—require the synthesis of a number of pieces of information. The idea of collecting information from several different places and putting them together in their own way, however, was not what students initially expected they would be doing. It was some time before they realized that they would never stumble on simple answers to their questions, but that they would have to create those answers from the information they did find. (The influence of textbook assignments was also reflected in students' surprise when they found out they didn't have to answer their questions in any particular order.)

Venn diagrams provide a way to organize information on similarities and differences.

One way that Amy addressed this problem was by having students keep a Venn diagram on their topic throughout their research. She began by demonstrating how to do this with the topic *schools*. She drew a diagram on the chalkboard, labeled one side "100 years ago" and the other "Today," and asked students what kind of information might go in each space. As they conducted their research, students recorded new information on their own diagrams. These proved useful when they moved into creating displays and writing their reports; they had collected information from various sources, and the Venn diagrams allowed them to view the information together in one place. (One drawback to using Venn diagrams was that they called attention only to the differences between two periods of time, rather than the actual process of change over the course of the last century.) Because they weren't used to synthesizing information from different sources, Amy modeled how the diagrams could help them: Using her diagram on *schools* again, she asked what conclusions they could reach—one hundred years ago children sat in desks at schools, and now we sit at tables; one hundred years ago students dressed up for school, and now we dress casually; and so on. Following class discussion, she worked with each group to help them use their own Venn diagrams in this way, and she particularly focused on how they would express those changes over time—composing compound sentences and using words like *then*, now, and *century*.

Teachers need to model how to draw conclusions from evidence.

Students need help seeing how information relates to their original questions.

Perhaps the most surprising challenge that Amy faced in helping students reach conclusions was getting them to see the connection between the re search and their displays and reports. Students frequently came to Amy after 10 or 15 minutes of work and said, "We're finished." Because they weren't used to collecting the kind of information that would help them draw conclusions, they had little idea when they had enough and when they didn't. One group investigating *work*, for example, told Amy they had done all the research they needed to do. She looked over their list of questions and found that one of them was, "How has the way they make shoes changed?" In answer, they had written down the word *shoemaker*, and they were now confident that they did not need to collect any further information on the topic. Amy asked if that told them what they needed to know to make their display or write their paper; they could tell by the tone of her voice that she didn't think it was enough, but they weren't sure what else was needed. She called their attention to the scoring guidelines for the project (see Fig. 7.2), particularly the section dealing with "use of details," and asked whether the word *shoemaker* gave them any details they would be able to use in their reports or presentation. They saw that it didn't, and Amy then gave them a way out of their dilemma—"Is this your research," she asked, "or just your brainstorming? I think this is just your brainstorming, and you still need to do more research to find out the details that you'll use." Although they were still somewhat disappointed that they weren't ready to start working on their display, they at least saw they needed more information to complete the assignment.

Similarly, when students finished their research and moved into the next phase of the project, nearly all of them ignored the notes they had taken. They simply began working on their reports without making any reference to what they had learned while doing research. Students in a different group investigating changes in work, for example, discussed the topic among themselves and then wrote, "People who had good jobs would make a dollar a day, and people who didn't have good jobs would make like a penny a day"—a statement that was completely unconnected to what they had found; they just made it up in the course of their discussion. Nearly every group of students repeated the same process: They wrote about how things changed "because it was neater" or "because people just liked it better," making no reference to what they had themselves discovered about changes. Again, Amy had to model for students how to use notes to draw conclusions and how to organize those in a report.

> Teachers need to model the use of notes to draw conclusions and organize reports.

	Points possible	Points awarded	Comments
Name _____ Points _____			
Physical setup: Attractive display, clear labels and captions, includes several historical artifacts or pictures	25		
Use of evidence: At least four different sources in display and written report, correctly lists where they came from	25		
Use of details: Clear and specific descriptions of historical items and how they were used	25		
Oral presentation: Effective explanation of the display; able to engage audience and answers questions	25		

FIG. 7.2. Checklist for evaluating History Museum display and report.

As we have noted, one of the goals of assessment is to help students develop an understanding of the standards of achievement so they can apply them to their own work. Indeed, one of the chief goals of instruction generally is to encourage students to plan and regulate their own learning. Students whose teachers tell them every detail of what to do and how to do it are ill prepared either for later learning or for life outside school. Successful students—and successful citizens—approach the world around them with curiosity, and they take charge of their own learning. They look to those in authority not so much to tell them what to do as to provide examples of what successful performances looks like. As Walt Keet's evaluation sheets in chapter 6 demonstrate, assessment can be an important tool in the process of developing such self-motivated and self-regulated learners. When clear standards are established before the beginning of an assignment, teachers and students can work together to reach those goals—and the teacher's role becomes one of supporting students' learning rather than directing it.

> Students should learn to plan and regulate their own learning.

This kind of self-directed learning was an important part of the History Museum project in Amy's classroom. Our emphasis on the pitfalls that students encountered may give the impression that this was a somewhat tedious or unexciting project, but nothing could be further from the truth. Students consistently stayed on task and made steady progress toward completing their work, and they were always ready to share with visitors and each other what they were finding out. The "feel" of the classroom was consistently open and relaxed despite the many obstacles students faced in learning about the purpose and nature of inquiry. One reason students felt comfortable with this process was the emphasis Amy placed on making them responsible for their own learning. At the beginning of the project, she distributed a detailed evaluation checklist (see Fig. 7.2), and she expected students to learn how to achieve the standards she had established. When their performance fell short—when, for example, a student thought he had completed his research after writing the word *shoemaker*—Amy responded not by criticizing students or giving them bad grades, but by showing them how to improve their work so that it more closely matched the evaluation checklist. Throughout the project, she made it clear that they were in charge of their learning and she was there to help them—thus each day, she asked students what stage of their project they were working on, what they were going to do next, and what their alternatives might be if they couldn't do the work they had planned. As we emphasized in chapter 6, students need to internalize the standards for achievement so that they know what they are trying to accomplish (and why), and Amy was largely successful in helping students make progress in that kind of metacognitive awareness. Near the end of the project, for example, she was reviewing paragraph structure with students and asked what they should do if they found they didn't have enough details to support the main idea of a paragraph. "Do more research," students agreed—a concept that would have been completely alien to them just two weeks earlier.

> Specific checklists can make evaluation standards clear to students.

> Evaluation checklists can help students monitor their own achievement.

It's important to recognize, though, that simply understanding a set of scoring guidelines will not motivate students to learn. Students might clearly fathom the meaning of a set of standards and still have no interest in achieving them; if the task is too hard, too easy, or too meaningless, students will not be likely to engage in any kind of self-regulated learning. Setting clear standards and helping students achieve them makes sense only when those standards relate to meaningful and authentic tasks. In this chapter, for example, one of the most important reasons students stayed interested and involved was that they knew their activities built toward their final performance—displays for their History Museum. These displays clearly were students' favorite part of their investigations, and they devoted careful attention to creating them—making sure they were visually appealing, easily understood, and full of interesting artifacts. And because they would be explaining their exhibits to other classes and to their parents and grandparents, they knew they had to understand their topics well enough to make these presentations and answer questions. Although teachers often ask students to imagine that they are writing or speaking for a particular audience (usually with mixed success), Amy's students really *were* preparing for an audience. Rather than imagining that someone didn't know anything about their topic, they were preparing their explanations for primary students who really didn't know anything about them. The authenticity of their expectations led them to plan presentations in which they took clear account of their audience with hands-on demonstrations and questions such as, "Do you know what these were used for?"

Assignments should have authentic purposes and audiences. *Scheurman & Newmann (1998)*

DEVELOPING AN UNDERSTANDING OF TIME AND CHRONOLOGY

Traditional history instruction is sometimes stereotyped as the incessant memorizing of dates. By this point in the book, we hope it's clear that our way of thinking about the topic is very different. Yet it's hard to deny that understanding time is an integral part of understanding history. In some important ways, the relationship between time and history is similar to the relationship between spelling and writing. Spelling can hardly be considered as important to writing as purpose, voice, or organization, and few teachers would spend as much time on spelling as on meaning-centered components of composition; yet they also know that students' writing will be far more effective if they eventually learn how to spell. Similarly, the importance of time pales in comparison to issues such as historical evidence, interpretation, agency, and significance, yet students' historical understanding will be more complete if they know when things happened. Just as spelling is a small but important part of writing, time is a small but important part of history.

One drawback to teaching students about time, though, is the temptation to confuse different aspects of the topic. Understanding historical time includes at least two separate components: being able to order moments in time (sometimes known as chronology) and being able to match moments in time to specific dates. Although at first these may seem similar, children are actually much more adept at the first. Our own research indicates that even children in kindergarten recognize that a picture of a covered wagon refers to a time longer ago than a picture with cars in it. Those in the primary grades can make even more complicated distinctions; as they get older, they become increasingly skilled at ordering historical pictures on the basis of clues in technology, fashion, and social roles. Children's chronological knowledge—their understanding of the order in which aspects of social and material life have changed—represents a very impressive area of prior knowledge.

Despite their knowledge of chronology, children's use of dates and other conventional markers of time—"the Depression," "the Colonial Era," and so on—is much less developed. Primary children know what dates sound like and usually know what the current year is, but they almost never associate periods in history with any particular years; they can put historical pictures in order, that is, but they don't match them with dates. By fourth grade, many children have begun to use some specific dates, most notably "the 1950s" and "the 1960s" (which generally refer interchangeably to the period ranging from poodle skirts to bell bottoms) and "the 1800s" (meaning a broad sweep of time including pioneers, the Civil War, and the Old West). By fifth and sixth grade, some (but not all) students can identify pictures from this century to within a decade and match pictures from the 1700s and 1800s with the appropriate century; occasionally students at this age use terms like "the Victorian era." These designations continue to be

Learning history does not mean memorizing dates.

Understanding time is a small but important part of history.

The research base for the following discussion of time can be found in Barton (1994, 2002), Barton & Levstik (1996), Downey (1994), Foster & Hoge (1999), Thornton & Vukelich (1988)

Children are better at sequencing historical periods than assigning dates or names to those periods.

Even older students rarely know the dates of political development and wars.

based mainly on clues in material and social life; even older students rarely know the dates of events such as wars or political developments.

Equating dates with an understanding of time, then, seriously underestimates students' abilities. Because younger children have so little knowledge of specific dates, and because even older ones can't readily identify the dates associated with events usually considered important in school, it's tempting to conclude that they don't understand time; such observations are sometimes used as justification for omitting history from the primary curriculum. In fact, however, most children have an extensive understanding of historical time—they just haven't learned specific dates yet. There are two important implications of these aspects of children's thinking.

First, dates and conventional time phrases (like "the Colonial Era") are unlikely to call forth any specific associations on the part of most students before fifth grade (nor for many after that point, either). Saying that something happened in "the 18th century," "1920," or even "about 30 years" ago doesn't mean anything to most children because those expressions don't match anything they can visualize. Early in the school year, for example, Amy happened to ask students if they thought there were televisions in 1980; most thought there were. She then asked if they thought televisions existed in 1970; the class was evenly split. Finally, she asked if there were any in 1960, and students were unanimous that nothing so modern could have been around so long ago. When students' knowledge of dates is as undeveloped as that, teachers cannot expect that using dates will help students know when something happened.

Dates generally do not allow students to visualize the time being referred to.

Instead of assuming that learning a date helps students know when something happened, teachers have to approach dates as concepts to be developed: They have to help students associate their visual images of history with the dates that correspond to them. Although Amy's students didn't think there were televisions in 1960, they could easily place a photograph from the 1960s between those from the 1950s and the 1970s. One of her goals, then, was for students to learn to use dates that went with their images of different time periods. In part, this involved constantly calling students' attention to the dates associated with the topics they were studying and asking them when they thought various developments took place (see, for example, the Artifact Think Sheet in Fig. 7.1). Even more important was the use of a "visual time line" on the wall of the classroom.

Teachers can help students associate their visual images of history with the corresponding dates.

Time lines can be found in any history text and on the walls of many classrooms. However, we believe that most time lines do little to develop students' understanding, because they provide no connection with prior knowledge. Time lines typically connect one thing students don't know much about—dates—with something else they don't know much about—wars and politics. The negative associations most people have with memorizing dates probably derives from just this shortcoming: Neither the date nor the event that went with it had any meaning. For a time line to be effective, it must build on students' prior knowledge—their visual understanding of changes in social and material life. In Amy's room, for example, two walls were taken up with a visual time line; this consisted of signs marking the decades from 1895 to the present with pictures placed at the appropriate points on the wall. As students brought in their own artifacts and photographs throughout the year, they added these to the time line as well. Soon after she put up the time line (and before she had even explained it to students), a striking phenomenon took place: Whenever Amy mentioned a date, in any context, students' heads would swing toward the time line—they were using it to find out what the date meant, to see for themselves how people dressed and what kind of machines they had in 1910 or 1940 or whatever. It was as if students were saying to themselves, "Oh, *that's* when 1940 was!" This visual time line served precisely the purpose we're advocating here: It helped students match dates to what they already knew. Such time lines should be as indispensable to elementary classrooms as world maps or reading corners. If students are

Most time lines do not allow students to make connections to their prior knowledge.

Visual time lines are an indispensable part of classrooms.

constantly exposed to the connection between dates and visual images, there is no reason they will not begin to develop an understanding of dates that will allow them to make sense of a statement like "World War II ended in 1945"—a statement that teachers may erroneously assume makes sense to students in the same way it does to them.

Students' prior knowledge of historical time has a second important implication: One of the principal purposes of instruction should be to help students further differentiate their categories of historical time—to break down broad periods like "close to now," "long ago," and "really long ago" into more finely detailed distinctions. Because students already have a basic understanding of some aspects of social and material life, these make a perfect starting point for instruction; the History Museum project in this chapter is a clear example of one such attempt to use what students already know to develop a more complete and nuanced understanding of change over time. Developing students' understanding of time means, in part, helping them to distinguish among the antebellum period, the Civil War, and the Old West instead of lumping them all together into one broad category of "the 1800s."

Instruction should help students make distinctions within broad categories of historical time.

One goal of such instruction should be to address a particularly common aspect of children's chronological thinking—their assumption of unilinear historical development. Children in the United States tend to assume that historical developments proceeded in a strict sequence—first one thing happened, then that period in history was over and everything changed. For example, they think that settlers came before cities, immigrants came before the first president, and so on. They fail to recognize that there were cities in some parts of the country at the same time people were settling on the frontier in other places, or that immigrants continued to arrive for hundreds of years after the American colonies were first settled by Europeans. Time lines (and the instruction that accompanies them) should be comparative, helping students to see what life was like for a variety of people at a given time. When students look at a date on a time line of American history, they should see more than a single image; they should see pictures drawn from several geographic regions and from the experiences of a variety of racial and ethnic groups, of women and men, and of working people as well as the wealthy. Helping students not only differentiate but also diversify their knowledge of historical time is a crucial but often overlooked purpose of instruction.

U.S. children often assume historical developments proceeded in a strictly linear sequence. Barton (1996a, 2001a), Barton & Levstik (1996)

Students should develop an understanding of the diverse images that may characterize any given time period.

EXTENSIONS

An obvious way to extend these History Museum projects is by varying the time period covered. Amy chose to have students investigate the last one hundred years primarily because she thought that would be the longest period of time for which students' families might provide information. Many families keep artifacts and tell stories that date back to the time of children's great-grandparents. Because elementary children are so often confused over what life was like before they were born, though, a teacher could just as easily plan the unit around changes over the last 50 years or even less. A primary teacher we know sets aside time for History Show and Tell. Each day a student brings in "something old" and describes what he or she has learned about it. The age of the items they bring in varies widely—from a 19th-century embroidery sampler to a five-year-old softball. Although this activity is not as extensive or systematic as the History Museum, it also develops students' understanding of historical time: By discussing the objects and placing them on an artifact time line in the classroom, students enhance their understanding of life at various times in the past. (One of the first things students realize is that "looking old"—like the beat-up softball—is not a direct indication of age.) Just as Amy's students did, students in this classroom

In History Show and Tell, students bring in and describe historical artifacts of varying ages.

develop an understanding of change over time and cease to think of the past as an undifferentiated period "long ago."

Students in the middle grades frequently study world history (or ancient civilizations specifically), and developing displays on change over time clearly fits well with such topics. If students fail to distinguish fully some period of time in American history, their distinctions in world history are even vaguer: One fourth grader described the entire pre-Colonial era as the time "back when God was around and everything." This impression is no doubt reinforced by instruction that races through the people and events of textbooks without ever really familiarizing students with the way people lived at different times in history. By investigating changes in daily life in the ancient world, medieval times, or the early modern era, students can develop more sophisticated understandings of the civilizations that they frequently rush through. This kind of project also lends itself to comparative time lines, in which students compare the changing ways of life in civilizations in China, Mali, Zimbabwe, Mesoamerica, Europe, and so on. Similarly, students studying state history would benefit more from creating displays on historic changes in their state than from trying to memorize the details of early political leaders or the adoption of the state flag.

The study of world history benefits from a focus on everyday life.

Passe & Whitley (1998)

Students in the middle grades can also devote more explicit attention to two aspects of historical change that largely were ignored by Amy's students. Most of the presentations in her class focused on aspects of material culture. Students occasionally touched on issues such as social relations—the *work* group, for example, included discussion of child labor, and the *fashion* group talked about changing expectations in women's appearance—but the main focus was always on physical changes as represented in photographs and artifacts. (This is not surprising, because as we have pointed out, elementary students tend to know more about these than any other aspect of change over time.) Students in the middle grades could be given a different set of topics from which to choose. Instead of investigating changes in material culture, they could examine the way social relations have changed over time—topics could include changing attitudes toward women, minorities, childhood, the poor, war, family structure, religion, labor, law, or the environment. Just as in Amy's class, these topics would involve students in asking questions, collecting information from people as well as printed sources, drawing conclusions, and making decisions about forms of presentation.

Students in the middle grades can focus on changing social relations.

Middle grades students also could focus attention on another aspect of change largely ignored in the History Museum project—the reasons for change. Students in Amy's class almost never devoted any attention to explaining why technology, fashion, work, or anything else had changed over time; whenever she pressed them for explanations, they either seemed to regard the changes as self-evident improvements ("They just figured it out") or were entirely baffled as to why the changes took place ("They just got tired of doing it that way, I guess"). If students have a teacher like Amy in fourth or fifth grade, however, and develop an understanding of the nature of change over time, their experiences in later grades can focus on helping them understand how those changes come about—particularly the way they are related to broader changes in culture, economy, or society.

Students can focus on the reasons for historical changes.

Students often think past society was different because people were lacking in knowledge.
Barton (1996a), Lee & Ashby (2000)

CONCLUSIONS

The projects described in this chapter represent several significant elements of the historical methods and instructional principles laid out in chapters 1 and 2. First, investigating changes in everyday life builds on the historical topics students usually know the most about: Even young children already have learned about changes in technology, fashion, and social roles from their relatives, the media, and popular culture generally. Investigating those topics further allows students to add depth and nuance to their understanding while dealing with familiar and comfortable content. Second, such projects engage students in genuine historical inquiry. Although young children who are still developing their reading skills will have trouble using some kinds of written primary sources—particularly from more remote time periods—analyzing photographs and artifacts allows them to use important historical materials in an authentic way. The questions that students develop, meanwhile, are not contrived, but derive naturally from their investigations and lead them to use a variety of other sources. Finally, directing such projects toward authentic audiences motivates students to develop the in-depth understanding that presentations or displays require.

As this chapter has made clear, of course, such authentic, disciplined inquiry is not easy; teachers must guide and support students at every step of the process—stimulating their interest, helping them develop questions, modeling procedures for collecting information, and so on. Yet the fact that teachers and students are so willing to stick with such projects attests to their potential for engaging students in meaningful historical learning.

These projects also prepare students for participatory democracy in two important ways. First, as we have noted throughout the chapter, students could not simply look up the answers to their questions—they had to find relevant information and draw their own conclusions from it. This is one of the most fundamental requirements of democratic participation: Citizens have to be able to develop ideas based on the careful consideration of evidence. In order to deliberate with others, we cannot rely solely on authority, tradition, or unreflective opinion, because others are likely to have their own authorities, traditions, and opinions. Neither can we simply make things up, even through students (and adults) often like to do so. When we deliberate together as members of a group, we must have reasons for our positions, and these reasons must be grounded in evidence, because otherwise we will have nothing to talk about and no way of bridging the gaps between us. In their History Museum Projects, students were learning to do exactly that—to base their assertions on evidence, and to make it clear how they arrived at those conclusions.

Barton & Levstik (2004)

A second contribution of these projects to democratic participation may be less obvious, but it represents an important advance over typical classroom activities. Often, students are asked to display their historical knowledge—by answering questions in class or on a quiz, for example, or by taking achievement tests—but such displays usually are designed only for the purpose of accountability: Did students read the chapter? Can they remember what they learned? Are schools covering the required content? Such displays have few benefits for the teaching of history, and they have no particular benefit for the students who take part in them. Yet in society at large, historical displays are common—at museums and historic sites, in historical reenactments, and so on—and many people enjoy such exhibitions. Projects like those described in this chapter are one way in which the displays of history in school can become more like such displays outside school. In their History Museum projects, students were displaying information for the benefit of others—their classmates, students in other classrooms, and their relatives. This is one of the basic ways in which people in our society participate in history: They pass along information about the past to others who don't already know about it. This gives meaning and purpose to the exhibition of historical knowledge: It is not done just for the purpose of accountability but because it helps other people learn. Sharing information in this way makes democratic participation richer and more complete.

Barton (2001b),
Barton & Levstik (2004)

Aliki. *A Medieval Feast*. Thomas Y. Crowell, 1983.

Bender, L. *Invention*. Alfred A. Knopf, 1991.

Bisel, S. C. *The Secrets of Vesuvius*. Scholastic, 1990.

Brooks, F. *Clothes and Fashion*. EDC Publishing, 1990.

Brooks, F., & Bond, S. *Food and Eating*. EDC Publishing, 1989.

Cahn, R., & Cahn, W. *No Time for School, No Time for Play: The Story of Child Labor in America*. Julian Messner, 1972.

Clare, J. D. *Living History: Pyramids of Ancient Egypt*. Harcourt, Brace, Jovanovich, 1992.

Cobb, V. *Brush, Comb, Scrub: Inventions to Keep You Clean*. Harper Trophy, 1989.

Cobb, V. *Snap, Button, Zip: Inventions to Keep Your Clothes On*. Harper Trophy, 1989.

Conrad, P. *Prairie Visions: The Life and Times of Solomon Butcher*. HarperCollins, 1991.

Cook, L. W. *When Great-Grandmother was a Little Girl*. Holt, Rinehart, & Winston, 1965.

Edom, H. *Home and Houses Long Ago*. Usborne Publishers, 1989.

Edom, H. *Travel and Transport*. Usborne Publishers, 1990.

Fisher, L. E. *The Schoolmasters*. Franklin Watts, 1967.

Fix, P. *Not So Very Long Ago: Life in a Small Country Village*. Dutton, 1994.

Freedman, R. *Children of the Wild West*. Houghton Mifflin, 1983.

Freedman, R. *Kids at Work: Lewis Hine and the Crusade Against Child Labor*. Clarion Books, 1994.

Fradon, D. *The King's Fool: A Book about Medieval and Renaissance Fools*. Dutton Children's Books, 1993.

Giblin, J. C. *From Hand to Mouth: Or, How We Invented Knives, Forks, Spoons, and Chopsticks and the Table Manners to Go with Them*. HarperCollins, 1987.

Giblin, J. C. *Let There Be Light: A Book About Windows*. HarperCollins, 1988.

Gumby, L. *Early Farm Life*. Crabtree Publishing Company, 1992.

Hamilton, V. *The Bells of Christmas*. Harcourt, Brace, & Jovanovich, 1983.

Hammond, T. *Sports*. Knopf, 1988.

Hart, G. *Ancient Egypt*. Knopf, 1990.

Hart, R. *English Life in Chaucer's Day*. G. P. Putnam's Sons, 1973.

Hart, R. *English Life in the Eighteenth Century*. G. P. Putnam's Sons, 1970.

Hart, R. *English Life in the Nineteenth Century*. G. P. Putnam's Sons, 1971.

Hart, R. *English Life in the Seventeenth Century*. G. P. Putnam's Sons, 1971.

Hart, R. *English Life in Tudor Times*. G. P. Putnam's Sons, 1972.

Haywood, J. *Work, Trade, and Farming Through the Ages*. Lorenz Books, 2001.

Hernández, X. *San Rafael: A Central American City through the Ages*. Houghton Mifflin, 1992.

Jackson, E. *Turn of the Century*. Charlesbridge, 1998.

Jackson, E. *Turn of the Century: Eleven Centuries of Children and Change*. Charlesbridge, 2003.

James, S. J. *Ancient Rome*. Alfred A. Knopf, 1990.

Kalman, B. *Early Settler Life* (series). Crabtree Publishing Company, 1991–1992.

Kalman, B. *Historic Communities* (series). Crabtree Publishing Company, 1992–1994.

Katz, W. L. *An Album of the Great Depression*. Franklin Watts, 1978.

Kentley, E. *Boat*. Alfred A. Knopf, 1990.

Kurjian, J. *In My Own Backyard*. Charlesbridge, 1993.

Lasker, J. *Merry Ever After: The Story of Two Medieval Weddings*. Viking Press, 1979.

Lauber, P. *What You Never Knew about Fingers, Forks, and Chopsticks*. Simon & Shuster, 1999.

Lessem, D. *The Iceman*. Crown Publishers, 1994.

Levinson, R. *I Go with My Family to Grandma's*. Dutton, 1992.

Loeper, J. J. *Going to School in 1876*. Atheneum, 1984.

Moser, B. *Fly! A Brief History of Flight Illustrated*. HarperCollins 1993.

McGovern, A. *If you lived 100 years ago*. Scholastic, 1999.

Nahum, A. *Flying Machines*. Alred A. Knopf, 1990.

Parker, S. *53½ Things That Changed the World and Some that Didn't*. Millbrook, 1995.

Perl, L. *Blue Monday and Friday the Thirteenth*. Clarion Books, 1986.

Perl, L. *From Top Hats to Baseball Caps, from Bustles to Blue Jeans: Why We Dress the Way We Do*. Clarion, 1990.

Platt, R. *Film*. Alfred A. Knopf, 1992.

Rowland-Warne, L. *Costume*. Alfred A. Knopf, 1992.

Sanchea, S. *The Luttrell Village: Country Life in the Middle Ages*. Thomas Y. Crowell, 1982.

Schroeder, A. *Ragtime Tumpie*. Little, Brown, 1989.

Steele, P. *Clothes and Crafts in Victorian Times*. Gareth Stevens, 2000.

Sturner, F. *What Did You Do When You Were a Kid? Pastimes from the Past*. St. Martin's Press, 1973.

Sutton, R. *Car.* Alfred A. Knopf, 1990.

Tanner, G., & Wood T. *At School.* A & C Black, 1992.

Tanner, G., & Wood, T. *Washing.* A & C Black, 1992.

Unstead, R. J. *See Inside a Castle.* Warwich Press, 1979.

Weaver, R., & Dale, R. *Machines in the Home.* Oxford University Press, 1992.

Wilkes, A. *A Farm Through Time: The History of a Farm from Medieval Times to the Present Day.* DK Publishing, 2001.

Wilson, L. *Daily Life in a Victorian House.* Puffin, 1993.

8

I HAVE NO EXPERIENCE WITH THIS!

Historical Inquiry in an Integrated Social Studies Setting

It is 10:00 A.M. on a surprisingly pleasant January day. A bank of windows along one wall lets in the sunshine; when several children complain that the room is too warm, Dehea Smith opens a window and a breeze moves through the room. The twenty-one children in Dehea's third-grade classroom are working at a variety of tasks. One group of three works with a set of geography materials, two children work at the computer, typing in their newsletter entry about the stage design they are working on for the school TV news program. Others work on a "Museum of the World" display that will organize some of the artifacts that the class has collected over the first semester of the year. Others are completing their "Morning Goals"—usually work in math or literature. The classroom is small and crowded. Children sit in groups of three, either at desks turned to face each other or at two round tables in the middle of the room. These are new groups, and the children have hung signs above each set of desks or table with their group name on it: Radical Red Rovers, Chkemy, Brown-eyed Tigers, and so forth. Earlier in the year, students had trouble working cooperatively. Over the first semester, Dehea assigned partners, occasionally moving into larger groups for some tasks. They have been working in groups of three since the new semester began. As the children finish up their work, Dehea passes out booklets entitled "Government is for Kids, Too!"

Dehea:	We've studied things far away, either in time or location—or both! Can you think of anything we've studied that was far away in location?
Several voices:	The rainforest!
Dehea:	Yes, rainforests are far away from here. What about something we've studied that was far away in time?
Lily:	Native Americans in the old days.
Dehea:	Right. It's interesting to study things that are far away from us, but it is also important to know something about things a little closer to home. There's also something else that will be different about this study. When we studied the rainforest, I picked many things that we were going to study. And when we studied Native Americans, Ms. Armstrong [student teacher] made a lot of the decisions about what questions we would investigate. But this time, you are going to make most of those decisions.
Kayla:	So, we're kinda like the teacher?
Dehea:	Well, you will certainly be doing some of the things that teachers often do.

Justin:	Alright!
Marshall:	We get to decide on the questions?
Dehea:	That's right. But in order to know what questions we want to answer, its good to find out what we already know. I'm curious to know what you already know about Lexington. For instance, how many of you have ever been to a place that's bigger than Lexington? [General discussion of places that are bigger.] Can you think of a place smaller than Lexington?
Rena:	Nicholasville.
Dehea:	How many have been there?
Justin:	I've been there, but I don't know if it's smaller. Seems like it, but I don't know for sure. [More discussion about how you can tell if a place is big or small.]
Dehea:	Hmm. How many of you have walked around downtown? Not just driven through. Really walked around. [About 11 hands go up—although the school is close to downtown, most of the children are bussed in from other parts of the city.] Well, let's brainstorm about what we already know. While I'm getting some paper, just look through—survey—the booklet I just gave you.
Tad:	Should we write any questions down?
Dehea:	Ah—good idea! Write down questions.
Amelia:	Can we use our research folders?
Dehea:	Another good idea. Use your research folders. [She places a large pad of chart paper on the board and waits a few minutes for students to look through the booklets. She walks through the room monitoring progress until it seems that most of the students have at least glanced through the booklet and written down a question or two.] OK, close your books. [Students turn their chairs to face the charts where Dehea waits to take dictation.] What are some of the places you knew about downtown?

The children start dictating a list of places: sports arena, theater, opera house, library, museums, hotels, park, banks, big buildings. Dehea looks over the list and notes that she thinks many of these places have something in common. She asks the students to take a couple of minutes to write what they think these downtown places have in common. As they work, she moves between groups, glancing over students' shoulders, commenting that "several people have seen different things," "keep thinking along those lines!," or "This is exciting! It tells me you're ready to learn what's *behind* all of this." Next, she collects their ideas, explaining that "if somebody says what you have on your list, check it off." Children mention that all except banks and buildings have something to do with entertainment, are popular with kids, involve action or fun. "Yes," Dehea agrees, "they solicit children to come. They invite you to come. But there are many other places downtown, too. We've got to decide on some questions to help us learn about these places, too." She tells the students that she will use "quick writing" [a term previously introduced to identify a form of note taking] as they dictate their questions. The first questions involve size and number: How many windows are there? What's the tallest building? The oldest building? But soon children move on: "Why do we need a mayor?" "Why are there taxes?" Dehea also intervenes to ask questions. "I was wondering, too, what *are* taxes?" or, after someone asks how big downtown is, she asks, "Why *is there* a downtown?" She then asks students to take five minutes and write down all the questions they can think of, sharing their work with their partner. Next, children categorize their questions, with Dehea transcribing comments, and asking them for key words to describe each category: government, history, structures, entertainment, people, geography, urban planning, and employment. Anna mentions that some of these categories overlap, and Dehea agrees.

Although critics have sometimes argued that schools should teach separate disciplines such as history rather than integrated fields such as social studies, there are sound cognitive and disciplinary reasons for teaching history in the larger context of social studies. First of all, disciplinary boundaries are increasingly permeable. Instead of being neatly defined as historians, anthropologists, political scientists, or the like, modern scholars more often tend to identify themselves with the problems or issues they address. Because so many of these issues cross traditional disciplinary boundaries, an integrated social studies approach is often a more authentic context for historical study. As we noted in chapter 1, such contexts support students' sense making in history. More authentic contexts provide examples of history-in-action rather than of history separated from action; students can see how historical thinking grows from and contributes to problem solving in the real world.

An integrated social studies approach can provide authentic contexts for studying history.

This chapter focuses on doing disciplined, reflective inquiry in the context of an integrated social studies unit. We begin with a common third-grade social studies topic, "communities," which often becomes little more than the "community helpers" we all remember from our elementary years. We visited the fire station, learned about doctors and dentists, police officers, and the safety patrol, but rarely went much beyond that. Dehea Smith, the teacher in the vignette that opened this chapter, also decided to focus on the concept of community but in a more substantive way that will involve students in a long-term set of inquiries into their community. Dehea has to align her curriculum with state and local mandates that define the goal of social studies as developing "contributing and knowledgeable citizens" who "understand and apply the content and concepts of the subdisciplines" of the field in their role as citizen.

National Council for the Social Studies (1994)

Disciplined, reflective inquiry occurs in integrated social studies contexts.

Kentucky's Core Content for Assessment (1997)

To meet these goals, instruction and assessment are supposed to focus on democratic principles, the structure and function of political, social, and economic systems, human and geographic interactions, cultural diversity, and historical perspective. Although this may seem overwhelming, if you go back to the vignette, you will see that on the very first day, Dehea's class inquiry touches on almost all of these aspects of social studies. This is especially apparent in the way in which her student organized their initial questions into broader categories. After lengthy discussion and debate, students select labels such as *government*, *history*, *structures*, *geography*, and *employment*. They argue that buildings, for instance, can be categorized as structures, but they also function as places of employment and entertainment, of government and historical interest. As Dehea puts the category headings on separate sheets of chart paper, she suggests that the students provide *key words* to help them remember what they have decided goes into each category. These key words also provide a good deal of information about how students understand each category at this point in their study, and they give Dehea some idea of where to place greater instructional emphasis. The *history* category, for instance, began with only a few questions focusing on finding the oldest building or street. There were no questions about the significance of these things, the sources of current problems, or even more generally how the city had changed over time. On the other hand, there were a number of government and urban planning questions—"What are taxes?" "Why do we need a mayor?" "Who decides on how a city looks?"—that lent themselves to historical as well as current treatment.

Teachers can coordinate local, state, and national standards.

Key words help students classify and organize data.

ALL QUESTIONS ARE NOT CREATED EQUAL: MOVING BEYOND THE SUPERFICIAL

If Dehea had stopped with the initial set of questions, the students probably could have completed their study in short order. Many of these first questions were superficial. As often happens in classrooms, one type of response can start a domino effect; when Julie asked "How many windows are downtown," Martin chimed in with "Well, then, how many *bricks* are downtown?" As did Amy in Chapter 7, Dehea reminded her students that good questions often start with "how" or "why," and this helped some, with one student asking "Why do we need a mayor?" after another suggested "Who is the mayor?" This type of ap-

Focusing students on important questions can be challenging with any age group. See for instance, Levstik & Groth (2004), Levstik, Henderson, & Schlarb (2005), VanSledright (2003).

proximation seems to be a common response as children struggle to frame substantial questions. Another response typical of this state of question development is the personalization of questions—"Why do *we* need a mayor" rather than "Why does a *community* need a mayor?" Of course a study of students' own community is more likely to elicit such statements of ownership as opposed to, say, a unit on rainforests.

As we have already noted, question generation is hard intellectual work, and Dehea was not satisfied with how things were going. "We spent all that time gathering facts on the last project, that they are just in that mode," she concluded. She had promised that on this project they could ask their own questions, but she did not want the study limited to mere fact gathering. Instead, she planned on emphasizing continuity and change in the city, how conflicts were resolved, and how even third graders could participate in their urban community. She decided to try another question-generating technique. First, she gave students a homework assignment: Interview people at home and ask them to suggest good questions to ask if someone wanted to learn about Lexington. Students were to decide which of these questions matched categories they had already developed and to identify any new categories they would need.

The next day, Dehea took each of the pieces of chart paper headed with the category labels and descriptions that had already been developed, put one at each work center around the room, divided the class into groups, and assigned each group to a different category. Their task was to edit the list of questions already generated, emphasizing *how* and *why* questions. Next, she told the students to rotate through the centers, adding to the charts all the new questions generated by their homework interviews. Again, they were to check for duplications and not write questions that were already listed. In the end, they created one new category: *miscellaneous*. As their work period ended, the students recorded the number of questions in each category, estimated the total, and then confirmed their estimation by adding category totals. They had generated 204 questions.

When students generate this volume of questions, they can easily become bogged down in trivia rather than engaged in substantial inquiry. There are several techniques for narrowing the scope of investigation to a more manageable size, including having children collapse several questions into one or letting students decide on a set of "most important" questions (see chap. 7 for other ideas). Dehea chose not to limit the number of questions. Instead, she noted that some of the questions could be easily answered; she suggested that students take the rest of that day's research time to see how many questions they could answer using the sources already in the room. She also reminded them to plan their record keeping: "Think about how you want to keep track of your answers first, then share your ideas with your partners."

This kind of metacognition—thinking about thinking—was a classroom constant. Dehea set aside time for full-class review of work plans, for individuals to consider how they could best organize their thinking, for students to share their thinking and planning with a peer, and, as you will see later in this chapter, for the development of metaphors to support children's visualization of tasks. After students had planned their work, they began sorting through the questions. Dehea made suggestions for sources they might use: phone books to find out what kinds of restaurants were downtown, maps to locate major geographic landmarks, and the *Lexington Answer Book* to find out where the courthouse was located. As the research period drew to a close, one group had answered all but two of the questions on their list, and most of the others had made substantial progress. "This is good information," Dehea told them. "Now, let's see what kinds of questions we have left." In the next few minutes, the class decided that they could eliminate some categories, concentrating more of their efforts on just a few. They also noted that each category contained several different types of questions:

Blythe (1989)

Short & Armstrong (1993)

A social studies approach emphasizes participation *(see e.g., National Council for the Social Studies, 1994).*

Students edit their own questions, emphasizing *how* and *why* questions.

Dickinson (1993)

Hyde & Bizar (1989)

Metaphors help students visualize tasks.

Lexington Answer Book (n.d.)

Categorizing questions helps focus research.

108

- questions that required a trip to the school library
- questions that required both library research and sources from outside the school
- questions that were "ridiculous"

Ridiculous questions included finding out how many bricks or windows there were downtown. "That would take forever to do!" Jason exclaimed. "It's just ridiculous!" Once they named the category, the students decided that they might answer some of these questions "just for fun," but they were not going to put much effort into them. They also edited a couple of *ridiculous* questions, made them more manageable, and moved them into the history and structures categories. The questions about windows and bricks, for instance, changed from *how many* windows or bricks to *what different styles* of windows and buildings could be found in Lexington. Members of the history group decided that they would see if window styles changed over time; members of the structures group thought they would see if the uses of buildings influenced their styles.

In a relatively short time, then, these third graders had honed their questions to a manageable and substantive list. They were able to quickly dispose of some that seemed initially interesting but had little significance, and focus on others that they decided were more important. It took time and patience to get to this point, but in the end, most of the students had a surer sense of what they were investigating and how their questions fit the larger theme of community. Given the opportunity and sufficient scaffolding, these students were able to distinguish between superficial and substantive questions. Dehea supported their efforts by allowing them time to work with the questions, sift and categorize them, debate and discuss their merits, do some initial investigation, and, finally, hammer out their own working definitions of categories. By their next research period, student inquiry was more focused, the theme of change over time began to emerge as a significant issue, and it was time to think about field trips and guest speakers.

FLEXIBILITY IS ESSENTIAL: BUILDING ON STUDENT DISCOVERIES

As Suling and Jason study maps of Lexington and the surrounding county, trying to locate water sources that might have enticed people to the area, they find two exciting pieces of information. First, they discover that the site of the first White settlement in the area was probably a spring close to their school. "Wow!" Suling exclaims. "That's a trip we need to take!" The librarian helps Jason find an old picture of the spring in a picture history book of Lexington, and Suling and Jason decide that they could make a copy of this "before" picture and then take "after" pictures if they visit the spring. Their second discovery is that a creek runs underneath part of the downtown area. Why would people want to bury a creek? Where did it come out? Who could they ask about this? They list their new questions in their research notebooks and go in search of their teacher.

As students conduct their inquiries and make discoveries, they need as many opportunities to pursue sources as possible. Because teachers cannot anticipate all the directions a study will take, flexibility and planning are essential. Before Dehea began the community study, for instance, she made a list of contact people for possible field trips and guest speakers. Obviously schools do not have unlimited access to field trips or outside experts. Choices must be made and made far enough in advance to ensure access at the necessary time. Dehea called several of her contacts before the unit started so that she knew what arrangements would need to be made. She also decided that the class would use public transportation for any field trips. This accomplished two things. First, transportation was a significant part of the community. It was also part of a community controversy over budget cuts that might eliminate bus routes and services for handicapped passengers. Second, the bus company required only one day's notice to pick up a whole class, whereas school buses had to be scheduled at the beginning of each school year. Dehea, then, was prepared for several pos-

With time, students can identify nonproductive questions.

Students may need help thinking about what questions have historical significance. (see e.g., Jorgensen, 1993)

Taking time for question development in the beginning of a study saves time later.

Flexibility and preplanning facilitate student inquiry.

K. A. Young (1994)

109

Planning for inquiry
should be conducted
jointly by teachers and
students. *(See e.g., Oyler,
1996; Wells & Chang-
Wells 1992; K. A. Young
1994.)*

Albert (1995)

Students need help in
deciding how to allocate
their research time.

Local history can draw on
a rich variety of local
sources.

sibilities. She felt strongly, however, that planning should be joint work. She wanted her students to be intentional in their thinking. "After all," she explained, "that's the only way they'll learn to do this on their own." One day, she noticed that some of the students seemed anxious to stop researching and pick a construction project—"Let's build a model of Lexington!" Dehea stopped the class and suggested they needed a "metaphor to help us think about our work."

Dehea began by drawing a metaphor on the board: a field of questions and, beneath the soil, information; a researcher digging for information, piling that information into a knapsack, and bringing it back to a "house of knowledge" where it was organized and used to answer questions. "Which part are we working on now?" she asked. The students agreed that they were digging, just beginning to fill their knapsacks. "Do you have enough in your knapsacks to really fill a house of knowledge?" she asked. Again, most of the students agreed that they needed more information before they were ready to build anything. Dehea told them to draw the metaphor in their research notebooks to remind them of their task. At each stage of work, then, she referred students back to this metaphor. Developing the metaphor helped students visualize the multistep task of reflective inquiry.

At one point, Dehea asked her students to stop and decide how best to allocate their remaining time and resources. "Make a list of sources you will need," she told them. "If we need to talk to people or visit downtown, we have to plan way ahead of time, and we'll have to make one trip answer a lot of questions. This will take a lot of planning and phone calling." As a group, then, the class made the plans listed in Table 8.1 (and recorded in each student's research notebook).

Although a field trip to McConnell Springs, the site of the first White settlement in Lexington, would have been nice, the city bus did not go there. Instead, the students decided to ask a representative of the "Save Our Spring" group to come to the class, show slides of the spring, talk about its history, and explain some of the problems encountered in trying to turn the area into a natural and historical park site. Although no speaker was available, the group sent a box full of materials for the students to use. In many ways, this was more productive in terms of Dehea's goals because the unsorted resources in the box made it necessary for students to develop their own interpretations.

TABLE 8.1

Class Constructed Work Plan for Part of Community Study

March 3: Bus trip downtown

      Purpose:

                1. Research in Kentucky Collection at the library (collection of newspapers, maps, photographs, and the like related to state and local history)

                2. Walking tour of downtown. Take pictures of structures and historic places

April 13: Bus trip to city council work session

      Purpose:

                1. See how city government works

                2. Find out what kind of problems the city council has to solve

                3. Tour government buildings

Visit from the Mayor (to be scheduled)

Visitor from McConnell Springs (to be scheduled)

Dehea wanted her students to understand some of the ways in which conflict shaped their community. The conflict over what responsibility the local government had in preserving both history and the natural environment seemed one possibility. In addition, several students decided they were interested in crime and weather-related problems in the community—topics that Dehea had not anticipated. In investigating whether crime had increased in Lexington, for instance, one group came upon an article reporting a public hanging in the city. The article included a gallows speech by the convicted murderer, pleading for other young men to avoid "strong drink and weapons." A second group, curious about why Lexington had few tornadoes or hurricanes, wrote to the regional weather service and discovered, among other things, that their city was on the eastern edge of "tornado alley" and that flooding was a much more common problem historically and currently. A major current conflict involved updating storm sewers, which did not seem particularly interesting until two students found a picture of a 1932 flood that inundated the downtown area. Although there had been heavy rainfall that day, the flooding was largely due to inadequate storm sewers. Both groups added new questions to ask the mayor.

> Conflict is an important element in any community's history.
>
> McGinnis (n.d.)

MAINTAINING FOCUS

Dehea reminds the students to take out their research notebooks, and there are a couple of moans.

"If you whine," she says, "there are consequences!"

"Oh, goody," Cheyenne says. "Research!"

There is general laughter as the students retrieve their notebooks. Dehea has noticed some falling off of interest in some of the groups, especially after a week of frequent interruptions. Momentum seems to be lost, and she wants to refocus the class on their research tasks.

"We're going to go back in the past this morning," she tells them. "You will need to take notes. Head your notes *The Quest for McConnell Springs*." Several heads go up in surprise. McConnell Springs is part of their study.

"I know where that is," Jason exclaims.

Dehea smiles, relieved that their interest seems to be reviving. "Now, let's refresh our memories. How do we take notes? Chad, how do you like to take notes?

"Don't write down everything they say."

"Just use phrases."

"Use abbreviations."

Dehea interjects a warning to write enough to "trigger your memory," and other students add that pictures can give clues.

"Don't concentrate on just one fact," Kelly adds.

Dehea turns on the video. "If you need me to stop, we can watch it again. Everybody ready? Let me get my notebook, so I can take notes, too."

The video is brief—a seven minute reenactment of the discovery and settlement of McConnell Springs. At its conclusion, Dehea asks the students to share their notes.

"Too short!" Karla cries. "I only got two notes."

"Want to see it again?" Dehea asks. The students ask for a replay, and Dehea reminds them to pay attention to the pictures. "Most of my notes came from the pictures!"

After the video has played through a second time, the class begins to discuss what they have learned. This time they have many more notes to share, and Dehea asks them if they could tell from the video what time of year it was. Initially, several of the students are convinced that it must have been fall. They also seem to think that the McConnell brothers are just visiting, not settling here. "Hmm," Dehea murmurs. "We'll need to discuss this!"

In the ensuing discussion, all children participate. If a child is silent too long, Dehea asks for his or her ideas and enforces the rules about not interrupting people when they are trying to formulate an opinion. Finally, Kelly says, "I don't think they're coming back 'cause they're claiming land. They'd come in the Spring, so they could clear the land and get their house built before the cold weather."

"Yeah," Jason agrees. "You can't count on luck. You have to be prepared."

Suling adds that "they need time to settle in."

At this point, Dehea introduces a contour map of the area around McConnell Springs along with several overlay maps that show how the area grew and changed, shifting eastward along the Town Branch, the creek that now runs under the city. The children lean forward to see the map, tracing the creek's flow and exclaiming when buildings they recognize from their trip downtown appear on the map.

Frequent interruptions can defuse students interest.

Because research takes time, and work in classrooms is frequently interrupted, sustaining inquiry can be a problem. Dehea, for instance, lost one week to Spring Break, another to statewide testing, and several days to the science fair, schoolwide assemblies, and similar events. It seemed that each time students became deeply involved, there was another interruption. Some of these interruptions were necessary, even interesting, breaks in routine, but their effect was to extend the community study to the point that students sometimes lost interest. Dehea found that regular whole-group presentations and discussions helped rekindle interest and kept students on task. She focused each of these whole-group experiences around a different aspect of the class study. In the prior excerpt, she focused on the process of note taking, but also on the interaction between the early settlers and their environment. Similarly, a discussion of the role of government preceded an interview with the mayor.

Pappas et al. (1999)

Perhaps one of the most striking aspects of these discussions was the time Dehea took to allow students to build interpretations based on the data they had been accumulating and the information presented in each of these whole-group experiences. It would have been much quicker, for instance, to simply tell the students that the first White settlers came in the spring. Instead, she engaged in a lengthy (30-minute) analysis of evidence that could support student assumptions about season, solicited conclusions—"I think it's early spring"—supporting evidence—"because they are dressed warmly, but there's no snow, and some leaves are on the trees"—and interpretations—"if you get there in the spring you have time to build up food for winter."

Building interpretations based on historical data takes time, especially with younger students.

Note, too, that Dehea worked along with the children, modeling the processes she wanted them to learn and then sharing her work as they did theirs. As the video played, for instance, she stood to the side, clipboard in hand, visibly taking notes. As students shared what they had written down, she would say, "Oh, yes. I wrote that down, too," or "Oh, I missed that. I think I'll add that to my notes, too." At other times, she would write notes to the class on the board—"Does anyone have a book with a picture of an old-fashioned radio?"—and students would respond by writing their name next to her question. By the end of the project, then, the blackboard became a center of communication where teacher and students could write notes without interrupting another group's work.

Jorgensen (1993), Lindquist (1995)

At the end of a research session, Dehea ran through the notes on the board, making sure inquiries were answered, notes made, or materials returned; then she erased the board. Other teachers use a large sheet of colored paper as a more permanent communications center. In either case, however, having such a system helps keep students focused on their own tasks with relatively few interruptions and gives the teacher a running record of current issues within and between groups.

Lindquist (1995)

NOW, WHAT DOES IT MEAN?

Interviewer: Hello, I'm Kelly James, here today with William, the famous criminal. Before we go on to your life, lets find out some things about general life in the 1800s. What were some of the places you saw or heard of as a child?

William:	On Main Street there was a business called Gibney and Cassell. It was run by Gibney and William H. Cassell.
Interviewer:	Yes, after a long time, it became Parcell's Department store. That was torn down in the late 1970s.
William:	It was? (acts surprised)
Interviewer:	Yes. It was made into an office/hotel building.
William:	One place I REALLY remember was the fourth Fayette County courthouse. I had my trial there. The courthouse was built in 1883 and 1884. It was designed by Thomas W. Boyd.
Interviewer:	That building was burned down in 1897. Lots of valuable oil paintings and a valuable sculpture by Joel T. Hart were lost in that fire. At this time, Lexington was pretty busy. Let's hear some about your life, William.
William:	When I was nine years old and I had to leave my parents was when I began my criminal life. I had to steal just to stay alive!
Interviewer:	No wonder you did such an awful thing!
William:	Before I was hung, I made a speech. The speech was a warning for young men to stay away from guns and alcohol. That's how my life got messed up.
Interviewer:	Since childhood was a bad experience for you, how do you feel it affected your adulthood?
William:	I felt like I didn't have a future so it didn't matter what I did.

At some point, researchers must draw at least tentative conclusions about their work. Dehea's third graders decided that they wanted to share what they had found with their parents through a series of skits. Each group was charged with writing a short script that "shows some of the most interesting things you have learned about Lexington." This turned out to be the most challenging aspect of the research. The students had accumulated lots of "facts" and had found answers to most of their questions, but deciding which pieces of information went together and whether any of it would be interesting or important to anyone else was difficult. As it turned out, however, what the students were most intimidated by was writing a script. This was somewhat surprising because they had written scripts for a puppet show about the rainforest earlier in the year and frequently wrote other types of stories and reports. As one of the boys explained, however, "We didn't all write the script for the puppet show. Some people worked on scenery, and some people gathered information and like that. I have no experience with this." His partner agreed, saying that she had never even been in a play and had no idea of what to put in the script.

Students need to develop a broad repertoire of ways to share what they have learned.

Cope & Kalantzes (1990), Jorgensen (1993), Lindquist (1995), Newkirk (1989)

At the end of one week of work, most of the children were still struggling. They knew what story they wanted to tell, but they tended to tell it in outline, leaving out all the information they had so painstakingly accumulated. The partners who had found out about the 1832 flood drafted a half-page script that involved waking up, shouting "Flood!," and swimming for their lives. Although this was certainly lively, it was short on historical information, the current connection that had captured their initial interest, and accuracy—the flood was only 3 feet deep; its major danger was typhoid rather than drowning. Similarly, the first draft of the group investigating crime in Lexington consisted of an interview with the criminal, William, in which he explained that the "happiest time [in his life] was when I was hung." Although William had actually said this in his gallows speech, the students' script provided no context for the statement. Two other groups wrote more substantial first drafts involving the founding of Lexington and city government.

First drafts are often only outlines of information.

Dehea looked over the students' drafts and suggested that they edit their scripts to make sure that each line included important information about their topic. "Oh," Cheyenne said, "We need facts in each line." This notion of anchoring each line of script in facts seemed to make a lot of sense to the students. As you can see from the script at the opening of this section—a third draft—the interview with the murderer took on a whole new dimension, introducing the audience to "general life in the 1880s" and then more specific information "about your life, William."

The pair who worked on the flood struggled for some time, finally working with a classroom volunteer to construct the outline and dictate the introduction in Fig. 8.1. At this point, the partners took over the writing on their own, explaining why flooding was a more frequent problem than tornadoes, describing what Lexington looked like in 1832, mentioning the deaths due to typhoid fever, and ending with one of the characters going down to City Hall to demand better storm sewers.

Because their grasp of dates was still shaky, another group became frustrated with figuring out the sequence of events. They needed to find out whether their main character would have been alive to witness some of the events they were putting in their script. With some urging, they constructed a time line to which they could refer when deciding what things could go in their script. Other groups found that they had not taken careful enough notes to add the details they needed for their scripts. This was particularly apparent when they were deciding on scenery. If a character was supposed to open a door, they wanted to know what the door might look like; if a character was supposed to be in a cabin, they needed to know what furniture and tools were inside. Because it was an authentic assessment, putting together a presentation made it clear to the students which aspects of their research they really understood, where they had holes in their data, and what pieces of information made convincing arguments for a particular perspective.

Geography:		Flood p. 207	
	Town Branch	Main things	
	Weather Letter		
	Size of city	Side things	
	Where was flood		
Skit:	Flood		
	Debate about sewers		
	How changed Lexington		
Needed:		Fake water	
	Story: Someone in the flood		
	Radio reporter telling people about the flood		
	Script: (Main idea) What reporter sees. Emergency! Flood Warning!		

Still stymied by the thought of what to write, students found it helpful to dictate the following introduction for their script

Narrator:

Where: Here we are in downtown Lexington

What it looks like: There used to me a beautiful creek here called Town Branch. Now, the creek is hidden underground. It runs underground through downtown Lexington under what will one day be Rupp Arena [Show map of Town Branch]

Why we are here: We are here to tell a story about the Town Branch creek and how Lexington finally got storm sewers. Travel back with us to the morning of August 2, 1932. We are in the home of Robert E. Mackenzie and his mother Alice Mackenzie, on Main Street in downtown Lexington.

FIG. 8.1.   Outline for script on the 1932 flood in Lexington, Kentucky.

TIME FOR REFLECTION AND ASSESSMENT

Third-grader Laine has been interviewing her classmates all week. She has a list of questions on a piece of loose-leaf paper attached to her clipboard.

"Are you ready to be interviewed?" she asks Jason and Suling.

"OK."

"Which of your questions took the most time to answer?"

Laine's interview goes on for some time. She is compiling the responses to use for an article about the research project on Lexington. As she interviews each group, the students pause to decide what things were hard, most interesting, or told them the most about Lexington. "Writing the script was hardest," Jason says. "And I'd never memorized lines before." For others, visiting the mayor and the trip downtown were most memorable. Alana describes how difficult it was for her to work with her partner. "We kept having different opinions about everything!" she says, although their final project is quite ambitious and involves taking Chelsea Clinton on an imaginary tour of Lexington. Taylor notes that he will make sure he writes down the important dates connected to events "so I can keep track of things better. I had this guy remembering things that happened before he was even born!" Finally, Stuart explains that he learned that "some things changed," but a lot of problems "just seem to be here all along."

As Laine's interview progresses, it becomes clear that, while her classmates found their recent study challenging, most of them also found it worthwhile and enjoyable. As Laine explains, "research is learning something. It's not just copying down information." These third graders also recognize that they are beginners, noting that next year they plan to improve in several areas. "I plan to improve on writing so that when I answer questions that need an explanation, I do a detailed explanation," Amara declares. Several of her classmates intend to practice "writing with more excitement" and "writing down what I think." Their comments reflect their struggles with interpretation. As one student notes, "it requires a lot of writing and thinking. You also have to go a lot of places just to figure one thing out. You have to make a lot of categories and lists." And, of course, once those categories and lists are created, students have to write down what they think it all means. This is a long-term project rather than a one-time event. In addition to considering children's performance in crafting one historical interpretation during one unit of instruction (see, for example, the suggestions in chap. 9), it also helps to consider their progress over time. Figure 8.2 provides one possible rubric for a more long-term assessment of student progress in developing supportable interpretations. Like the rubric in chapter 11 (Fig. 11.4), this is not intended to evaluate individual assignments. Instead, several examples of student-constructed interpretations—a script for a skit, for instance, along with samples of a student's notes, self-assessment, and video of the final production—might provide evidence for a student's location on the rubric. Not only does this information help Dehea understand how students are progressing individually and collectively, but it also helps her think about what further experiences her students might need as they learn to build supportable historical interpretations. This is part of what we mean by constructive assessment— thinking about teaching and learning as long-term enterprises rather than single events.

Self-reflection can be built into inquiry projects in different ways.
Hart (1999)

Levstik & Smith (1997)

Historical interpretation is a long-term project.
Gerwin & Zevin (2003), Levstik, Henderson, & Schlarb (2004), VanSledright (2003)

CONCLUSIONS

Dehea could have narrowed the focus of her community study to a more traditionally historical approach—the not uncommon "pioneers" unit. Instead, her work reflects a commitment to some of the principles outlined in the NCSS Standards document:

Novice	Developing	Proficient	Distinguished
Student provides a narrative that includes few historical referents or may simply provide a chronology of events. Student makes few causal links between events. Narrative may contain anachronisms, or judgments based on present day values. Student may rearrange chronology of events in order to forward a storyline.	Student includes some details that support the interpretation but may include anachronisms or make judgments based on present day values. Facts are not consistently related to each other or to a larger interpretive framework. Cause and effect relationships may be described but not supported by rich, historically grounded, details.	Student's interpretation is clear, coherent, and original (i.e., not copied from another source). It includes details that support the student's interpretation. The interpretation is plausible given the time and place depicted, and credible in terms of the history represented, given available information and level of experience of the student. The text (oral, written, visual) shows how facts are related to the student's larger interpretive framework, connecting a historical "effect" to possible causes.	Student's interpretation is clear, coherent, and original (i.e., not copied from another source). It is rich in the kinds of details that support student's interpretation. The interpretation is plausible given the time and place depicted, and credible in terms of the history represented. It is grounded in substantial historical data given available information and level of experience of the student. The text (oral, written, visual) shows how facts are related to each other and to the student's larger interpretive framework, connecting a historical "effect" to possible causes. Student acknowledges gaps in the historical record.

FIG. 8.2. Long-term rubric for historical interpretation.

- Teaching and learning integrate across the curriculum. Besides the integration of social studies disciplines such as history, geography, and political science, the students regularly drew on math and language arts and, especially in the reporting out phase, on the arts. As they reflected on their experiences as researchers, these third graders noted that many of their categories overlapped. "It was hard sometimes to decide if something was history, or like government, or maybe structures," commented one girl. Along with scholars from the various disciplines that comprise the social studies, they discovered that in-depth study of authentic issues frequently cuts across disciplinary boundaries and that it is often difficult to mark the place where one discipline begins and another ends.

- Students learn connected networks of knowledge, skills, beliefs, and attitudes that they will find useful both in and outside of school. In addition to learning to access information from print sources, students learned to use interviews, the built environment, and different types of maps. They gained experience in forming connected networks of knowledge and skills in putting together their presentations, as well as in reflecting on the process of inquiry.

Newmann et al. (1995)

- Teachers model seriousness of purpose and a thoughtful approach to inquiry and use instructional strategies designed to elicit and support similar qualities from students. Throughout the unit, Dehea modeled the practices she wanted students to learn and use. She also made sure that there were multiple opportunities for students to put these skills into action. Note taking, for instance, was not an exercise to be used at some future date. It was learned in a context where it was needed.

"Skills" are learned in context and through teacher modeling.

Students need to learn to discuss, agree, disagree, and support their ideas.

- Teachers show interest in and respect for students' thinking, but demand well-reasoned arguments rather than opinions voiced without adequate thought or commitment. A constant refrain throughout the community study was the emphasis on giving "facts and reasons to support your opinions." In addition, students were taught ways to agree and disagree that nurtured discussion rather than attacked individuals.

Historical study does not have to be organized chronologically over the school year.

Historical study puts current issues in historical context.

Clearly, history was a primary focus of the class' study. In fact, all but one of the group presentations were historical. Unlike studies of one period, however, this study shuttled between past and present. Sometimes this presented problems for children whose time sense was tenuous, but we think the benefits are considerable. First of all, students recognized the continuities in their community as well as the changes. They discovered that certain problems—flooding, for instance—persist over time. They were also able to make comparisons between current and historic issues such as crime and punishment. This helped put currently controversial issues into historical context. The constant comparison between past and present also encouraged students to determine historical significance at least in part on the basis of an event's impact on later times. Finally, we think the connections made between controversial issues, both historic and contemporary, and civic action are more likely to encourage students to see themselves and others as having historical agency—the power to make history. The next chapter deals more explicitly with issues of conflict, consensus, and historical agency in the history classroom.

Connecting historical and current issues can help students develop a sense of agency.

CHILDREN'S AND ADOLESCENT LITERATURE

Art and Architecture

Gaughenbaugh, M., & Camburn, H. *Old House, New House: A Child's Exploration of American Architectural Styles*. Preservation, 1994.

Manning, M. *A Ruined House*. Candlewick, 1994.

Wyeth, S. D. *Something Beautiful*. Delacorte, 1998.

Community Issues

Anderson, J. *Earth Keepers*. Gulliver Green, 1993.

Grossman, P. *Saturday Market*. Lothrop, 1994.

Kent, P. *Hidden Under the Ground: The World Beneath Your Feet*. Dutton, 1998.

Nichelason, M. G. *Homeless or Hopeless?* Lerner, 1994.

Showers, P. *Where Does the Garbage Go?* HarperCollins, 1993.

Communities Through Time

Ayoub, A., Binous, J., Gragueb, A., Mtimet, A., & Slim, H. *Umm El Madayan: An Islamic City Through the Ages*. Houghton, 1994.

Dorris, M. *Guests*. Hyperion, 1994.

Fix, P. *Not So Very Long Ago: Life in a Small Country Village*. Dutton, 1994.

Hall, D. *The Farm Summer, 1942*. Dial, 1994.

Levine, A. A. *Pearl Moscowitz's Last Stand*. Tambourine, 1994.

Millard, A. *A Street Through Time: A 12,000 Year Walk Through History*. DK Publishing, 1998.

Polacco, P. *Pink and Say*. Philomel, 1994.

Provensen, A., & Provensen, M. *Town and Country*. Browndeer, 1994.

Ray, M. L. *Shaker Boy*. Browndeer, 1994.

Sigerman, H. *Laborers for Liberty: American Women, (1865–1890)*. Oxford, 1994.

Sneve, V. D. H. *The Seminoles*. Holiday, 1994.

Wilson, K. *Earthquake!: San Francisco, 1906*. Steck-Vaughn, 1993.

Wilson, L. *Daily Life in a Victorian house*. Preservation, 1994.

People in Communities Around the World

Ancona, G. *Barrio: Jose's Neighborhood*. Harcourt Brace, 1998.

Ancona, G. *Pablo Remembers: The Fiesta of the Day of the Dead*. Lothrop, 1993.

Binch, C. *Gregory Cool*. Dial, 1994.

Calmenson, S. *Hotter Than a Hot Dog!* Little, 1994.

Carling, A. L. *Mama and Papa Have a Store*. Dial, 1998.

Chapman, R. *A Gift for Abuelita: Celebrating the Day of the Dead*. Rising Moon, 1998.

Chin, S. A. *Dragon Parade*. Steck-Vaughn, 1993.

Graff, N. P. *Where the River Runs: A Portrait of a Refugee Family*. Little, Brown, 1993.

Griffin, P. R. *The Brick House Burglars*. McElderry, 1994.

Jakobsen, K. *My New York*. Little, Brown, 1994.

Jenness, A. *Come Home With Me: A Multicultural Treasure Hunt*. New, 1994.

Keller, H. *Grandfather's Dream*. Greenwillow, 1993.

117

Kendall, R. *Russian Girl: Life in an Old Russian Town*. Scholastic, 1994.

Krull, K. *City Within a City: How Kids Live in New York's Chinatown,* 1994. Lodestar. (See also *The Other Side: How Kids Live in a California Latino Neighborhood*.)

Levinson, R. *Our Home Is the Sea*. Dutton, 1988.

Morris, A. *When Will the Fighting Stop? A Child's View of Jerusalem*. Atheneum, 1990.

Patrick, D. L. *The Car Washing Street*. Tambourine, 1994.

Roberts, D. *All Around Town: The Photographs of Samuel Roberts*. Holt, 1998.

Thiebaut, E. *My Village in Morocco: Mokhtar of the Atlas Mountains*. Silver Burdett, 1985.

Wright, D. K. *A Multicultural Portrait of Life in the Cities*. Cavendish, 1994.

9

WHY ISN'T THAT IN THE TEXTBOOK?

Fiction, Nonfiction, and Historical Thinking

As she comes in the door, Jennifer announces that there was team practice in answering social studies questions today. Each child made up a series of questions about the American Revolution, and these were used as part of a five-team contest. Jennifer's team tied for first place. "But this unit wasn't so good. All we did was learn about a few battles and fill in charts. I want to know a whole lot more!" She is particularly annoyed because so much of what she is learning in class either contradicts what she has read on her own or gives only part of the story.

"The text was talking about George Washington and how good he was to his soldiers. There was a part about Martha Washington knitting warm socks for the men, but in one of the books I read it said Washington had deserters at Valley Forge shot. Why wasn't that in the textbook? They just want you to think he was perfect."

This is not Jennifer's first encounter with the disjuncture between historical narratives and history texts. Earlier in the year, she announced during a small-group discussion that she thought Puritans were "cruel and stupid." Shocked, her classmate, William, called the teacher over and asked, "Do you know what Jennifer thinks!!"

"No," Mrs. Bainbridge answered.

"She thinks the Puritans were stupid!" William sputtered.

"Oh?" Mrs. Bainbridge smiled. "That's interesting. What made you decide that, Jennifer?"

Jennifer, having read two novels dealing with witchcraft in the early settlement and colonial periods, explained that Puritans had to be evil if they used religion as an excuse to torture and kill people. "They made their religion as bad as what they were trying to escape. It's wrong because you aren't the person to decide that … just because someone doesn't agree with you doesn't mean you have to kill them. And even if you were a person who didn't believe you would have to just act like you did, or you'd be in big trouble. They accused innocent people, and even if they were witches, they shouldn't have killed them. These people are supposed to believe in God, you know. Real religious. And God doesn't go around killing people."

Jennifer went on to argue that the textbook told "nothing interesting about the Puritans. They just said that the Puritans were very religious people who wanted to make religion more pure, and they didn't say anything about them, what they did bad … just that they were very organized people."

As we said earlier, historical stories are powerful cultural forces. They present historical interpretations in a memorable format; they also have a significant impact on children's historical thinking. It is commonplace to hear advocates of

Barber (1992), Blos (1993), Ehlers (1999), Levstik (1993), Olwell (1999)

119

Egan (1983, 1986),
Egan & Nadaner (1988)

History is more than a
story well told.

Barton (1996a), Levstik
(1995), VanSledright (1992)

Tunnell (1993)

For further discussion of
this issue, see also Bruner
(1986), Geertz (1983),
Kermode (1980),
Rabinowitz (1987),
Traugott & Pratt (1980),
Toolan (1988),
White (1980)

All narratives are created
within a sociocultural
framework.

Coerr (1994)

Narratives often make
connections between past
and present moral and
ethnical dilemmas.

Levstik (1989)

Coerr (1994)

Bruner (1986), Saul (1994)

Megill (1989, p. 633)

Depersonalized language
can also deproblematize
history.

Cushman (1994, p. 7)

history education claim that story, with its emphasis on human response to historical events, is the beginning of historical understanding. Moreover, a number of people argue that teaching history is largely a matter of presenting "a story well told." Clearly, narrative is a more powerful influence on Jennifer's historical thinking than her textbook. In fact, she judges the historical interpretation in her text and in her class work against the narrative history she reads independently. That she, or anyone else, should do this is not surprising. Stories are, after all, generally more compelling reading than textbooks. For centuries, historians have used narrative, and narrative devices, to order and assign cause and effect to events in the past. Yet Jennifer's experience indicates that the relationship among narrative, history, and historical understanding is more complex than appreciation of a story well told.

To begin with, defining what is meant by narrative is a challenge. Of course narratives are created and understood within a particular sociocultural context, so that definitions of narrative vary over time and between places and individuals. Generally, however, historical narratives are assumed to share certain elements with fictional stories and such nonfictional accounts as biographies, autobiographies, and traditional histories. They linguistically represent past experience, either real or imagined. Events in these narratives are expected to be connected—to have some point or conclusion. This may seem simple enough, but there is still quite a bit of difference between the grand narratives that present the rise and fall of empires and the narratives of individual agency Jennifer and others find so appealing, or even the more narrative textbooks now being published. And, because all narratives are created within a particular sociocultural context, no historical narrative (or any other genre for that matter) can possibly tell readers "the way it really was." Instead, narratives shape and interpret lives and events from the past, embedding them in a particular culture and often making direct parallels to the present. Consider, for example, how narrative shapes the events surrounding the destruction of Hiroshima in World War II. Perhaps you are familiar with Eleanor Coerr's book *Sadako*. (You may have read an earlier version, *Sadako and the Thousand Paper Cranes.)* Coerr does not simply lay out a chain of events and let readers make what interpretation they may. Instead, she carefully anchors her story in the details of one child's life and death to make a point about the present. The story has a clear moral—"This is our cry, this is our prayer: Peace in the world"—that resonates in the present as it gives meaning to the past. Compare this to Jennifer's experience with her history textbook: "The social studies book doesn't give you a lot of detail. You don't imagine yourself there because they're not doing it as if it were a person." For Jennifer, as for many children with whom we have worked, a narrative acts "as if it were a person" by particularizing and personalizing history. As Eleanor Coerr explains, "If you tell people that 200,000 died as a result of the bombing of Hiroshima, it doesn't have as much impact as the story of one little girl."

Neither a history textbook nor "battles and filling in charts" have this sense of personal agency. Listen to the depersonalized and lawlike voice so often used in textbooks: "*Whenever*, within a feudal system, towns and trade begin to grow …, *then* feudalism gives way to capitalism." This kind of language not only depersonalizes the transition from feudalism to capitalism, but it deproblematizes it as well. History, once again, is presented as the result of inexorable forces seemingly beyond human control. Compare that lawlike tone to the voice of Karen Cushman's *Catherine, Called Birdy*, describing a medieval manor during the same period:

> Today is quarter-rent day. My greedy father is near muzzle-witted with glee from the geese, silver pennies, and wagon loads of manure our tenants pay him. He guzzles ale and slaps his belly, laughing as he gathers in the rents. I like to sit near the table … and listen to the villagers complain about my father as they pay. I have gotten all my good insults and best swear words that way.

In this passage, the narrative voice is distinctly personal. Cushman touches on universal qualities—greed and gluttony, injustice, resentment, the need for dignity, and the capacity for fear and joy—as well as the economics of a medieval manor but locates them within a framework of human intentions. As *Catherine, Called Birdy* progresses, for instance, you discover that Catherine's father treats her with much the same greedy muzzle-wittedness as he does his tenants: He wants to marry her off like a "cheese sold to the highest bidder." He thinks a merchant would be a good choice because the newly developing towns are better off financially than small manors. Birdy, on the other hand, sets out to foil his attempts to arrange her life for his financial advantage. This small human drama contains many of the elements of the transition from feudalism to capitalism, but the narrative description of a greedy father swilling ale while his tenants suffer and selling his daughter to the highest bidder makes more intuitive sense than the distanced and lawlike explanations of the text (and it is much funnier!).

Cushman (1993, p. 7)

Of course not all historical narratives are either fictional or particularly personal. Increasingly, informational books for children present history in lively narrative (and nonnarrative) form. Russell Freedman's books on immigrant children, children of the Old West, and the like are certainly narrative—they tell a story (or stories) about American history—but they do not focus on a particular set of characters in the way that a biography or historical fiction might. Instead, Freedman weaves his story around the lives of people the reader may only meet for a moment.

Person & Cullinan (1992), Saul (1994)

Freedman (1980, 1983)

Milton Meltzer also writes nonfiction narrative history with a passion that captures readers' attention. He supports his narratives with personal accounts, as when he describes the work of children at Thomas Jefferson's Monticello nail factory. The factory was worked, he reports, by a dozen young slaves, ages 10 to 16. "They labored for twelve hours a day, six days a week. ... When several of the boys in his sweatshop ran off to freedom, Jefferson had them hunted down relentlessly and flogged when caught." Although this is not the story of a single child or even a single family, it certainly "tells it as if it were a person." In other words, Meltzer's and Freedman's works move beyond exposition—laying out the facts in order—to story—telling a tale "of common humanity ... to help young readers understand the world as it is, and to realize that we need not accept that world as it is given to us." Such narratives can help young readers see that, although the turn of historical events is not inevitable, economic, political, and social forces can sometimes overwhelm individual choice.

Well-written nonfictional narratives have voice and passion.

Meltzer (1994a, p. 24)

Meltzer (1994b, p. 21)

Historical events are influenced by more than individual choice.

Bardige (1988)

Part of the appeal of such narratives, as we have said, is that they have a moral. This is probably because the most readily available schema students have to bring to bear in understanding history are "human behavior" schema, where morality, or at least fairness, is often a central concern. In addition to being readily available, too, these schema are among the most fully developed, especially in young children. Moreover, they are particularly appropriate in understanding historical fiction, biography, and autobiography, based as they are on the particulars of human, and often child, behavior. Unfortunately, they are not equally useful in interpreting historical textbooks, in which individual human intentions and motivations are often replaced by political and economic analyses. As a result, students may find it more difficult to identify and recall these more analytical historical accounts without considerable assistance.

Barton (1997a), Brophy & VanSledright (1997), Carretero, Jacott, Limón, Manjón, & León (1994), Jacott, López-Manjón, & Carretero (1998), Levstik & Pappas (1987), Riviere, Núñez, Barquero, & Fontela (1998)

Because children have more readily available schema for interpreting some types of historical narrative, however, does not mean that these are the only texts they should read or that children are naturally critical readers of narratives. In fact, narrative is not the only history genre available to students, and the very accessibility of narratives may work against critical reading—if the narrative is intuitively right, its underlying historical interpretation is unlikely to elicit criticism. In addition, the ethical and moral context of the narratives we

Children are not naturally critical of historical narratives.

The moral content of narratives adds weight to their historical perspective.

Coerr (1994),
Cushman (1994)

O'Dell (1980),
Speare (1958)

Levstik (1989)

It can be very difficult to dislodge interpretations drawn from well-written narratives. *Levstik (1995)*

Collier & Collier (1974),
Forbes (1967), Fritz
(1967), Turner (1992)

Too often textbooks underestimate children's ability to handle complexity. *Ehlers (1999), Mayer (1999), Olwell (1999)*

An outline of events is rarely memorable or persuasive to students.

Degenhardt & McKay (1988)

Narrative can support informed and disciplined imaginative entry into history.

Teachers can honor children's search for truth while helping them become more analytical in their response to different historical perspectives.

Bardige (1988)

have described adds enormous weight to an author's historical perspective. Readers of books such as *Sadako* or *Catherine, Called Birdy* may find out how particular people lived their daily lives and that more than one point of view existed, but they are invited to sympathize with or at least understand the protagonist's point of view. When Jennifer read *Sarah Bishop* and *The Witch of Blackbird Pond,* she clearly identified with Sarah and Kit, the main characters in each book. Although she recognized that another view of the events was possible, she was still convinced that such a view "would be an awful story. ... They'd probably try and make it seem that the witches [Sarah and Kit are accused of witchcraft] were awful."

In other words, to the extent that young readers believe a story, they also read it as "telling what really happened." As Jennifer explains, "Even if it weren't all true, it could have been true, and it could have happened like that." This can make it hard to dislodge narrative interpretations, especially if no equally compelling case is made for alternative perspectives.

As she read different novels, Jennifer encountered a variety of historical perspectives on the American Revolution. In the Collier brothers' novel, *My Brother Sam Is Dead*, British and Loyalist sympathizers and the American Rebels commit atrocities, and there is little to choose between them. In Jean Fritz's *Early Thunder*, good and evil exist in both Loyalist and Rebel camps, and people of conscience choose where they think the most good must lie. Esther Forbes' *Johnny Tremain* presents a clear argument for the Rebel cause, and *Katie's Trunk* shows the Rebels as disgruntled marauders. It was clear to Jennifer that the textbook version was inadequate. The textbook, she declared, just said that "Americans were right but it doesn't tell you exactly why they were right, or why the British fought." She expected—and wanted—history to be interpretive and to involve moral issues. She wasn't interested in neutrality so much as in trying to understand why the two sides fought. You may think that the textbook does precisely that. It outlines the events leading up to rebellion and military conflict: taxation without representation, British control of the colonial economy, ideas about "unalienable rights." But these reasons, potent as they may be to historians, are not fully explanatory for students. From Jennifer's perspective, such explanations are neither persuasive nor memorable precisely because they ignore the human behavior schema we have already discussed.

Jennifer was angered by what she perceived as the single perspective taken by her textbook—Americans (Rebels) were right. In her reading, she had already encountered other perspectives and expected a more complete story. She wanted to be engaged by history, rather than distanced from it. Unfortunately, expository texts that emphasize greater and greater degrees of abstraction while trying to maintain a neutral or "objective" stance often distance students from history. Well-written, historically sound narratives (fiction as well as nonfiction), on the other hand, can support informed and disciplined imaginative entry into events—and help students make better sense out of expository texts. This is not sugarcoating the bitter pill of academic history, or turning history into one big storytelling session. Dealing explicitly with students' ethical sensitivities is, we think, more likely to make history a compelling part of the curriculum. This requires, however, a delicate balance between honoring children's search for historical truth and developing their recognition that other people in other times saw the world differently—not just from us, but from each other. Students do tend to value the "truthfulness" of historical narratives and use narrative interpretations as the standard against which other information is measured. What we are suggesting, then, is that a variety of good literature, combined with careful teacher facilitation, can help students see and understand the complexities that multiple historical perspectives suggest without sacrificing their ethical sensitivities and impulses.

SELECTING GOOD NARRATIVE HISTORY

Obviously, any piece of historical narrative is not as good as any other. In fact, if you read much historical fiction from the first half of the 20th century you might well wonder whether historical narratives have *any* relation to "what really happened." Geoffrey Trease, an author of historical fiction, listed just a few of the restrictions that applied to children's historical fiction in the 1950s: no liquor, no supernatural phenomenon, no undermining of authority, no parents with serious weaknesses, no realistic working-class speech (including even the mildest cursing), and no budding love affairs. As if these restrictions were not deadening enough, texts sprinkled with "prithees," "methinks," and the like produced historical caricatures rather than historically authentic characters. The historical realism of the type that garnered *Catherine, Called Birdy* a Newbery Honor award is a relative newcomer to children's literature. Unfortunately, the problems with historical fiction are not confined to the past. Some more recent fiction is also blatantly inaccurate, cursed with tunnel vision, and mired in romanticism. In other books, historical events are rearranged or facts are omitted to avoid controversy. A biography of Andrew Jackson, for instance, may barely mention the forced evacuation of the Cherokee, while books on Columbus often ignore the impact of exploration on the inhabitants of the "New World."

Trease (1983)

Historical realism in children's literature is a relative newcomer to the field.

Cushman (1994)

The teachers throughout this book rely heavily on historical fiction as well as informational books. Initially, most of them felt intimidated by the task of selecting historically accurate, well-written literature. They weren't all history majors and didn't always know the latest scholarship. Over the years, however, they developed selection criteria that worked for them. The following guidelines represent the kinds of considerations these teachers have found useful:

- Does the book tell a good story? Scholarship is not enough to carry historical fiction. If the narrative does not hold up, even the best-documented history will not matter. Ask yourself if the book you are considering tells a story that is interesting in its own right, blending fact and fiction so that the historical background is subordinate, but essential, to the story. In Margaree King Mitchell's *Uncle Jed's Barbershop*, living in the segregated South of the 1920s is the backdrop for a story of commitment to family, as well as dreams deferred and realized. Yet the backdrop is integral to the story. Segregation and economic collapse are the stage on which the story is played out:

    Even though I was unconscious, the doctors wouldn't look at me until they had finished with all the White patients....
    My daddy didn't have that kind of money. And the doctors wouldn't do the operation until they had the money.

Huck, Kiefer, & Hepler (2004)

A book must be good literature *and* good history.

Mitchell (1998)

- Is the story accurate and authentic in its historical detail, including the setting and the known events of history? Again, this attention to accuracy and authenticity must not detract from the story. Instead, the historical details should make the story ring true—not just in the description and use of material culture but also in the values and spirit of the time. As Karen Cushman notes, the differences between past and present run deeper than what people in the past ate, where (or when) they bathed, or who decided to marry whom. Historical people lived "in a place we can never go, made up of what they value, how they think, and what they believe is true and important and possible."

Children's fiction deserves the same attention to historical accuracy as nonfiction.

- Is the language authentic to the times? This is a challenging criterion. For one thing, the language of the past, even if it were English, is not the English spoken anywhere today. Instead of striving for complete authenticity, then, look for language that has the flavor of the times. Idioms, for instance, should be plausible given both the historical period and the characters. One of the delights of *Catherine, Called Birdy* is Birdy's experimentation with cursing. Her brother tells her that the king no longer says "Deus!" or "Corpus Bones!" as "ordinary folk do." Instead, he uses "God's breath!" Her brother adopts "God's feet." Not to be outdone, Birdy tries a different oath each day. First she tries "God's face," then "God's ears," and finally settles on "God's Thumb," "because thumbs are such important things and handy to use."

Cushman (1994, p. 165)

- Is the historical interpretation sound? Overly romanticized, outdated interpretations may be useful for comparison's sake but not for the core of literature to be used in class. Select several books representing the same topic from different perspectives and make sure that each perspective is supportable given what is currently known about the topic. Make

Completely authentic language is rarely possible in children's historical fiction. Look for the flavor of the times.

Avoid overly romanticized historical fiction.

Conley (1992)

sure characters act in accordance with these interpretations. In Robert Conley's *Nickajack,* the Cherokee nation has split into warring factions, some advocating resistance to the treaty that took away their homelands, others advocating cooperation and relocation. Conley based his story on recent scholarship about the period immediately following the "Trail of Tears." Its impact comes, at least in part, because of the inexorability of the central tragedy—the continuation of vengeance. In the last paragraph of the book, one character lies dying and his wife sinks to her knees: "The murderer's face was firmly etched in her mind. She would never forget it. This was not the end."

Conley (1992, p. 182)

- Whose voices are missing? Because literature is so powerful, it is important to select as many different, historically sound perspectives as possible. Think about who the participants in an event were and how those participants might have told their story. Traditional stories of the Westward Movement, for instance, have often been told from the perspective of white male pioneers moving from East to West. More recently, however, literature focusing on women, on Native Americans, and on Spanish perspectives have begun to appear. Jan Hudson's *Sweetgrass* and *Dawn Rider,* Liz Sonneborn's *The American West: An Illustrated History,* Julius Lester and Jerry Pinkney's *Black Cowboy, Wild Horses,* and Sollace Holtze's *A Circle Unbroken* are a small sample of some of the books now available that provide insight into the impact of culture clash in the American West.

Consider who the participants in an event might have been, and select literature to represent those perspectives.

Hudson (1989, 1990), Cornel (1993), Holtze (1988), Wright (1995), Burks (1998)

Well-written historical narratives speak to the present as well as about the past.

- Does the book provide insight and understanding into current issues as well as those in the past? As we said in the first chapter, history is not just about people in the past but also about the connections between past and present: How did people come to their current circumstances, and how might they shape the future? Well-written historical narratives speak to each of these conditions. It is no accident that as we struggle to come to terms with our collective histories, we rethink many aspects of the past and come to tell new stories about ourselves and others. A recounting of the building of the transcontinental railroad, for instance, is no longer a simple and single story of European Americans conquering the wilderness. Instead, it is also the story of Chinese and Irish immigrants, of displaced Native Americans, and of the fear and racism that accompanied expansion. As a result, Lawrence Yep's *Dragon's Gate,* or Yin and Soentpiet's *Coolies,* are not just about a young Chinese boy's experiences working on the railroad but about the struggle of many immigrants to survive in a new land.

Yep (1994), Yin & Soentpiet (2003)

As we emphasize throughout the book, students of history need experience with multiple historical genres. Fiction is certainly one of these genres, but so is informational (or nonfiction) literature. Sometimes adults assume that students prefer fiction to nonfiction, but we have not found this to be the case. Students not only hunger for information about their world, they crave expertise. Think about all the classroom experts on athletics, computers, music, cars, and the like. Many students regularly turn to informational sources in support of leisure pursuits. In classrooms where nonfiction is used in meaningful ways, students select it at least as often as they select fiction. Moreover, where inquiry is the basic approach to history, informational literature is an essential classroom resource.

Students need a variety of fiction and nonfiction.

Dayton-Sakari & Jobe (2003), Duke & Bennett-Armistead (2003), Kristo & Bamford (2004), Pappas (1991)

Ruby Yessin often starts the school day by reading and discussing nonfiction with her first grade class. During these times, illustrations are discussed, facts checked and questions raised about the authenticity of the information. A pop-up book of historical sailing vessels, for instance, fascinates her students and sends them to other books on Columbus to see if they accurately represent the Niña, Pinta, and Santa Maria. In Ruby's class, a child may be called upon to check with the librarian for further information or to use one of the reference books in the classroom to answer questions raised in reading an informational book. Children keep these books at their desks and are allowed to read them during "free reading time." In fact, several students prefer to check out informational books for home reading, too.

Levstik (1993)

When nonfiction receives the kind of attention usually accorded fiction, students respond with enthusiasm.

Extensive and intensive use of fiction and nonfiction builds a "web of meaning" in the classroom.

Many of these informational books are difficult for Ruby's students, but they read as much as they can and allow the teacher, their partners, or other adults to help them understand the rest. It is not unusual in the classroom for a visitor to be asked to read an informational book to a first grader intent on finding out about Shakers, Columbus, or China. Ruby explains that her extensive use of in-

124

formation literature is part of the "web of meaning" that she and the children are building. In her class, "finding out" is so highly valued that there is plenty of incentive for making use of nonfiction. Fortunately, there is more and more high quality nonfiction available for all ages. Just as with fiction, however, carful selection is important. While Ruby does a lot of book selection on her own, she also relies on recommendations from the school librarian and her colleagues. In general, Ruby uses the following selection criteria:

"Finding out" is a valued activity in inquiry-oriented classrooms.

- What are the qualifications of the author? A quick check of the "About the Author" page in a book or on the book's jacket will generally let you know what qualifications an author possesses. Sometimes an author is not an expert on a topic but has consulted with people who are and acknowledges them in the book. Jerry Stanley, for instance, is a history professor who knew a good deal about the background for Japanese internment during World War II, but his book, *I Am an American: A True Story of Japanese Internment,* relies heavily on interviews with Shi Nomura and other former internees. As a result of these firsthand recollections, Stanley's book has a greater degree of authenticity and sensitivity than he could have provided on his own.

Stanley (1994)

- How accurate and complete are the facts? It has been our experience that the most blatant errors in historical nonfiction have more to do with what is left out than with errors of fact. Books on Native Americans, for instance, too often deal only with life on the frontier or lump all Native peoples into one amorphous group of *Indians*. Books on traditional heroes may present one-sided portraits of such complex people as Abraham Lincoln or Martin Luther King, Jr. One way to guard against errors of either commission or omission is to invite students to compare different versions of historical people and events, noting where sources differ, and researching to find the most supportable facts. In addition, *Social Education* and *Hornbook* publish yearly reviews of children's literature by topic. *Social Education* confines its reviews to books specifically related to social studies topics, and *Hornbook* provides a more general guide with sections on social science, history, families, technology, and the like.

Even when the facts are accurate, check to see whether important information or perspectives are missing.

- Is the book up-to-date? Children in one primary classroom found a book in their collection that discussed the history of space travel, noting in its conclusion that one day man might walk on the moon. Though the children, who all knew full well that people had been to the moon and back several times, found this book amusing, other errors are more likely to go unnoticed. Children might not notice sweeping generalizations that identify an entire group of people as, for instance, thrifty or prone to violence. Illustrations may also misrepresent information. Far too many books on Thanksgiving, for instance, have the wrong Indians meeting the Pilgrims. Similarly, illustrations of prehistoric people assign gender roles—men creating rock art or cave paintings, for instance—when there is no archaeological evidence for assigning these roles to one gender rather than another. Checking publication dates is a good place to start in ascertaining whether a book is relatively current. Examining illustrations for datedness and stereotypes also helps. Nevertheless, some books will slip through with mistakes or misrepresentations. Don't toss them out. In an era of budget cutbacks and limited resources, even weak books have their uses. Encourage students to bring a critical eye to bear on their reading of all sorts of fact and fiction. Just remember that these books require teacher mediation. You will have to help students notice the errors, perhaps by contrasting different treatments of a subject as LeeAnn did when her class studied Columbus.

- Does the author distinguish between fact and supposition? One of the best examples of this is Jean Fritz' *The Double Life of Pocahontas*. Unlike books that tell a straightforward rescue story, Fritz acknowledges throughout the text that much of what we know about Pocahontas cannot be verified. In fact, she explains that there is little evidence that Pocahontas saved John Smith's life at all. In similar fashion, Kathy Pelta's *Discovering Christopher Columbus: How History is Invented* systematically deconstructs the Columbus story, explaining how and why this story has changed over time and what sources are known to exist. Some authors, including Russell Freedman, provide extensive endnotes that include sources, discussions of different interpretations, and other books students might want to read on the same topic. Be especially cautious about books that seem overly romanticized, too-good-to-be-true depictions of the past. Too often this means an author has uncritically accepted tradition, rather than critically analyzing sources to write good history.

Fritz (1983)

Pelta (1991)

Freedman (1993, 1994)

Check the author's notes for sources of additional information.

- How well is the book organized? Generally, an author's sense of purpose and prospective audience helps shape how a book is organized. A good deal of nonfiction will not be

Think about how the
readers will use the
nonfiction you select.

Miller & Miller (2003)

Saul (1994)

Meltzer (1994)

Kobrin (1995)

Bookbird is published
quarterly by the Inter-
national Board on Books
for Young People (IBBY).

Selection of good books is
not enough; organizing
their use is crucial.

Cushman (1994),
Fleischman (1992), Aliki
(1983), Macaulay (1977),
McDonald (1997),
Sancha (1990)

Book sets help organize
students' reading. Smith &
Barton (1997)

McKinley (1984)

Focusing student
attention on the historical
substance of literature
requires careful teacher
planning.

Keating (1994), Wells &
Chang-Wells (1992),
Atwell (1990)

Cushman (1994),
Fleischman (1992)

read cover to cover, or at least not in front-to-back order. Instead, readers of nonfiction often skip around, searching for a particular piece of information or explanation. Illustrations are very important in this search, and should complement and extend the information in the text. Captions should let readers know what they are seeing in clear and vivid language. Increasingly, authors and publishers of informational books include interactive features. *Journey of Hope: The Story of Irish Immigration to America,* for instance, includes pull-out primary source material such as letters, maps, and photographs along with fold-out pages of additional information. Think about how readers might use this book, and check for a useable index and table of contents.

- What literary distinction does the book have? A good piece of literature reveals the personal style of the author. As Milton Meltzer notes, if a writer is "indifferent, bored, stupid or mechanical" it will show in the work. The facts must be there, of course, but so must the author's voice and vision. The author shapes the facts, and in that shaping makes some facts more significant than others. Meltzer, for instance, could have simply described the tasks given to the young men working in Thomas Jefferson's nail factory and left out the personal cost of those tasks. Instead, his powerful authorial voice makes vivid the desperation of these young men: "The work was so repetitive, boring, mindless, and of course, payless that they did as little as possible … several of the boys in his sweatshop ran off to freedom.…" In a work of literary distinction, the author cares about the topic as, most likely, will the reader. For help in finding these kinds of books, check out *Eyeopeners II: Children's Books to Answer Children's Questions About the World Around Them,* a guide to informational books for children, and *Bookbird,* a journal specializing in international children's literature.

Selecting good books is, of course, just the beginning. Organizing their use is crucial to helping students appreciate the books they read as literature and as historical interpretations. Several teachers find *book sets* help students move beyond an attachment to a single perspective. A *book set* usually includes paired selections of fiction—Cushman's *Catherine, Called Birdy* and Fleischman's *The Whipping Boy* for a medieval study—and several informational books at different levels of difficulty—perhaps Aliki's *Medieval Wedding,* Macaulay's *Castle,* McDonalds's *How Would You Survive in the Middle Ages,* and Sancha's *The Luttrell Village: Country Life in the Middle Ages.* In Abby Mott's classroom, she combines book sets that the students read with at least one read-aloud novel. For the medieval unit, for instance, she chose McKinley's *The Outlaws of Sherwood,* a retelling of the Robin Hood legend that reinterprets the roles played by Robin and Marian. Sometimes students only read one of the paired books and the selection that Abby reads aloud serves as contrast. In the medieval set, however, both books are relatively short, so she required that students read both.

Abby discovered early on that simply assigning reading is not always motivating. After a couple of years of trying different techniques, she settled on several things that seemed to engage her students in discussing historical perspective. First, she found that dialogue journals provided an important opportunity for students to discuss their personal responses to their readings. In the dialogue journals, Abby and her students carry on a written conversation about the books they read or hear. Sometimes Abby asks students to respond to a specific question such as, "What do you think are the most important differences between your life and Birdy's?" This question might require little beyond reading *Catherine, Called Birdy* and thinking about how an adolescent's life has changed over time (or not). In other cases, she asks questions such as, "How accurate do you think Cushman's and Fleischman's depictions of the Middle Ages are?" and "What sources helped you answer this question?" These require more attention to the construction of a historical interpretation and encourage students to draw on the nonfiction sources in the book. Abby also found that peer discussion helped students move beyond their first impressions of a book. Because not all students necessarily read the books at the same time, she arranges two types of response groups of three to five students each. The first is a discussion opportunity for students who are reading the same book. Abby may start the group with a couple of questions or a problem that will require their reference to the book they are reading and will focus on both the literary and historical aspects of the book. In one group, for example, she asks students to select three passages that show how *Birdy* changes over the course of the book. In another, students search for passages that capture the differences between life in the manor and in the village. A third group selects historical descriptions from Birdy that can be supported by evidence from one of the informational books. Notice that the groups are not duplicating each other. Instead, each group is organized so that it will have something specific to contribute to a follow-up discussion among response groups.

The second type of response group mixes students who have read different books. The tasks for such a group might involve creating a list of medieval rules for child rearing, writing a description of medieval wedding customs that have current counterparts, making a comparison chart of the roles of different levels of medieval society, or creating a story map that locates each of the places described in the books. In one class, a group discussing child rearing practices was appalled at the level of violence directed against children. They collected current information about child abuse, found other books on child labor, and ended up making a chart of requirements for a "child-friendly world." Abby then gave them a copy of the U.N. Declaration on the Rights of Children and asked them to compare it to their own recommendations.

As you can see, some of these activities were relatively short term—writing a dialogue journal entry—whereas others became in-depth studies—the child rearing practices, for instance. Students had opportunities to share what they were thinking with their teacher and with small groups of their peers. In the small groups, most of that sharing happened in conversation. But not all students find this the most effective way to share what they know, and even in the most supportive environment not all students participate equally in conversation. As we discuss in chapter 13, honoring students' different ways of knowing is as important in history as in any other cognitive domain.

Abby discovered early in her teaching career that creating opportunities for students to respond to their reading using a variety of media resulted in richer historical thinking. During their medieval study, her seventh graders presented a reader's theater production, *Rent Day*, based in part on Aliki's *Medieval Wedding*, where the lives of a noble and his tenants are juxtaposed, and drawing on *Catherine, Called Birdy, Luttrell Village*, and the students' research in other books. In *Rent Day*, different characters living on a medieval manor describe their feelings about their lives, the people with whom they live, and the practice of paying rent to the lord of the manor. Another group created a mural styled after the Bayeaux tapestry, except that instead of depicting the Norman conquest, their tapestry contrasted life on the feudal manor with life in the newly created merchant towns. With help from their music teacher, another group put on a concert of recorder music that might have been heard in a medieval castle. One of the more interesting presentations involved the sale of Papal indulgences. Several students had focused on Birdy's brother, Edward, a monk working in a scriptorium, on her description of Jews forced to leave England, and on the religious activities at village fairs and in Birdy's home. In their research, they discovered that monks and priests sometimes sold indulgences—Papal forgiveness for mortal and venial sins committed for a set period of time. The students created illuminated "indulgences" for the characters in each book, including pictures of the torments of hell and the delights of heaven (authentic to illuminated manuscripts of the time) as well as descriptions of the sins each character needed to have forgiven (based on the students' analysis of the books they were reading).

As students worked on these projects, questions arose that sent them back to their reading. Sometimes debates would reignite as new information came to light. By arranging opportunities to encounter and reencounter a topic, Abby

Good questions facilitate response group discussions.

Zarnowski (1998), Maxim (1998), Wilhelm (1998)

When students read different books, discussions focus on comparison and contrast, as well as supportable arguments.

Gardner & Boix-Mansilla (1994)

Encourage a variety of ways to respond to history.

Aliki (1983), Cushman (1994), Sancha (1990)

Bickmore (1999), Levstik & Smith (1996), Wells & Chang-Wells (1992), Wilhelm (1998)

provided a context for communal construction of meaning. Students adjusted their ideas not just in response to the text or teacher comment, but on the basis of interactions with their peers. In addition, Abby encouraged reference to other sources of information. When a dispute over the accuracy of historical information arose, she arbitrated first by having students check each author's credentials and then by sending students to the library to look for confirming or disconfirming information. In doing so, she directed them to other history genres—art, primary sources, textbooks.

Finally, Abby used literature as a springboard to more in-depth inquiry. Based on their reading, students selected other topics to investigate. They were very interested in child rearing, general feudal practices, and the kinds of jobs people might do as adults, in addition to the usual fascination with knights, armor, King Arthur, and Robin Hood. These became individual and group projects that were presented at a medieval fair attended by parents and students from other grades. Notice that, although children began with a personal response to narrative—"It made me frustrated for Birdy" or "I thought that she should just run away with Perkin!"—they were also encouraged (indeed, required) to move beyond narrative. Their interest might be captured by a well-written story, but their responses were educated by a wide variety of genres.

"I DID NOT PANIC": CREATING HISTORICAL NARRATIVES

April 6, 1862

"Boom!" The cannon thundered across the sky. That's what happened on this bloody day. Even now the gunboats' cannon flash across the sky. I can hear the cry of wounded but nobody dares help them. I've heard the tales about bloody battles but none could be as bad as this! Men were falling all around me but I did not panic! The situation is grim but we'll hang on although General Sherman was wrong before, he's pulling us through.

So we Yanks ain't licked yet!

—Hugh B. McKay

Every piece of writing stands on the shoulders of all the literature that came before it. This is as true of your students' writing as it is of a published author's. Consider the sources for the prior diary entry. The fifth grader who wrote this heard *Thunder at Gettysburg* and *The Drummer Boy of Shiloh* and read actual diaries from the period. Relying largely on primary sources and historical narratives, he and his classmates reconstructed the life of a Union soldier injured at the Battle of Shiloh. Although this student is also in a classroom that overflows with books and in which he expects to write in a variety of genres, he has had little prior experience with primary sources. Nevertheless, narrative devices, including the use of dialect and first-person narration, are familiar and comfortable literary tools for him. Writing is an important way in which he and his classmates construct their own historical interpretations. Students who have not been similarly immersed in literature may be less likely to produce as literate a narrative, but all students can benefit from the opportunity to create historical narratives.

Pamela Vachon's fifth-grade students eagerly anticipated their upcoming study of the Civil War. In previous years, the study had included a reenactment of the Battle of Shiloh. A storage closet contained a tempting collection of military paraphernalia, including hats and flags that Pamela's predecessor had acquired as he visited historic sites. Unfortunately, as far as Pamela was concerned, the main thing that the students seemed to anticipate was the romance of feather cockades, gold tassels, and cardboard bayonets. She was especially surprised at how many of the students wanted to be Confederates. They were, after all, in a Union state and in an area that had sent many men to

Arbitrate rather than eliminate intellectual disputes.

Levstik (1998), Zarnowski (1998)

Literature is not the end of historical study; it is one source among many.

Gauch (1974), Clarke (1974)

All children can benefit from writing their own historical narratives.

fight for the Union. As it turned out, the appeal of the Confederacy had little to do with sympathy for the "lost cause." Instead, as Jacob, one of her students, explained, "The Confederate uniforms are better. Those big feathers are great!" Although there was no way to avoid reenacting the battle—it was a tradition started long before her entry into the school and involved all the fifth grades in the district—Pamela decided that she could better prepare her students to understand the historical context and the costs of war.

Pamela's students loved historical fiction, especially when she read aloud to them; they were also used to vigorous discussions of literature. When she introduced Arthur C. Clark's *The Drummer Boy of Shiloh*, they settled in their seats expectantly. As she finished the story and the students discussed their responses, Pamela called their attention to the list of questions they had previously developed for historical fiction:

Read aloud to students of all ages.

Clarke (1974)

- What would you need to know in order to write this story?
- Where would you find the necessary information?
- How does the author help you understand what the characters are feeling?
- What other options did the character have given this time and setting?
- Could this story have been told from another point of view?
- In what ways might this story have been different had it been set in our time and place?

Students can generate discussion questions for different historical genres.

With Clarke's vivid images of Shiloh as introduction, Pamela asked students to carefully analyze a portrait displayed on the overhead. This was a picture of a man from a small town in Ohio, she explained. What clues could they find to the time when this person lived? Did they think this was a wealthy or poor person? As the students made their observations, Pamela recorded them on sheets of chart paper. Next, she showed them a primary source—a surgeon's report on an injury. This document, she told them, was a piece of evidence to help them figure out the identity of the person in the picture. As a class, they discussed the document, listing new information and new questions that were raised.

Over the course of the next several days, Pamela introduced a variety of other sources that she had collected and organized in folders:

- Public Documents: Military records, surgeons' reports, and pension applications available from the National Archives.
- Family Records: Obituaries, a county history that included Hugh's family, and photographs. The pictures were from a family collection. The rest of the materials were from the county library and local historical society. Some collections also have photographs.
- Newspapers: Samples from Hugh's hometown paper included stories about secession, as well as farming news, recipes for sorghum and butter, advice, poetry, and local politics. Pamela's local library had old newspapers on microfilm; in some areas, these are kept in state and local historical societies or university libraries.
- Samples of Personal Writing: Other people witnessed the events Hugh lived through. Several diaries and collections of letters were available in the state historical society's manuscript collection as well as in periodicals such as *Civil War Times Illustrated*.
- Other Sources: Maps, drawings, photographs, and a time line of events from April 1861 through April 1865 provided a graphic framework for the other primary sources. Pamela used material from textbooks and photocopied pictures from Civil War histories.

Each day's work was organized around a set of questions related to the sources with which students worked. For the obituary of Hugh's mother, for instance, students were asked how many siblings Hugh had and what had happened to them by 1898. Pamela also moved between groups, helping them decipher antique penmanship or asking probing questions: Was this document sufficient evidence for a particular interpretation? What seemed to be the general feeling of the new soldiers as they marched South? Although each group worked with the same set of documents, their interpretations were often quite different, and discussions at the end of work sessions were lively. Pamela found that she needed to make rules for polite debate and discussion and finally spent time establishing ground rules for "supportable interpretations:"

- Evidence must be from a reliable source. Check publication date, author, possible bias.
- Interpretations should be true to the values and social rules of the time. Think about how people thought *then* not now.
- You cannot move historic events around just to suit your interpretation. You have to account for the facts.

Pamela reminded students that historians have similar arguments and that agreement was not required, although supportable interpretations were. She also found that, although students enjoyed the "decoding" aspect of reading primary sources, some sources just produced frustration. In deciding how to handle this, her students suggested developing a "primary source key," showing common forms of script for a specific time period. Pamela also decided that next time she would transcribe some of the most difficult sources.

Although some primary sources may need to be translated, most should be used as is.

Fulwiler (1982), Hartse & Short (1988), Short & Hartse (1996)

After each day's work, Pamela asked students to write a letter or diary entry based on what they had learned about Hugh. Writing encouraged students to think about what they knew and could support. It also required organizing information in some meaningful way. In the prior sample, the student author included details about the battle obtained from reading diary entries from other soldiers. He also incorporated an assessment of General Sherman based on a letter from another soldier. Another student discovered that field hospitals were used at Shiloh and incorporated that information into her story, along with details from the surgeon's report on Hugh's injury:

> Dear Diary,
>
> Today I got shot in the hand. My hand is almost completely destroyed. My middle finger is completely gone. I went to the field tent. The doctors did not do anything because there were other more important patients. I am not writing this diary entry, my best friend is. I am telling him what to write.

This type of writing certainly gives the teacher clues as to how well students understand source materials, but it also challenges children's notions of the romance of war. There was little in Hugh's story, or in any of the other sources, about feathers, sabers, and gold tassels. Instead, soldiers' letters and diaries describe rain and mud, terror, injury, and death. In one vivid diary entry, a young soldier described struggling to find a place to sleep with no shelter from the pouring rain and discovering in the morning that he had spent the night sleeping against a pile of amputated limbs discarded behind the field hospital. In response, a student wrote about April 7, 1862:

> Today is the worst day of my life. It seems as if all my friends are dead.... We are being picked off like grapes off a grape vine.

Although Pamela felt that her main purpose was achieved by having the students write diary entries or letters home, other teachers who have used primary sources find that the students benefit from the experience of writing a final, more comprehensive narrative. This takes time and access to all the sources that students have used throughout their project. One sixth-grade teacher has students write historical fiction based on the sources they have investigated. The characters do not have to be real, but the historical context must be authentic. This allows students to fill in the gaps in the historical record while remaining true to the period or situation.

Although young children can make less use of some types of written primary sources, they are perfectly capable of using art, artifacts, and interviews to write and illustrate biographies based on living people. Children's picture books can often suggest different techniques to use in creating biographies. One first grader, for instance, created postcards to tell the story of her uncle, a soldier stationed in Germany. The idea for postcards came from another book her teacher had read, *The Jolly Postman*.

Ahlberg & Ahlberg (1986)

ANALYZING STUDENTS' HISTORICAL NARRATIVES

As Pamela planned for the creation of historical narratives with her students, she considered different ways to assess their work. Although she intended to assess the *medium* or *surface* features of students' writing—control of grammatical structures, spelling, and the like—Pamela's main concern was with the *message* or *content* components of students' work. These included the use of sources to support interpretations, the completeness of the interpretations, the sequencing of events, and the degree to which interpretations were period appropriate, as well as students' facility with letter and diary genres. Along with many of the teachers you have already met in this book, Pamela had experience assessing students' written work *as writing*. She worried, however, about finding ways to assess *historical* writing. Pamela decided that she could adapt some literacy strategies to history. She began with the "ground rules" she had already developed with her students. Figure 9.1 shows the analysis sheet Pamela devel-

For more on assessing message and medium components of written work, see *Pappas et al. (1999)*

Students need feedback on the historical as well as literary aspects of their writing. *Marcello (1999)*

Student: Andrea	Date:
Questions	**Analysis/Observation**
How well does the student control the genre being attempted?	The first entry puts the action in the present tense, rather than as a reflection. The second entry sounds more "diary-like"—and very much like the Civil War diaries we read last week. She's picked up some of the language, too—"my dear Millie" and "determined woman." Still confusing desert/dessert. Is nonstandard spelling taken from other diaries or is it her own miscue?
Is the text historical? Could a reader identify the time, event, or issue depicted?	Andrea has made good use of the primary sources in each entry. She gives the reader some time markers (opening of Northwest Territory, Confederates closing in) as well as dating each entry. She is trying to capture the feelings of the time—seems to be making good use of the primary sources to help her think about what a person from that time might be feeling, thinking, concerned about.
Is information ordered to make sense? Is the order historically accurate?	I need to check on the desertion scenario in the first entry. Does Andrea have evidence for this? It seems too early in the war for desertion to be a big problem. I don't remember this in any of our sources. Perhaps she is using material from later in the war?
How well has the student used the available sources to build the interpretation?	Andrea seems good at reading sources for the emotional component, but doesn't always use them to provide telling historical detail. She doesn't name the "General" or talk much about why this battle is so difficult. Maybe this is a reflection of the kind of real diary entries she's been reading.
Suggestions: For Teacher	**For student conference:**
1. Write one diary entry as a class, demonstrating how to incorporate more historical detail in their writing.	1. Discuss which details are historically grounded, which are speculation.
2. Have discussion about chronology—i.e. was desertion an issue this early in the war? Make timeline of sources.	2. Look at several of the real diaries, discuss how a historian might use them to understand what was happening to ordinary people during this time. What questions could the diaries help answer? What things don't they tell us? Why?
3. Remind students that diary entries are written after events more often than during events—you probably wouldn't sit down and write in your diary while under attack.	

FIG. 9.1. **Assessment guidelines for historical writing.**

oped, along with her comments on the work of one of her students, Andrea. A sample of Andrea's writing is shown in Fig. 9.2.

These analysis sheets proved most useful in conferences with students, parents, and guardians. Sometimes Pamela organized students in small groups; sometimes she worked individually with students, especially if they were having difficulty with a particular aspect of the task of reconstructing Hugh McKay's life. Over several years, she experimented with a variety of ways to assess this project. The assessment sheet proved useful for the diary entries, but Pamela decided she needed some way to help students step back and view Hugh's experience in a larger historical context. As you look at the "final exam" question Pamela developed (Fig. 9.3), think about what this question would require of students and what scaffolding might be necessary to help them be successful. To begin with, the task asks students to *picture* history. Pamela encouraged students to use different mediums to create the three scenes— some used collage, others painted their scenes, while still others created three-dimensional dioramas. This sent them to the sources they had been using all along but required that they focus less on Hugh and more on the background—the geography, the placement of the people around Hugh, field hospitals, gunboats on the river, or life before or after Shiloh. Pamela also asked them to provide historical arguments for why each scene was significant and credible. As a result, students thought more carefully, not just about whether a scene was historically plausible or accurate, but about why it was historically important.

This kind of assessment is an integral part of learning to think historically. It benefits both students and teachers by promoting reflection on the content and process of doing history. It also encourages increasing levels of self-assessment and self-confidence on the part of students. As the grounds for building historical narratives are made more clear, students become better able to establish cri-

Assessment tasks often require careful scaffolding.

Historical arguments explain why an interpretation is significant and credible.

Alleman & Brophy (1999)

April 3, 1863

Dear Diary,

I am being fired at from all sides. It is still misty from last night's rain. I don't like war at all. I am now relising that it is a very bad thing. But I have to fight for the North. There are too many who have already desserted. I am thinking about deserting myself.

It is getting worse now. My friend Johnny died and was carried away with the many wounded. I can hear the wounded crying for help. The General is calling my regiment. I will have to leave.

(at night) The Confederates are closing in, but I can no longer fight. I write this now because I may not survive the surgery. A bullet tore through my hand. I think most of one finger is gone. Maybe I am lucky.

November 29, 1888

Dear Diary,

Today I will marry my dear Millie. Millie is a determined woman. She raised four children after the death of her first husband. Maybe it is because of her pioneer family. Her family moved here when the Northwest Territory first opened up. She knows how to face bad times and make the best of very little. Since I was sent home from the army I have had to do that too. I am lucky that I saved some money while I worked on the freighter in Colorado. I think I can make a good life for Millie and her children.

FIG. 9.2. Sample of student's historical writing.

Putting Hugh McKay in Perspective

A new play has been produced based on Hugh McKay's life. You are the set designer. Illustrate three scenes that you think would be important in helping theater-goers understand the historical setting for Hugh's experiences. Provide an explanation for why you have chosen each scene. Your explanation must show evidence that you understand the historical time in which Hugh lived.

FIG. 9.3. Final assessment of Hugh McKay Project.

teria for judging the merits of their own and others' work—the self-regulated learning discussed in chapter 7.

Finally, this kind of assessment provides a rich source of data for explaining student progress to parents and guardians. Just as checklists, rubrics, and analysis sheets make clear the parameters of a study to students, they also let parents and guardians know something about the work that engages their children. When questions arise about expectations or about the basis for evaluation, teachers explain a student's progress with reference to a variety of samples of work and their accompanying criteria. They can clearly demonstrate the relationship between those criteria and the student's work, and help parents or guardians understand where progress has already been made and where work remains to be done.

CONCLUSIONS

I will tell you something about stories …
They aren't just entertainment.
Don't be fooled.
            —Leslie Marmon Silko

Takaki (1993)

It is important in the development of any mature historical understanding that learners see history as a human enterprise made up of interpretations, subject to revision, and expressed through a variety of genres. The structure of narrative encourages readers to recognize the human aspects of history and, with some help, to develop a better sense of its interpretive and tentative aspects. In addition, narrative may help students maintain a balance between the abstractions of history as an intellectual exercise and history as an ongoing, participatory drama. But narrative is only one piece of the puzzle, for history is more than narrative. It is also learning to sift evidence before it has been shaped and interpreted. It is putting one's own time and place into a broader perspective and seeing oneself as making choices that are, cumulatively, historic.

History is expressed in a variety of genres—and students need experience in as many of them as possible.

Levstik (1995)

The task of the teacher is to help students judge the interpretations appearing in narrative, to make sense out of alternative points of view, and to make careful historical judgments. Questions of fact and interpretation raised in this context can be used to initiate historical inquiry, refer students to other sources, including the full array of nonnarrative genres, and provide a forum for the presentation of student interpretations. This, we think, is a crucial and often overlooked component to thinking and learning in history. This type of mediation also helps guard against the uncritical acceptance of literary constructions of history. The power of narrative is not an unmitigated good. As noted previously, a good story can mask bad history and blind students to other interpretations. Children are likely to believe bad history if the narrative is compelling and ignore good history if the narrative is insipid. This should serve as a caution to those currently recommending teaching history as a (often single) story well told. There is no evidence that a history curriculum based primarily on narrative and story telling is either good teaching or good history. As one of Jeanette Groth's students notes, different genres provide different historical insights. The text, she explains, "told exact dates, places, names and etc. Other sources provide more explanations of why something happened or why someone was famous. They give more details of actual reasoning and even feelings. For instance, I was *inside* on who wanted the states split up, and why." As you read through this book, you will notice that, although teachers use narrative in both its fictional and nonfictional forms, they also provide many other ways for students to think and learn in history.

The teacher's task is to help students make sense out of the literary and historical aspects of different written genres.
Levstik (1997), Mayer (1998), Olwell (1999)

Different genres provide different historical insights and serve different social and cultural purposes.

Albert (1995), Olwell (1999), Mayer (1999)

CHILDREN'S AND ADOLESCENT LITERATURE

Aliki, M. *Medieval Wedding*. HarperCollins, 1983.

Bruchac, J. *The Winter People*. Dial Books, 2002.

Burks, B. *Walks Alone*. Harcourt Brace, 1998.

Chaikin, M. *I Should Worry, I Should Care*. iUniverse, 2000.

Clarke, A. C. Drummer boy of Shiloh. In D. Roselle (Ed.), *Transformations II: Understanding American History Through Science Fiction* (pp. 13–23). Fawcett, 1974.

Coerr, E. *Sadako*. Putnam, 1994.

Collier, J., & Collier, L. *My Brother Sam is Dead*. Four Winds, 1974.

Conley, R. J. *Nickajack*. Doubleday, 1992.

Cornell, K. *These Lands Are Ours: Tecumseh's Fight for the Old Northwest*. Steck-Vaughn 1993.

Curtis, C. P. *Bud, Not Buddy*. Yearling, 2002.

Cushman, K. *Catherine, Called Birdy*. Clarion, 1994.

Fleischman, P. *Whipping Boy*. HarperCollins, 1992.

Forbes, E. *Johnny Tremain*. Houghton Mifflin, 1943.

Freedman, R. *Confucius: The Golden Rule*. Arthur A. Levine, 2002.

Freedman, R. *Kids at Work: Lewis Hine and the Crusade Against Child Labor*. Clarion, 1994.

Freedman, R. *Eleanor Roosevelt: A Life of Discovery*. Clarion, 1990.

Freedman, R. *Franklin Delano Roosevelt*. Clarion, 1990.

Freedman, R. *Children of the Wild West*. Clarion, 1983.

Freedman, R. *Immigrant Kids*. Dutton, 1980.

Fritz, J. *The Double Life of Pocahontas*. Putnam, 1983.

Gauch, P. L. *Thunder at Gettysburg*. Coward, McCann & Geohegan, 1974.

Haskins, J. *Black, Blue, & Gray*. Simon & Schuster, 1998.

Hesse, K. *Witness*. Scholastic, 2003.

Holtz, S. *A Circle Unbroken*. Clarion, 1988.

Hudson, J. *Sweetgrass*. Philomel, 1989.

Hudson, J. *Dawn Rider*. Philomel, 1990.

Hurmence, B. *Slavery Time When I Was Chillun*. Putnam, 1997.

Lester, J. *Black Cowboy, Wild Horses: A True Story*. Dial, 1998.

Macaulay, D. *Castle*. Houghton Mifflin, 1977.

McKinley, R. *The Outlaws of Sherwood*. Berkeley Publishing Group, 1989.

McKissack, P., & McKissack, F. *A Long Hard Journey: The Story of the Pullman Porter*. Walker, 1994.

Meltzer, M. *Cheap Raw Labor: How Our Youngest Workers are Exploited and Abused*. Viking, 1994.

Meltzer, M. *There Comes a Time: The Struggle for Civil Rights*. Random House, 2002.

Mitchell, M. K. *Uncle Jed's Barbershop*. Simon & Schuster, 1993.

O'Dell, S. *Sarah Bishop*. Houghton Mifflin, 1980.

Paulsen, G. *Soldier's Heart: A Novel of the Civil War*. Delacorte, 1998.

Pelta, K. *Discovering Christopher Columbus: How History Is Invented*. Lerner, 1991.

Parker, D. L. *Stolen Dreams: Portraits of Working Children*. Lerner, 1997.

Phillips, N. (Ed.). *In a Sacred Manner I Live: Native American Wisdom*. Clarion, 1997.

Rappaport, D. *We Are the Many: A Picture Book of American Indians*. HarperCollins, 2002.

Sancha, S. *The Luttrell Village: Country Life in the Middle Ages*. Crowell, 1990.

Sonneborn, L. *American West: An Illustrated History*. Scholastic, 2002.

Speare, E. G. *The Witch of Blackbird Pond*. Houghton Mifflin 1958.

Stanley, J. *I Am An American: The True Story of Japanese American Internment*. Crown, 1994.

Turner, A. *Katie's Trunk*. Macmillan, 1992.

Wright, C. C. (1995). *Wagon Train: A Family Goes West in 1865*. Holiday House.

Yep, L. *Dragon's Gate*. HarperCollins, 1994.

Yin & Soentpiet, C. *Coolies*. Puffin, 2003.

Viola, H. J. *It Is a Good Day to Die: Indian Eyewitnesses Tell the Story of the Battle of Little Bighorn*. Crown, 1998.

Zeinert, K. *Those Courageous Women of the Civil War*. Millbrook, 1998.

10

OH, GOOD! WE GET TO ARGUE

Putting Conflict in Context

Viktor Komac, an eighth-grade teacher from Ohio, attended a professional meeting at which the speaker mentioned that American children have few strategies for dealing with public conflicts. Having noticed that his own students had precisely this difficulty, he decided to begin the year by underlining the controversial nature of history and helping students develop skills in conflict management. He began by asking each student to bring in newspaper articles regarding current local, national, or world conflicts. He arranged a large bulletin board with four columns: *Conflict, Perspectives, Resolutions, Changes*. After students categorized the conflicts they had identified, Viktor asked them to read over the articles and see if they could identify at least two sides to each conflict. Next, students cut out letters to the editor, editorials, and articles representing these perspectives. Small groups formed around each of the conflicts. Their first task was to see if their textbook could provide any background information. The group investigating the conflict over altering an antidiscrimination law, for instance, found a section of their textbook on the Civil Rights movement useful. Another group discussing cutting funding for the arts found information on the establishment of governmental agencies such as the NEA and NEH useful. For the most part, however, their textbooks had little or nothing on their topics. Instead, they had to rely on other sources, especially newspapers and periodicals.

Viktor knew that as his students tried to juggle different sources, they would need help in keeping track of their work. Over the last several years, he had adapted several techniques to help students keep track of different perspectives on controversial issues. Figure 10.1 shows a discussion web used by a group studying the operation of a nearby nuclear power

Pro	Con
Cheaper, cleaner, power	*Danger of accidents*
Provide new jobs	*Jobs are hazardous*
Safer than mining	*Too close to schools and houses*
Will have safety features	*Lower value of homes*
Saves natural resources	*No safe way to get rid of waste*

POSSIBLE OUTCOMES

With Nuclear Power	Without Nuclear Power
1. All the "pro" things happen	*1. We continue to use current sources until they are all used up*
2. Cincinnati becomes like Chernoble	*2. Fuel costs keep rising because resources are scarce*
3. Nuclear waste pollutes ground water	*3. Scientists find a safer power source, before resources run out*
4. Other power companies go out of business or sell for less	

FIG. 10.1. Conflict: Should the nuclear power plant be operated?

plant. In this instance, the plant had already been built, and the controversy was over its operation, not its construction. As a result, students could go back to old newspapers to find out how the decision to build the plant had been made and what arguments were originally made against its construction. They could then compare current operation with the claims made for the plant in the past.

Viktor also asked each group to fill out two other forms to help students think about the historical significance of current conflicts. On a page headed "What Caused This?," students first identified a conflict and then wrote their best research-based guesses on what they thought caused the conflict. Another page headed "What Might This Mean?" asked students to explain what might be different tomorrow as a result of a current conflict. These two forms required that students infer both historical causes and possible current effects. Later, they compared these hypotheses against actual outcomes where those were available. When it appeared that a conflict was resolved, they listed the solution and discussed compromises, whose perspective won out, and the like. In the *Changes* column on the bulletin board, they listed evidence that either the conflict or its resolution created change. What difference did it make, for instance, when a controversial art show was closed down, an antidiscrimination law altered, or a new union contract signed? Finally, Viktor asked the students to use both forms to help them look into the future. Each group developed a 10-minute presentation *as if they were historians* explaining the conflict to people 50 years into the future. In their presentation, they were to explain the historical significance of the conflict they had studied from two perspectives: that of participants in the events, and that of a future historian. What did this conflict look like in its own time? What historical significance might it have later on in time?

Evans et al. (1999), Levstik (2000), Penyak & Duray (1999), White (1997)

We may long for consensus, but we live with conflict.

Hertzberg (1989), Levstik (1996), Lybarger (1990)

Engle (1970), Gordon (1990), Gutmann (987), Hess (2002b), Novick (1988), Parker (1991a), Zinn (1994)

Conflict is fundamental to democracy.

Avery (2002), Bickmore (2002), Evans et al. (1999), Parker (1991a, 1991b)

McGinnis (n.d.)

Many teachers are afraid to engage students in controversial topics such as this. They worry that their students will not be able to handle conflict, that parents and other will attack them if they try it, and that their task is to help students "get along." Not surprisingly, teachers who strive for harmony in disharmonious environments often long for consensus—some shared set of values—rather than conflict. In the 1940s and 1950s, American historians of the consensus school also tried to focus on uncovering a broadly shared set of values that, they argued, overrode ethnic and class distinctions. Much like current critics of multicultural education, these historians searched for something that could unify a diverse society. They, too, worried that diversity would cause fragmentation and that emphasizing conflict rather than consensus could lead to cynicism and the failure of citizens to participate in civic life. Echoes of the same charges and counter charges continue to be heard in current debates over the place of history in the social studies curriculum.

We, like Viktor and several other teachers in this book, argue a contrary position. Conflict is built into the fabric of our public and private lives. Democracy is rooted in a conflictual model. The American Declaration of Independence lays out a rationale for the right of people to overthrow governments that violate their rights, and the Bill of Rights begins with a guarantee of freedom of speech, including disagreeable speech. Democracies worldwide have similar foundations. Democratic governments are generally based on conflicting ideas, dissent, debate, negotiation, and even litigation. When we vote, the majority wins—we don't wait for everyone to agree. We also limit majority rule with laws intended to protect minority rights and we use a court system to adjudicate disputes. In addition, our own lives daily force us to recognize the reality of conflict in the world—whether it be terrorism at home and abroad, ethnic wars in Europe or Africa, calls for disunion in francophone Canada, disputes over prayer in schools in the United States, or disagreements about environmental issues. We live in a contentious world, yet research indicates that American students better understand the place of consensus than of conflict in our political system, are unsure of how conflict might be managed or resolved, or what happens when conflicts remain.

As you can see, assuming that conflict is something to avoid misunderstands and misrepresents both the foundations of democracy and the nature of much of the world. We suggest being more honest with students about both conflict and consensus. This requires shifting the focus of history instruction from an oversimplified emphasis on "progress"—every day in every way we are getting better and better—to more in-depth study of how groups and individuals now and in other times exercise power publicly and privately, how society deals with competing claims between order and protest and how political and social meanings are transmitted to individuals and groups. This certainly means that the history curriculum is more complex, but not that it disintegrates. Instead, the focus shifts from telling a mainstream narrative to studying the relationships between groups of people, recognizing their differing conceptions of social reality, and developing supportable interpretations based on that study. This is a perspective that shares substantial common ground with the Standards of the National Council for the Social Studies (NCSS). The authors of the NCSS Standards argue that students need "tools that will inform their decision-making processes," that "most issues, when famed from the perspective of two or more differing points of view, allow for a broader, more reasoned discussion rather than an immediate debate of one view versus an opposite view." We agree, but reasoned discussion requires considerable scaffolding before it becomes a comfortable part of students' intellectual repertoire.

Gabaccia (1997), Gerstle (1997), Hollinger (1997)

Gordon (1988), Gutmann (1976), Hess (2002a, 2002b), Sklar (1995), Takaki (1993)

LET'S TALK: PREPARING FOR REASONED DISCUSSION

It might seem that the last thing your students need is help with talking, but students really need exactly that if they are to participate in the kind of reasoned discussion of controversial issues that we have in mind. Unfortunately, this type of discussion rarely occurs in school. Instead, an *Initiation-Response-Evaluation (IRE)* pattern prevails. In IRE, the teacher asks a question (initiation), a student answers (response), and the teacher either accepts or corrects (evaluation) the response. Aside from game shows and, perhaps, courtrooms, there really isn't much "real world" call for this kind of talk. When people discuss the imposition of a dress code at a P.T.A. meeting, petition the zoning board for protection or development of land, debate the relative merits of a tobacco ban at a city council meeting, or serve on some other board, commission, or committee, they don't expect to be quizzed in this manner and would be rightfully annoyed if such a thing happened. On the other hand, civic life could certainly benefit if more of us learned to use evidence to support a position, listened respectfully when others differed with us, avoided ad hominem attacks, worked for consensus, and learned to live with disagreement. Most of the teachers in this book carefully plan for just this kind of experience by teaching *with* and *for* discussion.

Cazden (1988)

In teaching *with* discussion, teachers use discussion as an instructional technique in the service of some other purpose. They might, for instance, engage students in a discussion of Japanese internment, not so much to promote good discussion as to help students understand the perspectives of different participants at that historical moment. Most teachers assume that this kind of discussion will motivate student interest and should be part of their instructional repertoire. As Josh Elliott began his first year of teaching, he, too, wanted to use discussion as part of the required state history curriculum for his fourth-grade class. He thought that discussions would be interesting and engaging for his students, of course, but he also expected to use discussion to turn his disparate students into a more cohesive community of inquiry. Unfortunately, Josh's first few attempts at engaging his fourth graders in discussion fell flat. It wasn't that his students didn't like to talk; they argued about just about everything—until he tried to organize a discussion about the state history they were supposed to be studying. He asked a question. A painful silence ensued. He probed. Students

Teach *for* as well as *with* discussion.

mumbled and shifted in their seats. A few provided desultory responses. Before serious management problems erupted, Josh moved on to review a homework assignment, wondering all the while what had gone wrong.

Josh's experience is not unusual. It took some time and experimentation for him to begin teaching *for* discussion, so that he could better teach *with* it. Though teachers in this chapter and throughout this book support high-quality academic discussion in a number of ways, Josh organized by:

Hess (2002a, 2002b), Parker & Hess (2001)

- Carefully selecting discussion topics. Just as Dehea Smith (chap. 6) found that all questions weren't equally useful for inquiry, Josh quickly discovered that not all controversies were worth discussion. At one point, his students wanted to discuss the controversy over new state license plates, but Josh feared that pursuing a discussion of license plate illustration was unlikely to foster deep engagement with historical content. On the other hand, discussing the ways in which the region was represented—on license plates, among other things—met several curricular goals. Josh knew that the statewide assessment included questions about political cartoons; he also wanted his students to understand the historical roots and repercussions of regional images on present-day situations. He thought his students would benefit from discussing regional stereotyping because such historically rooted practices affected them and would likely continue to do so. Rather than discuss what should be on a license plate, students investigated the historical and current manifestations of regional stereotypes and discussed their impact on their state and region.

For recent scholarship on Appalachia that counters regional stereotypes. See, for instance, *Buck (2001), Weise (2001)*

- Preparing primary and secondary resources related to the topic. There's little point in discussion when participants lack sufficient resources to provide some common background information. As Josh soon discovered, there were plenty of primary and secondary resources to support discussion of regional stereotyping. He discovered cartoons and magazine illustrations, footage from movies and television, advertisements, and a wonderful set of photographs taken under the auspices of the Depression-era Works Progress Administration (W.P.A.) and Farm Service Administration (F.S.A.). Fortunately, many of these sources could be printed from the *American Memory* website. The availability of resources related to a discussion topic is crucial to a high-quality discussion—whether in the classroom or in other public arenas. Many topics generate considerable heat, but without sufficient resources to support intelligent discussion there is little light, learning, or understanding.
- Providing opportunities for small group background work. Initially, Josh hoped that he could save valuable time by giving students background material prior to class discussion. This just didn't work. Because they were unsure of exactly how to use materials, students tended not to look a them very carefully—if at all. As a result, Josh organized students into small groups to review selected resources. He began by presenting students with a proposition: Regional stereotypes make it difficult for people to respect groups and individuals from other regions. He asked students to work in small groups to find evidence for or against this proposition. First, students searched for regional representations. One group categorized a set of cartoons by types of stereotypes, another group looked for stereotypical images in a set of children's books, a third made a list of problems with stereotypes based on an article they read, and a fourth surveyed parents and other students about their ideas regarding different regions of the United States. Before they engaged in discussion with their peers, then, students had a rich array of background information to draw on, as well as at least a beginning understanding of different perspectives on the topic and proposition.

Hess (2002a)

Background study prepares students for discussion.

Developing evidence-based positions can be challenging, especially for younger students.

- Providing time to form at least a tentative position. Josh asked each group to write a position statement in response to his initial proposition. What evidence could they find of regional stereotypes, and what evidence did they have that these stereotypes might influence how people saw the region? If a group could not come to consensus, they were to describe their disagreement(s), along with any information that would clarify the nature of their disagreements. This turned out to be the most challenging task for his students. They could identify stereotypes, but they had trouble making a case that those stereotypes might influence people's thinking. They were unused to providing evidence for their own positions, and were often reluctant to provide arguments for an opposing view. Josh ended up teaching a minilesson on writing position papers. He first prepared a sample statement that reflected the problems students were having. Working in the school computer lab, he projected a copy of the paper on a screen and worked with students to edit it. He gave each student copies of the initial and final drafts to guide their future work. This turned out to be helpful for most of the students.

Over the course of the school year, Josh found that carefully structured small group discussions paved the way for richer full-class discussion. The small groups also had the advantage of involving more students more consistently then did full-class discussions. As students built confidence in the small groups, too, he noticed that more students spoke during whole-class discussions.

High quality academic discussions not only prepare students for participation in democratic debate and negotiation, they also support important aspects of historical thinking, including better understanding of historical agency. *Agency* refers to the power to act. As we have already mentioned, we are all participants in the ongoing drama of history. We are both the subjects of history and its agents. We make history by the collective activities of our lives, including our participation in both the enduring and ephemeral dilemmas of our times. Unfortunately, history instruction often loses exactly this sense of agency. To the extent that we make history seem both finished and inevitable, students have difficulty seeing themselves as having agency—the power to make history. Focusing disciplined, reflective inquiry on conflicts and persistent issues in history gives students practice, as the Social Studies Standards suggest, in discussing the arguments and evidence that surround such dilemmas, but it is also more likely to help students see themselves as having agency. Note, too, that the NCSS Standards argue for the importance of seeing issues from multiple perspectives. Part of developing a sense of one's own agency is recognizing that there are alternative positions and alternative actions that could be taken. Imagine trying to represent the current political climate in the United States to your grandchildren. What perspectives would you have to explain? If most conflicts had only two perspectives they might be easier to resolve, at least by voting, but there are obviously more than two ways of looking at such issues as military intervention in other countries, changes in affirmative action legislation, or deficit spending. A wide range of options and opinions are available to citizens in responding to each of these issues. One of the challenges facing history teachers is dealing with complex issues so that students develop both civic competence and a sense of historical agency.

den Heyer (2003)

Hahn & Tocci (1990), Kelly (1996)

For more on special challenges facing beginning teachers of history, see *Barton & Levstik (2003), Grant (2003), Selxas (1998, 1999), VanSledright (2002)*.

IT'S HAPPENING RIGHT NOW: STARTING WITH CURRENT EVENTS

Investigating current, unresolved issues has a sense of immediacy often lacking in historical study. Because they are unresolved, current issues encourage students to speculate about how conflicts might turn out—and provide a framework for analyzing other historical conflicts. Students learn to think about the options available to participants in a specific time and place, the likelihood that any particular option might be chosen, and the possible outcomes that might result. They learn to look for the decision makers—who has power, and how is it exercised? What can people distant from the immediate crisis do? How have such people reacted in the past? If, on the other hand, students perceive history as finished, it can be hard to get them involved in rethinking historic controversies, much less in thinking about what those controversies might have to do with their own lives.

Current conflicts encourage speculation about multiple causes and possible effects.

One option for teaching history, then, is to begin with controversies that are still unresolved. This was certainly Dehea Smith's (chap. 6) approach, and one of the reasons she preferred to teach history in an integrated social studies framework. She used current events to help students see how conflicts changed their community, and how groups and individuals influenced those changes. One current controversy—development of green space—was easily observed and lent itself to historic connections. Students could develop *before* and *after* illustrations to show shrinking green space, they could see how much construction altered their community, and they could debate whether devel-

Bennett & Spalding (1992), Foster (1999), Foster & Yeager (1999), Levstik, Henderson, & Schlarb (2004)

Teachers can work with librarians and other history interest groups to help students access different types of sources.

opment should be slowed, stopped or left unfettered. In addition, the public librarian showed children how to access maps and photographs, newspaper articles and blueprints showing how Lexington had coped with similar controversies in the past, and the local Trust for Historic Preservation provided boxes of primary and secondary materials, maps, photographs, children's literature, slides, and a videotape showing attempts to reclaim the site of the first town in the area. By the time the students began debating their first question, they had already accumulated a good deal of information. Dehea gathered the class in a circle on the floor:

> "Make the circle wide enough so that everyone can see and be seen," Dehea reminds her students.
>
> "Oh, good, we get to argue!" announces one of the boys.
>
> "Yes, I think we probably need an argument here, but remember that this is a special kind of argument," Dehea says, and then reviews the rules for turn taking, polite forms of disagreement, and the need for full participation [all clearly listed on a bright pink poster taped to the wall].
>
> For the next 25 minutes, the students discuss and debate issues surrounding the original settlement of Lexington. Twice Dehea intervenes to remind students to sit back in the circle so that no one's view is blocked. She also asks several students to provide information based on their reading, has one student read a passage from an informational text, and replays relevant parts of a video. It is clear that the discussion could go on longer, but the bell signals lunch break.

Constructive argument serves important functions in historical thinking.

Hahn & Tocci (1990), O'Reilly (1998), National Council for the Social Studies (1994)

Most of Dehea's third graders claimed to "love to argue," and Dehea worked hard to help them to do so in constructive ways. They could disagree about ideas, she said, and various opinions were always sought because "it helps to think out different opinions before we start," but students could not attack people or make fun of their ideas. "If we did that, no one would speak up, and then we wouldn't have as many good ideas to work with," Dehea reminded one student who said an idea was "stupid." In general, though, students used a discussion model that gave them two discussion templates. The first template began with a child saying, "I agree/disagree with _____ because _____." Considerable emphasis was placed on being able to give a solid reason for agreement or disagreement. The second template allowed students to agree with part of someone's idea but disagree with or modify another part. Thus, a sentence might begin, "I agree with _____ about _____, but I disagree about _____ because _____." Using these templates allowed for quick reminders when students violated the rules for debate. Sitting in a circle also helped, as everyone could see and be seen, and Dehea could make sure that everyone participated.

Templates for argument and debate help students formulate constructive discussion.

Older students sometimes chaff at such formulaic debates and can be especially intractable if they have had little experience dealing formally with controversy. Viktor preferred emphasizing the historical significance of controversies. Although students certainly engaged in debate, their work was most often organized around comparing how a conflict might look in its own time relative to what historical significance it might assume in the future. "It helps to get a little distance on 'hot' topics," he explains. "I ask them, 'How would a historian explain this controversy, or what would it look like to someone from another culture?' That makes them stop and think. Maybe not change their mind, but at least consider how it might look from another perspective."

Historical perspective helps students develop a broader view of current controversies.

Both Dehea's and Viktor's studies of local conflicts have the advantage of a wide variety of easily accessible resources, but students can also study more distant, although still current, conflicts. This often requires rethinking the kinds of sources that will be used for student inquiry. Billie Davis, a sixth-grade teacher responsible for helping her students make sense out of war in Bosnia, found that there were relatively few appropriate print resources for her students. Her sixth graders had little prior knowledge and some misconceptions about this part of

The way sources are organized can have an impact on their effectiveness.

140

the world, especially in relation to Bosnian Muslims. She decided to begin by introducing her students to Zlata, a child about their age living in Sarajevo. *Zlata's Diary*, a book somewhat similar to *The Diary of Anne Frank*, puts a human face on a historic tragedy. Because her students were less familiar with some of the names and places in *Zlata* than with *Anne Frank*, Billie decided to read parts of the diary aloud to them. Students read other passages silently and then performed others as reader's theatre. During reader's theatre, students selected passages that they thought demonstrated particular aspects of Zlata's life or of the war and read them dramatically, sometimes using solo voices interspersed with choral reading. The multiple readings and attention to timing, emphasis, and pronunciation required for these performances seemed to improve students' comprehension of the text. Nonetheless, some students still had difficulty picturing the geography of Zlata's homeland. Billie put a large map of the former Yugoslavia up on a bulletin board. As they read the diary, students located relevant places on the map. They also collected newspaper and magazine articles about the war and matched them to locations on the map.

Filipovic (1994), Frank (1989)

Pappas et al. (1999)

Zlata's Diary makes clear the frustrations of being a historical subject without feeling much agency. Before the war, Zlata took music lessons, went to school, loved MTV, and went skiing in the mountains around Sarajevo. Once the war starts, her world becomes a narrow, frightening place. The politicians she calls "the kids" lob shells onto her street, kill her friends, and make it necessary to spend nights in a rat-infested basement. Water and power are cut off; school is closed when the Serbs target schools for shelling. Most of Billie's students were easily caught up in the power of Zlata's story, unable to understand why someone did not stop the madness. Just as children often begin by thinking that people in the past were stupid, these sixth graders were convinced that only stupidity could explain the Serbs' behavior.

Literature can make a strong connection between otherwise distant people.

At first, students did not want to move beyond Zlata; they just wanted there to be a happy ending for her. "Those newspaper reporters should get her out of there!" one student declared. This response is, we think, an important component of historical thinking. Too often students are asked to leap past emotion to analysis. This can blunt student interest and cut off a healthy sense of outrage at injustice. Instead of dismissing her students' strong emotional response to the conflict that enmeshed Zlata, Billie provided an outlet for their feelings. Earlier in the year, she had introduced biographical poems. Now she reminded her students of the format they had used and asked them to write a poem about Zlata (see Fig. 10.2). Afterward, the students shared their poems (see Fig. 10.2), and Billie read portions of both *I Dream of Peace* ..., a book of poetry by the children of Sarajevo, and *I Never Saw Another Butterfly*, poems and artwork by children held at Terezin concentration camp during World War II.

Barton (1996a), Lee & Ashby (2000)

For further discussion of the bifurcation of emotion and reason in historical thinking, see *Barton & Levstik (2004), Burdige (1988), Kerber (1993)*; for discussion of historical empathy, see *Foster (1999), Lee (1978), Lee & Ashby (2000), Levstik (2000a), Portal (1987, 1990), Shemilt (1984), VanSledright (2000)*.

Garfield (1991)

Children of Yugoslavia Staff (1994), Statni Zidovske Museum, Prague (1984)

Writing and sharing their own poems and hearing the poetry of other children generated further conversation and pushed the students to think beyond Zlata and her family. Now they were more ready to step back a bit from their first emotional response and study the historical and current manifestations of interethnic and nationalist conflict: Why did these people start hating each other after such a long time? How had all these different people ended up in one country to begin with? Why couldn't the United Nations seem to stop the war? Could anyone help? It seemed that good people on both sides struggled to end the violence but had no power—no agency—to stop what was happening to them. Why was that?

Ashby, Lee, & Dickinson (1997)

Jolliffe (1987)

With these questions to guide them, the students were ready to make sense out of the background material their teacher had gathered. Unfortunately, most of the available resource material was a bit complex for sixth graders; there were interviews with leaders of different factions, magazine and newspaper articles, and videotapes of news coverage but few books or articles specifically for early adolescents. In addition, Billie's students were adamant

Biographical Poem Based on *Zlata's Diary*

Zlata
"Peace"
Loving, kind, hopeful, depressed
Lover of writing in her diary, peace, and letters
Who believed that there should always be
PEACE
Who wanted freedom, to stay with her family and
PEACE
Who used her pencil, her diary, and her brain power to write to Mimmy
Who gave love, Mimmy, and her words to the world
Who said, my childhood has been ripped away from me, stolen
Filipovic

FIG. 10.2. Biographical poems.

about not only wanting to *study* about Bosnia. They wanted to *do* something about it. They wanted other people to know about Zlata. This can be a sensitive point in many studies. It is not always possible to do something in quite the immediate sense that middle school students desire. In this case, however, Billie suggested that students prepare a program for the schoolwide television show that was broadcast each morning. This received enthusiastic agreement from most of the students and later from the principal. Billie was pleased because the news program could, in the long term, encourage a schoolwide response to the Bosnian crisis and, in the short term, provide additional focus for the kind of research she believed should precede such action. As reporters on the broadcast, students had a role to play that required both "investigative reporting" and "background briefings." Billie developed "briefing" packets for her students. These contained a two-page overview of "the Case of Bosnia-Hercegovina" that she adapted from materials available through ERIC. She gave a list of additional resources to each reporter, varying the list so that different students would have expertise in different areas and could be matched to appropriate print or visual materials. Billie also arranged for two visits from professors who specialized in Slavic Europe. Student reporters used the briefing packets to prepare questions for their guest experts.

Cox (1993)

The final television program, *The End of Childhood: Zlata's Sarajevo*, combined interview data, excerpts from *Zlata's Diary*, students' own poetry, and a comparison with Anne Frank and the Nazi holocaust. At the end of the pro-

142

gram, the students asked their schoolmates to contribute cards and letters to be sent to Sarajevo to let people there know they had not been forgotten. Not only did they create an interpretation of a historic event, they acted as historical agents, adding their voices to the international debate about the fate of Bosnia and its neighbors.

WHAT IF? IT COULD HAVE BEEN DIFFERENT

Historical agency is an important concept because it is the aspect of historical thinking that helps students see themselves as historical actors. Just as the actions of people in the past produced history, so too do students' actions today and tomorrow make history. History is real and current. Unfortunately, textbooks too often make the outcomes of historical conflicts seem inevitable. Think about all the times you memorized the three causes of the Civil War or the major events leading up to World War I. Taught this way, history seems inexorable—a train moving along a track of someone else's devising. Yet one of the fascinating aspects of history is how easily events could have gone otherwise. What if Lincoln had not gone to the theatre or Kennedy to Dallas? If African American parents had kept their children home, rather than let them face hatred and harassment in order to integrate schools? If Nelson Mandela had succumbed to his long imprisonment or Slobodan Milosevic had worked for peaceful coexistence between Serbia and its neighbors?

Gordon (1988), Gutman (1976), Loewen (1995), Sklar (1995), Takaki (1993), Thompson (1963)

As you might suspect by now, a train metaphor for history only works in retrospect. At any historic moment, all sorts of forces come into play. The economy takes a downturn and anti-immigration fervor mounts, a terrorist attack threatens peace negotiations, the development of home computing, email and fax changes how workplaces are organized, and changes in attitudes toward smoking alter social and economic relations. And just as students need to see how current conflicts can alter by the moment, they also need to recognize that historic conflicts could also have played out differently. Conflict may be inevitable in human interaction, but the outcomes are dependent on human agency. The Freedman's Bureau could have redistributed land in the American South instead of supporting a tenancy system in the wake of Civil War; former Liberian president, Charles Taylor, could have promoted peace and economic stability in Liberia rather than civil war. People make choices, singly and collectively. Sometimes they take stands against overwhelming obstacles. Sometimes they succumb to the basest motivations. Often they are unsure where reasonable solutions to dilemmas lie. In the end, however, each of these choices makes history. Speculating about the outcomes of current conflicts certainly helps students see the potential impact of such decisions.

Novick (1988)

Holt (1990)

A variety of factors, including individual choices, influence historical outcomes.

"What if" activities are another way to help students think more carefully about the impact of conflicts, inventions, and events in the past. Look at the list in Fig. 10.3, and think about the kind of background knowledge students might bring to each question, and the kind of research they would need to do in order to make better grounded speculations. "What if?" activities can also make vivid the longevity of historical dilemmas. Jim Farrell's eighth graders discovered this as they participated in a simulated Constitutional Convention with an interesting twist. The class had already studied the convention, along with the debates and compromises made to make the Constitution acceptable to its constituents. "Now," Mr. Farrell asked his students, "Consider what voices were left out of the original debates, and what difference those voices might have made. What if women or Native Peoples, African Americans or nonlandowners had been heard?" Groups of students were assigned different roles based on this discussion. Some represented the disenfranchised; others the original members of the convention. Rules were established (no filibustering allowed), and debate began.

Speculating about alternative outcomes helps students recognize that particular events are not inevitable.

Historical dilemmas are often longstanding.

143

What if . . . ?

• George Washington had been crowned king, as many wanted.

• The United Nations had not been created?

• The Equal Rights Amendment to the U.S. Constitution had passed?

• Television had never been invented?

• Constantine had not become a Christian?

• There had been no anti-apartheid boycott of South Africa?

• There was no First Amendment in the U.S. Constitution?

• Labor unions had never formed in the U.S.?

• The Moors had not been defeated by Isabella and Ferdinand of Spain?

• Europeans had not conquered the Americas?

FIG. 10.3. Speculating about alternative outcomes in history.

Contemporary issues challenge students to think differently about past and present.

Avery, Bird, Johnstone, Sullivan & Thrallhamer (1992), Bunton (1992), Kelly (1986), Sadker & Sadker (1991)

When history challenges our world view, it can be discomforting—and compelling.

Calclasure (1999), Evans et al. (1999), Gerwin & Zevin (2003), Levstik & Groth (2002), Parker (1991), Wade (1994)

Sometimes students found it hard to keep to the time period and use the arguments that might have been broached in 1787. For one thing, they discovered that some of these issues were very current. Gender turned out to be most volatile, because it touched on problems students faced in the school every day. Did the Constitution need an Equal Rights Amendment? If there had been such a thing in 1787, how would life in the United States have altered? As the debate progressed, students were amazed at how difficult these issues remained in their own lives. In fact, several students found the simulation disturbing and sometimes threatening. "There's no sense talking about the past," one student announced, after a heated debate on gender. "I don't like to pick sides. People just get mad all over again. We're all equal now. Let's be done with it." Another retorted, "There's still problems in this school and in this class. Maybe it should come out so we can deal with it." Similar controversy swirled around issues of race and class, with frequent conversational shuttling between past and present. One student declared that, because everyone was essentially alike, it did not matter who had been left out, and finally asked the teacher to "just tell us the information. Looking at all this controversial stuff is just confusing."

The student's responses and their sometimes-poignant discomfort are not unusual; rather, they are an indicator of how powerful historical study can be. Hard intellectual work, especially when it touches areas of current sensitivity, is not comfortable, but it can be compelling and memorable. As one student wrote about racism and sexism, "I always thought people back then just didn't know. They did, though. So do we, but we don't do anything about it either."

It would have been easy for Jim to back away from controversy and "just tell ... the information." Had he done so his students would have lost an opportunity to grapple with issues of historical agency not just in the past but also in their own lives. Certainly the class discussions did not cure current social problems, but some issues that had been taboo were now public and students had a language to use in describing and responding to them. In addition, pretending that such issues were not relevant or that there could be a simple right answer to persistent dilemmas would misrepresent history and undermine Jim's instructional goals. Jim's goal had been to prepare students to look at persistent issues in American history; the students made those issues their own and at least some of them found a degree of personal agency in the process.

144

IT ISN'T FINISHED YET: YOU CAN MAKE A DIFFERENCE

As we have said, one feature of historical agency is that things in the past could have been otherwise; an equally important aspect is that history is not final—some things can be undone. Certainly the bloodshed in the former Yugoslavia is evidence that hatreds long suppressed can be revived. In other cases, laws once passed—"separate but equal" or apartheid—can be revoked. And, perhaps more fundamentally, attitudes and beliefs—a "separate sphere" for women or the appropriateness of child labor—can alter. Choices are rarely finished. In Jeanette Groth's eighth-grade American history class, the students study the Bill of Rights. As an assessment, Jeanette assigns them the task of proving that one of the first 10 amendments to the Constitution still has a direct impact on their lives. One group, assigned to the First Amendment, produced a video that began with a mock news report. As the anchorperson began delivering the news, there was an interruption. A message flashed across the screen: "The President has declared a national emergency. All First Amendment Rights are suspended!" The anchorperson looked up from her desk: "Well, that means we're off the air!" The screen went dark. Moments later, the video showed a series of vignettes of life without the First Amendment: people being told they had to go to church (and which church they had to attend), a protester being led off to jail, and so forth. In each case, as the victims objected, they were reminded that the First Amendment no longer applied. At the close of the video, the students stood in front of an American flag and slowly read the First Amendment. Their video was certainly powerful and generated a good deal of discussion of possible limits on free expression that operated in their lives as well as in the United States as a whole.

Decisions made in the past can be changed in the present.

McGinnis (n.d.), National Council for the Social Studies (1994), Parker, Mueller & Wendling (1989)

Keller & Schillings (1987)

ASSESSING CONFLICT IN CONTEXT

Because students sometimes find discussions of conflict discomforting, it is especially important to provide them with opportunities to reflect on what they are learning. It is equally important to frame students' opportunities for reflection in ways that reinforce respect—not just for different perspectives but for thoughtful, supportable arguments and interpretations. As you have seen, the teachers in this book take seriously the challenge of finding ways to help students manage this kind of debate and disagreement. They are especially conscious of how easily assessment can stifle intellectual risk taking. As a result, they have developed a number of ways to encourage reflection and provide evaluations of student progress without leaving students feeling as if their ideas or opinions are under attack. Jeanette Groth has been particularly successful in this regard. In fact, one year, her middle school students voted her tests "most interesting"—a pretty amazing vote of confidence from often test-weary adolescents. Take a look at two of the challenges Jeanette sets her students:

Bickmore (1999)

- At the end of an eighth-grade unit on early culture contact in the Americas, students respond to this task: You have been invited to participate in KET's (a local educational television network) great debates in history show. In preparation, you have been asked to consider whether, in trying to help Native Americans, Bartolome did more harm than good. Write a paragraph to defend your position on this issue, then explain how this period in history may have affected your life today.
- In another class, students studying the Holocaust are asked to imagine the following scenario: You have been invited to be a guest speaker at a unity banquet. You have decided to focus on the Holocaust and anti-Semitism today. What would your speech include? How have our studies broadened your thinking on this topic?

You will notice that each task provides latitude for students to express different points of view about the history they have studied. Each question also asks students to make a connection between past and present—how has a historical period influenced life today? How has a particular study broadened students' thinking? Jeanette is careful to explain that their responses will not be assessed on the basis of the position they take on an issue but on the quality of the support they marshal in defense of a position.

Although there are many ways for students to express what they know and understand about historical conflicts and controversies, it often helps to introduce them to some of the social forms used to express and comment on different points of view. Sometimes Jeanette asks students to use these genres—cartoons, videotapes, pictures, and photographs—to explain either a particular position or alternate positions on historical conflicts. To ensure that she understands what her students are trying to communicate, she asks students to provide a key on the back of a cartoon or photograph. She finds that her students don't mind providing the key if it helps to make their point. They are generally appreciative of the opportunity to select a medium that allows them to best show what they know and want to make sure their teacher and peers fully understand the points they are trying to make. Jeanette also capitalizes on her students' interest in sharing their work with peers. "The pattern in my class," she explains, "is create, present, discuss." Repeated opportunities for students to explain their work—the "present and discuss" phases of this pattern—help students clarify their ideas. As they do so, Jeanette collects rich data on the progress of their thinking. During the "creation" phase, she informally observes student work, asks questions, and makes suggestions in regard to process and content. Observation and questioning also help her decide what kinds of "minilessons" need to be taught. If, for instance, students are struggling with a particular kind of source, Jeanette can plan for instruction directed at helping them better analyze or use the source. Similarly, she can identify other sources that might clarify a point, raise a new question, or present a different perspective. This kind of formative assessment is a crucial part of historical inquiry. No teacher can predict all the different turns an in-depth inquiry might take. Without careful monitoring of these turns, students can become frustrated and lose interest. Careful observation allows teachers to better anticipate students' needs and better scaffold their engagement with history.

The presentation and discussion phases are just as important as the creation phase in Jeanette's classroom. Once the students have a product—some form of historical interpretation or analysis—the opportunity to present that product to peers encourages more careful attention to the quality of the product. This only works, however, if presenters receive substantive feedback on their presentations and audience members have a reason to take the presentation seriously. Jeanette organizes presentations to maximize audience participation and provide useful feedback to presenters. "I always give them something to listen for," she explains. "Sometimes we put together an evaluation guide; sometimes we just list things on the board. But we always have something to focus on—to make sure they show their peers respect—for the work, of course, but for them as people, too." As students listen to their peers' presentation, they take notes. These notes, in turn, form the basis for follow-up discussion. During the discussion, the presenters are experts—they are expected to respond to questions, clarify points, and suggest places where further information might be located. In turn, they receive written feedback on their presentation from their peers (see Fig. 10.4). This feedback includes commentary on content and presentation style. Students discuss appropriate ways to offer and receive feedback, and Jeanette monitors and models both. In this way, assessment in the classroom becomes part of an ongoing, substantive conversation in which teacher and students work together to build shared understandings of the past.

Students need to learn the social forms for engaging in debate and discussion on controversial issues.

Seixas (1999)

Formative assessment helps teachers plan for and with their students.

Larson (1999)

Criteria for Presentation	Evaluation of Presentation
Connects to our unit of study	
Clearly communicates the content	
Provides interesting, accurate, and relevant details	
Identifies sources	
Keeps the audience's attention in positive ways	

FIG. 10.4.   Peer feedback form.

CONCLUSIONS

One of the functions of historical thinking is to help students make informed and reasoned decisions that promote personal as well as public good. When individuals begin to make such decisions, they are less likely to become the objects of manipulation and more likely to shape their own lives in dignity and respect for others. Individual decisions, however are not made in a vacuum. In contemporary U.S. culture, students often see violence modeled as a primary means of solving conflicts and problem solving rejected in favor of self-centered competition. It is not always easy or comfortable to alter these patterns, but we think it is worth the effort. If, as we argued in chapter 1, history is fundamentally controversial, then we have an obligation to help our students recognize and respond intelligently to controversy. If, in addition, democracy is based on a conflictual model of decision making, and if many of our public conflicts have historic roots, it becomes even more important to help students better understand how those conflicts played out historically and how they might participate in discussions about them. Finally, if exercising historical agency is embedded in how we respond to conflict and consensus, then we have another powerful argument for encouraging our students, not just to analyze conflicts but also to take reasoned and deliberate action to shape the future.

This chapter focused on two related aspects of historical thinking—recognizing the impact of conflict and consensus and understanding historical agency. In Dehea's class, these aspects were dealt with in the context of a social studies thematic unit on *community* (see chap. 8 for more detail on this unit). To help her students understand the impact of conflict and consensus in their community, she explicitly related public conflict management to classroom protocols. Her emphasis on metacognition—establishing metaphors to describe tasks, modeling procedures, and then asking students to analyze them, thinking aloud with students as they outlined the parameters of a "good argument"—provided cognitive touchstones for students new to inquiry into controversial issues. In addition, because the class focused on controversies in the local community, where they could interview relevant people, write to local officials, and survey participants in decision making, her students were initiated into the role of civic participant. Not only did they learn that other people have historic agency, but they practiced being agents themselves.

Historical agency influences how we respond to conflict and consensus.

Jim Farrell's students began with a more distant problem but found that some issues spread tentacles into the present. In their discomfort with the present manifestations of historic problems, some of the students rejected the role of historic agent; others embraced it. Like historic actors in the past, they made choices about how those issues would play out in their own lives. Jeanette Groth's students took the Bill of Rights and discovered that it was a living document that had a daily impact on their lives. In each of these classrooms, as well as in Viktor's and Billie's classes, disciplined, reflective inquiry helped students establish the significance of historic events and the impact of individual and collective agency—social participation—on the ways conflicts are managed. Although not every current or historic controversy requires such extensive treatment in the classroom, some issue, contention, or question lies at the heart of all historic inquiry. With no controversies, no questions to be resolved, and no perspectives to be understood, history is a lifeless thing—able to tell us little about an increasingly interdependent, complex, and controversial world.

Historical agency implies active civic participation.

CHILDREN'S AND ADOLESCENT LITERATURE

Nonfiction on Historical Controversies

Aaseng, N. *You Are the Supreme Court Justice*. Oliver, 1994. (Look for other titles in the "Great Decisions" series.)

Altman, L. J. *The Pullman Strike of 1894: Turning Point for American Labor*. Millbrook, 1994. (Look for other titles in the "Spotlight on American History" series.)

Ashabranner, B. *A New Frontier: The Peace Corps in Eastern Europe*. Cobblehill, 1994.

Children of Yugoslavia Staff. *I Dream of Peace*. HarperCollins, 1994.

Clinton, C. *The Black Soldier: 1942 to the Present*. Houghton Mifflin, 2000.

Colman, P. *Mother Jones and the March of the Mill Children*. Millbrook, 1994.

Filipovic, Z. *Zlata's Diary*. Viking ,1994.

Frank, A. *Anne Frank: The Diary of a Young Girl*. Doubleday, 1967.

Frank, A. *The Diary of Anne Frank: The Critical Edition*. Netherlands State Institute for War Documentation & Doubleday, 1989.

Freedman, R. *Kids at Work: Lewis Hine and the Crusade Against Child Labor*. Clarion, 1994.

Fritz, J. *The Double Life of Pocahontas*. Putnam, 1983.

Gay, K. *The New Power of Women in Politics*. Enslow, 1994. (Look for other titles in the "Issues in Focus" series.)

Hart, A. *Who Really Discovered America? Unraveling the Mystery and Solving the Puzzle*. Williamson, 2003.

Hoose, P. *We Were There, Too! Young People in History*. Farrar Straus & Giroux, 2001.

Howard, T. A., & Howard, S. *Kids Ending Hunger: What Can We Do?* Andrews & McMeel, 1992.

Knight, M. B. *Who Belongs Here? An American Story*. Tilbury, 1993.

Kuklin, S. *Iqbal Masih and the Crusaders Against Child Slavery*. Holt, 1998.

Lorbiecki, M. *Sister Anne's Hands*. Dial, 1998.

Meltzer, M. *Never to Forget: The Jews of the Holocaust*. Harpers, 1976.

Meltzer, M., & Cole, B. *The Eye of Conscience: Photographers and Social Change* (with 100 photographs by noted photographers, past and present). Fawcett, 1974.

O'Neill, L. A. *Little Rock: The Desegregation of Central High*. Millbrook, 1994. (Look for other books in the "Spotlight on American History" series.)

Robinet, H. G. *Forty Acres and a Mule*. Atheneum, 1998.

Springer, J. *Listen to Us: the World's Working Children*. Groundwood, 1998.

Statni Zidovske Museum, Prague. *I Never Saw Another Butterfly*. McGrawHill, 1964. (See also Bernstein, L. *Chichester Psalms: I Never Saw Another Butterfly*. Musicmasters, 1990.)

Sullivan, G. *The Day the Women Got the Vote: A Photo History of the Women's Rights Movement*. Scholastic, 1994.

Weisbrot, R. *Marching toward Freedom, 1957–1965: From the Founding of the Southern Christian Leadership Conference to the Assassination of Malcolm X*. Chelsea, 1994. (Look for other books in the "Milestones in Black American History" series.)

11

IN MY OPINION, IT COULD HAPPEN AGAIN

How Attitudes and Beliefs Have Changed Over Time

Throughout the year, Amy Leigh draws her fourth graders' attention to the way ideas, attitudes, values, and beliefs have changed over time. Near the beginning of the year, for example, the class investigates changes in names. After talking about their own first names, students collect information on names in their own, their parents', and their grandparents' generations—which names have become more or less common, how the length of names has changed, and how the reason for choosing names has changed. Students work in groups to record and analyze the data they collect, and they make presentations on their findings to the rest of the class. Afterward, they visit a nearby cemetery to collect information on names further back in time, and they examine 19th-century census records of Cherokee Indians and enslaved Africans for information on naming patterns among those populations.

Later in the year, Amy begins a unit on how social relations have changed over time. The class reads and discusses several works of children's literature that focus on attitudes toward racial, religious, and gender differences—works like *Teammates*, *The Number on My Grandfather's Arm*, *The Bracelet*, and *Bloomers!*—and students respond through activities such as simulated journals and written dialogues. Throughout this unit, Amy's focus is on the way people treat those who are different than themselves and the attitudes that underlie such treatment.

Later in the year, during a unit on life in Colonial America, students study the Salem witch trials. Amy begins by explaining how villagers' religious beliefs and their ideas about work and community influenced their attitudes toward each other. Over the next two weeks, students take on the roles of villagers and plan a simulated trial of a woman accused of witchcraft. Students have to plan their actions and statements based on the beliefs of people at the time. For example, witnesses decide what evidence would have been convincing to people at the time, and jurors decide what evidence would have convinced people then—not people today.

Being able to recognize the perspective of people in the past is a requirement for meaningful historical understanding. To understand why people acted as they did, it's necessary to be familiar with the cultural context that shaped their thoughts. Without examining the ideas, attitudes, values, and beliefs of people in history, their actions have no meaning. The development of racial slavery in British North America, for example, can only be understood with reference to Englishmen's ideas about the differences between themselves and Africans;

Historical thinking involves understanding the perspectives of people in the past. Lee (1978), Lee & Ashby (2001), Portal (1987), Shemilt (1984)

Jennings (1975), Jordan (1968)

the conquest of Native Americans by reference to ideas about what constituted civilization. Although advocates of a purely "factual" approach to the teaching of history sometimes claim that getting into the minds of people in the past is impossible—and therefore has no place in schools—nothing could be further from the truth. Most historical interpretations take into account people's motivations, and historians are careful to distinguish between those ideas that are based on contemporary attitudes and those that may have influenced people in the past. "Reading the present into the past"—explaining historic events by referring to contemporary standards—is a cardinal sin among historians; one cannot explain the actions of a medieval serf or lord, an 18th-century Japanese merchant, or a Texas farm woman in 1890 by pretending that they're all middle-class European Americans of the late 20th-century. Their worldviews, mentalities, and ideologies were different than those of people today, and those differences have to be taken into account—otherwise their actions may just seem stupid. Without understanding Salem villagers' attitudes toward God, the Devil, work, and community, for example, the practice of dunking someone in water to determine whether he or she was a witch looks like a flaw in logic. Most of us agree that there are no witches, and that even if there were, dunking them in water wouldn't prove much; if we apply our standards to Salem villagers, then, they all appear to be mentally defective.

Barton (2002), Barton & Levstik (1996), Levstik & Barton (1996)

And in fact, children often think precisely that until they have studied the perspectives of people in the past in more depth. We have emphasized that students come to school already knowing some things about how material life has changed over time—they quickly recognize historic clothes and technology, for example, and can even put them in a relatively accurate chronological sequence. But students' understanding of changes in ideas is much less sophisticated. They do know some things about the topic: They often recognize that people had different attitudes toward women and minorities in the past, and they may have learned that European settlers didn't consider Native Americans their equals. But they have rarely had the opportunity to see these attitudes as part of a coherent system of beliefs—one different from their own. Instead, they tend to think of them as idiosyncratic and inexplicable mistakes, and they generally conclude that people in the past weren't as smart as we are (similar to the way Billie's sixth graders in chap. 10 assumed Serbian aggression could only by explained by stupidity). By consistently asking students to think about why people did things differently in the past, though, Amy helps them develop a more complex understanding of how ideas have changed over time.

Historians avoid attributing contemporary attitudes to people in the past.

Many children know that attitudes toward race and gender were different in the past. Barton (1994)

Lee & Ashby (2001)

CHANGES IN NAMES

Students' belief that people in the past were stupid was often striking. While reading *Immigrant Kids*, for example, students in Tina Reynolds' class (chap. 5) began to discuss how people at the time washed their clothes; some thought they washed them in sinks because there were no washing machines, but one student was certain that there were indeed washing machines then—but that people were too stupid to use them! Clothing styles often inspired similar comments. For example, Tina found that students sometimes asserted that people long ago knew they were dressing "old fashioned" and realized that someday people would start doing things the right way. And in doing their family history projects, several students brought in their parents' high school yearbooks from the 1970s—"Why did they dress so nerdy?" they all wanted to know. The tendency of people in the 1970s to wear such obviously unattractive clothes led several students to conclude that "they must not have known it was picture day." Never having systematically explored the way ideas change over time, students had no way to explain polyester leisure suits other than outright ignorance.

Freedman (1980)

Children sometimes assume that people in the past were not as intelligent as people today. Barton (1996), Lee & Ashby (2001)

Without understanding that people in the past did not consider themselves stupid or old fashioned, it's difficult to understand much about history. If students think that people would have used washing machines if someone had just shown them how, or would have dressed differently if they had known how bad they looked, then studying the past must appear as an exercise in futility; all it shows is that people back then needed to be shaken until they got some sense. Fortunately, Amy has found it easy to move students beyond their initial belief in historical stupidity, and to help them recognize that people in the past considered themselves "normal," not old fashioned—that they saw things from a different perspective than we do. The Names project is the way she introduces students to this aspect of historical understanding.

The entire project was popular with students, and it provided a good transition from their personal and family histories (similar to those described in chaps. 4 and 5) to the History Museum projects in chapter 7. Students liked to talk about their names, and they usually had a great deal to say about them. Amy began the unit by reading the class *Wilfrid Gordon McDonald Partridge*, a book in which a boy makes friends with an elderly woman who also happens to have four names. In discussing the book, Amy asked students about their own names: Do any of you have four names? Do any of you have nicknames? Do you know how you got your name? Their response was passionate: They could barely stay in their seats, they were so excited about sharing what they knew about their names, whether they liked their names, and what they wished they had been named. For homework, each student had to find out three additional facts about his or her name—such as who they were named after or what they would have been named if they were the opposite sex—and share these in class the next day. They then used this information as the basis for essays that became part of their writing portfolios.

Having developed their interest in the topic, Amy later moved on to the more specifically historical aspects of the project. She asked whether they thought there were some names people used in the past that weren't common anymore, and most students could easily think of several—Gladys, Mabel, Thelma, Nola, and so on. They also thought there were some names that were common now—Tiffany, Amber, Crystal—that weren't used in the past, although they were less sure of their examples. Noting that most of their suggestions were women's names, Amy asked whether they thought women's names had changed more over time than men's. Although again they weren't sure, they thought they probably had. Finally, Amy asked whether they thought the reasons names were chosen were different in the past. Students were interested in the reasons for their own names, but most had no firm opinion on how those reasons may have been different in the past; a few suggested that more people were named after family members a long time ago.

Amy then introduced students to an assignment that would allow them to investigate these questions more systematically. She gave each student a data collection sheet (Fig. 11.1) on which they were to collect information on the names found in their generation, their parents', and their grandparents'. The next day, after giving students time to talk about what they had discovered, she divided them into groups and gave each group one of the following questions to answer:

- How have the reasons for men's names changed over time?
- How have the reasons for women's names changed over time?
- Are there some men's names that are found in only one generation or in all generations?
- Are there some women's names that are found in only one generation or in all generations?
- Have men's names gotten longer or shorter?
- Have women's names gotten longer or shorter?

Over the next week, students worked in groups to use their data sheets to answer these questions and design displays to communicate their findings.

Fox (1985)

Literature and personal connections can provide an introduction to the study of historical topics.

Students can use mathematical procedures to draw historical conclusions.

Generations

Yours (you, siblings, cousins)	Your parents' (parents, aunts, uncles)	Your grandparents' (grandparents, great aunts/uncles)
Name _____	Name _____	Name _____
Reason chosen:	Reason chosen:	Reason chosen:
___ liked the sound	___ liked the sound	___ liked the sound
___ named after relative	___ named after relative	___ named after relative
___ famous person	___ famous person	___ famous person
___ unknown	___ unknown	___ unknown
___ other _____	___ other _____	___ other _____
Name _____	Name _____	Name _____
Reason chosen:	Reason chosen:	Reason chosen:
___ liked the sound	___ liked the sound	___ liked the sound
___ named after relative	___ named after relative	___ named after relative
___ famous person	___ famous person	___ famous person
___ unknown	___ unknown	___ unknown
___ other _____	___ other _____	___ other _____
Name _____	Name _____	Name _____
Reason chosen:	Reason chosen:	Reason chosen:
___ liked the sound	___ liked the sound	___ liked the sound
___ named after relative	___ named after relative	___ named after relative
___ famous person	___ famous person	___ famous person
___ unknown	___ unknown	___ unknown
___ other _____	___ other _____	___ other _____
Name _____	Name _____	Name _____
Reason chosen:	Reason chosen:	Reason chosen:
___ liked the sound	___ liked the sound	___ liked the sound
___ named after relative	___ named after relative	___ named after relative
___ famous person	___ famous person	___ famous person
___ unknown	___ unknown	___ unknown
___ other _____	___ other _____	___ other _____

FIG. 11.1. Data collection chart.

The inquiry-oriented aspects of this project are obvious. But what does it have to do with recognizing the perspective of people in the past? This project did, in fact, go a long way toward helping students overcome their assumptions about the lack of intelligence long ago. As they were working on their projects, students frequently commented on some of the more unusual names they found, particularly in their grandparents' generation: "*Opal*, I like that name," or "*Cleatus*, I *know* nobody's named that anymore!" Whenever such comments arose, Amy asked why they thought those names weren't used anymore. Students' initial responses sometimes reflected their previous idea that people didn't know any better: "You wouldn't want to have a really cute boy, and name him *Oliver*, or a really cute girl, and name her *Pearl*." One student even suggested that people a long time ago didn't have enough education to be able to say all the letters of the alphabet, and thus couldn't pronounce all the names we can. But almost as soon as students made such suggestions, other students would correct them by pointing out that the names didn't sound funny back then, that they sounded perfectly normal or even "high tone"—and other students quickly agreed.

Perhaps because the topic was a simple one like names, or perhaps because the people being studied were their parents and grandparents, students began to understand that some things change just because fashion changes and not because people in the past couldn't see how stupid they were. After this project, whenever anyone in the class mentioned how unusual or perplexing something in history seemed, other students could be counted on to interject, "But it wouldn't seem that way to *them*, it just seems that way to us because we're not used to it." Moreover, students were quite conscious, and even proud, of their change in understanding: They knew they hadn't quite gotten it before and now they did. In addition to all the benefits of the process of historical inquiry, then, this project helped students begin to see how their own perspective differed from people in the past—a fundamental characteristic of historical understanding.

Students can understand that the perspectives of people in the past differed from their own.

CHANGES IN SOCIAL RELATIONS

There are, of course, more serious changes in perspective over time. Some of the most important involve the way people treat those who are different than themselves: Attitudes toward differences in race, religion, and gender have been responsible for many of history's most enduring and dramatic struggles. As noted in chapter 7, however, none of Amy's students chose to investigate changes in social relations during their History Museum projects. Instead, they focused on the aspects of everyday life they knew best—toys, clothes, cars, and so on. Amy knew that it would be her responsibility to expand students' understanding of changing perspectives on social relations, and for this, she relied primarily on children's literature.

Amy began this unit by asking students if any of them had ever wanted to do something and not been allowed. They all had examples, of course, and Amy listed these on the board, along with the reasons they had been given for not being able to do what they wanted. She then asked which reasons they thought were fair and which ones weren't. Most students saw that some reasons were fair even if they disagreed with them—not being able to have a slumber party until the same age as a sister, for example, or not being allowed to ride a motorbike because of the danger. Others they considered clearly unfair: One girl couldn't play soccer because she was a girl, while a boy couldn't stay overnight at his friend's house because the friend lived in a public housing project.

Personal experiences can provide an introduction to historical topics.

Amy had meant to spend this entire first lesson simply exploring the concepts of *fair* and *unfair* treatment and talking about how attitudes may influence people's treatment of each other. In the middle of the discussion, though, one student noted, "Hey, this sounds like prejudice and discrimination!" Several other students agreed with her, and Amy made the most of the opportunity—asking them if they knew of any times in history when people had been treated unfairly. One girl had recently read *Number the Stars* and *The Diary of Anne Frank*, and she explained how Jews had been treated unfairly "during the war." Another mentioned slaves being treated unfairly because of their color. Yet another student had read *Journey to Topaz* and explained that "the China people were treated bad just like the Jews." Students also suggested that Lincoln and Kennedy had been treated unfairly because they had been assassinated, and the class discussed the distinction between actions directed toward individuals—because of specific things they had done that others didn't like—and those toward entire groups. Nor did students simply consider these issues a thing of the past: They knew many examples, both from personal experience and from the media, of racial and sexual discrimination in the present.

Lowry (1990), Frank (1967), Uchida (1985)

Students sometimes recognize that prejudice and discrimination are contemporary problems.

This discussion indicates just how much historical knowledge children have. By fourth grade, many of them have encountered the topic of slavery while learning about Harriet Tubman and have heard words like *prejudice* and *discrimination* when studying Martin Luther King, Jr. Sources outside formal instruction provide an even wider range of information. Students often read historical fiction on their own, and the girl who had just read *Number the Stars* wasn't the only one who had heard about the Holocaust: Several others had recently seen news reports on television about its commemoration. Children sometimes also learn about how women and minorities were treated differently in the past from their relatives or other adults outside of school. Of course, this information is often lacking in context and elaboration, and students will benefit from learning that it was Japanese Americans (not "the China people") who were put in camps, and that both relocation and the Holocaust happened about 60 years ago, during World War II. The fact that children already are familiar with both the concept of prejudice and specific historical examples, though, makes it easier for them to examine new information on the topic.

Over the next few weeks, Amy read aloud a variety of books about people who had been treated differently because of racial, ethnic, political, or gender differences—books such as *Teammates* (about the integration of baseball), *The Lily Cupboard* and *The Number on My Grandfather's Arm* (about the Holocaust), *The Bracelet* and *Baseball Saved Us* (about the internment of Japanese Americans during World War II), *Bloomers!* (about the women's rights movement in the 19th century), *Nettie's Trip South* and *Christmas in the Big House, Christmas in the Quarters* (about slavery in the American South), and *Katie's Trunk* (about a Loyalist family during the American Revolution). Amy wanted students to achieve two main things during this unit—to understand the attitudes and beliefs that led to unfair treatment in the past, and to explain some of the ways people responded to such treatment. Nearly all the books directly addressed attitudes, so it was relatively easy to keep an ongoing class record of this information on a wall chart. For example, *Bloomers!* explained that men in the 19th century expected women to obey their husbands, and *The Number on My Grandfather's Arm* explained that many Germans thought Jews were to blame for all the country's problems. In most cases, students simply remembered what the books said and added that information to the chart. In a few cases, they elaborated on these explanations. For example, several thought that White Southerners were racist because it meant they could get other people to do their work for them, and others suggested men's attitudes toward women could be explained in much the same way. ("They didn't want to do anything around the house," as one student put it.) Although their understanding was still fairly simple, their explanations indicated they were beginning to see the connection between beliefs and the wider social context—rather than thinking of racism or sexism as inexplicable idiosyncrasies.

Interestingly, attitudes toward race and gender appeared easier for students to understand than other prejudices. Perhaps because these continue to be important issues today—or perhaps because they had learned more about them previously—students had few questions about such attitudes. They were interested in the specifics of slavery, in how Japanese Americans were treated in camps, and in what women could and couldn't do in the past, but none of them seemed to consider such treatment confusing; they knew that the beliefs of people in the past on these issues differed from their own. However, both the Holocaust and the treatment of Loyalists during the American Revolution inspired many more questions. Students didn't seem to understand why the Nazis would single out a religion for their attacks, nor did they ever quite understand how they knew who was Jewish and who wasn't. And although the story of *Katie's Trunk* (about Loyalists during the American Revolution) interested them, they were never sure who was on which side or what difference it made. In retrospect, Amy didn't consider their difficulties surprising, because understanding these episodes in history requires a much greater degree of background knowledge than they were likely to have. Moreover, we suspect that in regions where issues like religion form a more salient part of the community's diversity, students might more readily understand the prejudices that can accompany that aspect of identity.

154

The books Amy read to her class also provided an opportunity to compare the ways people have responded to mistreatment. After reading *Teammates*, for example, students pointed out that Jackie Robinson's main response was to put up with the abuse of the fans and other players, and to keep on doing his job. Amy also explained that, after he had established himself in the National League, Robinson began to speak out publicly on racial discrimination. The class recorded these responses on the wall chart, and when they read *Bloomers!*, they saw that women's reactions were similar to Robinson's: They put up with abuse, they kept on doing what they wanted, and they spoke out publicly. In several other books, the main response was either to hide or run away; this led to a discussion of what circumstances made one course of action wiser than another. Similarly, several books addressed the response of people not directly affected by mistreatment—PeeWee Reese in *Teammates*, for example, or Nettie and her brother in *Nettie's Trip South*—and the students discussed what people who witnessed discrimination could do about it. Studying such issues clearly relates to the civic ideals and practices that form a key element of national standards in the social studies.

National Council for the Social Studies (1994)

Students' initial response to most of the books was indignation: They were angry that anyone would mistreat others because of their race, religion, or gender. Amy encouraged them in their judgments about how wrong such actions were, but at first she worried their moral responses were so strong that they were failing genuinely to take the perspective of people in the past. Many of the activities she had planned for the class asked students to put themselves in the place of participants in these episodes and to make decisions about what they would have done—whether they would have tried to hide Jewish children in their homes during World War II, for example. At first students saw no reason to think they would have done otherwise (and frequently imagined themselves endowed with supernatural powers, able to hide every Jewish child in the Netherlands or to lead all the slaves to freedom). They argued that people were stupid not to know that everyone is the same, and they were sure they wouldn't have been that stupid if they were around then.

Such responses were similar to students' reaction to names like *Oliver*—why didn't they know any better? Rather than indicating a reversion to this earlier inability to understand the motivations of people in the past, Amy ultimately decided that they represented students' way of distancing themselves from the beliefs they were studying: They seemed to need this certainty as a way to demonstrate their own moral and ethical sensibility. Once they got past their initial discussions, students demonstrated a much more sophisticated inclination to take the perspective of people in history. After reading *The Lily Cupboard*, for example, students worked in pairs to complete decision charts (see Fig. 11.2) that listed the reasons for and against hiding Jewish families. Although all students ultimately decided they would have done so, they gave much more complicated reasons than they had initially, and they were careful to explain why they thought the benefits outweighed the potential dangers. Rather than seeing it as an obvious decision that no rational person could avoid, then, they came to consider it a complicated one that would have been difficult to make. Similarly, all the girls in the class were at first convinced that they too would have been an advocate for women's rights in the 19th century; on further reflection, however, some realized that their own attitudes as women might have been different then. As one girl said, "If it were *me* going back in time, I would have fought for women's rights, but if I had been a woman *then*, I might have been too afraid of what people would think."

See also Bardige (1988) and Levstik (1986b)

Decision charts allow students to record reasons for and against a course of action. For examples of other decision charts, see Alverman (1991).

Amy's use of graphic organizers was an important part of helping students think about these issues in more sophisticated ways. After reading *Teammates*, for example, students were assigned to write a simulated journal entry from the perspective of either Jackie Robinson or Pee Wee Reese. Before having them do

In simulated journals, students write diary-type entries from the perspective of people in history.

```
┌─────────────────────────────────────────────────┐
│  Question:                                        │
│                                                   │
│  ┌─────────────────────┐  ┌─────────────────────┐ │
│  │ Reasons for:        │  │ Reasons against:    │ │
│  │ _____    │  │ _____    │ │
│  │ _____    │  │ _____    │ │
│  │ _____    │  │ _____    │ │
│  │ _____    │  │ _____    │ │
│  │ _____    │  │ _____    │ │
│  │ _____    │  │ _____    │ │
│  └─────────────────────┘  └─────────────────────┘ │
│  Conclusion:                                      │
│                                                   │
└─────────────────────────────────────────────────┘
```

FIG. 11.2.   Decision chart.

that, though, she had them complete character webs for both Robinson and Reese (see Fig. 11.3). Students had to take these characteristics into account in their writing. Rather than simply a knee-jerk response, they had to try to make their journals reflective of the character traits they had identified. The webs, then, helped clarify how they could write from someone's perspective other than their own. Similarly, before writing a dialogue between Japanese Americans and the agents sent to detain them, students had to identify what goals each would have had and how they might have tried to reach them. Rather than stereotyping the characters as the embodiments of good and evil, students started to see them as real people who were probably concerned primarily with getting through the day. Instead of thinking that any sensible Japanese American would have started a violent confrontation (as they were at first sure they would have done themselves), they understood why many people might have gone along in the hopes that matters would be straightened out. It was the graphic organizers that Amy used that required students to stop, think, and organize what they knew instead of leaping to unhistorical conclusions.

We should point out that Amy was careful about the kinds of perspectives she asked students to take. She never asked them to put themselves in the place of people whose behavior she condemned: Students did not have to pretend to be Nazi soldiers, racist baseball fans, or slaveowners. Although there may have been historical merit in having them try to take those perspectives, she considered such activities too manipulative, and we agree. Many educators seem enamored of the simulation in which a class of students is divided by eye color (or some other arbitrary characteristic) and one group is encouraged to mistreat the other for a day—purportedly so they will have firsthand experience with discrimination. We see no value, however, in encouraging students to act in ways that are ethically repugnant. We think Amy's pattern of asking students to imagine they are witnessing mistreatment—rather than engaging in it themselves—is much more likely to develop an ethic of caring while still retaining the validity of historical perspective recognition.

On character webs, students record physical features, personality characteristics, and other traits.

In written dialogues, students work in pairs to create an imaginary conversation between two historical characters.

Graphic organizers can lead to more thoughtful written responses.

Noddings (1992)

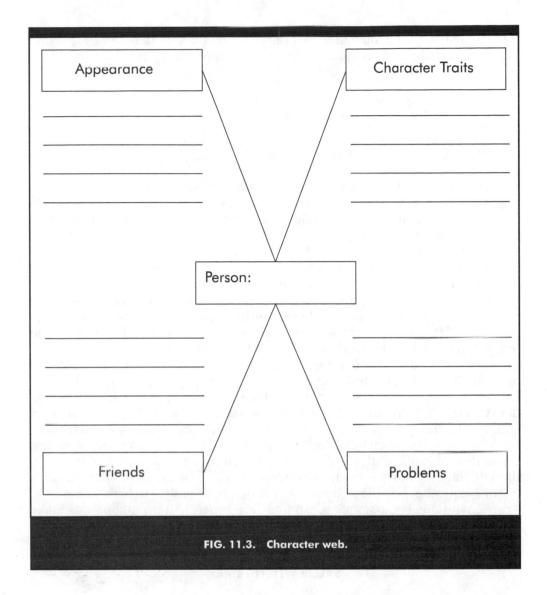

FIG. 11.3. Character web.

These response activities also demonstrate how teachers can avoid the temptation to "basalize" literature. Although many schools now buy trade books for use in classrooms, teachers often are at a loss as to what students can do with them. Traditional textbook programs come with a vast array of supplementary materials that can keep students busy for hours on end, but it's not always clear just what they should do after reading a chapter in a novel. Publishers have rushed in to fill this void, and teachers can now purchase dittos and blackline masters to accompany many well-known trade books. These materials too often mimic the worst features of textbook programs: They require students to copy definitions of vocabulary words, fill in blanks, and answer comprehension questions. With activities like these, students may learn to dislike reading good literature as much as they dislike reading textbooks.

In Amy's class, in contrast, students are asked to consider the content of what they read: They read literature to learn about themselves and the world. When the students have all read the same book, she has them write dialogues, perform skits, or write simulated journals—all activities in which they have to take what they have learned and extend their understanding by putting it in a new form. During their independent reading, on the other hand, students keep a dialogue journal in which they respond to the work they are reading. Because students often aren't sure what to write when journal assignments are completely unstructured, many teachers assign focused but open-ended questions for stu-

Students read literature to learn about themselves and the world.

In dialogue journals, students respond to literature, and teachers respond to students' observations.

dents to use in formulating their responses. Rhoda Coleman (see chaps. 2 and 12), for example, assigns students to choose from among the following questions after reading each chapter:

- What is your reaction to the events and words in this chapter?
- What questions do you have for the author or characters?
- What would you want to say to the author or characters?
- What predictions can you make about what will happen next?
- How does this chapter relate to your own experience?

Unlike commercial dittos, Amy's and Rhoda's activities help students understand what it means to engage with literature in authentic ways. When people read, they don't sit down and copy definitions or count syllables: They think about what they're reading—why an author wrote something the way she did, why a character acts as he does, how it relates to their own experiences. Students learn that reading is a way to grapple with issues that are significant and meaningful, not a prelude to easily graded school exercises.

This unit also encouraged students to see history itself as significant. We have sometimes heard people express hesitation at "exposing" young children to topics like the Holocaust or slavery out of concern that they are too innocent to learn about such violence. In our experience, however, most children have grown up on a steady diet of violent cartoons, movies, and television shows and are usually well acquainted with the most gory details of contemporary terrorism and warfare. Compared with the violence students see every day in the media, children's literature is quite tame. What most students have not been exposed to, though, is what motivates people to mistreat others or what could be done to prevent such behavior. Without the kind of reflection Amy provides, students may come to think of violence as natural and inevitable; in this unit, though, they see that people make decisions about their actions—they choose to mistreat others or they choose to condemn or resist such mistreatment. Armed with this understanding, students are much better equipped to make their own decisions in the future.

SALEM WITCH TRIALS

In studying the Salem witch trials, students encountered a set of beliefs that differed dramatically from their own. Amy began this topic in much the same way as she had the study of social relations. With students sitting on the carpet in the front of the room, she asked if any of them had ever been accused of something they hadn't done. Needless to say, students had a number of examples to volunteer, and the discussion of unfair accusations and how to counter them took up most of the first class. Much of this discussion focused on the reasons a person might be accused and the kinds of evidence that would be necessary to support or refute such accusations.

The next day, Amy (herself a descendant of Rebecca Nurse, who was hanged as a witch in Salem in 1692) began explaining the witchcraft accusations in 17th-century Salem village to students. She focused primarily on the villagers' religious beliefs—not only that witches were real but that idleness indicated a person was possessed by the devil. She also explained how a combination of physical disasters (such as an outbreak of smallpox and the death of livestock) and social tensions (revolving around the local church) made people particularly likely to look for someone on whom to blame their problems. Just as they had during previous lessons, students were eager to condemn these accusations—pointing out that witches don't really exist and that being lazy "doesn't mean that the devil is in you." Many were particularly upset by the connection of

witchcraft and religion: Because they were convinced that the existence of

witches is contrary to Christianity, they found it reprehensible that people justi-
fied their accusations by reference to the Bible. (In our experience, students often do not understand that beliefs within Christianity have changed over time or
even that beliefs vary from one denomination to another.)

Once again, though, this reaction seemed to be a way of distancing themselves from the people they were studying. Once they had demonstrated to their
own satisfaction how much more logical (and theologically pure) they were
than some of their ancestors, they were ready to enter more fully into the mind-
set of Salem villagers—a perspective necessary for the central activity of this
unit, the creation of a fictional witchcraft trial. Amy assigned students various
roles to play—accused and accusers, prosecutors, defense attorneys, jury
members, and witnesses for the prosecution and defense—and gave them general background information on their roles. (Because Amy's purpose was for
students to learn about the perspective of people in the past—rather than the
evolution of trial procedures—these roles more closely resembled contemporary courtrooms than the proceedings of 17th-century trials.)

There was no script for this trial; except for explaining procedures such as
who got to call their witnesses first, Amy left the development of the trial to the
students. For the next several days, they met in small groups to discuss their
roles and what they entailed. Jury members decided what kinds of evidence
they would listen for, witnesses wrote depositions on their knowledge of the accused, and attorneys planned their strategies. Of course, Amy was hardly idle
during this time. She constantly met with students to help them perfect their
plans. Through their discussions with her and their reading of the primary, secondary, and other sources she had provided, students largely were able to separate their contemporary perspectives from those of people at the time. For
example, jury members decided that they would look for marks on the body of
the accused, while defense attorneys prepared the accused to recite the Lord's
Prayer as evidence of her innocence.

Students can take
responsibility for
planning dramatic
activities.
Fines & Verrier (1974)

The trial itself was a big hit; several months later, most students said it was
their favorite activity of the entire year. Many did their best to dress the part—
judges wore black sweats to approximate robes—and several students used
what they knew about the language of the time (with the occasional lapse, as
when the defense attorney asked a witness why he thought the accused was "a
slimeball"). Meanwhile, the accused repeatedly erupted into fits during the trial.
Students' enthusiasm and flair notwithstanding, most of their learning had taken
place before this point—during the discussion and planning that led up to it. It
was while preparing what to say, what to ask, and what to listen for that students
were most actively engaged in learning about the period.

Drama is one of students'
favorite activities.

For this kind of activity to be a meaningful learning experience, students must
be given responsibility for creating the drama based on their investigation of the
issues of the day. Telling students to "role-play" George Washington is unlikely to
inspire in-depth research or consideration of alternative interpretations, and if
they are simply enacting a predetermined script, they may learn something
about acting but will probably gain little insight into the historical period under
study. With a script, the story is already in place, the characters and themes already set, and students have nothing to do but play their parts; when they are involved in creating a drama, though, they obviously have a much more active
role. Using role play and simulations as opportunities to play out different interpretations or constructions of events can support recognition of historical perspectives. This kind of drama demands historical inquiry, as students refine their
questions, consult evidence, consider a range of responses, test possibilities,
and examine the results. Without such inquiry, they could not have pulled off the
performance. They would have had little idea what to say, could not have responded to unanticipated questions, and would not have known where they
were going or how to get there.

Preparing for role play
requires learning about
the period under study.

Effective drama involves
students in inquiry.
Fines & Verrier (1974)

LONG-TERM ASSESSMENT OF HISTORICAL SKILLS

Teachers need to assess
the specifically historical
aspects of students' work.

As we have emphasized throughout this book, teachers need to assess students' understanding of history by focusing on the specifically historical aspects of their work. Teachers in chapters 4 to 6 emphasized students' understanding of historical concepts such as *causality, evidence*, and *significance*. In chapters 7 to 9, students grappled with more complicated historical projects, and assessment focused on the soundness of their historical *interpretations*; those projects not only included attention to causality, evidence, and significance but also to students' descriptions of change over time and their use of historically accurate details. In both chapter 10 and this chapter, we have highlighted the importance of another aspect of historical interpretation—*perspective recognition*.

Most historical skills can
only be measured along
a continuum.

Recognizing the perspective of people different than oneself, like most historical skills, can only be measured along a continuum; it is not a skill students lack one day and possess the next, like the ability to multiply fractions. When district or state curriculum guidelines are written as a series of discrete objectives, it is easy to regard them as a kind of checklist—Monday we'll teach understanding of time, Tuesday we'll do evidence, and Wednesday is perspective recognition. But like most important skills, perspective recognition cannot be taught, practiced, and mastered during the course of a single, seven-step lesson; it requires sustained attention in a variety of contexts over the course of many lessons, many units, and many years. As adults, for example, we still struggle to understand how people who were perceptive enough to write that "All men are created equal" could condone slavery, or how devout Christians could persecute and torture those whose beliefs or practices differed from their own. Assessing students' facility with perspective recognition, then, is not a matter of giving them 18 points out of 20 on a single assignment but of attempting to evaluate their gradual progress toward a complex and difficult component of sophisticated historical understanding.

Assessing such complex skills requires a more long-term approach than is typically found in the content areas, where one-day assignments and weekly tests predominate. The scoring rubric in Fig. 11.4 represents one way of thinking about the progress of students' recognition of historical perspectives. Like the rubric in chapter 8, it is not used to evaluate individual assignments (although it might be adapted for that purpose). On the contrary, a variety of individual assignments can be used to provide evidence for a student's location on the rubric. Amy's goal over the course of the year is for her students to move into at least the "Proficient" category. To assess whether they have done so, she gathers evidence from all the relevant assignments they have done—the "Names" project, literature response activities, the Salem witch trial reenactment, and so on. This evidence includes anecdotal records, graded assignments, and portfolio entries. The result of all this is not the assessment of an assignment, but the assessment of a student; it takes the form not of a numerical average but of a narrative report on that student's historical understanding.

Assessment should extend
over more than a single
school year.

The use of a long-term process like this illustrates another important characteristic of assessment—its ability to extend over more than one school year. Although schools have not traditionally put a premium on cross-grade organization and communication, many educators are becoming aware of the need to coordinate students' experiences over a number of years. For example, some schools are experimenting with "looping," where teachers change grades each year so they can stay with the same group of students as they progress through two or more levels. (We know one teacher who keeps the same set of students from Kindergarten through Grade 8.) Other schools have divided faculty into instructional teams that work together to guide students' learning over a number of years; although individual teachers may continue to have the same grade level each year, they take joint responsibility for a single group of students

160

as they move through primary, intermediate, or secondary school. In both models, teachers report the advantages of getting to know students better and of having a more developed sense of their prior academic progress. A long-term rubric such as that in Fig. 11.4 can help add continuity to such efforts. If such rubrics are used by all teachers in a team—from Grade 4 to Grade 6, for example, or Grade 6 to Grade 8, depending on school and team structures—teachers can develop a more consistent set of expectations for students' achievement and track their progress over more than a single year. Teachers consistently report that the joint development of such scoring guidelines helps them more clearly think through what they expect out of students.

Cross-grade school organization allows teachers to develop long-term relationships with students and better insights into their achievements.

Level	Indicators
Level 4 Distinguished	Student explains the actions of people in history by reference to the values, attitudes, beliefs, or experiences that were present at the time under study, including the ways in which they conflicted with each other or caused tensions; connects changes in behavior over time to a variety of interconnected factors, including changing values, beliefs, etc.; uses authentic language characteristic of the time, including slang, colloquialisms, and unusual or uncommon details; compares judgments based on values of the time and those based on contemporary values and suggests reasons for the differences
Level 3 Proficient	Student explains the actions of people in history by reference to the values, attitudes, beliefs, or experiences that were present at the time under study; connects changes in behavior over time to changing values, beliefs, etc.; uses language and details characteristic of the time; makes judgments based on values of the time
Level 2 Developing	Student recognizes historical differences in values, attitudes, beliefs, and experiences but does not completely connect these to changing behaviors; uses some language and details characteristic of the time, along with some anachronisms; makes judgments based on present-day values but recognizes that people in the past may not have shared those values
Level 1 Novice	Student explains the actions of people in history by reference to his/her own values, attitudes, beliefs, or experiences; cannot explain why people in the past acted differently than people in the present; uses language or other details characteristic of the present; makes judgments based on present-day values

FIG. 11.4. Long-term rubric for perspective recognition.

EXTENSIONS

Throughout this chapter, we have emphasized the importance of helping students gain insight into the perspectives of people in the past. Dramatic activities, simulated journals, and other responses to historical literature are particularly useful in involving students in deeper interactions with history, and these can easily be extended to a wide range of historical topics, events, and people. Although it is not always necessary to use literature as a starting point for role playing, it does have some advantages. First of all, literature generally attempts to get inside the head of characters, and readers come to understand at least some of the ideas and emotions that motivated people in the past. In addition, historical literature often incorporates personal idiosyncrasies that enrich characterization.

Literature highlights the ideas and motivations of people in history. O'Brien (1998)

For instance, Paul Fleischman's *Bull Run* consists of a series of monologues representing different perspectives on the Battle of Bull Run. A Southern officer recalls the first shots at Fort Sumter, a young boy tells of signing on as a drummer because he is too young to be a soldier, a Minnesota woman laments her father's harshness that sent her brother to war, and another young man signs on with the Confederacy because the army promises him a horse. This book naturally lends itself to dramatic presentation. In Dee Hallau's fifth-grade class, for example, she asks students to role-play characters from Fleischman's book. "These are people who never met each other," she tells her class. "Given what you have read about each of them, what might they say to each other? What questions might they ask each other? What questions would you want to ask them?" Three

Fleischman (1993)

students are selected and assigned roles. They come to the front of the room and sit at a table where they can see each other and be seen by their classmates. Dee asks the rest of the class to write questions on 3 × 5 index cards for the characters. She shuffles these, along with several questions she has written out, and then serves as moderator of the ensuing role play.

Note that students are not simply asked to "act like" a particular character. Instead, they are given a specific task to resolve as they think their character would have responded. They are allowed to refer back to the book, but few of the questions can be answered only by reference to Fleischman's novel. Instead, they have to think about what motivated a particular person and, given the time and circumstance, how that person might have answered questions such as "If you had it to do over again, would you still join the Confederacy/Union?" or "How much do you think slavery had to do with this war?" As the students respond from their characters' perspectives, Dee periodically stops and asks the class if they think a particular response is supportable, given their reading of the book, and students are encouraged to give each other suggestions. In addition, Dee occasionally switches role players so that most students have an opportunity both to ask questions and take on the perspective of one of the book's characters.

Some teachers also use historical roundtables, in which students take on the roles of specific individuals from history and other students serve as reporters who interview them. One roundtable discussion might include a mine worker, a family member, a union organizer, a mine owner, a scab, and a Pinkerton detective (hired to break up union activity). Using books such as *On Fire* and *The Thundering Voice of John L. Lewis* and movies like *Matewan* and *Harlan County U. S. A.*, students could investigate the personal and political goals that motivated each of these individuals, the practical concerns that restrained their actions, and the courses of action they chose. Such roundtables can also be organized around themes rather than specific events; one such roundtable might involve dialogue about independence movements among Gandhi (India), Jinah (Pakistan), Mandela (South Africa), Bolivar (South America), and Sam Adams (United States). Just as in the Salem witch trial drama, students would need a thorough understanding of diverse viewpoints to be able to carry out these projects.

The marginal notes read:

Students use what they know about specific characters to respond to questions.

In historical roundtables, students take on the roles of specific individuals from history.

Sebestyen (1985), Selvin (1969), Balson & Sayles (1987), Kopple (1976)

CONCLUSIONS

Understanding the perspectives of people in the past is a fundamental aspect of historical understanding, yet students often have given the topic little thought—assuming, for example, that people were too stupid to know better than to mistreat others or give their children names like Opal. But by reading and discussing literature, making comparisons to their own experiences, and engaging in response activities such as simulated journals, written dialogues, dialogue journals, and drama, students can come to understand the ideas, attitudes, and beliefs that underlay the actions of people in the past and see them as part of a larger social context.

Focusing on attitudes and beliefs calls attention to the enduring human dilemmas at the core of historical study.

Such a program of study is not merely an academic exercise but an important means to help students see history as meaningful and relevant. People still face the kinds of problems described in this chapter—how to get along with those from different backgrounds, how to explain social problems, and whether to engage in warfare. Focusing on the motivations that influence such decisions helps students see history not as inevitable, but as subject to human reason, and to see the *study* of history as a way to apply reason to contemporary problems. Many of Amy's students, in fact, drew precisely that conclusion: They thought people studied history so they would know what not to do in the future. They consistently pointed out that history was worth studying so that they would know not to mistreat African Americans, women, Jews, or immigrants. Although some elementary students have a limited perception of contemporary racism, prejudice, and discrimination, others know from the media or their own experiences that these are indeed enduring issues in society. When asked whether she thought people's attitudes were different today than in the past, for example, one sixth-grade girl in a racially mixed urban area—whose class had been reading literature on the Holocaust—pointed to the skinheads, Klan, and "other kooks" in her neighborhood and concluded that not much had changed. "In my opinion," she said, "It could happen again."

Barton & Smith (1994)

On the other hand, there's more to participatory democracy than dismissing other people as kooks, as tempting as that may be. In fact, those who are prejudiced against others because of their ethnicity, nationality, religion, or sexuality are likely to dismiss the rest of us as kooks. Fortunately, discrimination on the basis of some of these prejudices is illegal, but we all know that doesn't prevent prejudice, nor does it provide much guidance when new issues arise. Democratic deliberation requires that we engage meaningfully with people whose perspectives are different from our own, and this is possible only if we entertain the possibility that people with different worldviews may have reasons for their beliefs. Sometimes we may come to understand their perspectives even as we disagree with them, just as we can understand Salem villagers' belief in witchcraft without accepting it as our own. Other times we may never fully understand the beliefs of others, but in a democracy we have to accept their right to participate anyway; we must learn to work alongside those with whom we disagree—and they must learn to work with us. The students in this chapter began to develop such recognition: They learned that people in the past were not inferior versions of themselves, but intelligent human beings with different outlooks on what was moral, desirable, or just. We don't know if they will apply this recognition to people in the present, or what the impact will be if they do. We hope, however, that such understanding will help our democracy move beyond a competition between opposing perspectives; we hope that efforts at mutual understanding will lead to a future we all can live with.

Barton & Levstik (2004), Parker (2003)

CHILDREN'S AND ADOLESCENT LITERATURE

Women's Roles in Society

Blumberg, R. *Bloomers!* Bradbury Press, 1993.

Chang, I. *A Separate Battle: Women and the Civil War.* Lodestar, 1991.

Clinton, S. *The Story of Susan B. Anthony.* Children's Press, 1986.

Coleman, P. *Rosie the Riveter.* Crown, 1995.

Colman, P. *Where the Action Was: Women War Correspondents in World War II.* Crown Books, 2002.

Cullen-DuPont, K. *Elizabeth Cady Stanton and Women's Liberty.* Facts on File, 1992.

Dash, J. *We Shall Not Be Moved: The Women's Factory Strike of 1909.* Scholastic Press, 1996.

DePauw, L. G. *Founding Mothers: Women in America in the Revolutionary Era.* Houghton Mifflin, 1975.

Duffy, J. *Radical Red.* Charles Scribner's Sons, 1993.

Fritz, J. *You Want Women to Vote, Lizzie Stanton?* Putnam, 1995.

Hearne, B. *Seven Brave Women.* Greenwillow, 1997.

Hoople, C. G. *As I Saw It: Women Who Lived the American Adventure.* Dial Press, 1978.

Johnston, N. *Remember the Ladies.* Scholastic, 1995.

Kendall, M. E. *Failure is Impossible: The History of American Women's Rights.* Lerner, 2001.

Krull, K. *Lives of Extraordinary Women: Rulers, Rebels (And What the Neighbors Thought).* Harcourt Children's Books, 2000.

Landau, E. *Hidden Heroines and Women in American History.* Julian Messner, 1975.

McCully, E. A. *The Ballot Box Battle.* Knopf, 1996.

McCully, E. A. *The Bobbin Girl.* Dial, 1996.

Macy, S. *A Whole New Ball Game: The Story of the All-American Girls Professional Baseball League*. Henry Holt & Company, 1993.

O'Neal, Z. *A Long Way to Go*. Viking, 1990.

Pinkney, A. D. *Let It Shine: Stories of Black Women Freedom Fighters*. Gulliver, 2000.

Rappaport, D. *American Women: Their Lives in Their Words*. Thomas Y. Crowell, 1990.

Sullivan, G. *The Day that Women Got the Vote: A Photo History of the Women's Rights Movement*. Scholastic, 1994.

World War II Era and the Holocaust

Abells, C. B. *The Children We Remember*. Greenwillow, 1986.

Adler, D. A. *Hilde and Elie: Children of the Holocaust*. Holiday House, 1994.

Adler, D. A. *The Number on My Grandfather's Arm*. Union of American Hebrew Congregations, 1987.

Adler, D. A. *A Picture Book of Anne Frank*. Holiday House, 1993.

Avi. *Who Was That Masked Man, Anyway?* Orchard, 1992.

Bacharach, S. D. *Tell Them We Remember: The Story of the Holocaust*. Little, Brown, 1994.

Chaikin, M. *A Nightmare in History: The Holocaust, 1933–1945*. Houghton Mifflin, 1987.

Drukcer, M., & Halperin, M. *Jacob's Rescue: A Holocaust Story*. Bantam Doubleday Dell, 1993.

Finkelstein, N. H. *Remember Not to Forget: A Memory of the Holocaust*. Franklin Watts, 1985.

Frank, A. *Anne Frank: The Diary of a Young Girl*. Doubleday, 1967.

Friedman, I. R. *Escape or Die: True Stories of Young People Who Survived the Holocaust*. Addison-Wesley, 1982.

Fox, A. L., & Abraham-Podietz, E. *Ten Thousand Children: True Stories Told by Children Who Escaped the Holocaust on the Kindertansport*. Behrman House, 1998.

Greenfield, E. *Easter Parade*. Hyperion, 1998.

Greenfeld, H. *The Hidden Children*. Ticknor & Fields, 1993.

Hahn, M. D. *Following My Own Footsteps*. Clarion, 1996.

Isaacs, A. *Torn Thread*. Scholastic, 2000.

Jules, J. *The Grey Striped Shirt: How Grandma and Grandpa Survived the Holocaust*. Alef Design Group, 1993.

Kerr, J. *When Hitler Stole Pink Rabbit*. Dell, 1987.

Koehn, I. *Mischling, Second Degree: My Childhood in Nazi Germany*. Greenwillow Books, 1977.

Kuhn, B. *Angels of Mercy; The Army Nurses of World War II*. Atheneum, 1999.

Laird, C. *Shadow of the Wall*. Greenwillow Books, 1989.

Leigh, V. *Anne Frank*. Bookwright Press, 1986.

Leitner, I. *The Big Lie: A True Story*. Scholastic, 1992.

Lowry, L. *Number the Stars*. Dell, 1990.

Matas, C. *Daniel's Story*. Scholastic, 1993.

Meltzer, M. *Never to Forget: The Jews of the Holocaust*. Harper & Row, 1976.

Meltzer, M. *Rescue: The Story of How Gentiles Saved Jews in the Holocaust*. New York: Harper & Row, 1988.

Mochizuki, K. *Passage to Freedom: The Sugihara Story*. Lee & Low, 1997.

Oppenheim, S. L. *The Lily Cupboard*. HarperCollins, 1992.

Orlev, U. *The Man from the Other Side*. Houghton Mifflin, 1991.

Polacco, P. *The Butterfly*. Philomel, 2000.

Reeder, C. *Foster's War*. Scholastic, 1998.

Reiss, J. *The Journey Back*. HarperCollins, 1987.

Reiss, J. *The Upstairs Room*. HarperCollins, 1987.

Rinaldi, A. *Keep Smiling Through*. Harcourt, 1996.

Rogasky, B. *Smoke and Ashes: The Story of the Holocaust*. Holiday, 1988.

Rosenberg, M. B. *Hiding to Survive: Stories of Jewish Children Rescued from the Holocaust*. Clairon Books, 1994.

Taylor, J. L. *The Art of Keeping Cool*. Atheneum, 2000.

Toll, N. S. *Behind the Secret Window: A Memoir of a Hidden Childhood During World War Two*. Dial, 1993.

van der Rol, R., & Verhoeven, R. *Anne Frank: Beyond the Diary, a Photographic Remembrance*. Viking, 1993.

Vogle, I., & Vogel, M. *Bad Times, Good Times: A Personal Memoir*. Harcourt Brace Jovanovich, 1992.

Volavkova, H., Ed. *I Never Saw Another Butterfly: Children's Drawings and Poems from Terezin Concentration Camp, 1942–1944*.

Warren, A. *Surviving Hitler: A Boy in the Nazi Death Camps*. HarperCollins, 2001.

Wickham, M. *A Golden Age*. Smithsonian, 1996.

Yolen, J. *The Devil's Arithmetic*. Puffin, 1990.

Relocation of Japanese Americans During World War II

Allen, T. B. *Remember Pearl Harbor: American and Japanese Survivors Tell Their Stories.* National Geographic, 2001.

Bunting, E. *So Far From the Sea.* Clarion, 1998.

Cooper, M. L. *Fighting for Honor: Japanese Americans and World War II.* Houghton Mifflin, 2000.

Hamanaka, S. *The Journey: Japanese-Americans, Racism, and Renewal.* Orchard, 1990.

Levine, E. *A Fence Away From Freedom.* G. P. Putnam's Sons, 1995.

Mochizuki, K. *Baseball Saved Us.* Lee & Low Books, 1993.

Perl, L. *Behind Barbed Wire: The Story of Japanese-American Internment During World War II.* Benchmark Books, 2002.

Salisbury, G. *Under the Blood-Red Sun.* Delacorte, 1994.

Savin, M. *The Moonbridge.* Scholastic, 1992.

Stanley, J. *I Am an American: A True Story of Japanese Internment.* Crown, 1994.

Takashima, S. *A Child in Prison Camp.* Tundra Books, 1991.

Thesman, J. *Molly Donnelly.* Houghton Mifflin, 1993.

Tunnell, M. O., & Chilcoat, G. W. *The Children of Topaz: The Story of a Japanese-American Internment Camp.* Holiday, 1996.

Uchida, Y. *The Bracelet.* Philomel Books, 1993.

Uchida, Y. *Journey to Topaz.* Creative Arts, 1985.

Racism, Discrimination, and Civil Rights in American History

Bealer, A. W. *Only the Names Remain: The Cherokees and the Trail of Tears.* Little, Brown, 1972.

Duncan, A. F. *The National Civil Rights Museum Celebrates Everyday People.* Bridgewater Books, 1995.

Goldenbock, P. *Teammates.* Harcourt Brace, 1990.

Haskins, J. *The Day Martin Luther King, Jr. Was Shot: A Photo History of the Civil Rights Movement.* Scholastic, 1992.

Haskins, J. *The March on Washington.* HarperCollins, 1993.

Haskins, J. *The Scottsboro Boys.* Henry Holt, 1994.

Herlihy, D. *Ludie's Song.* Dial Books, 1988.

Jiménez, F. *Breaking Through.* Houghton Mifflin, 2001.

Levine, E. *Freedom's Children: Young Civil Rights Activists Tell Their Own Stories.* G. P. Putnam's Sons, 1993.

McKissack, P. *Goin' Someplace Special.* Atheneum, 2001.

McKissack, P. C., & McKissack, F. L. *Christmas in the Big House, Christmas in the Quarters.* Scholastic, 1994.

McKissack, P., & McKissack, F. L. *The Civil Rights Movement in America from 1965 to the Present.* Children's Press, 1991.

Meltzer, M. *Black Americans: A History in Their Own Words.* Crowell, 1984.

Meyer, C. *White Lilacs.* Harcourt, 1993.

Miller, W. *Richard Wright and the Library Card.* Lee & Low, 1997.

Myers, W. D. *Now is Your Time: The African-American Struggle for Freedom.* HarperCollins, 1991.

Siegel, B. *The Year They Walked: Rosa Parks and the Montgomery Bus Boycott.* Four Winds Press, 1992.

Taylor, M. D. *The Friendship.* Dial Books for Young Readers, 1987.

Taylor, M. D. *The Gold Cadillac.* Dial Books for Young Readers, 1987.

Taylor, M. D. *Let the Circle Be Unbroken.* Dial Books for Young Readers, 1981.

Taylor, M. D. *Mississippi Bridge.* Dial Books for Young Readers, 1990.

Taylor, M. D. *Roll of Thunder, Hear My Cry.* Dial, 1976.

Turner, A. *Nettie's Trip South.* Macmillan, 1987.

Walter, M. Pitts. *Mississippi Challenge.* Bradbury Press, 1992.

Wiles, D. *Freedom Summer.* Atheneum, 2001.

Yin. *Coolies.* Philomel, 2001.

For books on slavery, see the booklist at the end of chapter 12. For books on the Underground Railroad and on the experience of immigrants in the United States, see the booklist at the end of chapter 5.

Colonial Witchcraft Beliefs and Trials

Currie, S. *The Salem Witch Trials (History of the World)*. Kidhaven, 2002.

Dickinson, A. *The Salem Witchcraft Delusion, 1692: Have You Made No Contract with the Devil?* Franklin Watts, 1974.

Kohn, B. *Out of the Cauldron: A Short History of Witchcraft*. Holt, Rinehart, & Winston, 1972.

Lasky, K. *Beyond the Burning Time*. Scholastic, 1994.

Petry, A. *Tituba of Salem Village*. HarperCollins, 1991.

Rinaldi, A. *A Break with Charity: A Story About the Salem Witch Trials*. Harcourt Brace, 1992.

Rinaldi, A. *A Break with Charity: A Story about the Salem Witch Trials*. Gulliver Books, 2003.

Roach, M. K. *In the Days of the Salem Witchcraft Trials*. Houghton Mifflin, 1996.

Speare, E. G. *The Witch of Blackbird Pond*. Houghton Mifflin, 1986.

van der Linde, L. *The Devil in Salem Village*, 1992.

Woods, G. *The Salem Witchcraft Trials: A Headline Court Case*. Enslow, 2000.

Other Works in This Chapter

Flesichman, P. *Bull Run*. HarperCollins, 1993.

Fox, M. *Wilfrid Gordon McDonald Partridge*. Kane-Miller, 1985.

Freedman, R. *Immigrant Kids*. Scholastic, 1980.

Sebestyen, O. *On Fire*. Atlantic Monthly Press, 1985.

Selvin, D. F. *The Thundering Voice of John L. Lewis*. Lothrop, Lee, & Shepard, 1969.

Turner, A. *Katie's Trunk*. Macmillan, 1992.

12

NOSOTROS LA GENTE

Diverse Perspectives in American History

After reviewing the changes in the Virginia colony that led to an increased demand for labor, Rebecca Valbuena asks her fifth graders what they think of when they hear the word *slave*. Many of them have clear but fairly simple ideas, which Rebecca records on a chart— "they were whipped," "Black," "they had no freedom," "it was a long time ago," "they were always in chains." She explains that they are going to find out which of their ideas are correct and which they need to add to or change. After recording a list of their questions about slavery on another chart, she selects several students to perform Readers' Theater scripts based on firsthand accounts of the three passages of enslavement. After reading each selection, students brainstorm words to describe what slaves might have heard, seen, and touched, as well as what they might have said or felt. They then use these words and ideas to write poems from the perspective of enslaved Africans.

Over the course of this unit, students engage in several activities designed to extend and refine their understanding of slavery. In their second lesson, for example, they work in groups to develop a list of basic *human rights*—they suggest such things as privacy, being safe outside, speech, feelings, religion, clean air, nature, life, freedom, and "being yourself." She then shows them engravings of enslaved Africans and examples of slave codes from colonial Virginia; students compare these restrictions to their own list of rights and analyze why slave owners considered such measures necessary. The class concludes this lesson by discussing contemporary examples of violations of human rights; some students' families come from Guatemala and El Salvador and can supply examples from those countries, while others make comparisons to what they have learned at school about the Civil Rights movement, to media reports of events in Bosnia and Rwanda, or to their knowledge of topics—such as child abuse and sexual abuse—which rarely are discussed in school.

***

Rhoda Coleman's fifth graders begin their study of the Westward Movement of the mid-1800s by reading two selections from their basal series—one a collection of tall tales from the American West, the other a set of first-person accounts by Native Americans about the loss of their land. Earlier in the year, the class had studied the cultures of several Native American peoples, as well as the earliest contacts between Europeans and Native Americans, and so most students readily contribute to a Venn diagram comparing the perspectives of Native Americans and settlers. Before recess, students plot the routes of several of the major trails—such as the Oregon Trail and the National Road—on individual maps. After recess, Rhoda leads the class in beginning a KWL chart on the Westward movement— recording what they know already and what they want to know.

After lunch, Rhoda reads aloud from *Cassie's Journey*—an account of the trip west based primarily on women's diaries—and stops frequently to discuss the book with students.

Working in groups of three, students then develop a list of the hardships these settlers faced—either those they have just read about or others they know about or can imagine. After compiling a class list of these problems, Rhoda selects several students to be on the "Hot Seat"—to come to the front of the room to portray men, women, and children traveling west and to respond to questions from their classmates about the journey. They base some of their answers on what they have already learned today, while other questions are added to the KWL chart. Afterward, students write letters home from the perspectives of people on the journey, detailing where they are, what their hopes are, and what their think and feel. Over the next weeks, students will continue to listen to *Cassie's Journey* and other books, and they will use a variety of reference sources to investigate their questions and create simulated journals from the perspective of people on the trip west.

Many teachers must follow specific curriculum guidelines in teaching history.

Many teachers do not have the choice of studying the topics they or their students consider important; they don't have the option of exploring the Holocaust, Japanese American relocation, or the Salem witch trials. Particularly at fifth and eighth grades, when most states require American history to be taught, teachers are expected to cover the events that textbooks and curriculum guides have traditionally identified as the major events in the nation's past—early explorers, Colonial life, the American Revolution, the Westward Movement, and so on. Of course, these expectations are not unreasonable: We certainly hope that by the end of the middle grades, students will know about topics such as Europeans' encounter with Native Americans, the enslavement of African Americans, and the constitutional basis of American government. No one could understand "how we got here" without having a thorough acquaintance with these historical issues.

"Covering" content rarely leads to in-depth understanding.

Beck & McKeown (1991), McKeown & Beck (1994)

Unfortunately, studying the content traditionally found in textbooks often means using methods of instruction that revolve around those texts: assigning students to read a chapter on Monday, define vocabulary words on Tuesday, answer questions at the end of the chapter on Wednesday, review on Thursday, and take a test on Friday. In some schools, principals even require this sequence, week after week after week, to guarantee that the required curriculum is covered. It should be clear from our discussion in chapter 2 of how people learn that this kind of slavish and unimaginative use of textbooks guarantees something else entirely—that students will fail to understand either the content covered or the reason for covering it. Indeed, social studies texts are well known for their lack of readability. And in classrooms like Rhoda's and Rebecca's— where few students speak English as a native language—textbook reading in isolation would be practically unintelligible. Furthermore, because most of their students come from families who have immigrated to the United States only recently, the relevance of Jamestown or the Westward movement will need more explicit attention; few textbooks make it clear to a 10-year-old Tongan girl in Los Angeles what European Americans moving west in covered wagons have to do with her own life in the present.

California State Board of Education (1988)

Rhoda's and Rebecca's teaching shows how theory- and research-based methods of instruction can help students understand the content that too frequently is only "covered," and their approach shows that important historical principles can accompany such content. During the course of the year, for example, both Rebecca and Rhoda divide their social studies instruction into units that closely match the California state curriculum in history and social science—*The World and its Diversity* (including immigration and cultures around the world), *Cultures in Contact* (Native American cultures, European exploration, and Jamestown), *We the People* (slavery, Colonial life, the American Revolution, and the development of the Constitution), and *New Frontiers* (life in the new republic and the Westward movement). But neither teacher relies primarily on textbooks, nor do they value the simple coverage of information or amassing of facts. Instead, both Rebecca and Rhoda rely on literature and primary sources to develop students' understanding of content; in addition, they devote systematic attention to aspects of American history that are frequently ignored in textbook treatments—the multiple and often conflicting viewpoints on events that exist at any one time, for example, and the agency of people involved in past events. For their students, most of whose families have immigrated only recently from Mexico, Central America, Southeast Asia, or the Pacific Islands, America's history really does become a story of *Nosotros La Gente* (We the People): They study the thoughts, feelings, and actions of real people, and they learn about the diversity of perspectives and experiences that have been—and continue to be—part of our history.

PEOPLE IN AMERICAN HISTORY

Although textbooks typically focus on events—the taking of Fort Ticonderoga, Pickett's charge, the Wormley House agreement—most historians focus on people. In particular, historians examine the decisions people made in the past and how those decisions were affected by people's beliefs, their hopes, and their fears. It's not that historians don't study events as well, but an essential part of understanding events is knowing how they affected real people. Why did families start having fewer children in the early 18th century? Why did farmers join the Populist Party? How did Reconstruction affect the opportunities for former slaves in the South? For those who are not members of the academic discipline, the importance of people in history is even more pronounced—stories of courage, heroism, or simple endurance are more likely to strike a responsive chord than the analysis of political or legal affairs in history. Without the emphasis on people, history would be a highly abstract—and not particularly interesting—subject.

In the past three chapters, we have drawn attention to the importance of helping students make *human sense* of history, particularly through the use of various forms of narrative. Rebecca's and Rhoda's classrooms show how this perspective can be applied to many of the topics traditionally covered in American history courses. Just as in Amy Leigh's classroom (chap. 11), many of their activities require students to use what they have learned to put themselves in the place of historical actors. After reading accounts of enslavement, for example, Rebecca's students wrote "I Am" poems, in which they used a basic outline (Fig. 12.1) to explain what slaves might have heard, seen, felt, and so on. The examples in Fig. 12.2 show how students were able to draw conclusions not only about the physical environment in which slaves found themselves but also about the way those circumstances affected their thoughts and feelings. And later, in studying slave codes in the antebellum South, Rebecca had students do "Open Mind" activities: Using outlines of human heads, they listed potential ideas of slaves and slave owners.

Rhoda's "Hot Seat" activity is similar to Dee Hallau's role-playing activity in chapter 11. After students discussed the account of the Westward movement in *Cassie's Journey: Going West in the 1860s*, several of them took on the role of a family moving westward and answered questions about their feelings, motivations, and hardships. In doing so, they had to demonstrate not only their understanding of the circumstances of these trips, they also had to consider how they would have affected different members of a family. One of the main assignments for this unit, meanwhile, was for students to develop a simulated journal written from the perspective of someone moving west; these journals had to contain information on sights, weather, and events, as well as the writer's reaction to these. Again, this assignment required that students understand not only the factual content of the unit but also the way people reacted to their circumstances.

These perspective recognition assignments are a basic feature of instruction for most historical topics in Rhoda's and Rebecca's classrooms. In studying

Although textbooks focus on events, most historians focus on people.

Rosenzweig & Thelen (1998)

In "I Am" poems, students follow an outline to explain what people in history may have heard, seen, felt, and thought.

In "Open Mind" activities, students use outlines of human heads to list the ideas people in the past may have had.

Harvey (1988)

In a "Hot Seat," students take on the roles of people in history and respond to questions from other students.

Many historical topics lend themselves to perspective-recognition activities.

```
I am _____

I wonder _____

I hear _____

I see _____

I want _____

I am _____


I pretend _____

I feel _____

I touch _____

I worry _____

I cry _____

I am _____


I understand _____

I say _____

I dream _____
```

FIG. 12.1. "I Am ..." poem outline.

Jamestown, for example, students wrote broadsides advertising the colony to potential settlers in England; in doing so, they had to decide how to persuade a 17th-century Englishman to move to North America. (Phrases included, "Dost thou want to get rich?" and "Come hither. Perchance you will hit the big one.") In another assignment, they took the perspective of Jamestown settlers and wrote letters home to their families. And in studying the American Revolution, students wrote letters from the point of view of British soldiers stationed in Boston; created a colonial newspaper with news items, editorials, and interviews; and conducted debates between Patriots and Loyalists.

The "I Am" poems in Fig. 12.2 show the seriousness and passion with which students approached such assignments. In both classrooms, students consistently pointed to these kind of perspective recognition activities as one of the primary reasons they enjoyed studying history. Several noted that they hadn't liked history in previous years, when they were just reading about it from a book or writing about it on paper; what they liked, as one girl pointed out, was acting things out—pretending to be people in the past. A classmate agreed: "It gives you a chance to be in their places—how did it feel, like the real thing."

Students usually enjoy activities in which they take the perspective of people in the past.

USING LITERATURE AND PRIMARY SOURCES TO UNDERSTAND PEOPLE

As we have noted, historical fiction is a particularly effective way to help students recognize the perspective of people in the past. Fiction is inherently subjective in nature; it invites readers to put themselves in the place of the characters they read about. It is important to understand, however, that perspec-

170

I am African	I am an African
I wonder what is going to happen	I wonder if I'll ever go back home
I hear whipping	I hear the cries of relatives
I see white people	I see those evil people
I want to go home	I want my freedom
I am very sad	I am a slave
I pretend to be with my family	I pretend it's not so bad though it is
I feel very worried and confused	I feel really miserable without my people
I touch my irons	I touch nothing but chains
I worry about my family	I worry for my family
I cry because I'm very sad	I cry for the wooziness I feel
I am miserable	I am a prisoner
I understand nothing	I understand not a word they say
I say, Is this happening?	I say, You are the most hideous thing on Earth
I dream about my home in Africa	I dream that one day I'll have freedom
by Angela	by Genoveva

FIG. 12.2. "I Am ... " poems.

tive recognition activities are not simply exercises in creative writing, nor is their purpose to instill some vague sense of sympathy for people in the past; their purpose is to develop historical understanding, and therefore they must be based on evidence. Without emphasizing the role of evidence, such activities might amount to little more than asking students to imagine that they're elephants; because an elephant doesn't have human thoughts and feelings, anything students create is equally valid—there are no clear criteria for judging whether a student really recognizes the perspective of an elephant. People, however, can explain what they're thinking, and they leave behind both direct and indirect evidence of their ideas; these expressions of their perspectives form the basis for historical interpretations.

Both Rhoda and Rebecca connect their perspective recognition activities to primary sources. Rebecca, for example, had students write their "I Am" poems after having read and discussed firsthand accounts of Africans describing enslavement; in another lesson, students used advertisements for escaped slaves to make inferences about the life of slaves—concluding, for example, that because the advertisements sometimes noted that a slave could read, most probably could not. Similarly, Rhoda's students based their Hot Seat role play on literature based on the diaries of women who moved West in the mid-19th century, and their discussion of Native Americans' perspective on the loss of land was based on primary sources found in their basal readers and in *Wounded Knee: An Indian History of the American West.*

Students' own experiences often provide a valid basis for attempting to imagine the thoughts and feelings of people in the past. Despite all the differences in world view and experience between a Mexican American 10-year-old in the 1990s and a West African adult in the 1600s, their feelings about being separated from their families probably have some important similarities. At the same time,

Historical perspective-recognition depends on evidence.

Primary sources can provide insight into the perspectives of people in the past.

Brown (1975)

Students' own experiences can help them recognize the perspective of people in the past.

171

though, teachers must stress that part of the reason for such perspective activities is to understand how attitudes are both similar and different across time and place—and that these conclusions must be based on evidence. When Rhoda asked students how Native Americans felt about their loss of land, they initially reacted with their own intuitive judgments—"sad," "mad"—but she consistently directed their attention back to the primary sources they had been reading—"What did they say they felt?" she asked. Of course, students will not always be able to completely separate their own contemporary perspectives from those of people in the past: As we saw in the last chapter, there is always a tension between imagining what someone 200 years ago might have thought and what I would have thought if I had been alive then. Exercises in historical perspectives, however, help students expand their understanding so that they are no longer so limited to their own point of view. It is this emphasis on people—and the potential it holds for connecting them across time and space—that helps make the traditional topics in American history relevant for Rhoda's and Rebecca's students.

DIVERSITY IN AMERICAN HISTORY

North America has always consisted of widely diverse cultural groups, and the United States has been multicultural since its inception as a nation. Even before the first European explorers arrived, the native inhabitants of the continent spoke thousands of different languages and displayed an enormous range of cultural variation. Once European settlers arrived, the variety of people increased: Scandinavian, Dutch, German, English, French, and Scottish settlers populated the East Coast and interior waterways, while enslaved Africans further added to the Colonial population. By the mid-1800s, immigrants from Ireland, China, and Japan populated the coasts, while the conquest of Mexico resulted in the addition of millions of Latino residents in the Southwest. By the beginning of the 20th century, urban centers saw increasing numbers of residents from East and Central Europe, and immigration from Mexico, Central America, the Caribbean, Asia, the Pacific Islands, and, indeed, every region of the world continues to add to the greatest strength of the country—its diversity.

Many people do not think of U.S. history as including such diversity, yet people from a wide variety of backgrounds have always been central to the development of American society. Ours would be a radically different society without the contributions of any of the previously mentioned groups. European settlers could not have survived without the help of Native Americans, the southern plantation economy would never have developed without racial slavery, the American West would have taken a different course without the labor of its Chinese American, Japanese American, and Latino residents. And though it may come as a shock to some, women also have always contributed to the development of our society. We often hear that women don't show up much in texts because they haven't really done much in history—an observation that would come as a surprise to the millions of women who have given birth, done housework, farmed, worked in factories, operated businesses, become professionals, participated in political movements, and done all the other things that have produced contemporary society. American culture and society has always depended on the efforts of all segments of its population.

Although textbook publishers have begun to give increased attention to diversity, this attention is sometimes only at a superficial level; certainly most teachers cannot rely on their texts to present a significant account of the country's diversity. As long as women and minorities remain on the margins of the curriculum, the interactions and connections of the diverse people in our past will remain unclear. A meaningful understanding of American history requires the recognition that, at

Historical perspective recognition helps students make connections to people from different times and places.

America has always been multicultural. Takaki (1993)

Diversity is America's greatest strength.

People from all backgrounds have contributed to the development of American culture and society.

172

any given time, the country consisted of both men and women; of people from many different racial and ethnic backgrounds; of those who were rich, those who were poor, and everything in between. Understanding U.S. history means recognizing that people from these different backgrounds often had fundamentally different perspectives on the events of their day and that these perspectives frequently came into serious—even violent—conflict. As we've said, teaching history cannot be limited to a single story about the past—a story in which it appears that everyone agreed with each other in a kind of happy consensus, free of exploitation, repression, or conflict. Teachers must consistently devote attention to the diversity found in society at any given time and must take seriously the way perspectives on events differed among people.

People from different backgrounds had different perspectives on historical events.

Teachers must take responsibility for increasing attention to diversity. *Levstik & Groth (2002)*

Students need to study the variety of perspectives that existed at any given time in history.

This, too, is a constant feature of both Rebecca's and Rhoda's instruction. In all their historical units, they emphasize not only taking the perspective of people in the past, but taking the perspective of different people. In studying the Columbian encounter, for example, students write accounts from the perspective of Columbus, Columbus' crew, and Native Americans. In studying colonial Williamsburg, they learn about the lifestyles of the rich, poor, and "middling" segments of the population and about the different kinds of work done by men and women. In learning about the American Revolution, they conduct debates between Patriots and Loyalists and write editorials from each viewpoint. In studying slavery, they examine the perspective of slaves and slave owners. In studying the Westward movement, they look at the differences not only between settlers and Native Americans, but the differences among settlers. (See the literature list at the end of this chapter for books from differing perspectives.)

Children often fail to see this diversity in history and instead think of the past as a matter of simple and linear development. As pointed out in chapter 7, they often think that all people in the Colonial Era lived in log cabins or that everyone in the 1800s dressed in formal clothes all the time. Such perceptions are hardly surprising, given that students are rarely exposed to differences within a given time period. But when teachers consistently emphasize diversity and conflicting perspectives, it becomes a basic part of students' understanding of the past. When students in Rebecca's classroom first examined pictures from colonial Boston, for example, they quickly noted features such as the presence of African servants, the different kinds of work done by men and women, and the variety of economic classes depicted in some pictures. Similarly, students reading about the Westward Movement in Rhoda's class often stopped to point out how Native Americans would have viewed things differently—noting, for example, that what the settlers called a "new home" was already someone else's home. These are the kinds of observations we typically hear only from students who have been taught to look for such differences.

Students can learn to see diversity and conflicting perspectives as a basic characteristic of history.

Examining diverse experiences and conflicting perspectives, however, does not mean simply reversing the traditional story of American history—portraying it as the story of pathetic victimization rather than noble conquest. Doing so reinforces the perception that there is a single story out there—one in which women, minorities, and the poor play a generally subordinate and inferior (albeit sympathetic) role. Teachers are sometimes shocked, for example, when their African American students appear ashamed to hear about slavery: "It's their history," teachers ask, "so why aren't they proud of it?" We would argue that they're not proud of it because slavery and segregation are often the only time African Americans show up in school history; it's hard to be proud of your past when the only time you encounter it is in the context of someone beating up your forebears. Portraying people as victims—without choice, control, or initiative—is neither historically nor pedagogically sound. Part of the solution lies in making sure that African Americans don't appear only when studying slavery, Latinos only when studying farm workers, or Japanese Americans only when studying World War II. The curriculum must reflect the actual diversity that has existed throughout American history so that students see that African Americans have also been farmers and soldiers, women have been scientists and engineers, poor people have been politically active, and so on.

But just as important, instruction must respect the agency of people in the past. U.S. slavery is one of history's worst violations of human rights, and those enslaved were ruthlessly and cruelly victimized in countless ways. But the victimization involved in the slave system is very different than thinking of individuals solely as victims; portraying slaves as hapless and servile—even when doing so sympathetically—is a caricature that does nothing to illuminate life under slavery. Despite their lack of basic political and economic freedoms, slaves made lives for themselves—they married, had children, hunted, fished, raised gardens, learned skilled trades, and fought back against the slave system. Indeed, one of the most fascinating aspects of this period in history is the way people developed a vibrant and meaningful cultural tradition under trying circumstances—yet this is not always a part of the way the topic is presented in school.

Enslaved Africans and their descendants developed vibrant cultural traditions. Joyner (1984), Levine (1977)

In Rebecca's class, though, students studied not only how slavery violated human rights, but also how slaves adapted and survived. An important part of the unit, for example, focused on storytelling. Rebecca began by talking about how slaves had to survive in a new environment and how they passed on what they learned to each other and to their children. Students knew that some of the most important ways they themselves learn—schools and reading—weren't available to slaves, and Rebecca explained that storytelling fulfilled many of those same purposes. Students read several stories from *The People Could Fly* and other sources and discussed the lessons that each might have been meant to express. They concluded, for example, that one story demonstrated the importance of not telling everything you know—a lesson they thought was as useful today as during slavery. After learning about the elements of stories and storytelling, students wrote and performed their own stories designed to teach a lesson.

Hamilton (1985)

Students should see enslaved people not just as victims but as creative and insightful human beings.

These lessons portrayed slaves not as stereotypical victims, but as creative and insightful human beings—people who gained wisdom from their experiences and developed sophisticated art forms to convey those lessons. Through their own experience writing and performing stories, students saw just how difficult that was: They had to structure a story to teach a meaningful lesson, follow appropriate conventions, and learn techniques of performance. Finding out how much work and creativity was involved in such artistic products helped students see the richness and complexity of slave life, rather than perpetuating their initial stereotypes of slaves who were "always in chains." One student even pointed to this as his favorite activity during the course of the year: "It was something they did," he pointed out, "and we were doing the same thing."

BUILDING ON WHAT STUDENTS KNOW

The lessons described earlier are interesting and intellectually stimulating, and students' enthusiasm about history makes it clear how effective they are in keeping them interested. Nonetheless, all these lessons required serious and sustained effort by teachers and students. Because of their diverse backgrounds, for example, neither Rhoda nor Rebecca could assume that their students would have the prior knowledge to make sense of distant events in American history; as we pointed out in chapter 7, neither dates nor expressions like "the Colonial Era" are likely to call forth many specific associations for students from any background—much less those who have only recently immigrated to the country. Rhoda and Rebecca saw their first task, then, as helping students develop the schemas that would allow them to put topics like slavery and the Westward Movement in context. An important step in building that understanding, of course, was finding out what students already knew. Rebecca,

Teachers can help students develop the schemas they need to understand history.

for example, recorded students' ideas about slaves on a web in the front of the classroom; Rhoda listed what students knew about the Westward movement on a KWL chart. They did not limit such exercises to the beginning of new units, however; they also frequently structured individual lessons around students' prior knowledge—as, for example, when Rebecca had students develop a list of what they considered basic human rights before introducing slave codes, and then had them compare this to what they knew about contemporary human rights violations. Beginning lessons and units this way activated students' prior knowledge—it reminded them of what they already knew.

The collaborative nature of such activities is a critical part of this process. Asking an individual student what she knows about slavery or the Westward movement will usually prompt the response, "Nothing." But when they work together, each student's contribution reminds others of information they can add; often, students don't realize they have relevant knowledge until they hear their classmates' comments. In reading *Cassie's Journey,* for example, Rhoda asked students if they knew what buffalo chips were; only one student knew, but as soon as he explained what they were, others realized that they knew what they were used for—they just didn't know the term. Meaningful reading in the content areas depends on students' ability to call forth their background knowledge, and collaboration yields a much greater store of such information than individual activities would produce.

Such collaboration, we should point out, is often better accomplished in small groups—two to four students—than as a whole class (at least initially). Many students are hesitant to take risks before the entire class, and teachers sometimes find themselves calling on the same three or four students repeatedly. But working in small groups before coming together as a whole class helps more students contribute; those who are less confident—either of their language abilities or their knowledge—are more likely to take part in class discussion when they have had a chance to try out their ideas in small groups of peers first. Such collaboration, though, requires just as much direct instruction and scaffolding as academic content. Before Rhoda's students developed their list of hardships in small groups, for example, she asked them to review the standards of mutually respectful interaction, which they had been practicing for months. They mentioned using quite voices, listening to what others had to say, not hurting people's feelings, saying nice things, and remembering that "no idea's a bad idea."

Activities like webbing and KWL also have a purpose beyond activating students' prior knowledge: They give the teacher insight into what she needs to address in upcoming lessons and how much attention to devote to various aspects of the topic. Sometimes it becomes clear that students have already learned a great deal about a topic from relatives, the media, or their own reading. In chapter 11, for example, we saw how Amy discovered that her students were already so familiar with the concept of *prejudice* that some of the introductory content she had planned was unnecessary. Similarly, Rhoda had planned to spend more time developing students' understanding of transportation in the 1800s, but when she began by asking them if they could think of any differences between a covered wagon and a stagecoach, they quickly produced several dozen! (These vehicles are apparently such a staple feature of cartoons, movies, and television shows that students had already developed extensive—and relatively accurate—background knowledge about them.) It was only by allowing students to demonstrate this knowledge that Rhoda knew how much information to provide students. Effective instruction depends on giving students the opportunity to show what they already know and taking that knowledge seriously.

Other times, of course, students' knowledge is inaccurate or—more frequently—incomplete, and webs and KWL charts alert teachers to the information they need to address in upcoming lessons. Experienced teachers can

A web (also known as a *semantic map*) shows relationships among concepts and ideas.

Beginning with discussion, KWL charts, and webs activates students' prior knowledge.

Collaboration helps students activate their prior knowledge.

Small groups allow students to take more risks than whole-class discussion.

Learning to work together requires explicit instruction, modeling, and practice. *Cohen (1986), Johnson, Johnson, & Holubec (1993), Slavin (1995)*

Activities that activate prior knowledge provide teachers insight into students' understanding.

When teachers encourage students to share what they know, they must take that knowledge seriously.

Webs, KWL charts, and discussion provide teachers with information on misconceptions they need to address.

Webs and KWL charts can help students see how their understanding has changed.

Teachers accept students' ideas as approximations. *Pappas et al. (1999)*

Vosniadou & Brewer (1987)

Students modify their understanding based on new experiences.

Students should take responsibility for their own learning.

Seixas (1993a)

Teachers can encourage students to become self-directed learners.

anticipate many of students' ideas—that there are no more Native Americans, for example, or that slavery only existed at one point in time—and already will have prepared lessons to address these misconceptions. Other times, discussions reveal unexpected aspects of students' understanding. A teacher might not know ahead of time that students think slaves were always kept chained to each other, for example—yet if she doesn't address that misconception, they will have trouble understanding how slaves lived. Because she had students web out their ideas about slaves, Rebecca knew that she would have to include more information (especially visual images) on the daily life of slaves in upcoming lessons. As a consequence, when the class returned to their web at the end of the unit, they were quick to point out that they had been mistaken about slaves always being kept in chains. They not only learned new content but were able explicitly to track how their understanding of the topic had changed from the beginning of the unit to the end.

During such activities, teachers must accept students' ideas as approximations of more sophisticated understandings. Most of us are tempted to simply correct students whenever they say something that is factually inaccurate, but people don't modify their conceptual understanding just because someone tells them they're wrong. At best, they may place what they hear in school in a separate category of "school knowledge" unrelated to what they really know. (Young children, for example, often know that they're supposed to say that the world is round when they're at school, but they remain convinced that it's actually flat because that's what their experience tells them.) If school knowledge conflicts with the understanding students have gained elsewhere, they will believe it only if they can confirm it through new experiences. In Rebecca's classroom, reading firsthand accounts and looking at pictures of the daily life of enslaved families gave students new evidence about whether they were always kept in chains, and this gave them the chance to modify their own understanding. As a result, they were not only willing but even eager to point out their previous mistakes: They were proud that they knew more than they did before. If, on the other hand, Rebecca had simply told students, "No, slaves weren't always kept in chains, so I'm not going to write that on the web," she would have transformed a schema-building activity into nothing more than a pretest of factual details. Not only would students have learned little, but they probably would have stopped contributing to the discussion as well.

Finally, allowing students to decide on questions they want to answer during a unit helps place the responsibility for learning where it belongs—with the students. In previous chapters, we have explored the process of helping students develop questions to investigate. In most of those discussions, though, the topics under investigation were not ones usually covered by textbooks and curriculum guides—how medicine has changed over time, why people settled in our town, and so on. It would be difficult to learn about such topics without developing questions first. At first glance, it might appear that step is less important for "traditional" topics such as slavery or the Westward movement, which are already covered in textbooks. But one of the most serious problems with relying exclusively on texts is that it promotes the view that history—or any discipline—consists of a fixed body of knowledge, already discovered by others, and not open to investigation or interpretation. We hardly need to emphasize that such a perceptive is not psychologically, educationally, or historically valid. Teaching students that studying history means remembering what someone else says about the past misrepresents the nature of history and fails to help them learn the content. Encouraging students to develop their own questions and take responsibility for finding the answers, on the other hand, builds on the concerns about history that students bring with them to school and treats them as self-directed learners who can use a variety of resources to learn more. We have already pointed out that developing curriculum is not the sole job of either teacher or students but is a joint responsibility. Students are invariably interested in some things that teachers may consider only marginally significant—Where did settlers go to the bathroom? What kind of snakes were there?— while teachers will want to emphasize some things—such as the concept of human rights—that students might not have initiated on their own.

Of course, for students to investigate questions of their own choosing, they need access to a wide variety of resources. Textbooks and encyclopedias are unlikely to contain answers to questions about how people went to the bathroom on the Oregon Trail, and such works have the added disadvantage of being written in a style that students find difficult. Trade books like *Pioneers, The Oregon Trail,* and *The Westward Movement and Abolitionism* are well illustrated, written in readable prose, and include information on many aspects of everyday life. Having an assortment of literature available for students at all times also allows them to find answers to more informal questions that emerge during a unit. While writing letters back home from the trail west, for example, several students in Rhoda's class began to wonder whether people really did write letters and whether there was any way for them to be delivered. A quick check of *If You Traveled West in a Covered Wagon* revealed a section on precisely that topic, and students stopped their work and listened attentively as Rhoda read. In looking that up, meanwhile, other students came across a passage on the Pony Express, and several others became interested in that topic as well. Teachers cannot always anticipate what topics will interest students and so cannot plan lessons explicitly designed to address them. What they can do, though, is to make sure their classrooms have enough resources for students to find the answers they need. As Rhoda points out, "My room is more chaotic that way, but the learning is better."

SCAFFOLDING STUDENTS' UNDERSTANDING

As we have frequently noted, teachers must provide students with the structure they need to be successful. Creative and stimulating lessons sometimes fall apart when students begin independent or group assignments—hands fly up and the room is filled with cries of, "I don't know what to do!" The most imaginative, stimulating, creative assignments will yield few results if students aren't given the scaffolding to complete them. To build on the enthusiasm that effective presentations can produce, teachers have to help students make the transition to their own work. Having students design colonial newspapers, write "I Am" poems, or perform stories that teach lessons will not go smoothly unless the teacher shows them how to use what they are learning to complete their assignments.

One important means of scaffolding is through class discussion. Although students may listen or read carefully, they invariably learn more when their interaction with texts is accompanied by discussion with the teacher and other students. Rhoda, for example, stopped frequently while reading *Cassie's Journey*—several times on each page—to ask questions. Some questions simply checked for comprehension ("Do you know what buffalo chips are?"), but most were calculated to stimulate thoughtful analysis and discussion among students—such as, "If you were a kid traveling West and you could only take one thing, what would it be?" or "Why wouldn't you want to be at the end of the train of wagons?" Although some books benefit from uninterrupted reading, this kind of interaction is usually necessary when students are unfamiliar with the content. Especially with historical works—whether literature or primary sources—students depend on discussion to help them fully understand the context, to see the connection between events, and to gain insight into the perspectives of the people involved. The extremely high level of attention and participation when

Developing curriculum is the joint responsibility of teachers and students.

Fisher (1990), Katz (1993), Sandler (1994)

Levine (1986)

Students need structure to be successful.

Class discussion promotes interest and interaction.

Students understand texts better when they discuss them with teachers and with each other.
Pierce & Gilles (1993)

Rhoda and Rebecca read aloud is an indication of how much students benefit from such discussion; indeed, when we asked their students what advice they had for teaching history, several said that teachers shouldn't just read something out loud or tell students to read it—they should stop to talk about it so students will understand.

Concept development engages students in identifying the critical attributes of concepts through discussion of examples and non-examples. *Parker (1991d)*

Another important aspect of helping students understand what they study is *concept development*. Although this has been considered a basic part of social studies instruction for many years, we find it frequently overlooked in teaching history. Although students may be familiar with words for abstract concepts—*independence, religion, society,* and so on—they may not fully understand the ideas those words refer to. In preparing to study the American Revolution, for example, Rebecca knew that students would have to understand the concept of *rebellion*; as a result, she devoted an entire lesson to exploring the topic with them. She read examples of people who had been dissatisfied with something and had taken action, and read examples of people who had not taken action; the class discussed the similarities and differences among the examples, constructed a Venn diagram comparing them, and worked in groups to develop their own definitions of *rebellion*. Finally, they took events from their own lives and from the news and considered whether they could be classified as examples of rebellion. When they moved into the events leading up to the American Revolution, they frequently had occasion to refer back to these discussions. For historical topics to have meaning and relevance, students must have enough conceptual understanding to see how specific topics relate to broader themes and issues. Focusing on the concept of *human rights*, for example, helped students put their study of slavery into a broader context—one with relevance to many times and places.

Focusing on *concepts* as well as *topics* makes history more relevant.

Finally, graphic organizers are a key means by which both Rhoda and Rebecca help students build on what they know. Reading about enslavement may have produced a great many ideas, but most students would not have been able immediately to write a poem about an enslaved African's thoughts and feelings. Although the basic outline of the poem (Fig. 12.1) was one step in helping students get their ideas on paper, even more important was the graphic organizer the class filled out together: As they read and discussed each passage, they kept track of what a slave would have felt, seen, heard, and thought (Fig. 12.3). Similarly, even students who had studied the Westward movement in depth might have had trouble knowing what to write in a simulated journal. By leading students in webbing out their ideas beforehand (Fig. 12.4), Rhoda ensured that they would have many more words and ideas from which to draw.

Graphic organizers are a means of visually organizing information.

Enslaved Africans What they might have...					
	Felt	Heard	Seen	Said	Touched
First Passage					
Second Passage					
Third Passage					

FIG. 12.3. Enslavement graphic organizer.

FIG. 12.4. Planning web.

ASSESSING STUDENTS' KNOWLEDGE OF HISTORICAL CONTENT

Throughout this book, we have emphasized the assessment of students' historical skills—their ability to explain historical changes, use historical evidence, create historical interpretations, and so on. At some points, though, teachers will want to know not only how well students are mastering historical skills, but how well they are retaining specific content knowledge—the factual details of historical knowledge. The desire to assess how well students remember this content, however, does not mean that teachers must turn their back on the principles of constructive assessment, and it certainly does not mean that they should bombard them with multiple-choice tests, lists of items to be matched, or sentences in which they fill in blanks. Such tasks neither assess what students know nor improve the instructional process—they simply allow the teacher to shake loose a set of largely meaningless grades. The assessment of knowledge, like the assessment of skills, must play a constructive role in the class-

Assessment must play a constructive role in the classroom.

179

room—one that provides students and teachers with authentic information on how the schema-building process is coming along. Chapter 13 deals with the role the arts can play in assessing students' knowledge; in this chapter, we deal primarily with the use of writing.

Written language is one of the most common forms of evaluation, and in our experience, students often learn by writing in history. When combined with other forms of assessment, writing has tremendous potential for providing insight into what students know and can do. To provide constructive information on learning, written assignments must first and foremost be open ended: They must allow for a variety of correct responses. Good instruction (and good resources) usually present more information than any single student can be expected to remember; an open-ended assignment allows each student to draw from that body of information to reach conclusions or make evaluations. After studying the Westward Movement, for example, teachers should expect that students could give examples of the hardships faced by settlers; they should not expect, though, that all students would give the same examples. Different students will be interested in different details of their study, and thus the knowledge they retain will vary. This is not the same as saying that any answer is equally correct, because each response must make use of the facts, concepts, and relationships that have been covered in the unit.

One quick, basic way to assess students' understanding through writing is the use of "Magic Words" (see Fig. 12.5). Magic Words are prepositions and subordinating conjunctions; they're called "magic" not only because that sounds more exciting, but because their use magically improves the quality of writing. These words call attention to the relationships that lie at the heart of history—how one thing causes another, what events came before or after others, and so on—and using them requires that students demonstrate their understanding of relationships. Yet although preschoolers know and use most of these words in speech, they are rarely part of students' writing—at any age. When students are required to use them, though, they can do so with ease, and their writing then provides a great deal of insight into their understanding of the content they have learned. At the end of a lesson or unit, for example, Rebecca's students write several sentences about what they've learned; they can write anything at all about the topic, but each sentence has to contain a Magic Word. Thus, they have the opportunity to search through all the information they have gained to show what they know about time, causation, and so on. The following examples of Magic Word sentences come from her class and others:

Because the ground [at Jamestown] is watery, they can't plant corn.

Because Francis Drake stole money and land, he was a hero to England.

In a new settlement, slaves were in high demand because the colonists needed a lot of work done.

Although the Indians were not lazy and stupid, the Spanish thought they were.

Whenever a slave was bought, almost every time a family was split up.

Although the Indians lived here first, the Spanish said they owned the land.

After a woman was bought as a slave, she begged her master to buy her children too.

By expanding or narrowing the topic for assessment, teachers can vary the level of detail they obtain on student's understanding. For example, at the end of a unit on slavery, Rebecca might ask students to write 10 sentences on slavery using any of the Magic Words; after a week of studying the economic structure of slavery, she might be more specific and ask students to write five sentences on the economics of slavery and to use the word *because* in each. In either case, this strategy is a clear example of giving students the chance to show what they know rather than what they don't know: They must demon-

Daly (1989), Tierney, Carter, & Desai (1991)

Meaningful written assignments are open ended.

Although responses to open-ended tasks will differ, all must demonstrate knowledge of appropriate facts, concepts, and relationships.

Magic Words improve student's writing.

Magic Words call attention to the relationships that underlie historical interpretations. Barton (1996b)

Constructive assessment emphasizes what students know, not what they don't know.

180

about	because	for	though
above	before	from	through
across	behind	if	to
after	below	in	unless
against	beneath	in order that	until
along	beside	like	when
although	between	near	whenever
among	beyond	of	where
around	by	on	wherever
as	down	past	while
as if	during	since	with
at	except	so that	

Adapted from Barton (1996b)

FIG. 12.5. Magic words.

strate their understanding and retention of content, but they are not all expected to have learned exactly the same set of facts.

A more structured task is the use of open-ended questions. Such questions also allow for a range of possible answers, but they require a more focused response than Magic Words. Productive open-ended questions generally ask students to pull together different aspects of what they have learned in order to identify patterns, draw conclusions, or make evaluations. After studying the encounter between Native Americans and Columbus, for example, Rebecca asked students to explain what kind of personality Columbus had. One wrote that he was greedy and pointed to his quest for gold; another noted he was curious because he wanted to find a new way to Asia; yet another suggested he was hopeful because he kept going when he ran out of supplies. Each student responded differently, yet each had to use what he or she had learned to support a judgment about Columbus' personality. Similarly, Amy followed her History Museum projects by having students respond to the question, "How has the United States changed over the last 100 years?" Although each student used different examples, each had to draw on information to support a generalization about patterns of change.

> Open-ended questions ask students to identify patterns, draw conclusions, or make evaluations.

When used as assessment, such questions are sometimes called *performance tasks*. They evaluate whether the final product or performance sustains a supportable interpretation given the available information (and the level of experience of the writer); to do so, such writing must be grounded in substantial historical knowledge. This is not just a matter of getting the facts right, but of showing how those facts are related to each other and to the writer's larger interpretation. This is true even with the youngest writers. When LeeAnn's primary students wrote about Columbus, they included such telling details as Columbus "trading fake jewels for real gold" and kidnapping the Taino as support for their interpretation of his claim to fame. Although an older student might make a more complex argument, these young children are novices, and the fact that they marshal evidence to support a position is an important beginning point.

> Performance tasks are opportunities for students to present supportable interpretations.
>
> Historical writing must be grounded in substantial historical knowledge. *Newmann et al. (1995)*
>
> *Daley (1989), Graves (1983)*

Often, good written tasks ask students to organize what they have learned into forms other than expository sentences and paragraphs. After studying the Columbian encounter, for example, Rebecca had students write dialogues between a reporter and a student who was protesting either a school's Columbus

Day celebration or a school's cancellation of such a celebration. In writing the dialogue, students had to draw on their knowledge of why Columbus is regarded as either a villain or a hero—they had to use historical information to support a position on a contemporary social issue. Similarly, Amy had students write a dialogue between a Japanese American during World War II and the government agent sent to detain him or her; again, students had to use what they had learned to support a position in a real-life setting. Using information in this way leads to more meaningful writing—and better assessment—than simply trying to get students to reproduce a set of facts, definitions, or concepts.

Through writing, students can bring historical information to bear on contemporary issues.

Older students, of course, can produce more sophisticated arguments and interpretations. One of Walt's students, for instance, wrote a paper arguing for an "honest look at the evils of apartheid" by all South Africans. She used the United States' post-Reconstruction experiences as a counterexample, showing how ignoring or misrepresenting the past made it more difficult to correct historic injustices. Her paper showed her grasp of the major perspectives of participants in South Africa and the United States, as well as the degree of agency those participants might have in effecting change in race relations in their respective countries. Her writing was a credible piece of work, making good use of available sources and reflecting her richer experience with historical analysis. It is our observation that students like these—who have many opportunities to read and write in a variety of genres in the context of in-depth inquiry—create interesting, sophisticated historical writing that is more representative of authentic historical thinking than is ever demonstrated on most tests.

Experience with a wide variety of genres encourages richer historical thinking.

EXTENSIONS

All historical topics should include the study of diverse perspectives.

Throughout this chapter, we have emphasized the importance of focusing on the perspectives of people in the past and the diversity of experiences that have characterized any moment in history. For any topic a teacher wishes (or is required) to teach, she should ask herself, "Who else was involved in this, and what did they think about it?" In teaching about World War II, for example, it is important not to limit the focus to the battles and political leaders that may quickly leap to mind. The wealth of rich literature on the Holocaust suggests one meaningful way to focus on agency and diversity during the period; students would learn far more about humanity—and the relevance of history—by examining the personal choices people made in response to events than by reenacting the Battle of Midway. In addition, students might study the effect of the war on daily life in the United States and other countries; that topic could include attention to the relocation of Japanese Americans, integration of the military, changes in employment opportunities for women, American anti-Semitism and support for Hitler, and economic consequences of the war. All these have more important and far-reaching implications than following colored arrows on a map to trace troop movements.

Barton (1997a),
McKeown & Beck (1990),
VanSledright (1995)

Similarly, the American Revolution is one of the most frequently covered topics in both fifth and eighth grades, yet when asked about it later, students often remember only a string of unrelated people, events, and documents, and their understanding of its significance is limited to observations such as, "It's important so we wouldn't be bossed around by the queen anymore." Rarely do they learn that as many colonists opposed the war as supported it or that Patriots tarred and feathered Loyalists; rarely do they learn about the effect of the war on women, African Americans, or daily life in general. Nor do they learn that any account of the period is written from a particular point of view, that these perspectives vary from person to person, or that they change over time. Perhaps most significantly, students do not learn that creating such accounts requires the use of evidence, nor that such evidence can be examined critically. Rather than seeing the American Revolution as a pivotal and controversial event in their country's history, students are presented with a single, finished story—a story that has no clear immediacy and whose details they remember in only the most superficial way.

Students' historical understanding benefits when their study of the Revolution includes methods similar to Rebecca's and Rhoda's. In Amy Leigh's class, for example, students read and evaluated a dozen accounts of the Battle at Lexington Green, each written from a different perspective. They enjoyed the chance to evaluate the sources for bias—noting, for example, that Patriots would be more likely to claim the British fired first, and newspaper articles in London would do the opposite; that accounts written a week after the battle would be more reliable than the recollections of a former soldier 50 years later; and that a captured British soldier might change his account to please his captors. Having seen just how many details of the battle were in dispute, students then became indignant whenever they found books that asserted more certainty than in fact existed. They were thus becoming adept at asking the basic question of critical thought—How do I know if this is true?

P. Bennett (1967)

Analyzing and evaluating primary sources written from different perspectives helps students become critical readers. VanSledright (2002)

Similarly, students will gain a more complete understanding of the Revolution if they examine novels on the period written from a variety of perspectives—works like *My Brother Sam is Dead* (about a Loyalist family in which the eldest son joins the Continental army), *War Comes to Willy Freeman* (about a freed African American girl searching for her mother during the war), *An Enemy among Them* (about a Hessian soldier cared for by a German American Patriot family), and *The Fighting Ground,* about a boy who learns that fighting is not as heroic as he had imagined. By working in literature response groups, students can analyze and compare these novels and the perspectives they represent. But as we described in chapter 9, narrative can be a very powerful medium: Telling stories is a basic means by which people make sense of their world, and there is a tendency for students to regard what they have read without a critical eye. Students can thus use reference works like *The American Revolution, U.S. Kids History: Book of the American Revolution,* and *If You were There in 1776* to investigate the accuracy of the books they are reading. By comparing the information in these sources, students will learn more about historical inquiry and the effect of the Revolution on diverse groups of people than they would by reading a text passage or seeing a filmstrip on the Boston Tea Party.

Collier & Collier (1974, 1984), DeFord & Stout (1987), Avi (1984)

Brenner (1994), Carter (1992), Egger-Bovet & Smith-Baranzin (1994)

CONCLUSIONS

Many of the teachers in this book have almost complete control over their history curriculum, either because they teach in the primary grades—where there are few expectations for history content—or because their state curriculum focuses on outcomes rather than requiring specific topics at each grade level. Many teachers do not have that much responsibility for designing their curriculum; particularly in fourth grade and above, most teachers are required by official guidelines or informal (but very real) expectations to teach specific topics in state, U.S., or world history. As Rhoda and Rebecca demonstrate, though, teaching the required content of the curriculum does not mean following a textbook in lockstep fashion; principles of effective instruction and the elements of historical thinking can be applied to any topic a teacher wants or needs to teach.

At first glance, most of Rhoda's and Rebecca's students have little reason to be interested in the major events of American history. Most are immigrants from poor or working-class families; their ancestors rarely show up in stories of the British colonies, the Overland Trail, or the Civil War. But by focusing on human agency and multiple perspectives, Rhoda and Rebecca not only keep their students interested in U.S. history but also make it clear why the topic is relevant to them after all. Their students learn that the United States has always been diverse and that attention to any topic must include the experience of different ethnic groups, of men and women, of rich and poor. In addition, focusing on people—real human beings who live, work, play, create art, and make decisions—allows students to make connections across time and place—connections that at first might not be clear. By teaching history this way, Rhoda and Rebecca not only cover factual content but also help students see what historical understanding is and how it relates to their own lives.

The activities in this chapter also complicate the topic of historical perspective recognition in important ways. First, these teachers do not only try to help students understand "the" perspective of historical periods but to understand the variety of viewpoints that existed at any given time. Any historian will recognize that during any historical period, different people and groups held a variety of values, attitudes, and beliefs, and that they often came into conflict because of them. This recognition, however, often is overlooked in school history, and students are presented with an image of widespread consensus in which everyone held the same opinions on events of the day. Yet if students are going to take part in meaningful public discussion, they need to understand that differing perspectives are a normal part of social interaction. If students think that everyone in a given country or community agreed on public issues in the past, they will have few resources for understanding why people disagree today, and they will have little reason to take others' ideas seriously. The mistaken belief that people in the past adhered to a common set of values and attitudes does little to prepare students for citizenship in a pluralist democracy. The attention to diversity shown throughout this chapter may not guarantee that students will regard such pluralism as a good thing, but it should at least help them understand that it is unavoidable.

In addition, Rebecca's focus on human rights helps move students away from one of the drawbacks of perspective recognition: the belief that because historical actions can be explained, they cannot be condemned. We often hear people deny that moral judgments can be made about history; they say, "You have to understand how people thought back then." Thus the relocation of Japanese Americans cannot be denounced, because people were scared after Pearl Harbor; slavery cannot be condemned, because people really believed that individuals of African descent were inferior. Not only does this approach ignore the variety of perspectives in each historical period (abolitionists had different perspectives than slaveholders, and Japanese Americans weren't scared of themselves), it also makes democratic public action impossible, because it focuses only on the causes of historical events rather than their consequences. Understanding why people behaved as they did is important, but so too is evaluating the outcome of their actions, particularly if we hope to use history in ways that have enduring relevance. Thus, perspective recognition must be combined with analysis of democratic principles. Students need to learn more than "how people thought" in the 1940s; they need to learn that some White Americans used their prejudices to violate the constitutional rights of numerous other U.S. citizens. Not only does this provide a more complete historical account, it also provides a firmer basis for democratic deliberation. We may never share each others' perspectives, but we need standards for taking action in spite of our differing prejudices. Rebecca's emphasis on human rights provides one way of approaching this issue, and it provides students with a language for discussing democratic action.

Barton & Levstik (2004)

Barton & Levstik (2004)

CHILDREN'S AND ADOLESCENT LITERATURE

Life Under Slavery

Berry, J. *Ajeemah and His Son.* Harper-Collins, 1992.

Bial, R. *The Strength of These Arms: Life in the Slave Quarters.* Houghton Mifflin, 1997.

Buss, F. L. *Journey of the Sparrows.* Lodestar Books, 1991.

Chambers, V. *Amistad Rising: A Story of Freedom.* Harcourt Brace, 1998.

Diouf, S. A. *Growing Up in Slavery.* Millbrook Press, 2001.

Evitts, W. J. *Captive Bodies, Free Spirits: The Story of Southern Slavery.* Julian Messner, 1985.

Hamilton, V. *The People Could Fly.* Knopf, 1985.

Hansen, J. *The Captive.* Scholastic, 1994.

Haskins, J., & Benson, K. *Bound for America: The Forced Migration of Africans to the New World.* Lothrop, Lee, & Shepard, 1999.

Hopkinson, D. *Sweet Clara and the Freedom Quilt.* Knopf, 1993.

Hurmence, B. *Slavery Time When I Was Chillum.* G. P. Putnam's Sons, 1992.

Jacob, H. P. *The Diary of the Strawbridge Place.* Atheneum, 1978.

Johnson, D. *Now Let Me Fly: The Story of a Slave Family.* Macmillan, 1993.

Katz, W. L. *Breaking the Chains: African-American Slave Resistance.* Atheneum, 1990.

King, W. *Children of the Emancipation.* Carolrhoda, 2000.

Lester, J., & Brown, R. *From Slave Ship to Freedom Road.* Dial, 1998.

Lyons, M. E. *Letters from a Slave Girl: The Story of Harriet Jacobs.* Charles Scribner's Sons, 1992.

McKissack, P. C., & McKissack, F. L. *Christmas in the Big House, Christmas in the Quarters.* Scholastic, 1994.

McKissack, P. C. *A Picture of Freedom: The Diary of Clotee, a Slave Girl; Belmont Plantation, Virginia, 1859.* Scholastic, 1997.

Myers, W. D. *Now is Your Time: The African-American Struggle for Freedom.* HarperCollins, 1991.

Myers, W. D. *The Glory Field.* Scholastic, 1994.

Palmer, C. A. *The First Passage: Blacks in the Americas, 1502–1617.* Oxford University Press, 1995.

Paulson, G. *Nightjohn.* Bantam Doubleday Dell, 1993.

Stepto, M. Ed. *Our Song, Our Toil: The Story of American Slavery as Told by Slaves.* Millbrook, 1994.

Taylor, M. D. *The Land.* Phyllis Fogelman, 2001.

Turner, A. *Nettie's Trip South.* Macmillan, 1987.

Wyeth, S. D. *Freedom's Wings: Corey's Diary, Kentucky to Ohio, 1857.* Scholastic, 2001.

Zeinert, K. *The Amistad Slave Revolt and American Abolition.* Linnet, 1997.

For books dealing specifically with the Underground Railroad, see the book list at the end of chapter 5.

The American West and the Westward Movement

Ackerman, K. *Araminta's Paint Box.* Atheneum, 1990.

Alter, J. *Exploring and Mapping the American West (Cornerstones of Freedom).* Children's Book Press, 2001.

Bacon, M., & Blegen, D. *Bent's Fort: Crossroads of Cultures on the Santa Fe Trail.* Millbrook, 1995.

Blumberg, R. *Incredible Journey of Lewis and Clark.* Morrow, 1995.

Brown, D. *Wounded Knee: An Indian History of the American West.* Dell, 1975.

Bunting, E. *Dandelions.* Harcourt Brace, 1995.

Cushman, K. *The Ballad of Lucy Whipple.* Clarion, 1996.

Duncan, D. *The West: An Illustrated History for Children.* Little, Brown, 1996.

Fisher, L. E. *The Oregon Trail.* Holiday House, 1990.

Freedman, R. *Children of the Wild West.* Scholastic, 1983.

Furbee, M. R. *Outrageous Women of the American Frontier.* John Wiley & Sons, 2002.

Gregory, K. *Jenny of the Tetons.* Gulliver Books, 1981.

Harvey, B. *Cassie's Journey: Going West in the 1860s.* Holiday, 1988.

Jossee, B. M. *Lewis & Papa: Adventure on the Santa Fe Trail.* Chronicle Books, 1998.

Katz, W. L. *Black Women of the Old West.* Simon & Schuster, 1995.

Katz, W. L. *The Westward Movement and Abolitionism.* Steck-Vaughn, 1993.

Knight, A. S. *The Way West: Journal of a Pioneer Woman.* Simon & Schuster, 1993.

Kudlinski, K. *Facing West: A Story of the Oregon Trail.* Viking, 1996.

Lasky, K. *Beyond the Divide.* Macmillan, 1983.

Lasky, K. *The Bone Wars.* Morow Junior Books, 1988.

Laurgaard, R. K. *Patty Reed's Doll.* Tomato Enterprises, 1989.

Lewis, T. *Clipper Ship.* HarperTrophy, 1992.

Levine, E. *If You Traveled West in a Covered Wagon.* Scholastic, 1986.

Miller, B. M. *Buffalo Gals: Women of the Old West.* Lerner, 1995.

Russell, M. *Along the Santa Fe Trail: Marion Russell's Own Story.* Albert Whitman, 1993.

Sandler, M. W. *Pioneers.* HarperCollins, 1994.

Schlissel, L. *The Way West: Journal of a Pioneer Woman Based on Diaries of Mrs. Amelia Steward Knight.* Simon & Schuster, 1993.

Sonneborn, L. *American West: An Illustrated History.* Scholastic, 2002.

Stanley, J. *Hurry Freedom: African Americans in Gold Rush California.* Crown Publishing, 2000.

Steedman, S., & Bergin, M. *A Frontier Fort on the Oregon Trail.* Peter Bedrick Books, 1993.

Takaki, R. *Journey to Gold Mountain: The Chinese in 19th Century America.* Chelsea House, 1994.

Thomas, J. C. *I Have Heard of a Land.* HarperCollins, 1998.

Turner, A. *Grass Songs.* Harcourt, Brace, & Jovanovich, 1993.

van der Linde, L. *The Pony Express.* New Discovery Books, 1993.

Van Leeuwen, J. *Going West.* Dial, 1992.

Viola, H. J. *It Is a Good Day to Die: Indian Eyewitnesses Tell the Story of the Battle of Little Big Horn.* Crown, 1998.

Williams, D. *Grandma Essie's Covered Wagon.* Knopf, 1993.

Colonial America and the Revolutionary Era

Anderson, J. *A Williamsburg Household.* Clarion Books, 1988.

Avi. *The Fighting Ground.* J. B. Lippincott, 1984.

Avi. *Night Journeys.* Pantheon, 1979.

Brenner, B. *If You Were There in 1776.* Macmillan, 1994.

Brindell, D. F. *The Signers: The 56 Stories Behind the Declaration of Independence.* Walker, 2002.

Carter, A. R. *The American Revolution.* Franklin Watts, 1992.

Collier, J. L., & Collier, C. *The Bloody Country.* Four Winds Press, 1976.

Collier, J. L., & Collier, C. *Jump Ship to Freedom.* Delacorte Press, 1981.

Collier, J. L., & Collier, C. *My Brother Sam Is Dead.* Four Winds Press, 1974.

Collier, J. L., & Collier, C. *War Comes to Willie Freeman.* Dell, 1984.

Collier, J. L., & Collier, C. *Who Is Carrie?* Delacorte Press, 1984.

Corwin, J. H. *Colonial American Crafts: The Home.* Franklin Watts, 1989.

Curry, J. L. *Dark Shade.* Simon & Schuster, 1998.

Davis, B. *Black Heroes of the American Revolution.* Harcourt Brace, 1992.

DeFord, D. H., & Stout, H. S. *An Enemy Among Them.* Houghton Mifflin, 1987.

Egger-Bovet, H., & Smith-Baranzin, M. *U.S. Kids History: Book of the American Revolution.* Little, Brown, 1994.

Finlayson, A. *Greenhorn on the Frontier.* Frederick Warne & Company, 1974.

Finlayson, A. *Redcoat in Boston.* Frederick Warne & Company, 1971.

Fisher, L. E. *Colonial American Craftsmen: The Weavers.* Franklin Watts, 1966.

Haskins, J. *Building a New Land: African Americans in Colonial America.* HarperCollins, 2001.

Meltzer, M., Ed. *The American Revolutionaries: A History in Their Own Words, 1750–1800.* Thomas Y. Crowell, 1987.

Miller, B. M. *Growing Up in Revolution and the New Nation: 1775 to 1800 (Our America).* Lerner, 2003.

O'Dell, S. *Sarah Bishop.* Houghton Mifflin, 1980.

Perl, L. *Slumps, Grunts, and Snickerdoodles: What Colonial Americans Ate and Why.* Clarion, 1975.

Rinaldi, A. *Finishing Becca: A Story about Peggy Shippen and Benedict Arnold.* Harcourt Brace, 1994.

Rinaldi, A. *The Fifth of March: A Story of the Boston Massacre.* Harcourt Brace, 1993.

Sewall, M. *James Towne: Struggle for Survival.* Atheneum, 2001.

Turner, A. *Katie's Trunk.* Macmillan, 1992.

13

The Arts Make Us All Part of Humankind

Cognitive Pluralism in History Teaching and Learning

What makes a culture unique, where are the commonalities that we share if it isn't the arts? The arts make us all a part of humankind. When you think of learning as a whole instead of little pieces, the arts give you the whole picture. So, in seventh grade when I teach ancient civilizations, how could I teach about Greece and not teach about drama? How could I teach about Greece and not teach about architecture? And in eighth grade, it's really been interesting to watch the student who studied Mozart and found out that he was a contemporary of George Washington.... The arts also give us a window. Sometimes, we don't give students an opportunity to share with us what they do know because we restrict their vehicle of expression. If I only accept what they know about the Bill of Rights in written form, then I've eliminated children that want to share that information with me in a picture or a drama or those kinds of things. The arts give them a vehicle to share with me what they really do know. ... And sometimes you help a child develop areas they wouldn't have otherwise. They would have said that's not my strong suit, that's not something I do, but because it is a way that we express ourselves in the classroom—sometimes it's on some kind of assessment—that child makes an attempt to do it and becomes stronger as a result.

—Jeanette Groth, Middle School Teacher Grades 6, 7, & 8

Jeanette Groth's classroom is always full of art, music, and movement. When studying the Constitution, eighth-grade students carve feather pens, make ink (after finding a period recipe), and try their hands at drafting resolutions. A recording of Mozart's music using period instruments plays in the background as they work. A few weeks later, seventh graders transform the classroom into a medieval castle. Jeanette removes the classroom door and installs a "drawbridge" for the duration of their study. In her sixth-grade class, students make kente cloths and study the West African tradition of preserving history in the archives of a griot's memory. At other times, the arts of ancient Japan, Mali, and Mesopotamia compete for wall space with more recent images of American history. As one observer notes, the juxtaposition of images creates "harmonious chaos." Jeanette nods, "I like it because my room is mostly student created and so I think they feel comfortable with their own work, and I think it calls to mind things that they have learned." Three brief vignettes provide some of the flavor of Jeanette Groth's arts-infused curriculum.

***

"Jackdaw" is also the trade name for a series of historical primary source and activity packets.

Garrett is, he says, doing a "nonresearch paper" on Ulysses S. Grant for his eighth-grade American History class. His task is to study the life of Grant and then put together a "Jackdaw"—a packet of information and artifacts that will illuminate his subject. Jeanette's instructions direct him to "*visually represent* your topic, supply notes or photocopies of information with relevant details highlighted, provide pictures and replicas of relevant artifacts." "Then," Garrett says, "We get to present our Jackdaw to the class."

Jeanette explains that this assignment involves gathering all the sources for a research paper, "except you don't write the paper." Garrett compares it to an archaeological dig in reverse: Rather than presenting a written interpretation based on artifacts, he has to present interpretive artifacts based on written sources. So far he has decided to include a cigar and an empty whiskey bottle, along with a set of "letters from the field"—perhaps to Abraham Lincoln—and maps of Civil War campaigns.

***

The school choir is planning a program of Middle Eastern music that coincides with the sixth graders' study of the Middle East. Jeanette challenges her students: Use what you have learned about the Middle East to help the choir director develop the concert. As a follow-up assessment, Jeanette asks the students to develop program notes explaining what they considered to be the distinctive elements of Middle Eastern music. Students compare the smaller intervals, different rhythms, and instrumentations common to Middle Eastern music with those used in European music and discuss vocal sound production—comparing the "loose" throat vocalizations of Western music with the "tighter" throat more common to Middle Eastern music.

***

Jeanette's seventh graders are deeply involved in studying Islamic influences on Spain. The Alhambra, a fortress and castle in Granada, Spain, seems to be a perfect example of how war and conquest can disperse other aspects of culture, including art and architecture. Building a replica of the Alhambra might work, the students decide, but they really want visitors to be able to see, in detail, the kind of art introduced by the Moors—and they definitely want to try their hand at reproducing these artistic styles. Perhaps they could try some of the art and hang it around the room? Or they could do what they had seen students do last year with the medieval castle! Before long, the students turn their classroom into a replica of the Alhambra, complete with examples of Islamic art. Student guides conduct visitors on a tour of historic Moorish art and architecture, explaining its political and religious significance as they point out the distinctive style of portrait painting and mosaics. Although students are enthusiastic in their admiration for Islamic art and respectful of the culture that produced it, they are also impressed with their own production. Hannah smiles when complimented on her work, and says "It really is beautiful, isn't it?" She then points out some details of the time period they have included "because this style lets you know exactly when it was built."

Because she teaches all the sixth-, seventh-, and eighth-grade social studies in this small arts magnet school, Jeanette sees her students develop over time. She worries, too, about what will happen to them when they leave this school. "Some teachers are afraid to integrate the arts," Jeanette says. "They feel that they'll have more behavior problems. I think that the reverse is true, but I have trouble convincing people of that. They think they can't let children create a piece of music or a piece of art— that they'll miss some content because the arts are taking up their time. In reality, they are probably not going to be so frustrated in their learning. They see the whole picture. In other words, they may learn separate parts, but I want them to see how it fits in the whole. We may relate a concept from early in the year—early African and Indian slavery—and then that fits in with the picture of what happened in the Civil War, and then we might talk about what happens with a racial situation here."

The arts help students see the "whole picture." Groth & Albert (1997)

In our view, the arts are an integral part of history—part of what makes civilizations unique. Think about how rap music speaks to the life and experience of many young people today, how songs such as *Hair* or *Blowin' in the Wind* represented the counterculture or antiwar movements of the 1960s and 1970s in the

Albert (1995), Williams (1991)

United States, or how Picasso's *Guernica* powerfully interprets the horrors of the Spanish Civil War. Think, too, about the variety of official uses of art: commemorative stamps, memorial statues and monuments, political campaigns, and the like. As you look at the historical art in Fig. 13.1, consider how each artist attempts to manipulate your emotions. In the original artwork, lurid red and orange firelight illuminates the faces of Hitler and Hirohito, emphasizing the whites of Hitler's hypnotic eyes and the bit of liquid dripping from Hirohito's oversized teeth, conjuring up images of hell. Out of the black and red night, Hitler stares directly at the viewer; Hirohito shifts his view to the side, implying that he can see into the shadows. In the second example, the artist directs your eye to a mother and child. The lines are softer, and the picture is meant to recall the sentimentality and safety of a Madonna and child. In this instance, too, textual graphics call attention first to safety—she's good enough to be your baby's mother—and then to the point of the illustration—and she's good enough to vote with you.

The impact of each poster is greater, too, if you consider the historical context as well as the artistry of the rendering. Who was the audience for each piece of art? To what fears did each speak? The first, of course, is a World War II propaganda poster; the second a 1918 song sheet used to promote women's suffrage. As Jeanette explains, the "arts are situated in a historical context, in a culture, in a society. I think the arts can help the students speculate about what the purpose of a specific art form in a particular historical context or a particular historical time might be."

The arts are political as well as aesthetic.

Eisner (1988)

The arts exist in an historical context.

FIG. 13.1. Historical art.

189

THE ARTS ADDRESS SIGNIFICANT HISTORICAL QUESTIONS

Epstein (1994a, 1994d)

The historical arts help students address different questions than do more traditional print sources. A variety of print sources, for instance, might help students respond to a question such as: Could the conflicts between Native Americans and European Americans in the post Civil War era have been avoided? Students might read U.S. and Canadian government documents and census records, analyze statements by military leaders such as General Philip Sheridan ("The only good Indian is a dead Indian"), study U.S. government policies intended to destroy tribal cohesiveness ("Kill the Indian, save the man"), and consider Sitting Bull's call for his people not to surrender the sacred Black Hills ("We want no white men here. The Black Hills belong to me. If the whites try to take them, I will fight"). Using these sources, students could build and defend positions regarding the inevitability of hostility, develop an explanation of culture clash and its aftermath, or suggest alternatives to U.S. policy based on the Canadian example. These are important, but limited, questions to consider in making sense of this historical era.

Welch (1994)

Historical arts complement and extend more traditional historical sources.

Greene (1995)

By working with the historical arts, students focus on a different—though related—sort of historical question: What was it like to be a Sioux or one of their allies during the period surrounding the Battle of Little Big Horn? This question deals more explicitly with a people's "way of being in the world." Consider what sources students might use to answer this question. They might study examples of the decorative arts—clothing, basketry, body art—that evoke aspects of Sioux culture. They could use photographs taken of Sioux and Cheyenne children as they first entered boarding schools (separated from their families, tribal communities, and home language) and again after their long hair was shorn and their familiar clothing replaced by European style clothing. Photographs of an Arapaho camp, a Lakota woman, or a young warrior on horseback, free on the plains, could be juxtaposed with images of reservation life. Further, photographs of the massacre at Marias River, cartoons expressing outrage at Custer's defeat, posters for Buffalo Bill Cody's Wild West show, and Sioux artwork showing the death of Sitting Bull and Crazy Horse all provide insight into the human experience behind the myth of "Custer's last stand" and the eventual subjugation of the Sioux (and other Native peoples). These historical arts provide different vantage points from which to view history and make explicit the powerful emotions that often defy the power of words to fully express. This does not discount more traditional historical sources; rather, together they develop the "whole picture" that Jeanette seeks for her students.

The arts provide different historical vantage points.

Developing the whole picture is clearly important to Jeanette. Although her small classroom is often crowded with work from three different grades, she feels strongly that this apparent chaos really is harmonious. Students regularly see each other's work, borrow ideas from each other, and are reminded that the "separate parts" they study each year really do fit in a larger framework. In building this framework, Jeanette focuses on several aspects of the arts related to thinking and learning in history. First, she uses the arts as source material for historical study. This involves understanding and making judgments about art, as well as coming to appreciate art from different times and places. Second, she encourages (and regularly requires) students to use the arts as vehicles for the expression of their historical understanding. This is closely related to what Howard Gardner describes as the heart of arts education, "the capacity to handle, to use, to transform different artistic symbol systems—to *think with and in* the materials." Although these processes are interrelated in the context of Jeanette's classroom, it is useful to consider the separate contributions of the arts both as historical data and as ways to "think with and in" history.

The arts are data sources for history as well as vehicles for expressing historical understanding.

Brandt (1988a), Eisner (1988), Gardner (1988), Ranyi (1994)

THE ARTS AS SOURCE MATERIAL FOR HISTORICAL STUDY

The arts are primary source documents that tell us about the time and place in which they were produced. As Jeannette says, it is hard to imagine teaching about ancient Greece without reference to its art, literature, and architecture. Indeed, it should be equally difficult to imagine ignoring the rich artistry of such African empires as Benin or Mali or of the ancient Aztecs and Mayans. While much of Western knowledge of these civilizations was based on the reports of European explorers, each empire also left at least a partial record of its own worldview in its arts. An ivory mask from Benin, for instance, depicts a row of Portuguese sailors in a position intended to represent the power of the people of Benin over these strangers. Similarly, the art and architecture of the ancient Maya indicate a sophisticated understanding of math and astronomy, as well as a rich cosmology and elaborate social and political life. In North America, the art of Sioux and Cheyenne—pictures drawn in ledger books and on skins and fabric to explain events from the Native American perspective—provide eyewitness accounts of the plains wars in the late 1800s (see Fig. 13.2). The arts are sources of information on the content of these cultures, from clothing and recreation to religious beliefs and technology, from gender roles and child rearing practices to political and natural cataclysms. But the form of the arts is also historically important. Just as culture gives directions to art—providing religious ideas, for instance—so art shapes our perceptions of the world by embodying ideas in sensory images—a Russian Orthodox icon, perhaps. More

Zevins & Evans (1993)

Eisner (1998)

FIG. 13.2.   An unknown Hunkpapa Lakota artist's rendition of the arrest and killing of Sitting Bull (North Dakota Historical Society).

fully understanding history, then, means studying how the form and content of the arts express that history.

Although World War II posters and ledger art are primary sources—artifacts of the times in which they were created—the arts also function as secondary sources, interpreting other times and places. Perhaps you have seen the movie *Dances With Wolves*. It is certainly not a firsthand account of life among the Lakota or the U.S. Cavalry. Instead, it is a modern interpretation of the past, operating much as textbooks do by reinterpreting the past to a modern audience. In doing so, *Dances with Wolves* provides a commentary on what modern Americans are willing to tell themselves about this part of their past. In contrast to early "Westerns" where Native peoples were generally villainous and the cavalry rode to the rescue of white settlers, *Dances with Wolves* presents the Lakota as a heroic people stalked by the evil U.S. Cavalry. Such an interpretation probably tells us more about modern American society than it does about the complex lives of either the cavalry or the Lakota. Yet our students encounter history interpreted through the visual arts—pictures, films, art and artifacts, the built environment, television—all the time. Although we tend to emphasize the literary arts in school, our students' ideas of life on the American frontier or during the Eisenhower administration are at least as likely to be shaped by television shows such as *Little House on the Prairie* and *Happy Days*, or by movies such as *Dances with Wolves*, as by anything in a history text.

In Jeannette's classroom, she draws on music, dance, drama, literature, and the visual arts and feels strongly that each makes a contribution to her students' understanding of history and social studies. Her students expect the arts to be an integral part of their historical study. On the day that students try writing amendments to the U.S. Constitution using their newly carved quill pens and homemade ink, Jeannette turns down the lights. ("I would have used candles, but we aren't allowed to have them in school.") She plays a tape of Mozart's music to help establish a tone for student work. The class has already talked about Mozart and Washington as contemporaries, the kind of instruments available at the time, the places where that music might have been available, and the importance of music in the social life of the Revolutionary era. As the tape ends, students look up in the sudden stillness. "What happened?" asks one boy. "We need the music!" Jeanette restarts the tape and the class goes back to its labors, immersed in some of the sensory experiences of the age they are studying.

During the same unit on the Constitution, Jeanette reads excerpts from one of Jean Fritz' books, *Shh! We're Writing the Constitution*, shows a video of a play from the period and requires that students report on at least one source of information on the Constitution not already used in class. "What picture do you get from each of these sources?" she asks. "What images come to mind?" The students immediately respond with sensory images: "hot and muggy," "a lot of white haired, white men," "flies buzzing around, windows closed," "secretive." At this point, Jeanette introduces a large print of the signing of the Constitution and says:

> What we are looking at is a painting of the immediate setting of the writing of the Constitution. Now, when you look at this painting, I want you to use some of the work we have done with costume, with clothing, art, and things of the time period. You know there wasn't any CNN back during the writing of the Constitution. After the fact, an artist did a rendering of what he thought it would look like if you had been at the Constitutional convention. Now, you are the art critic. I want you to look at the painting and to evaluate it in terms of [she writes on the board]:
>
> What kind of job do you think the artist did? Did he make an accurate portrait of what happened at that time? Inaccurate? Why?
>
> Where is attention focused in the painting? What do you think the artist is trying to do here? What are the aesthetic elements of this painting? What are the political uses this painting might be put to?

Welch (1999)

Barton & Levstik (1996), Levstik & Barton (1996)

Albert (1994), Groth & Albert (1997)

Fritz (1987). See also Berkin (2002).

The arts develop sensory images of historical people, places, and events.

Working in small groups, the students begin noting details that conflict with other sources they have used. The men in the painting seem cooler and less uncomfortable than other sources indicated; curtains and windows are open, also contrary to most sources. They notice that George Washington is centered in the painting, the light focusing on him so that "he becomes the main figure," while the men who did most of the writing are minor figures in the painting. Carter explains that seeing the painting helped him visualize what the delegates looked like: "It really assisted me ... knowing which figure was which." Interestingly, he also mentions that, despite "knowing" how many delegates had been in attendance, "I didn't realize just how many delegates participated ... until I saw that picture. There were quite a few, you know."

Seeing often supports believing.

Carter's experience may be familiar to you. Think back to the first time you saw a favorite ballet, heard a soul stirring concert, or stood before a powerful piece of art—not on film or reproduced in a textbook, but live, perhaps in a theater, concert hall, gallery, or museum. Perhaps the experience jolted you out of familiar ways of seeing. You understood, to some degree, not just an event or idea, but a world of feelings. As you gained experience—perhaps heard a recording of the concert or saw the play performed a second time, you noticed dimensions of the work you missed the first time. These experiences enriched your feelings for the work; perhaps you also shared it with someone else and re-experienced it through their eyes. In a sense, this kind of aesthetic experience is a bit like unraveling a mystery—one in which there is no final scene where all is made clear. It engages both your intellect and your emotions, and often moves beyond the power of words to explain. As Isadora Duncan said, "If I could *tell* you what I mean, there would be no point in dancing."

Epstein (1994b, 1994c), Greene (1995), Kozma (1992), Winner (1982)

Goodman (1984), Rockefeller (1978), Selwyn (1995)

In history, too, there is an element of mystery, of searching for some key to explain not just what happened, but why it happened—what web of emotions, values, and ideas connects a set of events. Perhaps because of this air of mystery, students are likely to recognize voice and intention in the arts more readily than in textbooks. As students think about the mind behind the historical image, however, it is important to consider not only the viewpoint represented, but how the artist used her medium to express that viewpoint. An increasing number of children's books explore just this connection between artist and art, intention and action (see booklist at end of chapter). In *A Young Painter: The Life and Paintings of Wang Yani—China's Extraordinary Young Artist*, for instance, the relationship between Wang Yani's prodigious paintings, her life with her father, and her experiences growing up in China are explored. *Follow the Drinking Gourd,* a picture book for younger readers, explains how a song provided directions for African Americans escaping from slavery.

History and the arts share an element of mystery.

Brown, Collins, & Duguid (1989), Kozma (1991)

Epstein (1994b, 1994c), Gabella (1994)

Zhensun & Low (1991)

Winter (1988)

Unfortunately, the very thing that students find appealing—the emotion and intention of the arts—sometimes leads them to discount the arts as "biased." Students may assume that the world view of a textbook is "objective" precisely because it has, from their perspective, no recognizable voice or intention. This is not an argument against using the arts; rather, we think that an arts-infused curriculum in which children analyze the intentional nature of all modes of expression will help children think more carefully about the nature of historical perspective, wherever encountered.

Epstein (1994b, 1994c), Levstik & Pappas (1987)

Students should learn to recognize the voice and intention of all modes of expression.

Analyzing visual sources has several advantages for students. Unlike the events they represent, for instance, visual images are fixed in time. When you analyze a still image (or stop a moving one), you are undisturbed by the changing moment, by movement, or the emotional fluctuations that were part of the actual event. You can go back to an image repeatedly, searching its multiple dimensions, asking new questions, bringing new information and experience to bear. Of course, this presents its own set of problems. Something that was, in fact, ephemeral can gain undue significance simply because it was preserved. Think how easily a single photograph from your family album, taken out of con-

Levstik & Barton (1996), Mazur (1993), Olson (1974)

Visual images allow students to examine and reexamine historical moments.

Taking a historical
moment out of context
can lead to incomplete
interpretations.

text, could misrepresent your family history. We have all learned how power-fully a single image can capture public attention, either for good or ill. The photograph of a firefighter holding an injured child in the wake of a bombing speaks volumes about the tragic dimensions of this event. On the other hand, a photograph of Gerald Ford falling down a staircase during a campaign stop becomes emblematic of a larger political "clumsiness."

Winner (1982)

Dyson (1989)

Gardner (1982)

Children enter school having been exposed to an enormous variety of visual images. Although they may be more adept at making sense of animated computer art or cartoons than historical art, they already have a store of visual clues at their disposal. From their earliest years, sighted and hearing children infer relationships between visual and aural data and their own social situations and background experiences. In fact, many children communicate through the arts long before they achieve fluency with reading and writing, and may prefer drawing to writing despite increasing fluency in writing. In addition, children often have a rich visual symbology that helps them interpret their own and others' art. In Fig. 13.3, for instance, a seven-year-old's response to the *Little House* books uses only one word but incorporates many details from the story—high-button shoes, water pails, a barn with square nails, Laura's clothing—along with more iconographic symbols that were already part of the child's artistic shorthand—the imaginary house and yard and the bird.

FIG. 13.3. Visualizing the past.

As children gain more background knowledge in history (often from nonprint media), they use that information in their own artistic productions and in interpreting the historical arts. In general, they are more fluent in describing and interpreting material culture—technology, clothing, architecture, food—where they can make connections between the historical image and their own lives— or the lives they see displayed on television, in movies, and in books. Children looking at a photograph of a Victorian schoolroom, for instance, associated it with Samantha, a character (and doll) from the *American Girls* books and recognized various elements in the photograph based on their experience with these dolls and books. They also mistakenly identified a group of Iroquois as Romans because they mistook the blankets draped over the Iroquois' shoulders as "robes like Roman times." Their visual experience with Native peoples did not include wearing blankets in the way pictured, but they had recently seen illustrations of Roman togas in a history display created by older students.

Historical information can be garnered from many sources, including the media.

Barton & Levstik (1996)

It is clear that children in a variety of settings find the arts a rich part of their historical study. Old Town Elementary, a school not too far from the arts magnet school where Jeanette teaches, draws on one of the poorest populations in the city. Old Town has no special arts programming, and few of its teachers began their teaching careers with more than the rudimentary background in the arts provided by introductory undergraduate courses, yet the school overflows with art. Murals of pioneer life stretch down one hall, a display of masks produced by different cultures around the world hangs from the ceiling in the entryway, a huge three-dimensional dragon left over from a study of China lingers in a corner, and photographs of an Indonesian visitor demonstrating a lion dance to a group of primary children are displayed on a classroom door. In the first grade, students invite a guest to try her hand at brass rubbing. Several classmates are carefully rubbing crayons across paper-covered brass reliefs. The reliefs (raised images on a flat background) represent British historical figures; as the children rub their crayons across the surfaces of the reliefs, they comment on the images emerging on their paper, reminding each other of medieval symbology:

Levstik (1993)

The arts can speak across race, class, and cultural differences.

Erin: This one is a king.

David: He's a knight, cause he's got a sword, see?

Erin: Yeah, but there's a ... see down by his feet.

Aggie: A lion.

Erin: Uh-huh. That lion means he's a king. Kings get lions
          [this had been a small note on a picture seen earlier in the year].

Catrina: The lady's got something.

Jake: A dog.

Catrina: Yeah, a dog. She's not a queen, I don't think.

As the children continue their work, they rearrange these visual elements for their own purposes. Two of the boys label their rubbings in Norse (one of the artifacts they have been working with includes a Norse alphabet). Another girl turns her rubbings into stick puppets, and several others follow suit, intent on turning their work into a puppet show. David cuts out each of his figures and pastes them on different backgrounds, creating a picture that looks much like a medieval tapestry.

Students use visual arts for their own purposes.

In surrounding themselves and their students with the visual arts, these teachers, along with Jeanette, are learning to read the historical arts as well as teach with them. Their students analyze the arts from historical and aesthetic perspectives and learn to associate specific questions with each of these analytical stances. From a historical perspective, for instance, students look for the details of daily life, asking:

Students learn to read the arts historically and aesthetically.

Geoghegan (1994), Sautter (1990)

- What parts of life are shown? Young children studying changes in child rearing practices might study art for information on child labor, recreation, family activities, religious events, or schooling.
- What are the artist's feelings about these activities? A Norman Rockwell picture, for instance, celebrates certain aspects of family and small town life, while another artist might poke fun at small town insularity.

Students also consider the arts as social and political commentary. They ask questions such as:

- How do artists shape historical and political thinking? Older students might consider what works of art such as *The Rake's Progress*, *Guernica*, or *The World Upside Down* tell them about the social and political world of the artists.
- What themes seem to come in for the most artistic comment at any particular time? Students might compare political cartoons over time and chart common themes.
- How controversial might this commentary have been in its own time? Now? This question might send students to other sources to provide a context for their interpretations.

From an aesthetic perspective, students study how the elements of the arts relate to each other and to the historical content, asking:

- How does each artist approach the subject (style and technique)? Students might compare different artists' interpretations of the same idea, event, or emotion, as Jeanette's students did with the Constitutional Convention.
- What do these styles and techniques say about the world view of the people who create them? Younger children might study a group of cartoons of, say, Abraham Lincoln and discuss how each cartoonist has interpreted this historical figure.

As students apply these questions to the historical arts, they become better able to interpret the arts from historical and aesthetic perspectives.

IMAGINING IN YOUR MIND: LEARNING TO READ THE HISTORIC ARTS

You'd have to take this picture, imagine it in your mind, and go through time. Based on what you know, you come to a conclusion.

—Rodney, Grade 5

[Looking at a picture of a mass gathering in front of a large building] You have like protests about race … the soldier's uniforms, well it could be about like black rights … but I don't see any black people, but I guess they could be carrying the signs.

—Evan, Grade 5

[After looking at pictures of antebellum America] It looks real interesting because there's a lot of stuff in it that makes you think it's older, like it has lots of boats and old buildings in it, and a hot air balloon and it makes you think that it's older because the hot air balloon was invented a long time ago … and a lot of the people, it looks like they're homeless, they lost their homes. … I think it would just be neat to see what they did and talk to them and see what they'd look like and see what the land would look like without anybody on it.

—Haveli, Grade 6

Each of these students is eager to look carefully and "imagine in their minds" what might be going on in a piece of art. Students can become equally immersed in the details of a medieval tapestry, an intricately carved ivory sculpture from China, or Seurat's pointillism. Yet we have all followed along on museum tours where docents find it hard to keep children focused on even the most exquisite works of art. Feet get sore, attention wanders, the gift shop beckons, and art is ignored. Interest and attention to art, as with so many other things that adults think are good for children, has much to do with context—with attending to children's purposes.

As the teachers described in this chapter began making more use of the arts, they discovered that context really was crucial. Their students were more likely to immerse themselves in art if there was a reason for close attention. Each of the children quoted earlier, for example, had been asked to think about the time sequence of a set of visual images. They pored over the details of each picture, analyzing them for clues to the mystery of time. Other primary, intermediate, and middle school students enthusiastically responded to the same task, discussing the historical images, comparing pictures, and making reference to other sources of historical information. In other classes, students focus critical attention and discussion on selecting the images for a comparative time line.

Authentic tasks encourage close attention to the arts.

Barton (2001), Barton & Levstik (1996)

Making sense of the arts, like making sense of a written text, does not come automatically. Although we are probably born able to perceive patterns in different sensory modalities, experience and culture clearly influence how we interpret the arts. To a large extent, what we expect to see (or hear) influences what we do see (or hear). When something violates our expectations, we try to impose order on it, seeking to make sense out of our experiences. Although students certainly recognize some cultural ways of representing an object, idea, or emotion (downward curving lines indicate sadness, the forward lean of a figure indicates motion), there are others that are quite confusing. Young children who assume that a Japanese print depicts a wedding because the people wear white would certainly make a more supportable interpretation if they knew that, in Japan, white is generally the color of death and mourning. In the same way, children who learn some of the complex language of hand gestures typical of traditional Indonesian dancing are better able to appreciate the performance of an Indonesian dancer.

Gombrich (1974), Kennedy (1974), Mitchell (1995), Winner (1982)

Eisner (1988)

The kind of teacher mediation necessary to help students accomplish these tasks varies, of course, with the degree of familiarity the students have with the arts and their background knowledge of the history depicted. When Liza Flornoy was assigned to teach fourth grade, she knew her students would be studying their state's history. Because she had only recently arrived in the state, she was nervous about her competence in handling this curriculum. She had been quite successful in using the arts in her old school but had few resources for this new assignment. In addition, she was worried because she had been told that her school was "in transition"—redistricting was shifting the school population to include a more even balance of low- and middle-income students. Many of her students would be unfamiliar with the school and the surrounding neighborhood, and some, she had been told, would be actively hostile. When Liza expressed her concerns to her team teacher, Mrs. Kadahota suggested she look at state history materials developed by a local heritage group. Liza liked the emphasis on public art and thought that, with a few adjustments, the materials might work well. She decided to start with the built environment surrounding her school. This had several advantages. Because the school was located in the state capital, there were a number of buildings and monuments with obvious political and aesthetic significance. The school bordered an area of newly gentrified older homes, a small business and shopping district, and a public housing development, so there would be a variety of public art, from signs and gardens to architecture and graffiti. Liza did some background reading and began adapting the materials from the heritage council.

Helping students make sense of the arts requires attention to background knowledge.

Public art is generally free and accessible.

As she had expected, her students had little experience either with buildings and monuments as sources of historical information or with the neighborhood around the school, so Liza planned two introductory experiences on data retrieval. She began with a set of five slides of different types of public and private buildings and monuments in the area and introduced several themes that might be related to each building: privacy, values, culture, change over time, social behavior, creativity, and history. As she showed the slides, students identified evidence of each theme: an ornate plaster ceiling medallion for creativity, an electrified gas lamp as change over time, a recreation room for social behavior, family photographs as history, art and sculpture as both values and culture, and so forth. Liza then distributed data retrieval charts for the children to use in collecting information from a place of their own choosing—their own home, a favorite vacation spot, a store or recreation area. The data retrieval chart consisted of one sheet of paper. On the front, students filled in columns headed with each theme. On the back, they answered three questions about the building they selected: What is the purpose or function of the place you selected? How does the look, feel, and smell of this place make you think and feel? How important are the social things that happen there—how you are treated, whom you are with, what you do together (or apart)?

Not surprisingly, the children found that the categories listed on the data retrieval chart often overlapped. Two children listed the Bible as evidence of values, for instance, whereas another listed it as social behavior. Several children indicated that separate bedrooms for children was evidence of privacy. "Isn't that a value, too?" asked another child. "And what's the difference between history and change over time? Aren't they pretty much the same things?" Another child declared that "all of it is culture." As a result, the students altered the chart, limiting their categories to privacy, values, change over time, social behavior, and creativity. They also categorized buildings by use—commercial, educational, governmental, industrial, recreational, religious, residential, and transportation related—and compared how each theme was represented in each category. They noted that several buildings had changed categories over time. A former gas station, for instance, was now an ice cream parlor, and several residences had become commercial buildings. They began compiling a list of questions they wanted to investigate: What caused buildings to change use? Why were older buildings more elaborately decorated? Why were people paying so much more to move into older buildings, rather than buy newer houses in the suburbs? What did the graffiti on some of the buildings mean?

Next, Liza organized a study of two buildings within walking distance of the school. Each student received a research guide—directions for observations and data collection, as well as follow-up activities—a clipboard, and materials for sketching and texture rubbings, as well as a camera. Working in small groups, students collected data on each building. As you look at the task outlined in Fig. 13.4, notice that, although it includes elements of the arts, it also uses other forms of historical documentation such as interviews and printed information. Liza also asks her students to use this combination of data sources in their final product, requiring that students express their historical interpretations through visual images as well as different written genres

When the arts are an integral part of historical study, students are surrounded by a rich array of images that let them see what things looked like, what people did, how they did them, how people saw themselves or were seen by others. Art is studied as a product of human intention through which an artist or artists create alternate worlds and respond to the worlds created around them. From this perspective, making sense in art—just as in history—requires careful observation and a willingness to consider multiple interpretations. It is not enough, however, for children to be consumers of the historical arts; as they experience the multiple worlds expressed in the arts, they also need to express their own historical perspectives through the arts.

Teachers need to help students collect and organize data.

Built Environment Education Consortium (1990)

Specific questions help students organize data collection.

Initial data collection often generates more researchable questions.

Corwin (1991)

The arts should be an integral part of historical study.

Baggett (1989), Goodman (1984)

198

Step One: Observe

Carefully examine the building from as many angles and sides as possible. Look for the details and study the overall shape and size. Identify any sounds, smells, and tastes that may be associated with the building. Try to recognize the variety of building materials and textures related to the building. Look for any changes that may have occurred since its construction.

Step Two: Document

Answer as many of the following questions as possible from your observations.

1. Name of the building
2. Describe the location and setting of the building
3. What is the foundation material?
4. What are the building materials?
5. Sketch or film the different types of windows and doors, as well as decorative materials and designs used on the building.
6. Make texture rubbings of different parts of the building (check with me first!)
7. Are there any chimneys? How many? Draw a picture of the chimney.
8. Describe any signs or words on the building
9. What was the building built for?
10. How many stories (floors) does the building have?
11. Describe, draw or film any evidence of each of our themes.
12. What is the current use of the building?
13. Sketch a floor plan of the first floor of the building.

Step Three: Research

Be a historical detective! Find out as much as you can about the history of our buildings. You will have a chance to talk to a local historian, so think carefully about what questions you might want to ask her. You may also use materials in the folder marked "Built Environment."

Step Four: Interpret

We will be writing and producing a documentary on these buildings. As you plan your work, think about including the following:

1. A drawing or model of what you think the original setting of the building was.
2. Reenactments of some of the historical events this building "lived through."
3. An interview with the builder and/or original owners, discussing what the building meant to each of them.
4. Pictures and discussion of what this building means to the community today.
5. A poem or reader's theater showing what is unique or special about the building.

FIG. 13.4. Read-a-Building (adapted from materials developed by the Built Environment Education Consortium, 1990).

THE ARTS AS VEHICLES FOR EXPRESSING HISTORICAL UNDERSTANDING

Nathan stands before the class about to present his report on the French Revolution: "I kind of thought of it as looking like *The Highwayman* sounds ... sort of dark and dangerous." He holds up a charcoal drawing of a street scene in Paris. The paper is black, with white buildings whose faces (literally) stare down into the street or lean back with their windows (eyes) shut. In the street, white figures out of Munch's *The Scream* gather around a red guillotine.

***

Jeanette asks her students "What picture comes to your mind when you hear the words *living Constitution?* I'd like you to find different ways to express your ideas ... show why the Constitution has lasted so long. For us to be living, we need water, air, food, light. ... What kind of things does it take for the Constitution to be living?" One student responds by drawing the Constitution as an eagle in flight, with legs, wings, and beak. Another student writes:

Concepts of freedom

Open minds

Nation as one

States as a union
Timeless set of laws and rights
Ideas accepted
Thoughts spread
Understanding of citizen's desires
Time of brainstorming
Indifferent laws
Outstanding results
No one's rights denied.

Gardner (1990)

The arts provide a wider
expressive repertoire.

Opportunities to produce
art are as important as
opportunities to view art.

Art is a form of problem
solving and intellectual
risk taking.

Each of these students is learning to think *with* and *in* the arts. As they blend feeling and ideas to create art, they make their inner conceptions public. At the same time, the very process of selecting representations for their inner conceptions shapes students' historical understanding. Where otherwise students might have relied largely on written language to convey ideas, they now have a wider repertoire of forms and symbols available to them. And, as Jeanette notes, when class work includes the arts, "you can't remain an observer very easily. You have to become a participant and when you become a participant, you have a way of learning by doing."

Producing your own historical art is quite different than using the arts as historical data. It is like the difference between reading a novel and writing one. Making historical art, in particular, can seem like a very risky business to a youngster. Faced with the problem of combining the symbology of art and the requirements of history, students will need plenty of supportive instruction. It helps, then, to think of producing historical arts as both problem solving and intellectual risk taking, components of the inquiry based approach to history used throughout this book.

THE ARTS AS PROBLEM SOLVING

Jeanette has asked her eighth graders to represent a portion of the Constitution in some way that will make clear its most significant elements. She tells them to think first about what information they want to convey and then how best to represent it to their peers. Students work in four groups, first discussing the task and then drawing sketches to illustrate to each other how their ideas might best be presented. One group discusses the use of circles "because these things keep repeating." Another debates the appropriateness of cartoon characters that represent the different sides of an issue; a third sketches ideas, playing with spatial relationships, symbols, and colors. Individual groups divide up the work, sending a couple of students off to draw pictures, others to compose the text, and still others to mock up the full presentation on a piece of poster board. Jeanette moves between the groups, asking them questions and making suggestions. She asks one group if Congress has ever chosen a president who did not receive "a majority of the actual votes." She mentions to another group that all people did not receive equal rights in the original Constitution. "Look through the amendments. Whose rights are guaranteed later?" She also comments that one group "has a very good idea, here. Their chart gives you two alternatives; it tells you what happens when there is a majority and what happens when there isn't. How has this changed from the way the Constitution was originally written?" She asks another group if they copied an idea from another source or made it up themselves. "What does this mean?" she asks them. "Tell us about that."

The final products are an interesting mix of art and text. One group presents an illustrated flow chart of the 12th amendment to the U.S. Constitution (election of President and Vice-President). They have arranged a series of branching choices that must be made in electing the President and Vice President. At each decision point, they have an illustration showing some actual historical event that coincides with the decision that must be made. A hand dropping a vote into a ballot box illustrates the first step when electors meet. Further down the chart, an illustration of what happens when there is a majority vote shows Richard Nixon with his arms above his head, his fingers making the "V" for victory sign. A bubble over his head says "I am not a crook." Another illustration shows angry Congressmen negotiating the election of Thomas Jefferson.

Clearly, Jeanette's students do not do art as an afterthought to inquiry or as icing on an otherwise less palatable cake. Rather, art is fundamental to the way in which students solve problems in history. The problems that Jeanette sets for her students sometimes require a particular medium—perhaps a dramatization or the selection of music to fit a historical event or period—but more often require that students select their own form of representation. Notice that Jeanette has developed a vocabulary for this type of assignment. Her use of "represent," for instance, operates on several levels: It signals an arts-inclusive activity, refers back to the language used in students' art specific classes, and, finally, reminds the students that, in this instance, the arts are intended to represent historical content. As she moves between groups, she challenges students to better develop both the art and history in their representations. This can be a real challenge for a teacher, especially when one piece of the work is clearly stronger and better grounded than another. In one group, for instance, the students want to get on with the art without having to carefully construct the history. They confuse the statement of equality in the Declaration of Independence with the Constitution and are preparing an illustration that credits the Constitution with guaranteeing equal rights "to everyone." Jeanette sends them back to their historical sources and leaves them with the more complicated problem of deciding how to visually represent the ideal of universal political equality with the reality of inequity.

Note, too, how the students use the potential for double entendres in their art. The text on the chart for the Twelfth Amendment, for instance, is quite straightforward, explaining that when a majority of members of the electoral college vote for a candidate that person becomes President or Vice President. The accompanying illustration, however, shows Richard Nixon declaring both his victory and his innocence of wrongdoing. The juxtaposition of text and image speaks volumes about the students' perceptions of the challenges of the democratic process.

As historical problem solvers, then, Jeanette's students often transform linguistic information into visual representation. In doing so, they select and retrieve relevant information, generate ideas, and form new concepts. They ponder the organization of shapes and ideas, play with how colors influence each other, how to create spatial as well as historical depth, and how to indicate structural as well as historical relations. It takes courage for children to risk all this, especially in the face of possible misinterpretation by the adults who assess them.

THE ARTS AS INTELLECTUAL RISK TAKING

Representing ideas through the arts can seem quite risky, particularly to students used to more linguistic modes of expression. They may be unsure of the parameters within which they are working, of the language of interpretation, or the symbol systems open to them. In her work with high school students, Epstein found that students became more willing to discuss and use the arts as they observed that their teacher accepted and encouraged a range of interpretations. They also gained confidence as they listened to and learned from their peers. Our observations indicate that this is true of younger students as well. Elementary and middle school teachers find that students with little experience with the arts become quite concerned with "getting it right." In fact, some children become so uncomfortable with their inability to render an image with photographic accuracy that they are stymied in their ability to express themselves.

Epstein (1994b)

Gardner (1982)

201

It is not particularly useful at this point to tell students that there is more to art than realism. What seems to work more effectively is to give students choices in terms of medium, practice in using different media, and specific help so that they can create art that is satisfying to them. Dehea Smith found that her students loved to use the overhead projector to trace images that they then manipulated for their own purposes. They would draw the background to a picture, for example, and then use the overhead to trace a car or people, and so forth. This worked well early in the year, but their teacher also wanted them to be a bit more adventurous. For one project, then, she helped the students to develop a shadow puppet theater and play. She demonstrated how shadow puppets worked, showed them examples of shadow puppets from different cultures, and then set them to work making their own puppets. It soon became clear that their tiny figures with details drawn on were not going to show up effectively as shadows. Freed from the need to draw realistically, the students began paying attention to shape and space. They experimented with different materials, sizes of puppets, and distance from the screen. With well-timed suggestions from their teacher, the children developed an interesting set of props and puppets using a much wider array of materials than they had tried before. As the children became more confident with these images, their teacher encouraged them to add music and movement to their plays. She also asked the art teacher to teach the students specific techniques to satisfy their desire for realism. He worked with two-point perspective and figure drawing. Later in the year, a parent with some experience in stage design took the students to his studio and demonstrated simple techniques to make images feel peaceful, spooky, dangerous, and so forth. By the time the students painted their own stage sets for a series of historical skits, they were able to use some of the techniques they had learned and were more confident in expressing themselves artistically.

The art in children's literature can also serve as a beginning point in helping children experiment with different techniques. You might share a book with a distinctive technique—collage, charcoal, crayon resist—and then let students try their hand at the same technique. One class, fascinated with pop-up books, created pop-up illustrations for stories about early settlement in their community. Another class, after reading George Littlechild's *This Land Is My Land* (1993), in which the artist combines photographs, painting, resists, and realia, tried combining these elements. Littlechild's book is autobiographical, describing his life as a Cree and an artist. The children did much the same thing. They brought in family photographs, cut pictures from magazines, and found other images on the web that represented the story they wanted to tell. Their teacher photographed children in class, too. She digitized the photographs so that her students could select and print out the parts they wanted to use. The students drew illustrations in crayon resist and paint, and glued the pieces of photographs to their pictures. They added shells and bits of lace, as had Littlechild. One girl glued sand below a picture of a bare foot (cut from a magazine). She scratched birds into the crayoned sky, glued on cotton puff clouds, and titled her picture "My first walk on the beach." The result delighted her and inspired her classmates to try some of her techniques.

In a fifth-grade class where students had studied the art of the Sioux and Cheyenne, they decided to see whether they could show what they knew about a historic event using only pictures. One group decided that they would tell the story of the first Norse explorations of North America. Another gave a child's eye view of the Plymouth Colony, and a third presented a Chinese immigrant's view of building the transcontinental railroad. In creating these images, they went back through their history text as well as other sources they had used in studying American history. Their teacher suggested they also review some of the literature they had read on each of these topics, such as *Strange Footprints on the Land: Vikings in America, Meet the Real Pilgrims: Everyday Life on a Plymouth*

Collaboration with teachers in the arts enriches historical study.

Children's literature can be a rich source of visual art.

Kiefer (1995)

Littlechild (1993)

Check these sources for historical images: Smithsonian Institution at http://www.si.edu/history_and_culture/; National Archives at http://www.archives.gov/exhibit_hall/index.html; Library of Congress at http://www.memory.loc.gov/, or go to http://www.besthistorysites.net/USHistory.shtml for more possibilities for U.S. history.

Irwin (1980), Loeb (1979), Dillon (1986), Yep (1994)

Plantation in 1627, The Seekers, and *Dragon's Gate.* Although these books were not all richly illustrated, they reminded the students of the feelings as well as facts that might be represented in their drawings. A couple of the finished pictures were stick figure renditions of battles, but most provided interesting perspectives on how the students understood the events they had studied thus far. From a child's eye view, for instance, adults in Plymouth are huge, the forest threatening, plates and bowls often empty; Vikings sail between icebergs beneath a vast sky of stars with arrows pointing in the direction of a tiny North American island; Chinese men in baskets dangle next to ice covered mountains while their bosses sit warm and safe inside.

Literary imagery can inspire visual imagery.

An important feature of art infused classrooms is that children's artwork is on display. By carefully mounting and arranging students' work, teachers honor the intensity of effort and trust that went into its production. They find that art, like writing, thrives when it has a respectful audience and especially when that audience goes beyond the teacher. One Boston school displays children's art and writing so that adults will see it as they walk their youngsters to class each morning. As a father stops to admire a mural of life on the Great Plains, his daughter begins to explain her work to him, pointing out the decorations on tipis, the place where a smudged bear became a large bush, and so forth. Her classmates join her, eagerly sharing other features of the mural, and explaining how each element matched something they had learned about the people who lived on the Plains: "See, this is a buffalo. The tipis are made out of buffalo hide, and they use the horn and everything. That's why there's a buffalo painted on this tipi. It has a zigzag lightning thing going from its mouth. We saw that in a book we read. Want to see the book?" Meanwhile another parent compliments a child on how realistic the buffalo looks. "Oh," the child smiles. "We looked at lots of pictures. It was hard to find one that had a whole buffalo, though. At first it looked just like a horse with a *very* big head. Buffaloes have very strange shapes." Her friend explains that chickens are easier to draw, but she didn't think these Indians had chickens.

Displaying student art honors the students' problem solving and risk taking in an authentic way.

By displaying student work, teachers provide multiple audiences as well as multiple opportunities for students to discuss the aesthetic and historical choices they have made. Through these discussions, they are encouraged to be more experimental—turn bears into bushes if need be, care about historical accuracy, and not worry about an experiment that did not come out entirely as planned. In our experience, when student's artwork is displayed and discussed, students become more confident and produce much more interesting, historically sound artwork. As Jeanette explains:

> The arts give children who learn in a different way a lot of different opportunities to learn. I think that it gives them a chance to integrate material or to review what they learn in another way too. None of us has a single learning style. If I learn in a visual way and then again get to repeat it in an audio ways, its just strengthening my learning. I have another chance to learn. Sometimes you watch that here in the classroom. A child will seem to be over their head, and when you use a different form, it becomes something they can learn. It certainly provides more interest to teaching. It's more fun for me as a teacher and I think that makes it more interesting for the students. With the arts … you take what you learn into your being.

ASSESSMENT AND THE ARTS

As we noted earlier, most of the teachers with whom we work are reasonably comfortable assessing writing processes and products in history and often have established routines for selecting portfolio pieces and sharing student progress with parents and guardians. Although many of these teachers have also used the arts in teaching history, they are less sure of how to assess this aspect of their curriculum. In fact, however, many of the assessment issues teachers fear in the arts are similar to ones they are already successfully handling in writing. Just as

Hiebert & Hutchinson (1991), Marcello (1999)

Assessment in writing and the arts is often quite similar.

with writing, one issue is how to draw the line between credible and incredible interpretations or renditions. Sometimes, despite everyone's best efforts, students create artwork that reproduces stereotypes, ignores supportable historical interpretations, or is just silly. The work may be attractive or interesting artwork, but it is poor history. When you have worked hard to encourage students to take the risk and use the arts, this can be a real dilemma. How do you respond to the art without encouraging bad history and to the history without discouraging good art? This is particularly problematic when the teacher is insecure about assessing nonrepresentational art. At this point, it may seem easier to rely on linguistic modes of expression—just let students tell you what they know. But that, of course, is exactly what they are doing. They are letting you know that something is missing in their historical thinking. Epstein's work with high school students provides a useful way to think about responding to students' historical art. She argues that, just as with any written historical interpretation, students' work must be historically plausible or possible. In other words, the work must be both historically sound and historically bound.

Historically sound interpretations are those that are credible in terms of the history represented in the art. A picture depicting a bus driver happily inviting Rosa Parks to sit in the front of the bus (and not intended as satire) would not be true to events surrounding the Montgomery bus boycott. Such an interpretation, no matter how aesthetically pleasing, cannot be historically sound.

Historically bound interpretations are those that make sense within the broader historical context within which an event takes place. In other words, the interpretation is plausible given the time period and culture being studied. Although Jeanette's students did not know for sure that delegates to the Constitutional Convention listened to music by Mozart, it is plausible that they might have done so. In the same way, a fifth grader's representation of cowboys in the 1800s enjoying a televised football game is not historically bound—it would have been impossible for this activity to have taken place.

Jeanette deals with these issues in two ways. First, students participate in a number of activities that are presented to peers for discussion and suggestion. Although few of her students make blatant errors with historical soundness, they do sometimes have difficulty with historical boundedness. They have the specific events right, but there are anachronisms—usually items of material culture that would not have appeared in the particular time and place represented. By asking students to explain their work and respond to suggestions, Jeanette provides opportunities for students to self correct or put nonrepresentational art into historical context. Students also receive written peer evaluations of their work. These evaluations are based on a scoring rubric jointly developed by Jeanette and the students. The rubric addresses both the artistic and historical aspects of each performance. One expectation, for instance, is that the art must expand on any written information, not simply illustrate it. Thus, a poster explaining the electoral college has a straightforward text, but its illustrations comment on and expand the text through political cartoons. In another instance, a dance performance gives emotional weight to a reading from the Constitution.

After peer evaluation, Jeanette also provides feedback on the content as well as the form of presentation. She will compliment students for creative imagery on the one hand and tell them to recheck their historical interpretation on the other. Her students seem to understand the distinction and expect her critique to include both parts of their work. These are, after all, the same distinctions they are asked to make when they analyze other forms of historical art. In this sense, Jeanette insists that students give their own artwork the same respect and close reading accorded other artists.

Sometimes it is not essential that aesthetic merit be assessed, even when the arts are the medium of expression. Younger children especially may be

---

Epstein (1994a)

Epstein (1994a, 1994b, 1994c)

As with other historical genres, historical art can be assessed on its use of historical evidence.

Historical art can be assessed on its relationship to a broader historical context.

Anachronisms are ideas, events, or situations that are out of their proper historical time.

In explaining their own work, students have an opportunity to put that work in historical perspective or correct anachronisms.

Kornhaber & Gardner (1993)

Assessment addresses both historical and aesthetic aspects of performance.

Student work is worthy of the same respect and close reading accorded to other artists.

204

able to say what they know through the arts in ways they are not yet able to do linguistically. Thus, providing students with the opportunity to use the arts frees them to say more than they could otherwise manage. Especially with younger students, some teachers find *Sketch-to-Stretch* activities useful in helping students think about the historical soundness of their ideas. A Sketch-to-Stretch activity involves creating at least two different images of the same concept, event, or era. At the beginning of their study, children are asked to draw things they associate with some aspect of history. In one classroom, primary students drew things they associated with Africa *long ago* and things they associated with Africa *now*. Initial pictures combined elements of Disney's *The Lion King*, with jungle scenes, grass huts, and masks. One or two pictures included images of war and starvation. For the most part, however, there was little distinction between *long ago* and *now*. As they studied the history and culture of three different countries within Africa, students compared what they were learning with these first pictures. Sometimes they found elements that were accurate for a particular time and place. More often they found that many of the countries they were studying were quite different from their old ideas.

Dyson (1987)

As the unit progressed, the children drew new pictures of *long ago* and *now* for each of the countries. These new pictures combined images drawn from children's literature (*Shaka: King of the Zulus, Where Are You Going, Munyoni, Sundiata,* and *Mchesi Goes to Market*), slides, and photographs of each country. As children drew their new pictures, it was clear that their view of Africa was changing. Their *now* pictures concentrated on the contrast between urban and rural communities, whereas several of the "long ago" pictures depicted historical figures such as Shaka and Sundiata. Follow-up discussions allowed children to explain why they had included particular things in their pictures or left others out. There were still misunderstandings. One child drew a *now* picture of a young man from Chad who had visited the class. In the drawing, the young man and his sister ride an elephant to the student's school. As he shared his picture, the child explained: "I hope he comes visit our school again, but next time I want him to bring his sister and ride an elephant."

Stanley & Vennema (1988), Stock (1993), Wesniewski (1992), Sokoni (1991)

Sketch-to-stretch pictures allow teachers to see where students' misconceptions persist.

CONCLUSIONS

As you may have noticed by now, constructive evaluation shifts the focus from a remediation model for teaching and learning to the construction of a community of inquiry in which students rehearse, refine and revise, and communicate in a distinctive "voice" or style while solving substantive intellectual problems. Such an approach is closer to the way in which adults operate when they are working and is certainly more congruent with the ways in which teachers and students work throughout this book.

Johnston (1987), Newmann et al. (1995)

We have emphasized that the best assessment exercises have an authentic audience, and much of the work students have done in these classrooms clearly is directed at audiences beyond the teacher. We should also point out that some of the most meaningful assessment occurs when students are writing and creating art for themselves. The benefit of many of the techniques discussed throughout this book is that they give students a chance to demonstrate to themselves what they have learned. During a lesson or a unit, students may have picked up a great deal of information, but it often remains in a somewhat vague or disorganized form. Constructive evaluation provides a chance for students to reflect on their learning in order to identify organizing themes, patterns, and structures—it becomes a way for them to say, "Hey, I know what's going on here, and here's how I know it."

Dillon, E. *The Seekers.* Scribner's, 1986.

Fritz, J. *Shh! We're Writing the Constitution.* Putnam, 1987.

Irwin, C. Strange *Footprints on the Land: Vikings in America.* Harper, 1980.

Lawrence, J. *The Great Migration: An American Story.* The Museum of Modern Art, The Phillips Collection & HarperCollins, 1992.

Littlechild, G. *This Land Is My Land.* Children's Book Press, 1993.

Loeb, Robert H. *Meet the Pilgrims: Everyday life on a Plymouth plantation in 1627.* Clarion, 1979.

Wilder, L. I. *Little House on the Prairie.* Harper & Row, 1953.

Winter, J. *Follow the Drinking Gourd.* Knopf, 1988.

Yep, L. *Dragon's Gate.* HarperCollins, 1993.

Zhensun, Z., & Low, A. *The Life and Paintings of Wang Yani—China's Extraordinary Young Artist.* Scholastic, 1991.

Other Literature on the Historical Arts

Arenas, J. *The Key to Renaissance Art.* Lerner, 1990.

Braun, B. *A Weekend with Diego Rivera.* Rizzoli, 1994.

Chaucer, G. *Canterbury Tales.* (Selected and adapted by Barbara Cohen and illustrated by Trina Shart Hyman.) Lothrop, 1988.

Chrisp, P. *Welcome to the Globe: The Story of Shakespeare's Theater.* DK Publishing, 2000.

Davidson, R. *Take a Look: An Introduction to the Experience of Art.* Viking, 1994.

Duggleby, J. *Story Painter: The Life of Jacob Lawrence.* Chronicle, 1998.

Everett, G. *Li'l Sis and Uncle Willie: a Story Based on the Life and Paintings of William H. Johnson.* Rizzoli, 1992.

Finley, C. *Art of Japan: Wood-Block Color Prints.* Lerner, 1998.

Finley, C. *Art of the Far North: Inuit Sculpture, Drawing, and Printmaking.* Lerner, 1998.

Fisher, L. E. *Gutenberg.* Macmillan, 1930.

Freedman, R. *An Indian Winter.* Holiday House, 1992.

Garfunkel, T. *On Wings of Joy: The Story of Ballet from the Sixteenth Century to Today.* Little, 1994.

Gaughenbaugh, M., & Camburn H. *Old House, New House: A Child's Exploration of American Architectural Styles.* Preservation, 1994.

Glenn, P. B. *Under Every Roof: A Kids' Style and Field Guide to the Architecture of American Houses.* Preservation, 1993.

Herbert, J. *Leonardo Da Vinci for Kids: His Life and Ideas: 21 Activities.* Chicago Review, 1998.

Highwater, J. *Many Smokes, Many Moons: A Chronology of American Indian History Through Indian Art.* Lippincott, 1978.

Hunt, P. *Illuminations.* Bradbury, 1989.

Isaacson, P. M. *A Short Walk Around the Pyramids and Through the World of Art.* Knopf, 1993.

Lattimore, D. N. *The Sailor Who Captured the Sea: The Story of the Book of Kells.* HarperCollins, 1991.

Lazo, C. *Alice Walker: Freedom Writer.* Lerner, 2000.

Macaulay, D. *Castle.* Houghton Mifflin, 1977.

Monceaux, M. *Jazz: My Music, My People.* Knopf, 1994.

Moore, R. *Native Artists of Africa.* Muir, 1994.

Morley, J. *Shakespeare's Theater.* Bedrick, 1994.

Nickens, B. *Walking the Log: Memories of a Southern Childhood.* Rizzoli, 1994.

Niemark, A. E. *Diego Rivera: Artist of the People.* HarperCollins, 1994.

Normandin, C. (Ed.). *Spirit of the Cedar People: More Stories and Paintings of Chief Lelooska.* DK, 1998.

Orozco, J. (Selector/Arranger). *De Colores: And Other Latin American Folk Songs for Children.* Dutton, 1994.

Ross, S. *Shakespeare and Macbeth: The Story Behind the Play.* Viking, 1994.

Silverman, J. *Songs and Stories from the American Revolution.* Millbrook, 1994. (See also *The Blues, Work Songs, African Roots, Slave Songs.*)

Sullivan, G. *Mathew Brady: His Life and Photographs.* Cobblehill, 1994.

Turner, R. M. *Dorothea Lange.* Little, 1994.

Willard, N. *Pish, Posh, Said Hieronymous Bosch.* Harcourt Brace Jovanovich, 1991.

Wilson, E. B. *Bibles and Bestiaries: A Guide to Illuminated Manuscripts.* Farrar, 1994.

Winter, J. *Frida.* Arthur A. Levine, 2002.

Woolf, F. *Picture This: An Introduction to Twentieth Century Art.* Doubleday, 1993.

Yeck, J. L., & McGreevey, T. *Movie Westerns.* Lerner, 1994.

Books on African Nations

Ahiagble, G., & Meyer, L. *Master Weaver from Ghana*. Open Hand, 1998.

Barghusen, J. D. *Daily Life in Ancient and Modern Cairo*. Runestone, 2001.

Bess, C. *Story for a Black Night*. Mifflin, 1982.

Cheney, P. *The Land and People of Zimbabwe*. HarperCollins, 1990. (Additional volumes in this series deal with Kenya and South Africa.)

Cowen-Fletcher, J. *It Takes a Village*. Scholastic, 1994.

Gordon, S. *The Middle of Somewhere: A Story of South Africa*. Orchard, 1990.

Grifalconi, A. *The Village of Round and Square Houses*. Little, Brown, 1986.

Haskins, J. *Count Your Way Through Africa*. Carolrhoda, 1989.

Haskins, J., & Benson, K. *African Beginnings*. Lothrop, 1998.

Isadora, R. *At the Crossroads*. Greenwillow, 1991.

Jacobsen, K. *Zimbabwe*. New True Books, Houghton Children's Press, 1990.

Kanjoyah, J. N., & Mulima, S. *Our Location (Pupil Book for Standard 2)*. Longmans Kenya, 1989.

Knight, M. B., & Melnicove, M. *Africa is Not a Country*. Millbrook, 2000.

Kristensen, P., & Cameron, F. *We Live in South Africa*. Franklin Watts, 1985.

Levitin, S. *Dream Freedom*. Silver Whistle, 2000.

Levitan, S. *The Return*. Fawcett/Ballentine, 1987.

Lewin, T. *The Storytellers*. Lothrop, 1998.

Lundgren, G. *Malcolm's Villge*. Annick, 1983.

Margolies, B. *Rehema's Journey: A Visit to Tanzania*. Scholastic, 1990.

McKee, T. *No More Strangers Now: Young Voices from a New South Africa*. DK Ink, 1998.

Negash, A. *Haile Selassie*. Chelsea House, 1990.

Schrier, J. *On the Wings of Eagles: An Ethiopian Boy's Story*. Millbrook, 1998.

Sokoni, M. A. *Mchesi Goes to Market*. Nairobi, Kenya: Jacaranda Designs, LTD, 1991.

Stanley, D., & Vennema, P. *Shaka: King of the Zulus*. Morrow, 1998.

Stark, A. *Zimbabwe: A Treasure of Africa*. Dillon, 1986.

Steptoe, J. *Mufaros Beautiful Daughters*. Lothrop, Lee & Shepard, 1987.

Stock, C. *Where Are You Going, Manyoni?* Morrow, 1993.

Tadjo, V. *Lord of the Dance: An African Retelling*. HarperCollins, 1988.

Williams, K. L. *Galimoto*. Lothrop, Lee & Shepard, 1990.

Wesneiwski, D. *Sundiata*. Clarion, 1992.

Web Sites for Historical Sources

Smithsonian Institution at http://www.si.edu/history_and_culture/

National Archives at http://www.archives.gov/exhibit_hall/index.html

Library of Congress, American Memory at http://www.memory.loc.gov/

Best History Sites at http://www.besthistorysites.net/USHistory.shtml

Epilogue

Being human means thinking and feeling; it means reflecting on the past and visioning into the future. We experience; we give voice to that experience; others reflect on it and give it new form. That new form, in its turn, influences and shapes the way next generations experience their lives.

That is why history matters.

—Gerda Lerner (1997, p. 211)

As Lerner suggests, history always derives from the present—from the ways in which individuals at a given moment in time reflect on and give form to times past. Teaching and learning history is also about imagining a future in which we understand ourselves and others better, and that is the point of this book. The teachers with whom we have been privileged to work take this task quite seriously. In the elementary and middle school classrooms described here, history is not a grab-bag of tricks and gimmicks with no overarching frame of reference but an opportunity to reflect on the past and envision the future.

Sometimes people characterize alternatives to traditional approaches to history as throwing open the gates to the barbarians. They fear that where there are multiple "right" answers there are no "wrong" ones, that history becomes a complete fiction or simply a chronological arrangement of ungrounded opinions arrived at by group consensus and used to bolster spurious causes. We take a contrary point of view, arguing that thinking historically is fundamentally about judgment—about building and evaluating warranted or grounded interpretations. History, then, is not just opinion: It is interpretation grounded in evidence—hence the emphasis throughout this book on helping students learn how to gather and analyze information about the past.

Further, historical thinking and the construction of historical knowledge is a dynamic process that always takes place in a social context. We may make individual sense of the past, but we always do so in ways that are mediated by the cultural tools at our disposal, by the purposes for which those tools are employed, and by the multiple settings in which our sense making takes place. Among the procedures at our disposal, and one regularly used by the teachers in this book, is the development of a community of historical inquiry. In a community of inquiry, individuals jointly pursue a problem or question, share sources of information, share standards for evaluating that information, build and critique interpretations, and reflect on their findings. Students' historical understandings develop in and are shaped by this community. And their understandings will be different than those arising from more lecture- or textbook-based history instruction precisely because they developed in a context where students are responsible for putting their understanding to work—where they are responsible for explaining their thinking to interested others, for striving to be an "interested other" to their peers, and for keeping an open mind in regard to new evidence and alternative perspectives.

*Wertsch (1998),
Seixas (1999)*

Lerner (1997, p. 201)

This sort of agency—of believing in one's ability to take action—is crucial to our approach throughout this book. Agency in history is, of course, something we want students to learn about, but they are also agents in their own learning and in their own lives. They should be prepared to do something with what they learn. As we have argued throughout the book, this is the problem with simply telling history as a story—it leaves students unprepared to move beyond story into agency. As Gerda Lerner suggests, "a meaningful connection with the past demands, above all, active engagement. It demands imagination and empathy so that we can fathom worlds unlike our own, contexts far from those we know, ways of thinking and feeling that are alien to us. We must enter past worlds with curiosity and with respect." Knowing about the past then, is never enough—we must also care about the past, and care enough to use what we discover to make a better future.

We believe that students who do history in the ways described in this book are better prepared to care about history, and we believe they are better prepared to use history meaningfully in their lives. Doing this kind of history is no small challenge, either for students or teachers. It is, however, the challenge taken up by many of the teachers we know. Their willingness to work toward this kind of teaching and learning grows from a shared vision of their students (and themselves) as historical agents—reflecting on the past in order to act more wisely in the present, making more intelligent choices for the future, and expanding their vision of what it means to be human and humane.

In the end, we only capture moments in the lives and work of the diverse group of teachers and students portrayed in this book. For them, as for us, history is an exciting and ever-changing process of investigation and reflection. No one of these classrooms will look quite the same next year or the year after. As they read, travel, and participate in classes, seminars, workshops, and conferences, their approaches to investigating history with their students change and their own historical understandings deepen. LeeAnn, for instance, may not focus on Christopher Columbus next October, and Walt Keet will certainly change his approach to studying South Africa as that country's situation changes. Several of the teachers in this book face new challenges, too, as they move to new places or take on new assignments. Dehea Smith is now working in Florida, and Jeanette Groth moved to Ghana, where she is teaching and investigating the connections between history and citizenship education. All of this, of course makes teaching exciting—we are not forever bound by what we once knew. Rather, as the depth and breadth of our own experience and our reflection on that experience grows, so, too, does our teaching.

References

Adler, D. A. (1987). *The number on my grandfather's arm.* New York: Union of American Hebrew Congregations.

Adoff, A. (1970). *Malcolm X.* New York: Harper & Row.

Albert, M. (1995). *Impact of an arts-integrated social studies curriculum on eighth graders' thinking capacities.* Unpublished doctoral dissertation, University of Kentucky, Lexington.

Aliki, M. (1983). *Medieval wedding.* New York: HarperCollins.

Alleman, J., & Brophy, J. (1998). Assessment in a social constructivist classroom. *Social Education, 62,* 32–34.

Alleman, J., & Brophy, J. (1999). Current trends and practices in social studies assessment for the early grades. *Social Studies and the Young Learner, 11*(4), 15–17.

Allen, J. (Ed.). (1998). *Class actions: Teaching for social justice in elementary and middle schools.* New York: Teachers College Press.

Alvermann, D. (1991). The discussion web: A graphic aid for learning across the curriculum. *The Reading Teacher, 45,* 92–99.

American Memory. http://www.memory.loc.gov/.

Anderson, L. (1990). A rationale for global education. In K. Tye (Ed.), *Global education: From thought to action* (pp. 13–34). Alexandria, VA: Association for Supervision and Curriculum Development.

Angell, A. V. (2004). Making peace in elementary classrooms: A case for class meetings. *Theory and Research in Social Education, 32,* 98–104.

Appleby, J., Hunt, L., & Jacob, M. (1994). *Telling the truth about history.* New York: Norton.

Arnheim, R. (1981). *Visual thinking.* Berkeley: University of California Press.

Asbhy, R., & Lee, P. J. (1998, April). *Information, opinion, and beyond.* Paper presented at the annual meeting of the American Educational Research Association, San Diego.

Ashby, R., Lee, P., & Dickinson, A. (1997). How children explain the "why" of history: The Chata research project on teaching history. *Social Education, 61,* 17–21.

Atwell, N. (1987). *In the middle: Writing, reading, and learning with adolescents.* Upper Montclair, NJ: Boynton/Cook.

Avery, P. (2002). Political socialization, tolerance, and sexual identity. *Theory and Research in Social Education, 30,* 190–197.

Avery, P., Bird, K., Johnstone, S., Sullivan, J. L., & Thalhammer, K. (1992). Exploring political tolerance with adolescents. *Theory and Research in Social Education, 20,* 386–420.

Avi. (1984). *The fighting ground.* New York: J. B. Lippincott.

Axtell, J. (1992). *Beyond 1492: Encounters in colonial North America.* New York: Oxford.

Baggett, P. (1989). Understanding verbal and visual messages. In H. Mandle & J. Levin (Eds.), *Knowledge acquisition from text and pictures* (pp. 101–124). Amsterdam, NY: Elsevier.

Bakhtin, M. M. (1986). *Speech genres and other late essays* (V. W. McGee, Trans.). Austin: University of Texas Press.

Baldwin, J. (1988). A talk to teachers. In R. Simonson & S. Walker (Eds.), *Multi-cultural literacy* (pp. 3–12). Saint Paul, MN: Graywolf.

Balson, M. (Producer), & Sayles, J. (Writer/Director). (1987). *Matewan* [Motion Picture]. United States: Cinecom International Films.

Bamford, R. A., & Kristo, J. V. (1998). *Making facts come alive: Choosing quality nonfiction literature K–8*. Norwood, MA: Christopher-Gordon.

Barber, B. J. (1984). *Strong democracy: Participatory politics for a new age*. Berkeley, CA: University of California Press.

Barber, B. J. (1992). *An aristocracy of everyone: The politics of education and the future of America*. New York: Ballantine.

Bardige, B. (1988). Things so finely human: Moral sensibilities at risk in adolescence. In C. Gilligan, J. V. Ward, & J. M. Taylor (Eds.), *Mapping the moral domain: A contribution of women's thinking to psychological theory and education* (pp. 87–110). Cambridge, MA: Harvard University Press.

Barton, K. C. (1994). *Historical understanding among elementary children*. Unpublished doctoral dissertation, University of Kentucky, Lexington.

Barton, K. C. (1995, April). *"My mom taught me": The situated nature of historical understanding*. Paper presented at the annual meeting of the American Educational Research Association, San Francisco.

Barton, K. C. (1996a). Narrative simplifications in elementary children's historical understanding. In J. Brophy (Ed.), *Advances in Research on Teaching: Vol. 6. Teaching and Learning History* (pp. 51–83). Greenwich, CT: JAI Press.

Barton, K. C. (1996b). Using magic words to teach social studies. *Social Studies and the Young Learner, 9*(2), 5–8.

Barton, K. C. (1997a). "Bossed around by the Queen": Elementary students' understanding of individuals and institutions in history. *Journal of Curriculum and Supervision, 12*, 290–314.

Barton, K. C. (1997b). "I just kinda know": Elementary students' ideas about historical evidence. *Theory and Research in Social Education, 25*, 407–430.

Barton, K. C. (2001a). A sociocultural perspective on children's understanding of historical change: Comparative findings from Northern Ireland and the United States. *American Educational Research Journal, 38*, 881–913.

Barton, K. C. (2001b). "You'd be wanting to know about the past": Social contexts of children's historical understanding in Northern Ireland and the United States. *Comparative Education, 37*, 89–106.

Barton, K. C. (2002). "Oh, that's a tricky piece!": Children, mediated action, and the tools of historical time. *Elementary School Journal, 103*, 161–185.

Barton, K. C., & Levstik, L. S. (1996). "Back when God was around and everything": The development of elementary children's understanding of historical time. *American Educational Research Journal, 33*, 419–454.

Barton, K. C., & Levstik, L. S. (1998). "It wasn't a good part of history": National identity and students' explanations of historical significance. *Teachers College Record, 99*, 478–513.

Barton, K. C., & Levstik, L. S. (2003). Why don't more teachers engage students in interpretation? *Social Education, 67*, 358–361.

Barton, K. C., & Levstik, L. S. (2004). *Teaching history for the common good*. Mahwah, NJ: Lawrence Erlbaum Associates.

Barton, K. C., & McCully, A. (2005). History, identity and the school curriculum in Northern Irelenad: An empirical study of secondary students' ideas and perspectives. *Journal of Curriculum Studies, 37*, 85–116.

Barton, K. C., & Smith, L. A. (1994, November). *Historical fiction in the middle grades*. Paper presented to the Annual meeting of the College and University Faculty Assembly, National Council for the Social Studies, Phoenix.

Beck, I. L., & McKeown, M. G. (1991). Social studies texts are hard to understand: Mediating some of the difficulties. *Language Arts, 68*, 482–490.

Bennett, C., & Spalding, E. (1992). Teaching the social studies: Multiple approaches for multiple perspectives. *Theory and Research in Social Education, 20*, 263–292.

Bennett, P. S. (1967). *What happened on Lexington Green: An inquiry into the nature and methods of history. Teacher and student manuals*. Washington, DC: Office of Education, Bureau of Research. (Eric Document Reproduction Service No. ED 032 333)

Bestor, A. (1953). Anti-intellectualism in the schools. *New Republic, 128*, 11–13.

Berkin, C. (2003). *A brilliant solution: Inventing the American Constitution*. Orlando, FL: Harcourt.

Bickmore, K. (1993). Learning inclusion/inclusion in learning: Citizenship education for a pluralistic society. *Theory and Research in Social Education, 21*, 341–384.

Bickmore, K. (1999). Elementary curriculum about conflict resolution: Can children handle global politics? *Theory and Research in Social Education, 27*, 45–69.

Bickmore, K. (2004). Discipline for democracy? School districts' management of conflict and social exclusion. *Theory and Research in Social Education, 32*, 75–95.

Blos, J. (1993). Perspectives on historical fiction. In M. O. Tunnell & R. Ammon (Eds.), *The story of ourselves: Teaching history through children's literature* (pp. 11–18). Portsmouth, NH: Heinemann.

Blumberg, R. (1993). *Bloomers!* New York: Bradbury.

Blythe, J. (1988). *History 5–9.* London: Hoddger & Stoughton.

Blythe, J. (1989). *History in primary schools: A practical approach for teachers of 5- to 11-year-old children.* Philadelphia: Open University Press.

Boatner, M. M. (1969). *The Civil War dictionary.* New York: David McKay.

Boner, P. (1995). New nation, new history: The history workshop in South Africa, 1977–1994. *Journal of American History, 81,* 977–985.

Boyd, D. (1989). *Film and the interpretive process: A study of Blow-up, Rashomon on, Citizen Kane 8 ½, Vertigo and Persona.* New York: Peter Lang.

Bradley Commission on History in Schools. (1989). Building a history curriculum: Guidelines for teaching. In P. Gagnon & The Bradley Commission on History in the Schools (Eds.), *Historical literacy: The case for history in American education* (pp. 16–47). New York: Macmillan.

Brandt, R. (1988a). On assessment in the arts: A conversation with Howard Gardner. *Educational Leadership, 45*(4), 30–34.

Brandt, R. (1988b). On discipline-based art education: A conversation with Elliot Eisner. *Educational Leadership, 45*(4), 6–9.

Brenner, B. (1994). *If you were there in 1776.* New York: Macmillan.

Bresnick-Perry, R. (1992). *Letters from Rifka.* New York: Henry Holt.

Britton, J. (1987). *Writing and reading in the classroom* (Tech. Rep. No. 8). Washington, DC: Office of Educational Research and Improvement (ERIC Document Reproduction Service No. ED 287 169).

Brooks, J. G., & Brooks, M. G. (1993). *In search of understanding: The case for constructivist classrooms.* Alexandria, VA: Association for Supervision and Curriculum Development.

Brophy, J. (1990). Teaching social studies for understanding and higher-order application. *The Elementary School Journal, 90,* 351–417.

Brophy, J., & VanSledright, B. (1997). *Teaching and learning history in elementary schools.* New York: Teachers College Press.

Brophy, J., VanSledright, B. A., & Bredin, N. (1992). Fifth graders' ideas about history expressed before and after their introduction to the subject. *Theory and Research in Social Education, 20,* 440–489.

Brophy, J., VanSledright, B., & Bredin, N. (1993). What do entering fifth graders know about U.S. history? *Journal of Social Studies Research, 16/17,* 2–19.

Brown, D. (1975). *Wounded Knee: An Indian history of the American West.* (Adapted for young readers by Amy Ehrlich from Dee Brown's *Bury my heart at Wounded Knee.*) New York: Dell.

Brown, J. S., Collins, A., & Duguid, P. (1989). Situated cognition and the culture of learning. *Educational Researcher, 18*(1), 32–42.

Bruer, J. (1993). Schools for thought: A science of learning in the classroom. Cambridge, MA: MIT Press.

Bruner, J. (1986). *Actual minds, possible worlds.* Cambridge, MA: Harvard University Press.

Buah, F. K. (1998). *A history of Ghana: Revised and updated.* London: McMillan.

Buck, P. (2001). *Worked to the bone.* New York: Monthly Review Press.

Built Environment Educational Consortium. (1990). *Assessment tasks submitted to the Kentucky Council on School Performance Standards.* Unpublished report.

Burks, B. (1998). *Walks alone.* New York: Harcourt Brace.

Burton, R. J. (1991). *Inventing the flat earth: Columbus and modern historians.* New York: Praeger.

Caine, R. N., & Caine, G. (1994). *Making connections: Teaching and the human brain.* New York: Addison-Wesley.

California State Board of Education. (1988). *History–social science framework for California public schools, kindergarten through grade twelve.* Sacramento: Author.

Carey, S. (1985). *Conceptual change in childhood.* Cambridge, MA: MIT Press.

Carlisle, M. (1995). Talking history. *Magazine of History, 9*(2), 57–59.

Carretero, M., Jacott, L., Limón, M., Manjón, A. L., & León, J. A. (1994). Historical knowledge: Cognitive and instructional implications. In M. Carretero & J. F. Voss (Eds.), *Cognitive and instructional processes in history and social sciences* (pp. 357–376). Hillsdale, NJ: Lawrence Erlbaum Associates.

Carter, A. R. (1992). *The American Revolution.* New York: Franklin Watts.

Casanova, U. (1995). An exchange of views on "The great speckled bird." *Educational Researcher, 24*(6), 22.

Cazden, C. B. (1988). *Classroom discourse: The language of teaching and learning.* Portsmouth, NH: Heinemann.

Cheney, L. V. (1987). *American memory: A report on the humanities in the nation's public schools.* Washington, DC: National Endowment for the Humanities.

Chi, M. T. H. (1976). Short-term memory limitations in children: Capacity or processing deficits? *Memory and Cognition, 4,* 559–572.

Chi, M. T. H., Feltovich, P., & Glaser, R. (1981). Categorization and representation of physics problems by experts and novices. *Cognitive Science, 5*, 121–152.

Chua, A. (2003). *World on fire: How exporting free market democracy breeds ethnic hatred and global instability*. New York: Doubleday.

Children of Yugoslavia Staff. (1994). *I dream of peace …*. New York: HarperCollins.

Clarke, A. C. (1974). The drummer boy of Shiloh. In D. Roselle (Ed.), *Transformations: II. Understanding American history through science fiction* (pp. 13–23). New York: Fawcett.

Coerr, E. (1994). *Sadako*. New York: Putnam.

Cohen, D. W. (1994). *The combing of history*. Chicago: University of Chicago Press.

Cohen, E. G. (1986). *Designing groupwork: Strategies for the heterogeneous classroom*. New York: Teachers College Press.

Collier, J. L., & Collier, C. (1974). *My brother Sam is dead*. New York: Four Winds Press.

Collier, J. L., & Collier, C. (1984). *War comes to Willy Freeman*. New York: Dell.

Collingwood, R. G. (1961). *The idea of history*. London: Oxford University Press.

Conley, R. (1992). *Nightjack*. Garden City, NY: Doubleday.

Conrad, P. (1991). *Prairie visions: The life and times of Solomon Butcher*. New York: HarperCollins.

Cook, L. W. (1965). *When great-grandmother was a little girl*. New York: Holt, Rinehart, & Winston.

Cooper, H. (2002). *History in the early years* (2nd ed.). New York: Routledge Falmer.

Cope, B., & Kalantzes, M. (1990). Literacy in the social sciences. In F. Christie (Ed.), *Literacy for a changing world* (pp. 118–142). Hawthorne, Victoria: Australian Council for Educational Research.

Cornbleth, C., & Waugh, D. (1995). *The great speckled bird: Multicultural politics and educational policy making*. New York: St. Martin's Press.

Cornel, K. (1993). *These lands are ours: Tecumseh's fight for the Old Northwest*. Austin, TX: Steck-Vaughn.

Corwin, S. (1991). *Art as a tool for learning United States history*. Champaign-Urbana, IL: National Arts Education Research Center, University of Illinois.

Cox, J. K. (1993). *Teaching about conflict and crisis in the former Yugoslavia: The case of Bosnia-Hercegovina*. (ERIC Document Reproduction Service No. ED 377 139)

Crocco, M. (1997). Making time for women's history: When your survey course is already filled to overflowing. *Social Education, 6*, 32–37.

Crocco, M. (1998). Putting the actors back on stage: Oral history in the secondary school classroom. *The Social Studies, 89*, 19–24.

Crook, J. B. (1988). Where have all the heroes gone? In V. Rogers, A. D. Roberts, & T. P. Weinland (Eds.), *Teaching social studies: Portraits from the classroom* (Bulletin No. 82, pp. 36–41). Washington, DC: National Council for the Social Studies.

Culclasure, S. (1999). *The past as liberation from history*. New York: Lang.

Curriculum Research and Development Division, Ministry of Education. (1987). *Pupil's book 1: Social studies for junior secondary schools*. Legon-Accra, Ghana: Adwinsa Publications.

Cushman, K. (1994). *Catherine, called Birdy*. New York: Clarion.

Cuthbertson, G. (1995). Racial attraction: Tracing the historiographical alliances between South Africa and the United States. *Journal of American History, 81*, 1123–1136.

Daly, E. (Ed.). (1989). *Monitoring children's language development: Holistic assessment in the classroom*. Portsmouth, NH: Heinemann.

Daniels, H. (2002). *Literature circles: Voice and choice in book clubs and reading groups*. Portland, ME: Stenhouse Publishers.

Danto, A. C. (1965). *Analytical philosophy of history*. Cambridge, England: Cambridge University Press.

DeFord, D. H., & Stout, H. S. (1987). *An enemy among them*. Boston: Houghton Mifflin.

Degenhardt, M., & McKay, E. (1988). Imagination and education for intercultural understanding. In K. Egan & D. Nadaner (Eds.), *Imagination and education* (pp. 237–255). New York: Teachers College Press.

Delouche, R. (Ed.). (1992). *Illustrated history of Europe: A unique portrait of Europe's common history*. New York: Henry Holt.

den Heyer, K. (2003). Between every "now" and "then": A role for the study of historical agency in history and citizenship education. *Theory and Research in Social Education, 31*, 411–434.

Dewey, J. (1929). *The quest for certainty: A study of the relation of knowledge and action*. New York: Minton, Balch.

Dewey, J. (1933). *How we think: A restatement of the relation of reflective thinking to the educative process*. New York: Heath.

Dewey, J. (1956). *The child and the curriculum* and *The school and society*. Chicago: University of Chicago Press.

Dewey, J. (1958). *Art as experience.* New York: Capricorn Books.

Dickinson, A. K., & Lee, P. J. (1984).Making sense of history. In A. K. Dickenson, P. J. Lee, & P. J. Rogers (Eds.), *Learning history* (pp. 117–153). London: Heinemann.

Dickinson, J. (1993). Children's perspectives on talk: Building a learning community. In K. M. Pierce & C. J. Gilles (Eds.), *Cycles of meaning: Exploring the potential of talk in learning communities* (pp. 99–116). Portsmouth, NH: Heinemann.

Dillon, E. (1986). *The seekers.* New York: Scribners.

Donaldson, M. (1978). *Children's minds.* New York: Norton.

Downey, M. (Ed.). (1982). *Teaching American history: New directions* (Bulletin No. 67). Washington, DC: National Council for the Social Studies.

Downey, M. (Ed.). (1985). *History in the schools* (Bulletin No. 74). Washington, DC: National Council for the Social Studies.

Downey, M. (1994, April). *After the dinosaurs: Elementary children's chronological thinking.* Paper presented at the annual meeting of the American Educational Research Association, New Orleans, LA.

Downey, M., & Levstik, L. S. (1991). Teaching and learning history. In J. Shaver (Ed.), *Handbook of research on social studies teaching and learning* (pp. 400–410). New York: Macmillan.

Downs, A. (1993). Breathing life into the past: The creation of history units using trade books. In M. O. Tunnell & R. Ammon (Eds.), *The story of ourselves: Teaching history through children's literature* (pp. 137–146). Portsmouth, NH: Heinemann.

Duckworth, E. (1987). *"The having of wonderful ideas" and other essays on teaching and learning.* New York: Teachers College Press.

Duke, N. K., & Bennett-Armistead, S. (2003). *Reading and writing informational texts in primary grades: Research-based practices.* New York: Scholastic Professional Books.

Dunn, R., & Griggs, S. A. (1988). *Learning styles: Quiet revolution in American secondary schools.* Reston, VA: National Association of Secondary School Principals.

Dyson, A. H. (1987). Individual differences in beginning composing: An orchestral vision of learning to compose. *Written Communication, 9,* 411–442.

Dyson, A. H. (1989). *Multiple worlds of child writers: Friends learning to write.* New York: Teachers College Press.

Egan, K. (1983). Accumulating history. *History and Theory, Belkeft 22,* 66–80.

Egan, K. (1986). *Teaching as storytelling: An alternative approach to teaching and curriculum in the elementary school.* Chicago: University of Chicago Press.

Egan, K., & Nadaner, D. (Eds.). (1988). *Imagination and education.* New York: Teachers College Press.

Egger-Bovet, H., & Smith-Baranzin, M. (1994). *U.S. kids history: Book of the American Revolution.* Boston: Little, Brown.

Ehlers, M. G. (1999). "No pictures in my head": The uses of literature in the development of historical understanding. *Magazine of History, 13*(2), 5–9.

Eisner, E. (1988). *The role of discipline-based art education in America's schools.* Los Angeles: Getty Center for Education in the Arts.

Eisner, E. (1991). *The enlightened eye: Qualitative inquiry and the enhancement of educational practice.* New York: Macmillan.

Elshtain, J. B. (1981). *Public man, private woman: Women in social and political thought.* Princeton, NJ: Princeton University Press.

Engle, S. (1970). The future of social studies education and the National Council for the Social Studies. *Social Education, 34,* 778–781.

Epstein, T. L. (1991). Equity in educational experiences and outcomes. *Magazine of History, 6,* 35–40.

Epstein, T. L. (1993). Why teach history to the young? In M. Tunnel & R. Ammon (Eds.), *The story of ourselves: Teaching history through children's literature* (pp. 1–8). Portsmouth, NH: Heinemann.

Epstein, T. L. (1994a). "America Revised" revisited: Adolescents' attitudes toward a United States history textbook. *Social Education, 58,* 41–44.

Epstein, T. L. (1994b, April). *Makes no difference if you're black or white? African-American and European-American adolescents' perspectives on historical significance and historical sources.* Paper presented at the annual meeting of the American Educational Research Association, New Orleans, LA.

Epstein, T. L. (1994c). The arts of history: An analysis of secondary school students' interpretations of the arts in historical contexts. *Journal of Curriculum and Supervision, 9,* 174–194.

Epstein, T. L. (1994d). Sometimes a shining moment: High school students' representations of history through the arts. *Social Education, 58,* 136–141.

Epstein, T. L. (1994e). Tales from two textbooks: A comparison of the civil rights movement in two secondary history textbooks. *The Social Studies, 85,* 121–126.

Evans, R. W. (1988). Lessons from history: Teacher and student conceptions of the meaning of history. *Theory and Research in Social Education, 16*, 203–225.

Evans, R. W. (1989). Diane Ravitch and the revival of history: A critique. *The Social Studies, 80*, 85–88.

Evans, R. W., Avery, P. G., & Pederson, P. V. (1999). Taboo topics: Cultural restraint on teaching social issues. *The Social Studies, 90*, 219.

Fertig, G. (2003). Using biographies to explore social justice in U.S. history. *Social Studies and the Young Learner, 16*(1), 9–12.

Filipovic, Z. (1994). *Zlata's diary*. New York: Viking.

Fines, J., & Verrier, R. (1974). *The drama of history: An experiment in co-operative teaching*. London: New University Education.

Fisher, L. E. (1990). *The Oregon trail*. New York: Holiday House.

Flack, J. D. (1992). *Lives of promise: Studies in biography and family history*. Englewood, CO: Teacher Ideas Press.

Flannery, K. T. (1995). *The emperor's new clothes: Literature, literacy, and the ideology of style*. Pittsburgh: University of Pittsburgh Press.

Fleischman, P. (1992). *The whipping boy*. New York: HarperCollins.

Fleischman, P. (1993). *Bull Run*. New York: HarperCollins.

Forbes, E. (1967). *Johnny Tremain*. Boston: Houghton Mifflin.

Foster, S. J. (1999). Using historical empathy to excite students about the study of history: Can you empathize with Neville Chamberlain? *The Social Studies, 90*, 18–24.

Foster, S. J. (2001). Historical empathy in theory and practiced: Some final thoughts. In O. L. Davis, Elizabeth A. Yeager, & Stuart J. Foster (Eds.) *Historical empathy and perspective taking in the social studies* (pp. 167–181). Lanham, MD: Rowman and Littlefield.

Foster, S. J., & Hoge, J. D. (1999). Thinking aloud about history: Children's and adolescents' responses to historical photographs. *Theory and Research in Social Education, 27*, 179–214.

Foster, S. J., & Yeager, E. A. (1999). "You've got to put together the pieces": English twelve-year-olds encounter and learn from historical evidence. *Journal of Curriculum and Supervision, 14*, 286–317.

Fox, M. (1985). *Wilfrid Gordon McDonald Partridge*. New York: Kane-Miller.

Fox, R. A., Jr. (1993). *Archaeology, History, and Custer's Last Battle*. Norman: University of Oklahoma Press.

Frank, A. (1967). *Anne Frank: The diary of a young girl*. Garden City, NY: Doubleday.

Frank, A. (1989). *The diary of Anne Frank: The critical edition*. Garden City, NY: Doubleday.

Fredericks, A. D., & Rasinski, T. V. (1990). Involving parents in the assessment process. *The Reading Teacher, 44*, 346–349.

Freedman, R. (1980). *Immigrant kids*. New York: Dutton.

Freedman, R. (1983). *Children of the Wild West*. New York: Clarion.

Freedman, R. (1990). *Franklin Delano Roosevelt*. New York: Clarion.

Freedman, R. (1993). *Eleanor Roosevelt: A life of discovery*. New York: Scholastic.

Freedman, R. (1994). *Kids at work: Lewis Hine and the crusade against child labor*. New York: Clarion.

Freeman, E., & Person, D. G. (Eds.). (1992). *Using nonfiction trade books in the elementary classroom: From ants to zeppelins*. Champaign-Urbana, IL: National Council of Teachers of English.

Fritz, J. (1967). *Early thunder*. New York: Coward-McCann.

Fritz, J. (1983). *The double life of Pocahontas*. New York: Putnam.

Fritz, J. (1987). *Shh! We're writing the constitution*. New York: Putnam.

Fulwiler, T. (1982). Writing: An act of cognition. In C. W. Griffin (Ed.), *New directions for teaching and learning: No. 12. Teaching writing in all disciplines* (pp. 15–26). San Francisco: Jossey-Bass.

Gabaccia, D. R. (1997). Liberty, coercion, and the making of immigration historians. *Journal of American History, 84*, 570–575.

Gabella, M. S. (1994). Beyond the looking glass: Bringing students into the conversation of historical inquiry. *Theory and Research in Social Education, 22*, 340–363.

Gaddis, J. L. (2002). *The landscape of history: How historians map the past*. NY: Oxford University Press.

Gagnon, P., & The Bradley Commission on History in the Schools. (Eds.). (1989). *Historical literacy: The case for history in American education*. New York: Macmillan.

Gallie, W. B. (1964). *Philosophy and the historical understanding*. New York: Schocken.

Gardner, H. (1982). *Art, mind, and brain: A cognitive approach to creativity*. New York: Basic Books.

Gardner, H. (1983). *Frames of mind: The theory of multiple intelligences*. New York: Basic Books.

Gardner, H. (1988). Toward more effective arts education. *Journal of Aesthetic Education, 22*, 158–166.

Gardner, H. (1990). *Art education and human development* (Occasional paper No. 3). Los Angeles: Getty Center for Education in the Arts. (Eric Document Reproduction Service No. ED 336 315)

Gardner, H. (1991a). The tensions between education and development. *Journal of Moral Education, 20,* 113–125.

Gardner, H. (1991b). *The unschooled mind: How children think and how schools should teach.* New York: Basic Books.

Gardner, H., & Boix-Mansilla, V. (1994). Teaching for understanding in the disciplines—and beyond. *Teachers College Record, 96,* 198–218.

Garfield, S. (1991). Building self-esteem through poetry. *The Reading Teacher, 44,* 616–617.

Garrison, W. (2003). Democracy, experience, and education: Promoting a continued capacity for growth. *Phi Delta Kappan, 84*(7), 525–529.

Garza, C. L. (1990). *Family Pictures/Cuadros de familia.* Emeryville, CA: Children's Book Press.

Gauch, P. L. (1974). *Thunder at Gettysburg.* New York: Coward, McCann, & Geohegan.

Geertz, C. (1983). *Local knowledge: Further essays in interpretive anthropology.* New York: Basic Books.

Geoghegan, W. (1994). Re-placing the arts in education. *Phi Delta Kappan, 75,* 456–458.

Gerstle, G. (1997). Liberty, coercion, and the making of Americans. *Journal of American History, 84,* 524–558.

Gerwin, D., & Zevin, J. (2003). *Teaching U.S. history as mystery.* Portsmouth, NH: Heinemann.

Golenbock, P. (1990). *Teammates.* Orlando, FL: Harcourt Brace.

Gombrich, E. H. (1974). The visual image. In D. R. Olson (Ed.), *Media and symbols: The forms of expression, communication, and education.* Yearbook of the National Society for the Study of Education, New Series No. 73, part 1 (pp. 241–270). Chicago: University of Chicago Press.

Gonzales, C. T. (1987). *Quanah Parker: Great chief of the Comanches.* Austin, TX: Eakin Press.

Good, T. L., & Brophy, J. E. (1999). *Looking in classrooms* (8th ed.). New York: HarperCollins.

Goodman, N. (1984). *Of mind and other matters.* Cambridge, MA: Harvard University Press.

Goodrich, H. (1996/1997). Understanding rubrics. *Educational Leadership, 54,* 14–17.

Gordon, L. (1988). *Heroes of their own lives: The politics and history of family violence, Boston 1880–1960.* New York: Viking.

Gordon, L. (1990). U.S. women's history. In E. Foner (Ed.), *The new American history* (pp. 185–210). Philadelphia: Temple.

Grant, S. G. (2003). *History lessons: Teaching, learning, and testing in U.S. high school classrooms.* Mahwah, NJ: Lawrence Erlbaum Associates.

Graves, D. (1983). *Writing: Teachers and children at work.* Exeter, NH: Heinemann.

Greene, M. (1993a). Beyond insularity: Releasing the voices. *College ESL, 3*(1), 1–14.

Greene, M. (1993b). The passions of pluralism: Multiculturalism and the expanding community. *Educational Researcher, 2*(1), 13–18.

Greene, M. (1995). Art and imagination: Reclaiming the sense of possibility. *Phi Delta Kappan, 76,* 378–382.

Greenfield, E. (1977). *Mary McLeod Bethune.* New York: HarperCollins.

Griffin, A. F. (1992). *A philosophical approach to the subject-matter preparation of teachers of history.* Washington, DC: National Council for the Social Studies.

Groth, J. L., & Albert, M. (1997). Arts alive in the development of historical thinking. *Social Education, 61,* 42–44.

Gutman, H. G. (1976). *The black family in slavery and freedom: 1750–1925.* New York: Pantheon.

Gutmann, A. (1987). *Democratic education.* Princeton, NJ: Princeton University Press.

Hahn, C. (1998). *Becoming political.* Albany: SUNY Press.

Hahn, C. L., & Tocci, C. M. (1990). Classroom climate and controversial issues discussion: A five nation study. *Theory and Research in Social Education, 18,* 344–362.

Hamilton, V. (1985). *The people could fly.* New York: Knopf.

Hammond, T. (1988). *Sports.* New York: Knopf.

Harnett, P. (1993). Identifying progression in children's understanding: The use of visual materials to assess primary school children's learning in history. *Cambridge Journal of Education, 23,* 137–154.

Harnett, P. (1995, September). *Questions about the past: Children's responses to visual materials in primary history.* Paper presented at the annual meeting of the British Educational Research Association, Bath University, England.

Harp, B. (1993). Principles of assessment and evaluation in whole language classrooms. In B. Harp (Ed.), *Assessment and evaluation in whole language programs* (pp. 37–52). Norwood, MA: Christopher-Gordon.

Harste, J. C., & Short, K. G. (1988). *Creating classrooms for authors: The reading-writing connection*. Portsmouth, NH: Heinemann.

Hart, D. (1994). *Authentic assessment: A handbook for educators*. Menlo Park, CA: Addison-Wesley.

Hart, D. (1999). Opening assessment to our students. *Social Education, 65*, 343–345.

Harvey, B. (1988). *Cassie's journey: Going west in the 1860s*. New York: Holiday House.

Harvey, K. D., Harjo, L. D., & Jackson, J. K. (1990). Introduction. In K. D. Harvey, L. D. Harjo, & J. K. Jackson (Eds.), *Teaching about Native Americans* (Bulletin No. 84, pp. 1–7). Washington, DC: National Council for the Social Studies.

Henson, J. (1993). The tie that binds: The role of talk in defining community. In K. M. Pierce & C. J. Gilles (Eds.), *Cycles of meaning: Exploring the potential of talk in learning communities* (pp. 37–57). Portsmouth, NH: Heinemann.

Hepler, S. (1991). Talking our way to literacy in the classroom community. *The New Advocate, 4*, 179–191.

Hertzberg, H. W. (1981). *Social studies reform: 1880–1980*. Boulder, CO: Social Science Education Consortium. (ERIC Document Reproduction Service No. 211 429)

Hertzberg, H. W. (1989). History and progressivism: A century of reform proposals. In P. Gagnon & the Bradley Commission on History in the Schools (Eds.), *Historical literacy: The case for history in American education* (pp. 68–89). Boston: Houghton Mifflin.

Hess, D. (2002a). Teaching controversial public issues discussions: Learning from skilled teachers. *Theory and Research in Social Education, 30*, 10–41.

Hess, D. (2002b). Teaching to public controversy in a democracy. In J. J. Patrick & R. S. Leming (Eds.), *Education in democracy for Social Studies teachers: Principles and practices for the improvement of teacher education*. Bloomington, IN: ERIC/ChESS.

Hesse, K. (1992). *Leaving for America*. New York: Henry Holt.

Hickey, M. G. (1997). Bloomers, bell bottoms, and hula hoops: Artifact collections aid children's historical interpretation. *Social Education, 61*, 293–299.

Hiebert, E. H., & Hutchinson, T. A. (1991). Research directions: The current state of alternative assessments for policy and instructional uses. *Language Arts, 68*, 662–668.

Hirsch, E. D. (1987). *Cultural literacy: What every American needs to know*. Boston: Houghton Mifflin.

Hollinger, D. A. (1997). National solidarity at the end of the twentieth century: Reflections on the United States and liberal nationalism. *Journal of American History, 84*, 559–569.

Holt, T. C. (1990a). African-American history. In E. Foner (Ed.), *The new American history* (pp. 211–232.). Philadelphia: Temple.

Holt, T. C. (1990b). *Thinking historically: Narrative, imagination, and understanding*. NY: College Entrance Examination Boards.

Hostetler, K. (1999). Conversation is not the answer: Moral education as hermeneutical understanding. *Journal of Curriculum Studies, 31*, 463–478.

Hotze, S. (1988). *A circle unbroken*. New York: Clarion.

Huck, C., Hepler, S., Hickman, J., & Kiefer, B. (1996). *Children's literature in the elementary school*. New York: McGraw Hill.

Husbands, C., Kitson, A., & Pendry, A. (2003). *Understanding history teaching*. Philadelphia: Open University Press.

Husbands, C. T. (1996). *What is history teaching? Language, ideas, and meaning in learning about the past*. Philadelphia: Open University Press.

Hudson, J. (1989). *Sweetgrass*. New York: Philomel.

Hudson, J. (1990). *Dawn rider*. New York: Philomel.

Hyde, A. A., & Bizar, M. (1989). *Thinking in context: Teaching cognitive processes across the elementary curriculum*. New York: Longman.

Irwin, C. (1980). *Strange footprints on the land: Vikings in America*. New York: Harper.

Jacott, L., López-Manjón, A., & Carretero, M. (1998). Generating explanations in history. In J. F. Voss & M. Carretero (Eds.), *International review of history education: Vol. 2. Learning and reasoning in history* (pp. 294–306). London: Woburn.

Jackson, B. D. (2003). Education reform as if student agency mattered: Academic icrocultures and student identity. *Phi Delta Kappan, 84*, 579–585.

Jennings, F. (1975). *The invasion of America: Indians, colonialism, and the cant of conquest*. Chapel Hill: University of North Carolina Press.

Jobe, R., & Dayton-Sakari, M. (2003). *Info-kids: How to use nonfiction to turn reluctant readers into enthusiastic learners*. Markham, Ontario: Pembroke Publishers, Ltd.

Johnson, D. W., Johnson, R. T., & Holubec, E. J. (1993). *Circles of learning: Cooperation in the classroom* (4th ed.). Edina, MN: Interaction Book Company.

Johnston, P. (1987). Teachers as evaluation experts. *The Reading Teacher, 40*, 744–748.

Johnston, P. (1992). *Constructive evaluation of literate activity*. New York: Longman.

Jolliffe, D. A. (1987). A social educator's guide to teaching writing. *Theory and Research in Social Education, 15*, 89–104.

Jordan, W. D. (1968). *White over black: American attitudes toward the Negro, 1550–1812.* Chapel Hill: University of North Carolina Press.

Jorgensen, K. L. (1993). *History workshop: Reconstructing the past with elementary students.* Portsmouth, NH: Heinemann.

Joyner, C. (1984). *Down by the riverside: A South Carolina slave community.* Urbana: University of Illinois Press.

Kammen, M. (1991). *Mystic chords of memory: The transformation of tradition in American culture.* New York: Knopf.

Kansteiner, W. (1993). Hayden White's critique of the writing of history. *History and Theory, 32,* 273–293.

Katz, W. L. (1993). *The Westward movement and abolitionism.* Austin, TX: Steck-Vaughn.

Keating, C. (1994). Promoting growth through dialogue journals. In G. Wells (Ed.), *Changing schools from within: Creating communities of inquiry* (pp. 217–236). Portsmouth, NH: Heinemann.

Keedy, J. L., Flemin, T. G., Wheat, D. L., & Gentry, R. B. (1998). Students as meaning-makers and the quest for the common school: A micro-ethnography of a U.S. history classroom. *Journal of Curriculum Studies, 30,* 619–645.

Keefe, J. W. (1987). *Learning style: Theory and practice.* Reston, VA: National Association of Secondary School Principals.

Keegan, S., & Shrake, K. (1991). Literature study groups: An alternative to ability grouping. *The Reading Teacher, 44,* 542–547.

Keller, C. W., & Schillings, D. L. (Eds.). (1987). *Teaching about the Constitution* (Bulletin No. 80). Washington, DC: National Council for the Social Studies.

Kelly, T. E. (1986). Discussing controversial issues: Four perspectives on the teacher's role. *Theory and Research in Social Education, 14,* 113–138.

Kennedy, J. M. (1974). Icons and information. In D. R. Olson (Ed.), *Media and symbols: The forms of expression, communication, and education.* Yearbook of the National Society for the Study of Education, New Series No. 73, part 1 (pp. 241–270). Chicago: University of Chicago Press.

Kentucky Council on School Performance Standards. (1991). *Kentucky's learning goals and valued outcomes* (Tech. Rep.). Frankfort, KY: Author.

Kentucky Department of Education. (1999). *Sharpen your child's writing skills: A guidebook for parents.* Frankfort, KY: Division of Curriculum Development, Kenucky Department of Education. http://www.kde.state.ky.us/oapd/curric/portfolios/SharpenWritingSkills.asp

Kentucky's Core Content for Assessment. http://www.education.ky.gov/KDE/Default.htm

Kentucky's Six Learning Goals, Kentucky Department of Eduction. Revised, 1994, KRS#158.6451.

Kerber, L. (1993). Some cautionary words for historians. In M. J. Larrabee (Ed.), *An ethic of care: Feminist and interdisciplinary perspectives* (pp. 102–107). New York: Routledge.

Kermode, F. (1980). Secrets and narrative sequence. *Critical Inquiry, 7,* 83–101.

Kessler-Harris, A. (1990). Social history. In E. Foner (Ed.), *The new American history* (pp. 163–184). Philadelphia: Temple.

Kiefer, B. (1995). *The potential of picturebooks: From visual literacy to aesthetic understanding.* Englewood Cliffs, NJ: Merrill.

Knight, P. (1989). Empathy: Concept, confusion and consequences in a national curriculum. *Oxford Review of Education, 15,* 42–43.

Kobrin, B. (1988). *Eyeopeners: How to choose and use children's books about real people, places, and things.* New York: Viking.

Kobrin, B. (1995). *Eyeopeners II: Children's books to answer children's questions about the world around them.* New York: Scholastic.

Kopple, B. (Producer and Director). (1976). *Harlan County USA* [Motion picture]. United States: Cabin Creek Films.

Kornhaber, M., & Gardner, H. (1993). *Varieties of excellence: Identifying and assessing children's talents* (Opinion paper BBB12599). Pleasantville: Aaron Diamond Foundation.

Kozma, R. (1991). Learning with media. *Review of Educational Research, 61,* 179–211.

Kristo, J. V., & Bamford, R. A. (2004). *Non-fiction in focus: A comprehensive framework for helping students become independent readers and writers of nonfiction, K–6.* New York: Scholastic Professional Books.

Larson, B. E. (1999). Influences on social studies teachers' use of classroom discussion. *The Social Studies, 90,* 125–132.

Lave, J., & Wenger, E. (1991). *Situated learning: Legitimate peripheral participation.* New York: Cambridge University Press.

Lawrence, J. (1992). *The great migration: An American story.* New York: HarperCollins.

Lee, P. J. (1978). Explanation and understanding in history. In A. K. Dickinson & P. J. Lee (Eds.), *Historical teaching and historical understanding* (pp. 72–93). London: Heinemann.

Lee, P. J., & Ashby, R. (2000). Empathy, perspective taking and historical understanding. In O. L. Davis, Jr., E. A. Yeager, & S. J. Foster (Eds.), *Development of historical empathy and perspective taking in the social studies*. Lanham, MD: Rowman & Littlefield.

Leinhardt, G. (1994). A time to be mindful. In G. Leinhardt, I. O. Beck, & C. Stainton (Eds.), *Teaching and learning in history* (pp. 209–255). Hillsdale, NJ: Lawrence Erlbaum Associates.

Lemke, J. (1991). *Talking science: Language, learning, and values* (pp. 183–213). Norwood, NJ: Ablex.

Lerner, G. (1997). *Why history matters*. New York: Oxford University Press.

Levine, E. (1986). *If you traveled west in a covered wagon*. New York: Scholastic.

Levine, E. (1993). *If your name was changed at Ellis Island*. New York: Scholastic.

Levine, L. W. (1977). *Black culture and black consciousness: Afro-American folk thought from slavery to freedom*. New York: Oxford University Press.

Levinson, R. (1985). *Watch the stars come out*. New York: Dutton.

Levinson, R. (1992). *I go with my family to Grandma's*. New York: Dutton.

Levstik, L. S. (1986a). History from the bottom up. *Social Education, 50,* 1–7 (insert).

Levstik, L. S. (1986b). The relationship between historical response and narrative in a sixth–grade classroom. *Theory and Research in Social Education, 14,* 1–19.

Levstik, L. S. (1989). Historical narrative and the young reader. *Theory into Practice, 28,* 114–119.

Levstik, L. S. (1993). Building a sense of history in a first grade classroom. In J. Brophy (Ed.), *Advances in research on teaching: Vol. 4. Research in elementary social studies* (pp. 1–31). Greenwich, CT: JAI Press.

Levstik, L. S. (1995). Narrative constructions: Cultural frames for history. *The Social Studies, 86,* 113–116.

Levstik, L. S. (1996a). NCSS and the teaching of history. In O. L. Davis (Ed.), *NCSS in retrospect* (Bulletin 92, pp. 21–34). Washington, DC: National Council for the Social Studies.

Levstik, L. S. (1996b). Negotiating the history landscape. *Theory and Research in Social Education, 24,* 393–397.

Levstik, L. S. (1999). "The boys we know; The girls in our school": Early adolescents understanding of women's historical significance. *International Journal of Social Studies, 12*(2), 19–34.

Levstik, L. S. (2000). Articulating the silences: Teachers' and adolescents' conceptions of historical significance. In P. Stearns, S. Wineburg, & P. Seixas (Eds.), *Teaching, learning, and knowing history*. New York: New York University Press.

Levstik, L. S. (2001a). Crossing the Empty Spaces: Perspective-Taking in New Zealand Adolescents' Understanding of National History. In O. L. Davis Jr., E. A. Yeager, & S. J. Foster (Eds.), *Development of historical empathy and perspective taking in the social studies*. Lanham, MD: Rowman & Littlefield.

Levstik, L. S. (2001b). Daily acts of ordinary courage: Gender equitable practice in the social studies classroom. In K. deMarrais (Ed.), *Gender equitable practice in middle schools*. Mahwah, NJ: Lawrence Erlbaum Associates.

Levstik, L. S. (2003). "To fling my arms wide": Students learning about the world through nonfiction. In R. A. Bamford & J. V. Kristo (Eds.), *Making facts come alive: Choosing quality nonfiction literature K–8* (pp. 221–234). Norwood, MA: Christopher-Gordon.

Levstik, L. S., & Barton, K. C. (1996). "They still use some of their past": Historical saliences in elementary children's chronological thinking. *Journal of Curriculum Studies, 28,* 531–576.

Levstik, L. S., & Groth, J. (2002). "Scary thing, being an eighth grader": Exploring gender and sexuality in a middle school U.S. history unit. *Theory and Research in Social Education, 30,* 233–254.

Levstik, L. S., & Groth, J. (2005). "Ruled by our own people": Ghanaian adolescents' conceptions of citizenship in a pluralist democracy. *Teachers College Record, 107,* 563–586.

Levstik, L. S., Henderson, A. G., & Schlarb, J. (2002). Digging for clues: An archaeological exploration of historical cognition. In P. Gordon, P. Lee, & R. Ashby (Eds.), *International Review of History Education*. London: Routledge Falmer.

Levstik, L. S., & Pappas, C. C. (1987). Exploring the development of historical understanding. *Journal of Research and Development in Education, 21,* 1–15.

Levstik, L. S., & Smith, D. B. (1996). "I've never done this before": Building a community of historical inquiry in a third-grade classroom. In J. Brophy (Ed.), *Advances in Research on Teaching: Teaching and Learning History, Vol. 6.* Greenwich, CT: JAI Press.

Levstik, L. S., & Smith, D. B. (1997). "I have learned a whole lot this year and it would take a lifetime to write it all": Beginning historical inquiry in a third grade classroom. *Social Science Record, 34,* 8–14.

Lexington Answer Book. (n.d.). Lexington, KY: Lexington-Fayette Urban County Government.

Lindquist, T. (1995). *Seeing the whole through social studies*. Portsmouth, NH: Heinemann.

Linenthal, E. T. (1994). Committing history in public. *Journal of American History, 81*, 986–991.

Lipscomb, G. (2002). Eighth graders' impressions of the Civil War: Using technology in the history classroom. *Education, Communication and Information, 2*, 51–67.

Littlechild, L. (1993). *This land is my land*. Emeryville, CA: Children's Book Press.

Loeb, R. H. (1979). *Meet the real Pilgrims: Everyday life on a Plymouth plantation in 1627*. New York: Clarion.

Loewen, J. W. (1995). *Lies my teacher told me*. New York: New Press.

Lowenthal, D. (1998). *The heritage crusade and the spoils of history*. Cambridge, England: Cambridge University Press.

Lowry, L. (1990). *Number the stars*. New York: Dell.

Lybarger, M. B. (1990). The historiography of social studies: Retrospect, circumspect, and prospect. In J. Shaver (Ed.), *Handbook of research on social studies teaching and learning* (pp. 3–26). New York: Macmillan.

Macaulay, D. (1977). *Castle*. Boston: Houghton Mifflin.

Mahood, W. (1987). Metaphors in social studies instruction. *Theory and Research in Social Education, 15*, 285–297.

Marcello, J. S. (1999). A teacher's reflections on teaching and assessing in a standards-based classroom. *Social Education, 65*, 338–342.

Mayer, R. H. (1998). Connective narrative and historical thinking: A research-based approach to teaching history. *Social Education, 62*, 97–100.

Mayer, R. H. (1999). Use the story of Anne Hutchinson to teach historical thinking. *The Social Studies, 90*, 105–109.

Mazur, J. (1993). *Interpretation and use of visuals in an interactive multimedia fiction program*. Unpublished doctoral dissertation, Cornell University, Ithaca, New York.

McGinnis, K. (n.d.). *Educating for a just society: Grades 7–12*. St. Louis: The Institute for Peace and Justice.

McKeown, M. G., & Beck, I. L. (1990). The assessment and characterization of young learners' knowledge of a topic in history. *American Educational Research Journal, 27*, 688–726.

McKeown, M. G., & Beck, I. L. (1994). Making sense of accounts of history: Why young students don't and how they might. In G. Leinhardt, I. O. Beck, & C. Stainton (Eds.), *Teaching and learning in history* (pp. 1–26). Hillsdale, NJ: Lawrence Erlbaum Associates.

McKinley, R. (1989). *The outlaws of Sherwood*. New York: Berkeley Publishing Group.

McKissack, P., & McKissack, F. L. (1994). *Christmas in the big house, Christmas in the quarters*. New York: Scholastic.

Megill, A. (1989). Recounting the past: "Description," explanation, and narrative in historiography. *American Historical Review, 94*, 627–653.

Meltzer, M. (1994a). *Cheap raw labor: How our youngest workers are exploited and abused*. New York: Viking.

Meltzer, M. (1994b). *Nonfiction for the classroom: Milton Meltzer on writing, history, and social responsibility*. New York: Teachers College Press.

Merryfield, M. (1995). Response to Banks. *Theory and Research in Social Education, 23*, 21–26.

Merryfield, M. (1997). A framework for teacher education in global perspectives. In M. Merryfield, E. Jarchow, & S. Pickert (Eds.), *Preparing teachers to teach global perspectives: A handbook for teacher education* (pp. 1–24). Thousand Oaks, CA: Corwin.

Merryfield, M., & Wilson, A. H. (2004). *Teaching Social Studies for global understanding*. Washington, DC: National Council for the Social Studies.

Miller, A., & Coen, D. (1994). The case for music in the schools. *Phi Delta Kappan, 75*, 459–461.

Milson, A. J., Brantley, S. M. (1999). Theme-based portfolio assessment in social studies teacher education. *Social Education, 63*(6), 374–377.

Mitchell, W. J. T. (1995). *Picture theory: Essays on visual and verbal representation*. Chicago: University of Chicago Press.

Mizell, L., Benett, S., Bowman, B., & Morin, L. (1993). Different ways of seeing: Teaching in an anti-racist school. In T. Perry & J. W. Fraser (Eds.), *Freedom's plow: Teaching in the multicultural classroom* (pp. 27–46). New York: Routledge.

Mochizuki. (1993). *Baseball saved us*. New York: Lee & Low.

Moffett, J. (1968). *Teaching the universe of discourse*. Boston: Houghton Mifflin.

Moser, S. (2001). Archaeological representation: The visual conventions for constructing knowledge about the past. In I. Hodder (Ed.), *Archaeological theory today* (pp. 262–283). Cambridge, England: Polity Press.

Naidoo, B. (1986). *Journey to Jo'burg*. New York: Harper.

Naidoo, B. (1989). *Chain of fire*. New York: Lippincott.

Nash, G., Crabtree, C., & Dunn, R. (1997). *History on trial: Culture wars and the teaching of the past*. New York: Knopf.

Nasir, S. N., & Saxe, G. B. (2003). Ethnic and academic identities: A cultural practice perspective on emerging tensions and their management in the lives of minority students. *Educational Researcher, 32*(5), 14–18.

National Council for the Social Studies. (1994). *Expectations of Excellence: Curriculum Standards for Social Studies* (Bulletin No. 89). Washington, DC: Author.

National Council for the Social Studies Focus Group on the NEH History Standards. (1993). *Response to the History Standards.* Unpublished report.

National Council of Teachers of Mathematics. (1989). *Curriculum and evaluation standards for school mathematics.* Reston, VA: Author.

National History Standards Project. (1994a). *National standards for United States history: Exploring the American experience.* Los Angeles: National Center for History in the Schools.

National History Standards Project. (1994b). *National standards for world history: Exploring paths to the present.* Los Angeles: National Center for History in the Schools.

National Research Council. (1996). *National Science Education Standards.* Washington, DC: National Academy Press.

Neuman, S. (1992). Is learning from media distinctive? Examining children's inferencing strategies. *American Educational Research Journal, 29,* 119–140.

Newkirk, T. (1989). *More than stories: The range of children's writings.* Portsmouth, NH: Heinemann.

Newmann, F. M., Secada, W. G., & Wehlage, G. G. (1995). *A guide to authentic instruction and assessment: Vision, standards and scoring.* Madison, WI: Wisconsin Center for Education Research.

Nickell, P. (1999). The issue of subjectivity in authentic social studies assessment. *Social Education, 65,* 353–355.

Ninsin, K. A. (1996). *Ghana's Political Transition, 1990–1993*; Selected Documents. Accra, Ghana: Freedom Publications.

Noddings, N. (1992). *The challenge to care in schools: An alternative approach to education.* New York: Teachers College Press.

Novick, P. (1988). *That noble dream: The "objectivity question" and the American historical profession.* New York: Cambridge University Press.

O'Brien, J. (1998). Using literary themes to develop historical perspective. *The Social Studies, 89,* 276–280.

Oddleifson, E. (1994). What do we want our schools to do? *Phi Delta Kappan, 75,* 446–452.

O'Dell, S. (1980). *Sarah Bishop.* Boston: Houghton Mifflin.

Ogle, D. M. (1986). K-W-L: A teaching model that develops active reading of expository text. *Reading Teacher, 39,* 564–570.

Olson, D. R. (Ed.). (1974). *Media and symbols: The forms of expression, communication, and education.* Yearbook of the National Society for the Study of Education, New Series No. 73, part 1. Chicago: University of Chicago Press.

Olwell, R. B. (1999). Use narrative to teach middle school students about Reconstruction. *The Social Studies, 90,* 205–208.

Oppenheim, S. L. (1992). *The lily cupboard.* New York: HarperCollins.

O'Reilly, R. (1998). What would you do? Constructing decision-making guidelines through historical problems. *Social Education, 61,* 46–49.

Oyler, C. (1996). *Making room for students: Sharing teacher authority in Room 104.* New York: Teachers College Press.

Pappas, C. C. (1991). Fostering full access to literacy by including information books. *Language Arts, 68,* 449–462.

Pappas, C. C., Kiefer, B. Z., & Levstik, L. S. (1999). *An integrated language perspective in the elementary school: An action approach* (3rd ed.). New York: Longman.

Parker, W. C. (1991a). A final response: Searching for the middle. *Social Education, 55,* 27–28, 65.

Parker, W. C. (1991b). Helping students think about public issues: Instruction versus prompting. *Social Education, 55,* 41–44.

Parker, W. C. (1991c). Teaching an IDEA. *Social Studies and the Young Learner, 3*(3), 11–13.

Parker, W. (1996). "Advanced" ideas about democracy: Toward a pluralist conception of citizen education. *Teachers College Record, 98,* 104–125.

Parker, W. C. (2003). *Teaching democracy: Unity and diversity in public life.* New York: Teachers College Press.

Parker, W. C., & Hess, D. (2001). Teaching with and for discussion. *Teaching and Teacher Education, 17,* 273–289.

Parker, W., Mueller, M., & Wendling, L. (1989). Critical reasoning on civic issues. *Theory and Research in Social Education, 27,* 7–32.

Parks, R. (1992). *Rosa Parks: My story.* New York: Dial.

Passe, J., & Whitley, I. (1998). The best museum for kids? The one they build themselves! *The Social Studies, 89,* 183–185.

Payne, C. M. (2003). More than a symbol of freedom: Education for liberation and democracy. *Phi Delta Kappan, 85*, 22–33.

Peace Corps World Wise Schools. (1998). *Looking at ourselves and others*. Washington, DC: Peace Corps.

Peetoom, B. (1991, August). *The Bible and whole language*. Paper presented to the Whole Language Umbrella Conference, Phoenix, AZ.

Pelta, K. (1991). *Discovering Christopher Columbus: How history is invented*. Minneapolis, MN: Lerner.

Penyak, L. M., & Duray, P. B. (1999). Oral history and problematic questions promote issues-centered education. *The Social Studies, 90*, 68–71.

Perfetti, C. A., Britt, M. A., & Georgi, M. A. (1995). *Text-based learning and reasoning: Studies in history*. Hillsdale, NJ: Lawrence Erlbaum Associates.

Person, D. G., & Cullinan, B. E. (1992). Windows through time: Literature of the social studies. In E. Freeman & D. G. Person (Eds.), *Using nonfiction trade books in the elementary classroom: From ants to zeppelins* (pp. 65–75). Champaign-Urbana: National Council of Teachers of English.

Piaget, J. (1952). *The origins of intelligence in children*. New York: International Universities Press.

Pierce, K. M., & Gilles, C. J. (Eds.). (1993). *Cycles of meaning: Exploring the potential of talk in learning communities*. Portsmouth, NH: Heinemann.

Popham, J. W. (1997). What's wrong—and what's right—with rubrics. *Educational Leadership, 55*, 72–75.

Portal, C. (1987). Empathy as an objective for history teaching. In C. Portal (Ed.), *The history curriculum for teachers* (pp. 89–99). London: Falmer.

Prawat, R. S. (1989a). Promoting access to knowledge, strategy, and disposition in students: A research synthesis. *Review of Educational Research, 59*, 1–41.

Prawat, R. S. (1989b). Teaching for understanding: Three key attributes. *Teaching and Teacher Education, 5*, 315–328.

Putnam, R. D. (2000). *Bowling alone: The collapse and revival of American community*. New York: Simon and Schuster, 2000.

Purves, A. C. (1990). *The scribal society: An essay on literacy and schooling in the information age*. New York: Longman.

Rabinowitz, P. J. (1987). *Before reading: Narrative conventions and the politics of interpretation*. Ithaca, NY: Cornell University Press.

Ravitch, D., & Finn, C. E. (1987). *What do our 17-year-olds know? A report on the first national assessment of history and literature*. New York: Harper & Row.

Ravitch, D., & Schlesinger, A. (1990). Statement of the committee of scholars in defense of history. *Perspectives, 28*(7), 15.

Reardon, S. J. (1988). The development of critical readers: A look into the classroom. *The New Advocate, 1*, 52–61.

Reiff, J. C. (1992). *Learning styles*. Washington, DC: National Education Association.

Renyi, J. (1994). The arts and humanities in American Education. *Phi Delta Kappan, 75*, 438–445.

Resnick, L. B. (1987). The 1987 presidential address: Learning in school and out. *Educational Research, 16*(9), 13–20.

Richard, J. J. (1993). Classroom tapestry: A practitioner's perspective on multicultural education. In T. Perry & J. W. Fraser (Eds.), *Freedom's plow: Teaching in the multicultural classroom* (pp. 47–63). New York: Routledge.

Ricoeur, R. (1984). *Hermeneutics and the human sciences: Essays on language, action, and interpretation* (J. B. Thompson, Trans.). New York: Cambridge University Press.

Rivière, A., Núñez, M., Barquero, B., & Fontela, F. (1998). Influence of intentional and personal factors in recalling historical texts: A developmental perspective. In J. F. Voss & M. Carretero (Eds.), *International review of history education: Vol. 2. Learning and reasoning in history* (pp. 214–226). London: Woburn.

Rockefeller, D. (1978). The arts in American education. *Today's Education, 67*(2), 33–38.

Rogoff, B. (1990). *Apprenticeship in thinking: Cognitive development in social context*. New York: Oxford University Press.

Rouet, J., Marron, M. A., Perfetti, C. A., & Favart, M. (1998). Understanding historical controversies: Students' evaluation and use of documentary evidence. In J. F. Voss & M. Carretero (Eds.), *International Review of History Education: Vol. 2. Learning and reasoning in history* (pp. 95–116). London: Woburn.

Rosenzweig, R., & Thelen, D. (1998). *The presence of the past: Popular uses of history in American life*. New York: Columbia University Press.

Rowland-Warne, L. (1992). *Costume*. New York: Knopf.

Sadker, M., & Sadker, D. (1994). *Failing at fairness: How America's schools cheat girls*. New York: Scribner's.

Sancha, S. (1990). *The Luttrell village: Country life in the middle ages.* New York: Crowell.

Sandler, M. W. (1994). *Pioneers.* New York: HarperCollins.

Saul, E. E. (Ed.). (1994). *Nonfiction for the classroom: Milton Meltzer on writing, history, and social responsibility.* New York: Teachers College Press.

Sautter, R. C. (1990). An arts education school reform strategy. *Phi Delta Kappan, 75,* 432–437.

Scheurman, G., & Newmann, F. M. (1998). Authentic intellectual work in social studies: Putting performance before pedagogy. *Social Education, 62,* 23–25.

Schroeder, A. (1989). *Ragtime Tumpie.* Boston: Little, Brown.

Schug, M. C., & Berry, R. (Eds.). (1984). *Community study: Applications and opportunities* (Bulletin No. 73). Washington, DC: National Council for the Social Studies.

Schuster, M. R., & VanDyne, S. (1998). Placing women in the liberal arts: Stages of curriculum transformation. In C. A. Wayshner & H. S. Gelfond (Eds.), *Minding women: Reshaping the educational realm.* Cambridge, MA: Harvard University Press.

Scott, D. D., Fox, R. A., Jr., Connor, M. A., & Harmon, D. (2000). *Archaeological perspectives on the Battle of the Little Bighorn.* Norman: University of Oklahoma Press.

Sebestyen, O. (1985). *On fire.* Boston: Atlantic Monthly Press.

Segall, A. (1999). Critical history: Implication for history/social studies education. *Theory and Research in Social Education, 27,* 358–374.

Selvsin, D. F. (1969). *The thundering voice of John L. Lewis.* New York: Lothrop, Lee, & Shepard.

Seixas, P. (1993a). The community of inquiry as a basis for knowledge and learning: The case of history. *American Educational Research Journal, 30,* 305–324.

Seixas, P. (1993b). Historical understanding among adolescents in a multicultural setting. *Curriculum Inquiry, 23,* 301–327.

Seixas, P. (1993c). Parallel crises: History and the social studies curriculum in the USA. *Journal of Curriculum Studies, 25,* 235–250.

Seixas, P. (1994a). *Margins and sidebars: Problems in students' understanding of significance in world history.* Unpublished manuscript.

Seixas, P. (1994b). Students' understanding of historical significance. *Theory and Research in Social Education, 22,* 281–304.

Seixas, P. (1998). Student teachers thinking historically. *Theory and Research in Social Education, 26,* 310–341.

Seixas, P. (1999). Beyond "content" & "pedagogy": In search of a way to talk about history education. *Journal of Curriculum Studies, 31,* 317–337.

Selwyn, D. (1995). *Arts and humanities in the Social Studies* (Bulletin No. 90). Washington, DC: National Council for the Social Studies.

Shaara, M. (1974). *The killer angels.* New York: McKay.

Shama, S. (1992). *Dead certainties: Unwarranted speculations.* New York: Vintage.

Shemilt, D. (1980). *Evaluation study: Schools council history 13–16 project.* Edinburgh: Holmes McDougall.

Shemilt, D. (1984). Beauty and the philosopher: Empathy in history and classroom. In A. K. Dickinson, P. J. Lee, & P. J. Rogers (Eds.), *Learning history* (pp. 39–83). London: Heinemann.

Shemilt, D. (1987). Adolescent ideas about evidence and methodology in history. In C. Portal (Ed.), *The history curriculum for teachers* (pp. 29–61). London: Falmer.

Shepherd, L. A. (1991). Negative policies for dealing with diversity: When does assessment and diagnosis turn into sorting and segregation? In E. H. Hiebert (Ed.), *Literacy for a diverse society: Perspectives, practices, and policies* (pp. 279–298). New York: Teachers College Press.

Short, K. G., & Armstrong, J. (1993). "More than facts": Exploring the role of talk in classroom inquiry. In K. M. Pierce & C. J. Gilles (Eds.), *Cycles of meaning: Exploring the potential of talk in learning communities* (pp. 119–137). Portsmouth, NH: Heinemann.

Short, K. G., & Harste, J. C. (1996). *Creating classrooms for authors and inquirers.* Portsmouth, NH: Heinemann.

Shug, M. C., & Cross, B. (1998). The dark side of curriculum integration. *The Social Studies, 89,* 54–57.

Sklar, K. K. (1995). *Florence Kelley & the nation's work: The rise of women's political culture, 1830–1900.* New Haven, CT & London, UK: Yale University Press.

Slavin, R. E. (1995). *Cooperative learning: Theory, research, and practice* (2nd ed.). Boston: Allyn & Bacon.

Smith, L. A., & Barton, K. C. (1997). Practical issues in literature study groups: Getting the most out of historical fiction in the middle grades. *Social Science Record, 34,* 27–31.

Sokoni, M. A. (1991). *Mchesi goes to market.* Nairobi, Kenya: Jacaranda Designs.

Sosniak, L. A., & Stodolsky, S. S. (1993). Making connections: Social studies education in an urban fourth-grade classroom. In J. Brophy (Ed.), *Advances in research on teaching: Vol. 4. Research in elementary social studies* (pp. 71–100). Greenwich, CT: JAI Press.

224

Speare, G. E. (1958). *The witch of Blackbird Pond.* Boston: Houghton Mifflin.

Stanley, D., & Vennema, P. (1988). *Shaka: King of the Zulus.* New York: Morrow.

Stanley, F. (1991). *The last princess: The story of Princess Ka'inlani of Hawai'i.* New York: Four Winds.

Stanley, J. (1994). *I am an American: A true story of Japanese internment.* New York: Crown.

Statni Zidovske Museum, Prague. (1964). *I never saw another butterfly.* New York: McGraw Hill.

Sternberg, R. J., & Horvath, J. A. (1995). A prototype view of expert teaching. *Educational Researcher, 24*(6), 9–17.

Stock, M. A. (1993). *Where are you going, Manyoni?* New York: Morrow.

Stockdale, K., & Kauffman, G. (1994). *Primary sources: Strategies for finding and using original sources.* Logan, IA: Perfection Learning Co.

Streitmatter, J. (1994). *Toward gender equity in the classroom: Everyday teachers' beliefs and practices.* Albany: State University of New York Press.

Sturner, F. (1973). *What did you do when you were a kid? Pastimes from the past.* New York: St. Martin's.

Sutton, R. (1990). *Car.* New York: Knopf.

Swales, J. M. (1990). *Genre analysis: English in academic and research settings.* New York: Cambridge University Press.

Takaki, R. (1993). *A different mirror: A history of multicultural America.* Boston: Little, Brown.

Taylor, D. (1993). *From the child's point of view.* Portsmouth, NH: Heinemann.

Temple, C., Nathan, R., Temple, F., & Burrus, N. A. (1993). *The beginnings of writing.* Boston: Allyn & Bacon.

Thelen, D. (1995). The practice of history. *Journal of American History, 81,* 933–960.

Thompson, E. P. (1963). *The making of the English working class.* New York: Pantheon.

Thornberg, L., & Brophy, J. (1992, November). *Early elementary students' thinking about Native Americans and their encounters with Europeans.* Paper presented to the annual meeting of the College and University Faculty Assembly, National Council for the Social Studies, Detroit.

Thornton, S. J. (1990). Should we be teaching more history? *Theory and Research in Social Education, 18,* 53–60.

Thornton, S. J. (1991). Teacher as curricular-instructional gatekeeper in social studies. In J. P. Shaver (Ed.), *Handbook of research on social studies teaching and learning* (pp. 237–248). New York: Macmillan.

Thornton, S. J. (2001a). Educating the educators: Rethinking subject matter and methods. *Theory Into Practice, 40,* 75–78.

Thornton, S. J. (2001b). Subject specific teaching methods: History. In J. Brophy (Ed.), *Advances in research on teaching, Vol. 8. Subject-specific instructional methods and activities* (pp. 291–314). New York: Elsevier Science.

Thornton, S. J., & Vukelich, R. (1988). Effects of children's understanding of time concepts on historical understanding. *Theory and Research in Social Education, 16,* 69–82.

Tierney, R. J., Carter, M. A., & Desai, L. E. (1991). *Portfolio assessment in the reading-writing classroom.* Norwood, MA: Christopher-Gordon.

Todorov, T. (1982). *Theories of the symbol.* Ithaca, NY: Cornell University Press.

Todorov, T. (1984). *The conquest of America: The question of the other.* New York: Harper & Row.

Toolan, M. J. (1988). *Narrative: A critical linguistic introduction.* New York: Routledge.

Torney-Purta, J. (1991). Schema theory and cognitive psychology: Implications for social studies. *Theory and Research in Social Education, 19,* 189–210.

Traugott, E. C., & Pratt, M. L. (1980). *Linguistics for students of literature.* New York: Harcourt Brace.

Trease, G. (1983). Fifty years on: A writer looks back. *Children's Literature in Education, 14,* 149–159.

Trout, L. (1982). Native American history: New images and ideas. In M. T. Downey (Ed.), *Teaching American history: New directions* (Bulletin No. 67, pp. 91–112). Washington, DC: National Council for the Social Studies.

Tuchman, B. W. (1981). *Practicing history.* New York: Knopf.

Tunnell, M. O. (1993). Unmasking the fiction of history: Children's historical literature comes of age. In O. M. Tunnell & R. Ammon (Eds.), *The story of ourselves: Teaching history through children's literature* (pp. 79–90). Portsmouth, NH: Heinemann.

Tunnell, M. O., & Ammon, R. (Eds.). (1993). *The story of ourselves: Teaching history through children's literature.* Portsmouth, NH: Heinemann.

Turner, A. (1987). *Nettie's trip south.* New York: Macmillan

Turner, A. (1992). *Katie's trunk.* New York: Macmillan.

Uchida, Y. (1985). *Journey to Topaz.* Berkeley, CA: Creative Arts.

Uchida, Y. (1993). *The bracelet.* New York: Philomel Books.

Van Oers, B., & Wardukker, W. (1999). On becoming an authentic learner: Semiotic activity in the early grades. *Journal of Curriculum Studies, 31*, 229–249.

VanSledright, B. A. (1995). "I don't remember—the ideas are all jumbled in my head": 8th graders' reconstructions of colonial American history. *Journal of Curriculum and Supervision, 10*, 317–345.

VanSledright, B. A. (1996). Studying colonization in eighth grade: What can it teach us about the learning context of current reforms. *Theory and Research in Social Education, 24* 107–145.

VanSledright, B. A. (1997). And Santayana lives on: Students' views on the purposes for studying American history. *Journal of Curriculum Studies, 29*, 529–557.

VanSledright, B. A. (1997/1998). On the importance of historical positionality to thinking about and teaching history. *The International Journal of Social Education, 12*(2), 1–18.

VanSledright, B. A. (2000). From empathic regard to self-understanding: Im/positionality, empathy, and historical contextualization. In O. L. Davis Jr., E. A. Yeager, & S. J. Foster (Eds.), *Development of historical empathy and perspective taking in the social studies.* Lanham, MD: Rowman & Littlefield.

VanSledright, B. A., & Brophy, J. (1992). Storytelling, imagination, and fanciful elaboration in children's historical reconstructions. *American Educational Research Journal, 29*, 837–859.

VanSledright, B. A., & Kelly, C. (1998). Reading American history: The influence of multiple sources on six fifth graders. *Elementary School Journal, 98*, 239–265.

Vosniadou, S., & Brewer, W. F. (1987). Theories of knowledge restructuring in development. *Review of Educational Research, 57*, 51–67.

Vygotsky, L. (1978). *Mind in society: The development of higher psychological processes.* Cambridge, MA: Harvard University Press.

Wade, R. C. (1994). Conceptual change in elementary social studies: A case study of fourth graders' understanding of human rights. *Theory and Research in Social Education, 22*, 74–95.

Weise, R. S. (2001). *Grasping at independence: Debt, male authority, and mineral rights in Appalachian Kentucky, 1850–1915.* Knoxville: University of Tennessee Press.

Welch, J. (1994). *Killing Custer: The battle of the Little Bighorn and the fate of the Plains Indians.* New York: Norton.

Wellman, H. M., & Gelman, S. A. (1992). Cognitive development: Foundational theories of core domains. *Annual Review of Psychology, 43*, 337–375.

Wells, C. G. (1986). *The meaning makers: Children learning language and using language to learn.* Portsmouth, NH: Heinemann.

Wells, C. G. (1999). *Dialogic inquiry: Towards a sociocultural practice and theory of education.* New York: Cambridge.

Wells, C. G., & Chang-Wells, G. L. (1992). *Constructing knowledge together: Classrooms as centers of inquiry and literacy.* Portsmouth, NH: Heinemann.

Wertsch, J. V. (1998). *Mind as action.* New York: Oxford University Press.

Wesniewski, D. (1992). *Sundiata.* New York: Clarion.

Wexler-Sherman, C., Gardner, H., & Feldman, D. H. (1988). A pluralistic view of early assessment: The project spectrum approach. *Theory Into Practice, 27*, 77–83.

White, M. (1965). *Foundations of historical knowledge.* New York: Harper & Row.

White, H. (1978). *Tropics of discourse: Essays in cultural criticism.* Baltimore: Johns Hopkins University Press.

White, H. (1980). The value of narrativity in the representation of reality. *Critical Inquiry, 7*, 5–27.

White, H. (1982). The politics of historical interpretation: Discipline and desublimation. *Critical Inquiry, 9*, 113–137.

White, H. (1984). The question of narrative in contemporary historical theory. *History and Theory, 23*, 1–33.

White, H. (1992). Historical emplotment and the question of truth. In S. Friedlander (Ed.), *Probing the limits of representation: Nazism and the "final solution"* (pp. 37–53). Cambridge, MA: Harvard University Press.

White, J. J. (1997). Teaching about cultural diversity. In C. Kottak, J. J. White, R. H. Furlow, & P. C. Rice (Eds.), *The teaching of anthropology: Problems, issues, and decisions* (pp. 7–76). Mountain View, CA: Mayfield Publishing.

White, M. (1965). *Foundations of historical knowledge.* New York: Harper & Row.

Whittington, D. (1991). What have 17-year-olds known in the past? *American Educational Research Journal, 28*, 759–780.

Wiggins, G. (1989). A true test: Toward authentic and equitable assessment. *Phi Delta Kappan, 70*, 703–713.

Wiggins, G. (1992). *The case for authentic assessment.* Washington, DC: United States Department of Education, Office of Educational Research and Improvement, Educational Resources Information Center.

Wiggins, G. P. (1993). *Assessing student performance: Exploring the purpose and limits of testing.* San Francisco: Jossey-Bass.

Wilde, O. (1982). *The artist as critic: Critical writings of Oscar Wilde.* Chicago: University of Chicago Press.

Wilder, L. I. (1953). *Little house on the prairie.* New York: Harper & Row.

Williams, H. M. (1991). *The language of civilization: The vital role of the arts in education.* Washington, DC: President's Committee on the Arts and the Humanities.

Willinsky, J. (1998). *Learning to divide the world: Education at empire's end.* Minneapolis: University of Minnesota Press.

Wilson, A. H. (1983). A case study of two teachers with cross-cultural experience—They know more. *Educational Research Quarterly, 8,* 78–85.

Wilton, S. (1993). Newer biographies are "better than before." In M. Zarnowski & A. F. Gallagher (Eds.), *Children's literature and social studies: Selecting and using notable books in the classroom* (pp. 16–19). Dubuque, IA: Kendall/Hunt.

Wineburg, S. S. (1991). On the reading of historical texts: Notes on the breach between school and academy. *American Educational Research Journal, 28,* 495–519.

Winner, E. (1982). *Invented worlds: The psychology of the arts.* Cambridge, MA: Harvard University Press.

Winter, J. (1988). *Follow the drinking gourd.* New York: Knopf.

Winter, J. (1991). *Diego.* New York: Knopf.

Wood, D. (1998). *How children think and learn: The social contexts of cognitive development* (2nd ed.). Malden, MA: Blackwell.

Wright, C. C. (1995). *Wagon train: A family goes west in 1865.* New York: Holiday House.

Yeager, E., & Davis, O. L., Jr. (1996). Classroom teachers thinking about historical texts: An exploratory study. *Theory and Research in Social Education, 24,* 146–166.

Yeager, E. A., Foster, S. J., Maley, S. D., Anderson, T., & Morris, J. W., III. (1998). Why people in the past acted as they did: An exploratory study in historical empathy. *International Journal of Social Education, 13,* 8–24.

Yep, L. (1994). *Dragon's gate.* New York: HarperCollins.

Yin. (2001). *Coolies.* New York: Philomel.

Young, C. (1994). Change and innovation in history curriculum: A perspective on the New South Wales experience. In K. J. Kennedy, O. F. Watts, & G. McDonald (Eds.), *Citizenship education for a new age* (pp. 29–46). Queensland, Australia: The University of Southern Queensland Press.

Young, K. A. (1994). *Constructing buildings, bridges, and minds: Building an integrated curriculum through social studies.* Portsmouth, NH: Heinemann.

Zarnowski, M. (2003). It's more than dates and places: How nonfiction contributes to understanding social studies. In R. Bamford & J. Kristo (Eds.), *Making facts come alive: Choosing quality nonfiction literature K–8* (pp. 121–140) Norwood, MA: Christopher-Gordon.

Zhensun, J., & Low, A. (1991). *A young painter: The life and paintings of Wang Yani-China's extraordinary young artist.* New York: Scholastic.

Zinn, H. (1990). *Declarations of independence: Cross-examining American ideology.* New York: HarperCollins.

Zinn, H. (1994). *You can't be neutral on a moving train.* Boston: Beacon.

INDEX

230